The British Revolution, 1629–1660

British Studies Series

General Editor JEREMY BLACK

Alan Booth **The British Economy in the Twentieth Century**
John Charmley **A History of Conservative Politics, 1900–1996**
David Childs **Britain since 1939 (2nd edn)**
John Davis **A History of Britain, 1885–1939**
David Eastwood **Government and Community in the English Provinces, 1700–1870**
Philip Edwards **The Making of the Modern English State, 1460–1660**
W. H. Fraser **A History of British Trade Unionism, 1700–1998**
John Garrard **Democratisation in Britain: Elites, Civil Society and Reform since 1800**
Brian Hill **The Early Parties and Politics in Britain, 1688–1832**
Katrina Honeyman **Women, Gender and Industrialisation in England, 1700–1870**
Kevin Jefferys **Retreat from New Jerusalem: British Politics, 1951–1964**
T. A. Jenkins **The Liberal Ascendancy, 1830–1886**
David Loades **Power in Tudor England**
Ian Machin **The Rise of Democracy in Britain, 1830–1918**
Allan I. Macinnes **The British Revolution, 1629–1660**
Alexander Murdoch **British History, 1660–1832: National Identity and Local Culture**
Anthony Musson and W. M. Ormrod **The Evolution of English Justice: Law, Politics and Society in the Fourteenth Century**
Murray G.H. Pittock **Inventing and Resisting Britain: Cultural Identities in Britain and Ireland, 1685–1789**
Nick Smart **The National Government, 1931–40**
Howard Temperley **Britain and America since Independence**
Andrew Thorpe **A History of the British Labour Party (2nd edn)**

British Studies Series
Series Standing Order
ISBN 0–333–71691–4 hardcover
ISBN 0–333–69332–9 paperback
(outside North America only)

You can receive future titles in this series as they are published by placing a standing order. Please contact your bookseller or, in case of difficulty, write to us at the address below with your name and address, the title of the series and the ISBN quoted above.

Customer Services Department, Macmillan Distribution Ltd
Houndmills, Basingstoke, Hampshire RG21 6XS, England

The British Revolution, 1629–1660

Allan I. Macinnes

First published 2005 by
PALGRAVE MACMILLAN
Houndmills, Basingstoke, Hampshire RG21 6XS and
175 Fifth Avenue, New York, N.Y. 10010
Companies and representatives throughout the world

PALGRAVE MACMILLAN is the global academic imprint of the Palgrave Macmillan division of St. Martin's Press, LLC and of Palgrave Macmillan Ltd. Macmillan® is a registered trademark in the United States, United Kingdom and other countries. Palgrave is a registered trademark in the European Union and other countries.

ISBN 0–333–59749–4 hardback
ISBN 0–333–59750–8 paperback

This book is printed on paper suitable for recycling and made from fully managed and sustained forest sources.

A catalogue record for this book is available from the British Library.

Library of Congress Cataloging-in-Publication Data
Macinnes, Allan I.
      The British revolution, 1629–1660/Allan I, Macinnes.
          p.   cm. – (British studies series)
      Includes bibliographical references (p.) and index.
      ISBN 0–333–59749–4 – ISBN 0–333–59750–8 (pbk.)
          1. Great Britain – History – Puritan Revolution, 1642–1660.   2.
      Great Britain – History – Charles I, 1625–1649.   I. Title.   II. British
      studies series (Palgrave Macmillan (Firm))

      DA405.M28   2004
      941.06'2–dc22

                                                                2004050002

      10   9   8   7   6   5   4   3   2   1
      14   13   12   11   10   09   08   07   06   05
Printed in China

To Tine

Contents

Acknowledgements

This book would not have been possible without the immense support of a considerable number of people and institutions. In the course of my personal researches I have been assisted by major research grants from the British Academy which facilitated my access to the archives at Inveraray Castle in Argyllshire at Dumfries House in Ayrshire and at Buckminster, Grantham, Lincolnshire. For permission to work in these archives I am indebted respectively to the Trustees of the 10th Duke of Argyll, the late Marquess of Bute and the Tollemache family. A special debt is owed to Alastair Campbell of Airds, the chief executive of the Clan Campbell, for his constructive guidance and to Linda Fryer, my former research assistant, for her assiduous labour and organisational flair. My work at the Huntington Library was aided by a renewed research fellowship in 2001 and by generous assistance and advice from Roy Ritchie and Mary Robertson. Much of the writing up and reworking of the contents was done at the University of Chicago during my spell as Visiting Professor of British History. I am particularly grateful to the collegiate support I received from Steve Pincus and the undergraduate and graduate students I taught at the outset of 2003. My spell in Chicago also allowed me access to the Newberry Library, where the staff were unfailingly helpful, as they were at the Folger Library in Washington D.C. and the New York Public Library. The Rigsarkivet in Copenhagen is the most relaxed atmosphere for archival study in which I have been privileged to work. It could well provide refresher courses in how to avoid the bureaucracy that afflicts the National Archives of Scotland in Edinburgh. Nevertheless, the staff there do provide a helpful service, as is also manifestly the case at the British Library in London, the National Library of Scotland in Edinburgh, the Mitchell Library in Glasgow, Northumbria Archives in Berwick-upon-Tweed, Tyne & Wear Archives in Newcastle, Glasgow University Archives, Edinburgh University Library and, above all, Aberdeen University Library and Special Collections. Material collated from the royal archives in Belgium and Sweden was provided unstintingly by Steve Murdoch and Alexia Grosjean, my former graduate students and colleagues in the Research Institute of Irish and Scottish Studies (RIISS) at Aberdeen, now at the University of St Andrews.

My other graduate students at Aberdeen who have provided much appreciated intellectual and technical support towards this book are Linas Eriksonas, Ali Cathcart and David Menary. I have also welcomed the opportunity to try out my evolving ideas of the British Revolution in my undergraduate honours class on the Three Kingdoms in the Seventeenth Century at Aberdeen. In the course of many conversations and the flying of not a few kites I have benefited immeasurably from the advice and assistance provided by John Adamson, Sarah Barber, Peter Davidson, Steven Ellis, Karen Kupperman, Peter Lake, David Scott, Kevin Sharpe, Jane Stevenson, Kariann Yokota and John Young. A special debt is owed to my sparring comrade, Art Williamson, and to my close working colleagues at Aberdeen, Tom Devine and George Watson. Janet Hendry, the administrator at RIISS, has again proved invaluable in the final preparations of the typescript. I should like also to thank Terka Acton and Sonya Barker at Palgrave Macmillan for their encouragement and forbearance and my marvellously helpful copy-editor, Katy Coutts. However, I must lay sole claim to the sins of commission and omission in the final production of this book, which would not have been achievable without the love and support of my wife, Tine Wanning.

Abbreviations

AHR	*American Historical Review*
APS	*Acts of the Parliament of Scotland*, ed. T. Thomson and C. Innes, 12 vols (Edinburgh, 1814–72)
AUL	Aberdeen University Library
BL	British Library, London
CSP, Domestic	*Calendar of State Papers Domestic Series, of the reign of Charles I*, ed. J. Bruce and W.D. Hamilton, 17 vols (London, 1858–82)
CSP, Venetian	*Calendar of State Papers and Manuscripts relating to English Affairs existing in the Archives and Collections of Venice, and in other Libraries of Northern Italy*, ed. A.B. Hinds (London, 1913–23)
DH	Dumfries House, Cumnock, Ayrshire
DR	Dansk Rigsarkivet, Copenhagen
EHR	*English Historical Review*
EUL	Edinburgh University Library
HJ	*Historical Journal*
HL	Huntington Library, San Marino, California
HMC	Historical Manuscripts Commission
ICA	Inveraray Castle Archives, Inveraray, Argyllshire
IHS	*Irish Historical Studies*
NAS	National Archives of Scotland, Edinburgh
NLS	National Library of Scotland, Edinburgh
PRO	Public Record Office, London
RPCS	*Registers of the Privy Council of Scotland*, 1st ser., ed. D. Masson, 14 vols (Edinburgh, 1877–98); 2nd ser., ed. D. Masson and P.H. Brown, 8 vols (Edinburgh, 1899–1908)
SHR	*Scottish Historical Review*
TFA	Tollemache Family Archives, Buckminster, Grantham, Lincolnshire
TKUA	Tyske Kancellis Udenrigske Afdeling
TWA	Tyne & Wear Archives, Newcastle

Introduction: The British Problem

The regal union of 1603 installed the Stuarts as the first truly British dynasty. Then as now there has been relatively little difficulty for the Scots, the Irish and the Welsh in differentiating between the respective histories of their own countries and that of Britain. In terms of population, wealth and apparatus of government Britain was at least ten times larger than Scotland, Ireland and Wales. Conversely, the similar resources of England were only augmented by a tenth with the addition of a British dimension. As a result, the English have tended to make no substantive intellectual, commercial or political distinction between England and Britain, either in a domestic or an imperial context. Conflicting perceptions of unequal magnitude between Scotland, Ireland and Wales on the one hand and England on the other are at the root of the British problem. Moreover, this problem has been as much historiographic as historic.[1]

Well into the twentieth century, the historiography of England and Wales, Scotland and Ireland as multiple kingdoms was dominated by the Whig tradition of progressive empiricism. This tradition, which placed greater emphasis on narrative than theory, came under siege from radical, revisionist, ideological and methodological attacks led by English and American historians. In the case of Scotland and Ireland, and to a lesser extent Wales, a further nationalist dimension became evident in the historical onslaught on the Whig tradition, even though the West British tendencies in Ireland were never as pronounced as the North British nature of Scottish Whiggery.[2] Notwithstanding the recent vogue for 'New British Histories', has the Whig tradition survived the historiographic siege? Current historiographic concerns appear preoccupied with the Stuart court and baronial power, with religious establishments and with the resolution of political divergences through institutional union. These concerns suggest the emergence of neo-Whiggery rather than a comprehensive revision of British history in terms of either a unified realm or the constituent parts of the British Isles. Indeed, what

1

is new about British history other than a change in terminology? 'New British Histories' have accorded primacy to state formation, civil wars and national identities. Does this mark a distinctive shift in focus away from the nation building of the Whig tradition?[3]

The deficiencies of the Whig tradition can be summed up in its insularity, its introspection and its disconnected domestic and imperial historiography. These manifest deficiencies also characterise the 'New British Histories'. An overwhelmingly anglocentric perspective tends to disregard or discount separate Scottish and Irish links – confessional, mercantile and military – to the continent.[4] The European context that is largely absent from British history cannot be filled adequately by reliance on calendars of state papers or British diplomatic correspondence. Secondary reading is certainly a help, but of limited value if that reading is conducted solely through the medium of English.[5] Insularity and introspection are by no means the preserve of anglocentric historians, however.[6] In Scotland, these characteristics have now even been rationalised as devolved British history.[7] In Ireland, insularity has been corrected, not eradicated, by attempts to identify the forerunner of the Irish Free State in the chaotic Confederation of Irish Catholics during the 1640s.[8] The inclusion of Scottish and Irish illustrations to supplement an English narrative constitutes neither the writing of British history nor the advancing of comparative studies.[9] The distinctive contributions of Scotland and Ireland must be integrated fully into domestic and imperial history.[10] At the same time, political thought must interact with the political process if the prospect of an integrated British history is ever to be accomplished.[11]

An integrated approach to British history requires wider contextualising rather than deeper problematising. Revolution in all three Stuart kingdoms during the mid-seventeenth century must be set within not only a European but also a transoceanic context. Such a setting must resolve awkward, even antithetical, issues. Advocacy of a British revolution needs to connect and compare developments in England and Wales, Scotland and Ireland. Simultaneously, these developments have to relate to the court that ruled over the Stuarts' British dominions after 1603.[12] Historical analysis must also take account of the differing meanings of words within those dominions.

Thus, the notion of commonwealth, classically *res publica*, was not the same in all three kingdoms. Indeed, the only time a unified meaning prevailed throughout the British Isles was when it was imposed by English dominance in the 1650s. Yet this commonwealth, constituted after the execution of Charles I in 1649, marked the breach rather than the unity of crown and community traditionally associated with the meaning of the word in England. Paradoxically, the English regicides promoted a concept of commonwealth more akin to the Scottish version that had prevailed when a Protestant Reformation had been achieved in defiance of monarchy in 1560. Large-scale migration to and commercial interaction with Poland–Lithuania from the late sixteenth century onwards ensured that the Scots had developed not only a non-anglocentric, but also a more international, awareness of alternative commonwealths.[13] By the mid-seventeenth century, Scotland's closest trading partner was the United Provinces. Throughout the 1620s, Thomas Scott, the Anglo-Scottish polemicist and Puritan, broadcast the mercantile and godly virtues the Dutch commonwealth derived from federative union.[14]

Political union is likewise open to more diverse federative interpretations than that of the parliamentary incorporation that still prevails in most of the British Isles. Nevertheless, the latter concept of union remains part of a grand narrative if not a manifest British destiny for the 'New British Histories' as for their Whig predecessors. England had effectively absorbed Cornwall and Wales by 1543. Parliamentary incorporation was complemented by administrative cohesion in church and state and by the political integration of the ruling elites. Cultural distinctiveness embellished rather than threatened political union. Despite being declared a subordinate kingdom in 1541, Ireland was not incorporated into a composite English kingdom. Successive Tudor monarchs failed to accomplish conquest and achieved little integration beyond the English Pale, effectively Dublin and its hinterland. The limited advent of the Protestant Reformation in Ireland further compounded this failure. In this situation, cultural distinctiveness remained threatening.[15] From such an anglocentric perspective, the regal union of 1603 still tends to be viewed as marking a transitional stage from a composite English to a unified British kingdom. Thus, the accession of James VI of Scotland to the English throne in 1603 paved the way for the parliamentary incorporation known as the United Kingdom of Great Britain in 1707, a process disrupted but not halted by revolution and civil war in the mid-seventeenth century.[16]

The prevailing anglocentric perspective contends that disruption commenced with the launching of the personal rule of Charles I in 1629 and ended with the restoration of his son, Charles II, in 1660. However, an integrated British approach is necessary to determine why the ostensibly stable rule of a Stuart monarch in England was terminated by his subjects in Scotland and Ireland between 1638 and 1641.[17] Certainly, the revolution in England was characterised by provincialism, by political and religious polarisation, by apprehensions over the collapse of government and by cultural alienation from the court that led to partisan and internecine conflict.[18] But can such introspection be sustained? England was hardly immune to intrusive influences from elsewhere in the British Isles. Should England be viewed as impervious to the military upheaval known as the Thirty Years War that dominated European politics from 1618 to 1648? Indeed, was control over the British political agenda always exercised from England?

From a non-anglocentric perspective, disruption commenced with the imposition of administrative, social and religious uniformity throughout the British Isles from 1629 and concluded with the constitutional settlements that cemented Scotland as well as Ireland as satellite states in 1660. While it can be tempting to define this latter perspective as Celtic, this would be both anachronistic and misleading: anachronistic, because the term 'Celtic' was essentially a product of the Welsh-inspired reaction to the triumphalist Whig appropriation of the term 'British' between the 'Glorious Revolution' of 1688–91 and the parliamentary union of 1707;[19] misleading, because 'Celtic' suggests peripheral rather than integral participation in the civil wars of the 1640s and 1650s.[20]

These decades of political and religious turmoil, bloody conflict, and social and ideological upheaval throughout England, Scotland and Ireland constituted a British revolution that can be perceived not just as the product of war(s) in or of the three kingdoms.[21] The Scottish Covenanters who instigated revolution against Charles I with covert Swedish backing in 1638, the Irish Confederates who subsequently looked to France, Spain and the papacy to sustain their rebellion, and later the Cromwellian Commonwealth, all viewed the civil wars as a fight for the three kingdoms. From this perspective, civil wars within the British Isles were part of the wider European theatre of the Thirty Years War.[22] As a further antidote to English provincialism, the Covenanting movement in Scotland adopted a proactive role in promoting federative alliances with the United Provinces and Sweden as well as with England between 1640 and 1645. Scotland, a new Israel, was preparing the ground not just for European but for global reordering once the forces of godliness had vanquished those of the Antichrist.[23]

Within the British Isles, comparative history has tended towards multifarious discussions on issues of identity. At one level, this has afforded some scope for Gaelic correctives to anglocentric Britishness; at another, to the sharper definition of diverse interests within the three kingdoms, most notably in identifying the English rather than the British interest in Ireland manifest by the Restoration.[24] Simultaneously, seemingly competing identities have been resolved by a multilayered approach which takes account of time, place and employment as well as country of birth or naturalisation. This approach carries added value when applied to the wider Stuart world of the seventeenth century which strove to bridge European and transoceanic developments.[25]

Among the enterprising few capable of crossing that bridge in the seventeenth century were three Scots whose critiques of local and national affairs were enhanced by their experiences beyond the British Isles in a frontier world in which commercial and religious entrepreneurship took precedence over nationality. The first was Patrick Copeland from Aberdeen, who joined the English East India Company as a naval chaplain in 1613. Having travelled to Japan and China as well as India, he subsequently settled in Virginia, the Bahamas and Bermuda. His experiences of the East and West Indies convinced him that the Stuart dominions were bound by ties of godliness and education no less than by empire and entrepreneurship. Inspired by Dutch initiatives to promote Protestantism in Amboyna, his conviction that a similar strategy would spread Christianity to the American Indians led to his raising funds for a Virginia College from the Cape of Good Hope in 1621, efforts which were renewed on his return to London in the following year. His educational framework was also to include the children of settlers and even servants of the East India Company. Despite his own personal commitment as a colonist and his election as rector of the proposed college, his pedagogical innovation did not take root in the Chesapeake. But he did become a sponsor of education in New England, with donations to Harvard complementing his endeavours to establish Eluthera as an exemplary civilised community in the Bahamas by 1647. At the same time, he had established the first chair of divinity in 1616, in the recently founded Marischall College, Aberdeen's second university. Until his death in 1651, Copeland remained an assiduous, but discreet, critic of the town council for their notorious parsimony and embezzlement of public funds.[26]

The second case is that of John Durie from Edinburgh, who was reared in Scotland, educated in the United Provinces and France, married in Ireland, and eventually became a resident cleric in England. Having begun his career as pastor to the British mercantile community at Elbing in Prussia in 1624, he was drawn into the extensive intellectual network

of Samuel Hartlib, a merchant, pietist and educationalist with an ency-
clopedic mind who relocated to England from 1628.[27] Inspired by the
Hartlib circle, in which he became a major figure, Durie dedicated his
life to a peaceful accommodation between the Reformed (Calvinist) and
Lutheran traditions. Throughout the 1630s, he strove unflinchingly to
gather support for confessional union between Calvinists and Lutherans
by his chronically underfunded, peripatetic endeavours in Germany,
Poland–Lithuania and Sweden. His claim to speak for 'the British
Churches' was a subtle, but nonetheless subversive, challenge to the hegemonic Anglican agenda then being pursued by William Laud, the Archbishop of Canterbury, in all three Stuart kingdoms, their American
colonies and among exiled mercantile communities from Muscovy to the
Moluccas. Linked to Durie's promotion of confessional confederation
against Habsburg imperialism was the prospect that the exiled family of
Elizabeth Stuart, the 'Winter Queen' of Bohemia and sister of Charles
I, could be restored to the Palatinate, from which they had been ousted
at the beginning of the Thirty Years War.[28]

The third Scot was William Lithgow from Lanark on the Clyde, probably the most travelled adventurer from the British Isles in the early seventeenth century. In the course of nineteen years he travelled through
Europe, explored Africa and made his way overland through Persia to
the frontiers of India. His journeys established that 30,000 Scots and
their families had migrated to Poland–Lithuania. This figure has not
only stood up to demographic scrutiny, but was instrumental in persuading the Scottish courtier Sir William Alexander of Menstrie to lobby
for a Scottish colony as part of the British endeavours in the Americas
during the 1620s. In the course of three epic journeys Lithgow claimed
to have visited 48 kingdoms, 21 republics, 10 absolute principalities and
200 islands. He also fell into the clutches of the Spanish Inquisition when
he was accused of spying at Malaga in 1626. A celebrated self-publicist
– he called himself 'the Bonaventure of Europe, Asia and Africa' –
Lithgow, in the course of a poetic peregrination in 1618, encouraged the
future king, as Prince of Great Britain, to concentrate on uniting his
kingdoms rather than seeking conquests in foreign places.[29]

Fourteen years later, Lithgow concluded his last journey with a tour
of Scotland in which he lamented the drain on Scottish resources occasioned by absentee nobles and gentry attending on absentee monarchy at the British court. When Charles I made his belated coronation
visit to his native kingdom in 1633, the cosmopolitan Lithgow issued a
prescient admonition that sharply demarcated the interests of the court

from those of the Scottish Commonwealth. In 1637, he diverted from sailing to Russia to cover the siege of Breda in the United Provinces. His detailed journal of military manoeuvres, techniques and precedents for surrenders in the Thirty Years War demonstrated a ready expertise that he subsequently deployed in the service of the Covenanting movement, which instigated the revolution in the three kingdoms. He resurfaced in London in 1643, as part of the contingent of Scottish veterans training the parliamentary forces, training that was instrumental in establishing the professionalism evident in the New Model Army by 1645. Somewhat discomfited by the English lack of respect for the Scottish veterans once their programme of military training was complete – a lack of respect with a long historiographic echo[30] – he contented himself with providing the Scottish Covenanters with a detailed blueprint of fortifications and other defensive topographical features that would allow them to seize the metropolis should the need arise.[31]

Such wider contextualising of British history cannot be just geographic. It must take account of apocalyptic visions as well as baronial politics, commercial networks as well as confessional allegiances, representative images as well as written texts. This contextualising is particularly pertinent to perceptions that were definitively British and potentially revolutionary in the mid-seventeenth century.

1 British Perceptions

The British interests of the Stuart monarchy and those of the three kingdoms of England, Scotland and Ireland diverged markedly in the mid-
seventeenth century. In determining if there was a British revolution
between 1629 and 1660, governmental, ideological and confessional
upheavals are key elements; so is the threat, if not the accomplishment,
of social reconstruction. But contemporaneous perceptions of both
Britain and revolutionary change have also to be taken into account, particularly when these perceptions were reinforced by providential and
prophetic interpretations of events. There is also a need to reconnect
public policy with political thought. Integral to this process is an awareness of the rival formulations of Britain and the British Isles as perceived
in England, Scotland and Ireland. These processes, which clashed awkwardly and at times bloodily between 1629 and 1660, can be categorised
as the Britannic, the Scottish, the Irish and the Gothic. In varying
degrees, the first three represent inclusive British perceptions that can be
deemed respectively the imperial, the confederal and the associate. The
last, based on the supremacy of the English parliament and the common
law, was an exclusive perception that proved least accommodating to the
others.[1]

The Britannic

The Britannic formulation, which was essentially imperial, was rooted
in the determination of James VI of Scotland to project himself as James
I of Great Britain and Ireland. Rather than retain the Scottish Stewart
as the founding surname of the first encompassing British dynasty,
he took over the Francophile adaptation of Stuart patented by
his mother, Mary, Queen of Scots. His first issue of coinage proclaimed
him as Emperor of Great Britain. Non-anglocentric sensibilities
were partially accommodated on the flags, seals and emblems projecting
the Stuarts as an imperial British dynasty, not just as rulers of
multiple kingdoms. Thus, the maps drawn by John Speed from

1611 were embossed with a composite imperial emblem representing the three kingdoms of England, Scotland and Ireland as well as the Stuart's inherited English claim on France. The royal standard featured three English lions set against three French lilies on both the top left and bottom right quarterings; the lion rampart of Scotland was placed on the top right and the Irish harp on the bottom left.[2] This Britannic resolve of James I had firm intellectual roots in his ancient and native kingdom, not least because tangible British harmony enabled the Scots to counter traditional English claims to suzerainty. Indeed, aspirations for union, which were given a particular fillip by the Protestant Reformation in both Scotland and England, had a long pedigree founded on the concept of empire that had exclusive sovereignty within the British Isles.[3] At the same time, traditional English dominance of the three kingdoms, characterised by the interchanging of Britain for England, was a contemporaneous historiographic problem rooted in medieval myth refocused by Renaissance scholarship.

The anglocentric dominance of British history rested on Norman–Welsh myth making of the twelfth century, most notably the fabrications of Giraldus Cambrensis and Geoffrey of Monmouth. The Britannic construct was derived from Brut, the epic Trojan hero who moved to Rome before progressing through Gaul, from where he and his followers settled the whole of the British Isles. Although Britain was divided up among the successors of Brut during the first millennium BC, anglocentric dominance was reasserted under Roman occupation. Constantine the Great, who spread Christianity throughout the Roman Empire and transferred the capital from Rome to Byzantium at the outset of the fourth century AD, was both born and acclaimed emperor in Britain. Following the fall of Rome, the Britons were subject to invasions from Picts, Scots and Saxons that forced them to the margins in Wales and Cornwall. However, King Arthur had led a British revival in the early sixth century, which expanded his dominion throughout the British Isles and into France. Successive conquests by Saxons, Danes and Norsemen tied epic British heroism to the march of civility as institutionalised through kingship, the common law and post-Reformation Protestantism. This mythical Britannic perception was reinforced by Welsh antiquarians, keen to identify Wales as the enduring heartland of the original Britons, as well as by English chroniclers like Raphael Holinshed and mercantile adventurers like John Dee during the sixteenth century. The formulation of a territorially expansive Britain was rationalised by the antiquarian William Camden, in his final version of *Britannia* prepared in 1607.[4]

Although Camden regarded the figure of Brut as mythic and without scholarly credibility, his humanistic conception of Britain underwrote English claims to be an exclusive empire. For the English were an elect Protestant nation with a Christian tradition under an episcopacy unbeholden to Rome but deemed erastian through its close ties to the monarchy and the state. Conquest and invasion had refined their civilising mission. Thus, London, the old Roman foundation, was now the metropolitan capital of a composite British empire whose territories encompassed the Anglo-Saxon heptarchy (the ancient division of seven regional kingdoms) as well as Wales and Cornwall. This composite empire could not only lay claim to Ireland but also to that part of Scotland formerly held by the Picts. Though barbarians, they were not like the Irish and Scots of irredeemable Gothic stock, but actually Britons who had lived outside the boundaries of Roman civilisation – the classical demarcation which ensured that such redeemable Gothic influences as the Saxons, the Danes and the Norsemen had enriched rather than destroyed Britain. These northern boundaries, which were settled at the Forth–Clyde division of Scotland, conformed to the division between the ancient Scottish kingdom of Alba and the Saxon kingdom of Northumbria. Following his accession to the English throne, the founder of the Stuart dynasty certainly felt his imperial vanity was enhanced by the notion that he was the fabled heir to both Constantine the Great and King Arthur as well as the more prosaic Tudors. At the same time, the repeated print runs of Camden's *Britannia* throughout the seventeenth century fuelled rather than dispelled English claims to superiority over Scotland and Ireland as well as Wales.[5]

That the three kingdoms actually constituted an imperial composite was illustrated graphically by the cartographer John Speed, whose *Theatre of the British Empire*, first published in 1611, remained the template for the subsequent mapping of Great Britain and Ireland for much of the seventeenth century. Following Camden, England was depicted as a composite kingdom based on the Anglo-Saxon heptarchy. Scotland was also a composite of the Scots, the Picts and the Isles; Ireland of its four provinces of Munster, Leinster, Connacht and Ulster together with Meath; and even Wales had a tripartite division of North, South and Powys. Abridged versions of Speed's maps issued from 1632, though purportedly depicting England and Wales, Scotland and Ireland as multiple kingdoms, still adhered to the basic structure of a composite empire.[6] This composite, Britannic representation of Camden and Speed, which effectively appended Scotland, Ireland and the rest of the British Isles onto detailed topographical descriptions of the English and Welsh shires, was accorded international recognition by the leading Dutch cartographer, Wilhelm Blaeu. His map of *Britannia* was published posthumously in 1645.[7] In like manner, when the work of the earlier great Dutch cartographer Gerard Mercator was 'Englished' in 1635, his map of England, Scotland and Ireland first published in 1595 was re-titled the Isles of Britain. In this work, dedicated to the 'Gentrie of Great Brittaine', the commonwealth of Scotland was second only to the English in terms of greatness, while Ireland remained a dependent kingdom whose development was restricted by the limited advance of civilisation beyond the English Pale.[8]

In representing a male Britannia as barbarous but noble, then refined by Saxons, Danes and Normans in the guise of classical heroes, Speed was illustrating the importance of progressive civility to the Stuart dynasty's imperial project. Indeed, the association of nobility with British patriotism as a heroic activity was a noted feature of artistic endorsement for early Stuart imperialism, as is evident from the masques of Ben Jonson and Thomas Carew, from the portraiture of Sir Anthony van Dyke, and from the set designs and commemorative architecture of Inigo Jones. Such classically inspired representations of imperial monarchy were by no means incompatible with the prevailing chivalric codes of honour sustained and refashioned at the polycentric courts of James I and his son, Charles I.[9] The influx of classical ideas on civic responsibilities and duties, particularly the virtues of public service allied to private scholarship, derived primarily from the revived interest in such Stoics as Cicero, Tacitus and Seneca. Received humanist teachings on the public good and the place of direct action had shaped the historical thinking of Camden and his associates, who included such antiquarians as the librarian and intellectual facilitator Sir Robert Cotton and artistic disciples such as Jonson. Neo-stoicism, as it had emerged in France and the Netherlands in response to the political polarisation and confessional intensity of the Wars of Religion in the sixteenth century, offered a more reflective moral perspective than the hitherto prevailing pragmatism in state affairs attributed primarily to the writings of Machiavelli.[10]

For Camden and his associates, the admonitions by Tacitus against corruption and duplicity at the centre of power inspired their neo-stoic commitment to a Stuart Britain intent on the fundamental religious and ethical reform of a body politic that had become jaded and corrupted in the later years of Elizabethan England. Their intention was not to alter the constitution, but to inspire good governance in the interests of moderation, harmony and equilibrium: that is, to uphold monarchical government but not arbitrary rule. So long as the body politic was not degenerately or irredeemably corrupted, literary and artistic criticism sustained the moral virtue of the Britannic perspective. This supportive view was carried not just to the English provinces, but throughout the British dominions by courtiers, their retainers and clients. At the same time, newsletters and transcripts in manuscript carried copy of court and other current affairs which circumvented restrictions on the printing of domestic news that was tightly controlled by the privy or governing councils in all three kingdoms prior to the 1640s.[11] In practical terms, the neo-stoic stance can be identified with apprehensions about the harmful impact of Spanish infiltration at the Stuart courts and, after the outbreak of the Thirty Years War in 1618, with the vigorous defence of Protestantism in continental Europe. However, neo-stoicism was not necessarily about political reform from within. Indeed, the teaching of Seneca favoured withdrawal from the corruptions of public life in favour of private scholarly and aesthetic pursuits, a teaching which encouraged passive obedience towards imperial monarchy.[12]

Perhaps one of the foremost British examples of this passive stance was the Scottish intellectual Sir William Drummond of Hawthornden, an irenicist or proponent of peaceful accommodations who used history didactically to avoid confrontation with the Stuart monarchy. He prepared his memorials of state affairs under the five successive Stewart kings called James from 1423 to 1540 to serve as a warning to Charles I against taking discriminatory action against disaffected members of the Scottish nobility. In like manner, Sir Robert Cotton had written a history of the twelfth-century English king Henry III to attack the pernicious influence of royal favourites under James I. However, the literary output of Drummond of Hawthornden, like that of his close literary correspondent at court, Sir William Alexander of Menstrie (the future Earl of Stirling), used English, not Scots, as the complement to Latin in the pursuit of civility, a practice also followed by James I himself after 1603.[13] Thus, the Authorised Version of the Bible produced under James's imprimatur in 1611 endorsed his imperial vision of godly monarchy and his resolve that English should be the prescribed language of Reformed civility throughout his British dominions.

As a firm advocate of the view that monarchy was divinely interposed between God and civil society, James I of Great Britain viewed dynastic consolidation as the first step towards perfect union under an imperial monarchy. Such a union opened up the prospect of British leadership in a Protestant Europe battling to resist Antichrist in the form of the papacy and the whole panoply of the Counter-Reformation. This imperial vision of godly monarchy, enunciated initially in *The True Lawe of Free Monarchies* (1597), was followed by *Basilikon Doron* (1599), essentially a manifesto for James's dynasty's divine right to succeed to the English throne. On the one hand, James drew demonstrably on traditional English claims to be an empire free from papal control. On the other hand, he rebutted Presbyterian claims to the autonomy of the Scottish Kirk, whereby government through bishops, the erastian preference of imperial monarchy, faced replacement by an autonomous hierarchy of ecclesiastical courts.[14]

Accordingly, while James I glorified in portraying himself as Constantine *redivivus*, his main preference was for biblical rather than classical analogies, and most notably for his idealisation as Great Britain's Solomon. This idealisation was solemnised by the sermon given at his state funeral on 7 May 1625 and was visually commemorated ten years later in the ceiling painting by the Flemish maestro Peter Paul Rubens that constituted the centrepiece of the Banqueting House in Whitehall designed by Inigo Jones. In this painting James, the imperial monarch, is attended by two female supplicants and a baby boy standing before his throne awaiting judgement, not in biblical terms of deciding maternity, but in celebrating his paternalistic creation of a new British child through his unification of Scotland and England.[15]

The Scottish

In effecting this union, James had also brought into play Scottish origin myths. Largely the product of the Wars of Independence of the late thirteenth and fourteenth centuries, these Scottish myths borrowed heavily from Irish origin mythology, the first to be articulated within the multiple kingdoms from the eleventh century. In contrast to the Roman imperial element, which the English shared with other aggressive northern powers in early modern Europe, the Scottish myths stressed civic origins.[16] Gathelus of Athens, having journeyed to Egypt, married Scota, daughter of the Pharaoh, shortly before Moses led the Israeli exodus. In the wake of the Pharaoh's destruction in the Red Sea, Gathelus and Scota wandered to Iberia from whence their heirs moved to Ireland and then to Scotland, where an autonomous kingdom was established in 330 BC under Fergus son of Ferchar, a contemporary of Alexander the Great. Around AD 403, having overcome an alliance of Romans and Picts which temporarily forced their return to Ireland, Fergus son of Earc re-established the kingdom of the Scots, which was expanded under Kenneth MacAlpine in 843 to include that of the Picts. Despite continuing English hostility, their descendants went on to consolidate the borders of Scotland from the Solway to the Tweed in the eleventh century. This legend underwrote not only Scottish pretensions to the longest unbroken line of kings in Europe, but also the imperial aspirations of their Stewart monarchy. For Achaius, the 65th King of Scots, was leagued in friendship, not clientage, with Charlemagne, the Holy Roman Emperor, around 790, a league which laid the foundation of the 'auld alliance' between Scotland and France that was consolidated by the Wars of Independence. The advent of the Reformation gave added significance to the legend – for the spread of Christianity from the Scots to the Picts by Columba and his followers during the sixth century was viewed as proto-Presbyterianism untrammelled by either erastian episcopacy or Rome.

Fergus MacEarc, who actually ruled around AD 500, was the first authentic King of Scots. His designation as 40th in line from Fergus MacFerchar was a fabrication notably embellished by Hector Boece, first principal of King's College, Aberdeen, in his *Scotorum Historiae* of 1527, when Anglo-Scottish relations had degenerated in view of the real prospect of an English conquest of Scotland. Six years earlier, Boece's fellow countryman and Sorbonne scholar John Mair had proposed an alternative strategy offering permanent resolution for Anglo-Scottish conflict. His *Historia Maioris Britannia* discounted the mythical origins of both countries, rejected English claims to superiority, and distanced him from his country's xenophobia towards England. Mair was an eloquent advocate of British union through dynastic alliance such as that between James IV of Scotland and Margaret Tudor of England in 1503, an alliance that eventually brought their great-grandchild James VI to the English throne. James was notably indebted to Mair's imperial vision of a composite British empire. However, this vision requires wider international contextualising, especially as the Spanish monarchy had already established an Iberian world empire when the Stuart dynasty commenced its British project.[17]

Mair was the principal Iberian apologist within the three kingdoms. However, the main opponents of world empire within the three kingdoms were also Scots, especially John Knox from a biblical and apocalyptic perspective and George Buchanan, the foremost classical exponent of aristocratic republicanism. The Scottish formulation was anti-imperial but by no means antipathetic to a greater Britain. Both viewed post-Reformation Scotland as a virtuous commonwealth that should be open to wider federative arrangements to counter universal monarchy. Buchanan, though no less sceptical than Camden about mythic origins, had firmed up Boece's fabricated line of kings in order to demonstrate the capacity of the Scottish commonwealth to remove tyrannical monarchs. In marked contrast to Camden's imperial perception of continuity and stability through virtuous monarchy, Buchanan stressed that an elective monarchy had depended on the consent of the political community. This notion of popular sovereignty, basic to Buchanan's conception of civic humanism, had its roots in Cicero's questioning of the legitimacy of government. Buchanan's advocacy of the right of resistance to monarchy, which upheld trusteeship over sovereignty in *De Iure Regnis apud Scotus dialogus* (1579), made the book a ready target for proscription by successive Stuarts.[18]

The fundamental reconfiguration of Britain was also a prime concern of Andrew Melville, humanist, educational reformer and founder of Scottish Presbyterianism, as indeed it was of Edmund Spenser, whose perceptions of English rule in Ireland, however demonised by contemporary historicists, are only problematic if viewed in an insular context.[19] Spenser, like Melville, viewed the constituent parts of the British Isles as distinctive but supportive elements in the great war against the Iberian world empire. It was Melville who first suggested that the imperial Britannic be moderated by the confederal Scottish perspective. In a pastoral eulogy on the birth of Prince Henry, eldest son of James VI, in 1594, he anticipated that the future regal union would join Scotland and England in a united commonwealth of the Scoto-Britannic people. This new commonwealth, however, would be but the first step in a grand confederation of free Protestant states.

David Hume of Godscroft, the leading Presbyterian intellectual in Jacobean Britain, was no less committed to the full integration of Britain. In 1605 he promoted the idea of a complete political and religious union that would lead to the fusion of the British peoples. Nonetheless, the creation of a universal British commonwealth under the Stuart dynasty to challenge Spain and the papacy sat awkwardly with the aristocratic republic which he, like Buchanan, idealised. The Iberian menace pointed to new political directions that were not necessarily liberating. As a civic humanist vigorously opposed to withdrawal from public life yet reluctant to condone outright resistance to monarchy, Hume had no clear alternative to counteract the non-cooperation of the Stuart monarchy with his vision. Paradoxically, Hume contributed ultimately, if uneasily, to the intellectual foundations for the British destiny of the Stuart dynasty. Buchanan, on the other hand, had afforded an incisive and unequivocal critique of hierarchic and imperial kingship to which the Scottish Covenanters proved notably receptive when instigating revolt against Charles I.[20]

A unique added ingredient to Scottish thinking on state formation and the promotion of patriotism was the celebration and commemoration of virtuous worthies, of scholars and soldiers as well as monarchs, a practice inspired by the attributes of classical heroism as propounded by both Ovid and Cicero. This classical conception was given political currency and enduring popular appeal through the first print run from the extant manuscripts of *The Wallace*, composed by Blind Harry in the fifteenth century as a heroic complement to *The Bruce* by John Barbour in the previous century. Published in 1570 in the aftermath of Reformation and civil war, and during a regency government, the selfless life of the martyred William Wallace, resistance fighter and upholder of the Scottish Commonwealth, came just a year before the printed life of Robert the Bruce, the perjured king who successfully consolidated the Scottish opposition to English hegemony during the Wars of Independence. As Buchanan was well aware in his reconstructed Scottish history, Wallace provided a historical example of lawful resistance while Bruce supported his advocacy of an independent, consensual monarchy. Thereafter the practice of printing heroic narratives in times of political upheaval became a unique and radical feature of the Scottish formulation. Further print runs of *The Wallace* in 1594 marked the high point and conclusion of the first phase of Presbyterian dominance in the Kirk of Scotland, when the national hero was enlisted to bolster Presbyterian convictions that Scotland was a chosen nation. It was no accident that a reprint of the heroic epic recalling the feats of Wallace was commissioned for publication by the Scottish Covenanters in 1640, in order to sustain a popular patriotism during the decisive phase of the Bishops' Wars against Charles I.[21]

These awkward if not always antithetical Britannic and Scottish perspectives gained international recognition. When seeking a distinctive counterpoint to the composite delineation of Great Britain by Camden and Speed, Dutch typographers and cartographers turned to Buchanan, supplemented by Boece. In 1627, Bonaventure and Abraham Elzevirus published a topographical compilation, *Respublica, sive Status Regni Scotiae et Hiberniae*. Their selective representation, together with a summative history of the 'auld alliance' with France, underlined Scotland's status as a classical commonwealth independent of England. For Ireland, however, the evidence drawn predominantly from Camden and Speed was loaded in favour of its status as an English dependency. This difference was sustained by the publication of Joan Blaeu's *Grand Atlas*, in which Scotland was covered in book 12 of the Amsterdam edition of 1654, while Ireland, though recognised as a distinct European entity in book 13, was published as a supplement. The accompanying topographical sections were prepared primarily by Sir Robert Gordon of Stralloch, an Aberdeenshire laird firmly wedded to the Graeco-Egyptian origins of the Scots, to the antiquity of the Scottish kingdom and to the emphatic rebuttal of Camden.[22]

When Christian IV of Denmark, the brother-in-law of James I and uncle to Charles I, decided on a national history in Latin for the international commemoration of his country in general and of his Oldenburg dynasty in particular, he actually commissioned two historiographers royal to undertake the task. His first choice was a Dutch scholar with Danish roots, Johannes Pontanus, a long-standing acquaintance of Camden. However, his narrative, published in 1631 as *Rerum Danicarum historia*, borrowed primarily from Buchanan and ended in 1448, prior to the accession of the Oldenburgs. He was duly superseded by another Dutch scholar, Johannes Meursius, who completed a more succinct two-volume *Historica Danica* by 1638, which was more supportive to the imperial aspirations of the Oldenburgs and their endeavours to resist Swedish claims to the province of Scania and the dependent kingdom of Norway.[23]

The Irish

Neither the Dutch nor the Danes had ready access to the one work of Renaissance scholarship that served as a corrective to both the antiquarian pretensions of the Scots and the hegemonic claims of the anglocentric Britons. *Foras Feasa ar Éirinn* by Séathrún Céitinn (Geoffrey Keating), the principal text for the Irish formulation, was a history purged of fable but written in Irish around 1634 and subsequently circulated in manuscript only. Keating's refutation of the kingship line fabricated by Boece and Buchanan was part of his wider rejection of the claim that Irish kings were ever dependent on Arthur or any other king of the Britons. Ireland was never part of any foreign dominion prior to the incursion of the Normans from England at the behest of the papacy in the twelfth century. At the same time, his underlying historical purpose was to demonstrate that Ireland was not a barbaric backwater requiring civilisation through conquest, plantation and the imposition of English common law, as argued by Camden's fellow antiquarian and the English attorney-general for Ireland, Sir John Davies.[24]

In the common classical Gaelic tradition, both the native Irish and the Scots who migrated from Ireland were designated the *Gael* and all other inhabitants and invaders within Britain and Ireland were deemed the *Gall*. The Gael was associated with epic heroism, scholarship and fidelity and the Gall with the foreign and alien cultures that had come initially through the Gallic visits of Brutus and were perpetuated in Britain by the invasions of the Romans, the Saxons, the Danes and the Normans. Thus, Camden's civilising mission of the Britons against the Irish and the Scottish Goths was turned on its head. The Irish were comparable to any nation in Europe in terms of valour, learning and steadfastness in the Catholic faith. But Keating, as befitting a descendant of an Old English family, was also concerned to ensure that due place was given to the contribution of the *Sean-Gallaibh* as well as of the Gaelic Irish in sustaining Catholicism. Both groups should be designated *Éireannaigh* – that is, the Catholic Irish – in contrast to the *Nua-Gallaibh*, effectively the Protestant settlers who arrived as New English under the Tudors and as New British under the Stuarts. Nonetheless, this Catholic nation building remained located within the contexts of Britain and Ireland as multiple kingdoms.

Keating's perspective on constitutional relations within the three kingdoms was not so much imperial or even federative as associative. Although validating the national dynamic that gave rise to the Irish Confederation of Catholics during the 1640s, Keating was primarily concerned to legitimise the Irish acceptability of the Stuart dynasty.[25] Thus Charles I, like his father before him, should be recognised as the true king of Ireland, and in turn, Ireland should be accorded the same status as England and Scotland in her constitutional association with the Stuart dynasty – as a free, not a dependent, kingdom. Indeed, this process of legitimisation ensured that the Catholic Confederation sought rapprochement with Charles I as the legitimate king of Ireland through-out the 1640s.[26]

The shift from a Tudor to a Stuart dynasty in 1603 was particularly welcomed in Ireland. The rights of the Tudors to Ireland were due more to acquisition than assimilation through free association. James I, however, could claim direct descent not only from Fergus MacEarc, who had arrived from Ulster as first king of the Scottish Gaels, but also from the kings of the other provinces of Munster, Leinster and Connacht. His right to the high kingship of Ireland was endorsed theologically. Under the leadership of Peter Lombard, Archbishop of Armagh, the Roman Catholic Church in Ireland taught that James, despite his Protestantism, was *de iure* King of Ireland and entitled to temporal allegiance. This allegiance was eagerly affirmed by the Irish parliament in 1613, notwithstanding the writings of continental Jesuits that a heretical monarch could be deposed at papal instigation – writings which moved James to a vigorous defence of his independent empire to which unequivocal allegiance was owed by all subjects whether Catholic or Protestant.[27] Plantations in Ulster, Munster and Connacht soon dashed Irish Catholics' hopes that allegiance to the Stuart dynasty would be reciprocated by liberty of conscience. Nonetheless, Keating and other clerical agents of the Counter-Reformation validated the aims of the Catholic political elite for an accommodation with the crown that would associate Ireland as an equal partner, not as a confessionally disadvantaged satellite, within a composite British empire.[28]

The Gothic

The endeavours of James I to effect not only regal union but the full integration of his British dominions provoked an English backlash, publicly evident in the historical dramas written to be performed on the London stage after 1603. The severing of English nationhood from its institutional roots is an integral part of the tragedy of *Macbeth*, in which William Shakespeare extolled an exclusive patriotism that England was in danger of losing by sleepwalking into British union. James I favoured an inclusive, Britannic political discourse which sat awkwardly with the anglocentric exclusivity favoured by Elizabeth and supported by received Calvinist claims that England was an elect nation. Whereas Elizabeth had advantageously gendered her exercise of power as a chaste protector of the English nation, James saw himself as the husband and the whole isle of Britain as his wife. English purity and, indeed, the virtue of common law had to be protected from the endeavours of James to promote complete British union.[29]

In the process of shifting the language of English nationhood away from monarchy to the common law as the protector of the English people, the stage was reinforcing the antiquarian message of the Gothic formulation. The formative role of the Anglo-Saxons in the constitutional history of England led Camden's associates, Sir Henry Spelman and John Selden, to play down British continuity from the Romans to the Normans. Unlike the splenetic attorney-general for England, Sir Edward Coke, who contended an immutable and continuous tradition in the common law from the time of the Britons, Spelman and Selden argued for the foundations of common law in the transmission of the immemorial Gothic predilection for liberty and constitutional assemblies during the Anglo-Saxon incursions of the fifth century. Institutional and cultural continuity in English life had been preserved despite Danish incursions in the ninth century and the Norman Conquest of 1066. Indeed, notwithstanding the stress on hereditary and authoritarian monarchy associated with this conquest, the Normans had facilitated the refinement of the constitutional assemblies of the Saxons into the parliaments that guaranteed English laws and liberties.[30] The rehabilitation of the Anglo-Saxon contribution through its positive identification with Gothic virtues, which could be represented chronologically rather than mythologically, has been attributed primarily to Richard Verstegan. His work on the *Restitution of Decayed Intelligence*, first published in 1605, was dedicated to James I in terms which excluded any other Britannic, Scottish or Irish perspective, 'as descendant of chiefest blood royal of our ancient English-Saxon kings'. Verstegan solidified the association of the Gothic virtues of the Germanic peoples with the migration of the Anglo-Saxons, which was the formative influence in fashioning the 'most noble and renowned English nation'.[31]

However, the humanist rehabilitation of Gothic civility was actually instigated in the mid-sixteenth century by Joannus and Olaus Magnus, and aided visually by the latter's *Carta Marina* (1539). The Magnus brothers, who served successively as the Roman Catholic bishops of Uppsala in exile on account of the Lutheran Reformation in Sweden, built upon the claims of Jordanes in the sixth century and Isidore of Seville in the seventh: that the Goths were direct descendants of Noah; that as the aboriginal people from Scandza, they spread over Europe and Asia; and that Sweden constituted the true heartland of the Goths, a people associated with a heroic civilisation that predated that of either Greece or Rome. The moral and physical superiority of the Goths was confirmed by their formative role in the destruction of the Roman empire in the fifth century. These same civilised virtues upheld the Swedish break from the Kalmar Union with Denmark and Norway in the early fifteenth century and the right of the Swedish monarchy – elective but continuous from times immemorial – to lay claim to both Scania and Norway as territories settled by direct descendants of the Goths. Their work in Latin, which was composed during the 1530s but not published for another two decades, first in Rome, then in Paris, Antwerp and Basle, had a reported currency in England by 1559.[32] England and Scotland were both identified as nations created from the Gothic diaspora. Joannus having claimed that the imperial aspirations of the Danish monarchy were without legal foundation and not just arbitrary but tyrannical, his Gothic rebuttal of 1536 was considered notably inflammatory during the Kalmar War of 1611–13, when Christian IV struggled to hold off Swedish territorial acquisitiveness. Furthermore, as the Magnus brothers offered a precedent for this acquisitiveness in the Scottish wresting of Orkney and Shetland from Denmark in the mid-fifteenth century, Christian's cordial relationship with his brother-in-law James I was strained by the latter's final annexation of the northern isles to the Scottish crown during the Kalmar War.[33]

Following on from the Magnus brothers, Verstegan had claimed Tacitus as a primary source for Gothic antiquity. For Tacitus had identified the distinctive moral virtue of the Germanic peoples, whose aversion to arbitrary and hereditary government contrasted starkly with the duplicity, corruption and tyranny among the political elite prior to the fall of imperial Rome. This subversive commentary of Tacitus in relation to monarchy and imperialism found particular favour with Spelman and Selden. At the same time, Verstegan's stress on the positive civilising influence of the post-Roman Goths in shaping the nebulous but ancient constitution of England found a receptive audience among such fellow members of the Society of Antiquaries as Camden, Cotton and Speed. However, James I was not impressed with their investigations into English parliamentary development, and he had that Elizabethan foundation wound up in 1614.

The Britannic concept of imperial monarchy promoted by the early Stuarts was exclusive in asserting sovereignty free from the interference of the papacy or other foreign power, but inclusive in the organic sense of involving not just England and Wales, but Scotland and

Ireland as well. The Gothic proponents of English greatness through the supremacy of the common law placed contractual emphasis on rights, liberties and privileges which were applicable to all freeborn Englishmen, but which were exclusively English at the expense of differing Scottish legal traditions or Irish customs. Where the Anglo-Saxon invasion was held to be qualitatively different from that of the Romans, Danes and Normans was that the civilisation of England was advanced through the expulsion of the Britons. Thus the Welsh, the inspirational proponents of the Britannic formulation, were written out of the Gothic. The Welsh could be held to have acquired civility through assimilation into the expanding English state in the sixteenth century, an argument that also underwrote expulsion and plantation in Ireland. Scotland's putative Gothic past was not endorsed by institutional development comparable to that of England.[34]

The extent to which non-anglocentric interests could be accommodated within the English body politic was the historic nub of the British problem. In formulating his Britannic concept of *ius imperium*, James I drew a cardinal distinction between the theoretically absolute powers of an imperial monarch and the empirical exercise of political entente through personal forbearance. On the one hand, James upheld the common law of England, whose tradition was based on precedent and case law reinforced by parliamentary enactment. On the other hand, he also drew on the Scottish tradition of civil (or Roman) law, which was based on principles of jurisprudence as perceived practically, though not always systematically, through 'practicks' into which were incorporated decisions by privy and judicial councils as by conventions of the political estates meeting in lieu of a parliament. In the former tradition, the English parliament was the supreme and sole legislature for matters of state. In the latter tradition, the Scottish parliament was the supreme, but not the sole, legislative body. Civil law as received in Scotland made an integral distinction between *ius regis*, as a universal concept relating to the whole framework of government, and *lex regis*, as a relative concept covering the specific acts, statutes or customs made in different societies by magistrates or rulers. Whereas *lex* was alterable when required for the common welfare, *ius* was a permanent feature of the fundamental law that not only governed the succession of the Stuarts, but was issued usually with the consent of the political nation or sustained by immemorial custom. Without *ius*, the key to civility, as the natural bond of human society, Scotland could not be an independent kingdom or Britain a true empire.[35]

The principal propagator of this distinction between *ius* and *lex* was Sir Thomas Craig of Riccarton, the leading Scottish jurist and one of the joint parliamentary commissioners charged by James I to negotiate the actual terms for full and complete union from 1604. As close agreement was apparent on the fundamentals of *ius* in both Scotland and England, Riccarton contended that there need be no insurmountable obstacle to the harmonising of civil and common laws. James had admonished the English parliament in 1607 that the civil framework of government in Scotland should not be sacrificed to an imperial construct in which English common law would invariably predominate. James had also ridiculed any suggestion that Scotland should be garrisoned like a Spanish province. But he rather tactlessly made comparisons with Sicily and Naples, which provoked the Scottish Estates to temper their support for a unified British empire if it resulted in their governance by a viceroy or deputy. The more obvious, albeit implicit, exemplar was not Spain's Italian provinces but the English dependency of Ireland.

Despite Riccarton's prompting on the joint commission, perfect union tended to be interpreted on the English side as the full integration of both government and laws. The more gradualist position in favour of political and commercial integration also came under sustained attack from vested legal and mercantile interests in the English parliament of 1606–7. Four years of fitful negotiations by the joint commissioners eventually foundered on the back of English concepts of political hegemony and parliamentary supremacy.[36] The English had been required, when extending their authority in Ireland as later when arguing for closed seas around the king's British dominions, to temper common law with civil law. Nonetheless, there was a marked aversion by the autumn of 1607 to accepting any innovative arrangement for union that neither accorded supremacy nor deferred ultimately to common law, the quintessentially Gothic basis of English parliamentary privileges, religious liberties and rights of property.[37]

The strained resolution of Colvin's Case under English law in 1608 accorded common nationality to all those born within Britain since the regal union. In promoting this objective as attorney-general for England, Sir Francis Bacon argued before the House of Commons that the benefit of conceding naturalisation to the Scots was the undoubted association of the three kingdoms on English terms: that is, by assimilation through the spread of the common law rather than by an accommodation with the civil law of Scotland. In establishing the *ius imperium* of the Stuarts, James had sought to accommodate the separate legal traditions by leavening the relativism of the common law with Scottish fundamentalism. Bacon was arguing for an expansion of the composite English kingdom that had absorbed Wales and Cornwall in the sixteenth century, not for the creation of a composite British empire. The spread of the common law to Scotland would enhance the security of England by making permanent the sundering of the 'auld alliance' with France. In arguing that British civility was tied strategically to English security, he was underscoring the case made by Sir John Davies, that the imposition of the common law would not only reduce Ireland to obedience, but also cut off the threat of invasion from Spain. Indeed, for Bacon, having Scotland united and Ireland reduced through the common law was the constitutional bedrock of English greatness as an elect kingdom capable of global expansion.[38]

Such a Gothic perspective as favoured by common lawyers and parliamentarians, like the Britannic as espoused by the early Stuarts, was undoubtedly anglocentric. But the imperial vision of the early Stuarts ensured that Britain was always something more than England. For the English common lawyers who regulated government and the parliamentarians who voted supply, Britain *was* England. The Gothic was potentially the most revolutionary of the four rival perspectives as it not only disregarded the Scottish and the Irish, but also threatened to reduce three kingdoms to one kingdom with two satellite states. Only the Scottish perspective offered a radical alternative, the federative restructuring of Britain; yet in that Ireland was to remain an English dependency. The Britannic, the Gothic and the Scottish shared a common Protestantism for which the Irish perspective was essentially disruptive and unobtainable without recourse to violence.

These awkward, even antithetical, perspectives which constituted the British problem had a further defining element. Regardless of confessional differences, each perspective claimed the backing of providence and prophecy in seeking to influence public support for the status quo or revolution.

Providence and Prophecy

The rival perspectives that constituted the British problem were not only founded on Renaissance scholarship but were also propagated through providence and prophecy. These revelatory features of God's divine purpose, which were rooted in the Judaic–Christian tradition, cut across the confessional divide opened up by the Reformation. The revealed will of God was explained in contractual terms to his people by covenanting. Divine revelation was further enhanced by miracles. As a religious counter to classical auguries of fortune and fate, providentialism upheld God's plan for the universe, whether applied generally to nations or specifically to individuals. Richard Boyle, 1st Earl of Cork, who had risen from the ranks of a minor Kent family in the 1590s to become one of the richest men in the British Isles by the 1630s, penned an autobiography which demonstrated how providence had worked inherently to his spiritual and material benefit. God's majesty, evident through his manifest conferral of blessings and punishments, motivated mankind regardless of social standing or economic resources to strive collectively for grace and seek individual assurance of salvation. In the Reformed teaching dominated by Calvinism throughout the British Isles, individual providence confirmed the predestined salvation of the elect notwithstanding the reprobate tendencies of the majority of their nation. At the same time, the wholescale striving of a nation to live gracefully was indicative of their general status as a chosen people.[39]

Covenant or federal theology mitigated the impersonal and absolute sovereignty of God in moving individuals and nations to demonstrate their faith through purposeful works as well as graceful living. This theology, which had a particular appeal to evangelical Protestants from Transylvania to New England, emphasised the contractual relationship between God and man rather than the stark Calvinist reliance on election by divine decree. Predestination and, thereby, man's ultimate dependence on divine grace was not denied. The true believer proved his or her election by covenanting with God, not by exercising his or her free will to choose salvation. Divine grace moved man to covenant. But once man had so banded himself to God he was assured of election.

Miracles were inexplicable occurrences brought about by divine intervention that demonstrated mankind's limited capacity to comprehend ordained judgements. In Reformed teaching, miracles were achieved without the intercession of saints or angels and made manifest the necessity of obeying the will of God. The miraculous acquisition of divine favour had to be balanced against the terrible wrath that accompanied its loss. Miracles signalling the imminent deliverance of the elect mitigated rather than negated their prolonged suffering to secure salvation. The reprobate remained damned. Protestant pulpits throughout the Stuart's dominions carried the prophetic warning that national apostasy assured heavenly vengeance.[40]

Biblical prophecy offered a divine explanation for natural occurrences such as famine, pestilence and war as harbingers of God's wrath on reprobate peoples. Famine in Scotland during 1623, followed by plague in England on the death of James I in 1625 (a recurrence of that experienced at the regal union in 1603) and an outbreak of dearth and cattle disease in Ireland three years later, served as the prophetic context for George Wither's warning to 'the British nation' in 1628. According to Wither, endemic impiety was occasioning the blanketing of Britain by a storm cloud that presaged the spread of war from continental Europe which would bring further death and destruction.[41] At the same time, the predictions within the book of Revelation became a touchstone not only for the progress of the Protestant Reformation in northern Europe, but also for British political reconfiguration as the first step towards apocalyptic world reordering. Such prophesying revealed the footsteps of providence in preparing a way for the conversion of the Jews to Christianity.[42]

Astrology provided a partial complement by offering a systematic, if cryptic, methodology for studying the heavens to interpret portents such as comets and eclipses. The general interpretation of current conditions, whether political, social or environmental, was deemed the province of natural astrology. Specific interpretations of future private and public developments based on individual astral readings – as through horoscopes – were viewed as judicial astrology. Leading practitioners of the natural as well as the judicial claimed they pursued Christian astrology that accorded with providentialism and prophecy. Natural astrology claimed a close association with natural philosophy and astronomy. Indeed, Johannes Kepler, a pioneer of the laws of motion, was lauded more for his prediction of the European conflagration known as the Thirty Years War, a prediction that coincided with the regal union of 1603. Judicial astrology was more pragmatic and less scientific. Its favourable reception was compounded by the popularity of secular or non-biblical prophecy. Secular prophecy did have religious roots, however, having first been attributed to the saints of the early church, such as Patrick, Columba and Malachy, then to wizards such as Merlin, William Ambrose and Thomas the Rhymer. Historical chroniclers drawn overwhelmingly from religious orders in the early and high middle ages, such as Bede, Geoffrey of Monmouth and Giraldus Cambrensis, passed on the utterances of the saints and wizards. Thus secular prophecy was woven into the fabric of the myth making that had shaped the Britannic, Irish, Scottish and Gothic perspectives. Secular prophecy, which was deliberately opaque and ambiguous, had the immeasurable merit of being recyclable. Select revelations were readily updated and adapted to the sweeping political and religious changes that characterised the British Isles in the mid-seventeenth century.[43]

Although prophecy was integrally bound up with political partisanship between 1629 and 1660, it has tended to be associated with the exotic and the quixotic sectarianism exhibited by the fringe groupings that ranged from the Quakers and the Ranters through to the Seekers and the Fifth Monarchists and on to the Diggers and the Muggletonians.[44] Despite its close if not always amicable association with such legal and natural philosophers as Francis Bacon, John Selden and Elias Ashmole, prophecy has also been deemed unscientific in an English context.[45] The prominent role of women seers – from Ursula (Mother) Shipton at the English Reformation to Lady Eleanor Audley (alias Davies and later Douglas) in the reign of Charles I – has been attributed to their negotiation of a public space in which to venture opinions on current affairs that were denied conventional outlets through their marginalisation in public life.[46] However, marginality was certainly not a feature of the work of either seer, which proved highly adaptable to editorial reinterpretation to suit changing political circumstances in the 1640s and 1650s. Moreover, to emphasise prophecy as an aspect of feminist expression is to undervalue the contemporaneous outpouring of women's commentaries on political and social affairs in both print and manuscript.[47]

The philosophical centrality of providence and prophecy to political life was upheld by the leading European jurist of the early seventeenth century. Hugo de Groot, alias Grotius, saw God's providential hand in both the conserving and the altering of empires and commonwealths. Further proof for his discourse was sought in miracles and predictions that were authenticated historically. For in well-established kingdoms, as in commonwealths, 'nothing is want to be done beside the Common Laws, unless by the Will of the Supreme Governor'. Predictions not only came from Hebrew prophets, but were also supported classically by Greek and Roman oracles and, more recently and famously, by the Mexicans and Peruvians foretelling the arrival of the Spaniards and the calamities that ensued for the native peoples in Latin America.[48]

Providence and prophecy were integral aspects not of a vulgar, but of a vernacular, culture that covered all the languages in the British Isles. Enhanced but not stimulated by the removal of censorship at the outset of the 1640s, providential and prophetic texts were circulated in manuscript as well as in print through almanacs, tracts, engravings and, above all, chapbooks in England. This material, though focused on London and designed primarily for 'the south parts of Great Britain', was also imported into Scotland and Ireland.[49] Chapbooks also circulated in the Scots language, while vernacular poetry in Scottish and Irish Gaelic developed a cutting edge in political and social criticism. In part, Irish poetry was stimulated by the Counter-Reformation, but like other vernacular texts it was responding primarily to the unprecedented demand for ideological, military and financial commitment in all three kingdoms during the 1640s.[50] Vernacular commentaries deploying providence and prophecy served as propaganda counterpoints to both the pulpits and official proclamations, and were no less influential in conditioning public opinion than the newsletters and broadsheets that flourished at the time. Vernacular commentaries, moreover, were less susceptible to influence by the political elite. Yet they also shaped public perceptions throughout the British Isles and conditioned the constituent peoples to anticipate and respond to change. Overturning the established order through violence, upheaval, convulsion and, ultimately, revolution was divinely destined.[51]

Prior to the outbreak of the Bishops' Wars in Scotland in 1639, providence and prophecy were deployed in domestic, international and transoceanic contexts. Domestically, vernacular commentaries warned of divine wrath through famine, plague and war. Internationally, they were on guard against the external threat from the Habsburgs, the papacy, and other forces of the Antichrist. Globally, but primarily in the transatlantic setting, they celebrated the establishment of colonies or the deliverance of merchant adventurers in less than hospitable environments from the Caribbean and New England to Greenland. During the 1640s, providence and prophecy were utilised principally in a vernacular context that was both British and revolutionary. They were applied by partisans of all sides to the outcome of battles won and lost or occasionally avoided. They consoled the elect with the divine assurance of salvation despite the reprobate behaviour of the majority that brought about military setbacks and even massacres. They justified political purging and regime changes in the name of godliness. They confirmed the favoured nation status of all three kingdoms during the civil wars. During the 1650s, providence and prophecy upheld the special position of fortress England, assailed as it was both internally and externally by ungodly influences. They anticipated the Restoration of Charles II in 1660. Above all, their staple inclusion in vernacular commentaries publicised and propagated the increasingly bloody perceptions that constituted the British problem.[52]

Antipathetic Applications

Irish perceptions legitimising the Stuarts as the true heirs to the three kingdoms drew not only on genealogical tradition, but also on such associated mechanisms as providence and prophecy – the same mechanisms that ensured that the Catholic Confederation would seek a political accommodation with Charles I throughout the 1640s.[53] At the same time, the providential role of the Irish people as a distinctive entity within the Stuart dominions, which was reinvigorated by vernacular poetry, was notably enhanced by the teachings of the Franciscan Order, the main missionary force for the Counter-Reformation, which allied a liberation theology to a civic covenant. Its Irish College of St Anthony of Padua at Louvain was founded in the wake of the flight of the leading Gaelic earls of Ulster into Habsburg service in the Spanish Netherlands. Less concerned with inward repentance than with national deliverance, providence and prophecy in Ireland were linked to the struggle of the Jewish Maccabees, the Old Testament sect that fought to keep Israel pure from the external corruption associated with imperial conquest. In particular, the heroic endeavour of Judas Maccabeus to deliver the Hebrew people was harnessed to the teaching of the thirteenth-century Franciscan theorist John Duns Scotus. Political authority was based not on divine right kingship, but on the social consensus which bound a people together in a political commonwealth.

These teachings, in which the children of Israel in search of deliverance from oppression assumed the bardic guise of *Clann Israel*, inspired Owen Roe O'Neill, the nephew of the expropriated Hugh, Earl of Tyrone, to mobilise the Irish brigades in exile. His first endeavour, to secure Spanish backing for an invasion of Ireland in 1627, never got off the drawing board, primarily because of Habsburg concerns about reconciling the rival territorial factions that made up this Irish enterprise. However, O'Neill's next endeavour, for which he secured the release of Irish forces from Habsburg service, was to instigate the Irish rebellion in October 1641, not in opposition to Charles I, but to liberate the kingdom. The rebellious native Irish and Old English forces merged themselves into a Confederation resolved to accommodate provincial allegiances and reconcile territorial rivalries. The Confederation of Irish Catholics was duly instituted at Kilkenny in March 1642.[54]

The rooting of resistance in biblical prophecy and the association of the troubles of the Catholic Irish with the struggles of the Israelites was an inspirational counter to the Britannic portrayal of colonising and conquest in Ireland as aspects of classical civility. Nonetheless, as during the Nine Years War against Tudor rule, which collapsed in 1601, the Britannic forces arrayed against Irish rebellion in the 1640s were no more averse to drawing on secular prophecy and, in particular, astrology to decide locations of battles and to attest the invincibility of their forces. Secular prophecy, however, offered a mixed message for Irish perceptions favouring national deliverance. On the one hand, a prophecy attributed to Merlin which predicted disaster for the English in Ireland as the culmination of over 70 years of catastrophe from the Reformation was circulating in vernacular Irish well in advance of the rebellion in 1641. On the other hand, the Nine Years War had given currency to prophecies that only the Scots would defeat the Irish, a prophecy which acquired particular potency when the Covenanters moved forces into Ulster within two months of the Catholic Confederacy being established at Kilkenny.[55]

Notwithstanding strictures from both Roman Catholic and Protestant clerics against secular prophecy, James Ussher, who became the Anglican primate in Ireland as Archbishop of Armagh, quoted Mother Shipton and other prophets extensively when composing his *Britannicarum Ecclesiarum Antiquitates* of 1639. This publication coincided with the outbreak of the Bishops' Wars, when the prophecies of Mother Shipton, regarding the outbreak of war in the spring which the Scots would bring into England, had a potent vernacular currency.[56] Although Ussher himself made no claim to be a seer, he gained a considerable posthumous reputation as a prophet from the 1650s. His summative warning in a sermon at Dublin in 1601, that Ireland faced 40 years of judgement, was heralded as foretelling the Irish rebellion. His further warning in a sermon at Cambridge in 1625 about the consuming flames of wickedness was interpreted as predicting that the newly crowned Charles I would be confronted by war for his three kingdoms.[57] Ussher's primary concern, however, was not the propagation of prophecy based on biblical and secular texts but the endorsement of the Britannic vision of a godly monarchy as a matter of urgency. For the confidence in the ultimate victory of the godly over Antichrist, which inspired Calvinists throughout Britain, stood in marked contrast to Protestant perceptions in Ireland, that in the last days Antichrist would be at its strongest and the godly would be threatened with their greatest sufferings and persecution.[58] Accordingly, Ussher was among the more earnest of the Protestant episcopate in the three kingdoms who endorsed, with varying degrees of enthusiasm, the imperial concept of British union as advocated by James I.[59]

John Thornborough, Bishop of Bristol, viewed the providential reunification of the British empire under a godly monarch as an occasion of great happiness that would be perfected by the eventual merging of the constituent identities of England and Scotland into a composite British nation.[60] James I himself had sponsored the publication of two works in Scotland that sought to ally providence and prophecy to his Britannic project. The claims of an anonymous English apologist that the miraculous and happy union between England and Scotland would prove expeditious and profitable to both nations, and stop unnecessary wars, were reprinted in Edinburgh in 1604. This attempt to convince the Scottish Estates to participate, without equivocation, in the creation of 'the moste opulent, strong and entire Empire of the worlde', which would be capable of transatlantic confrontation with Spain and the papacy, was made redundant by the failure of the English parliament to support political incorporation.[61] Nonetheless, James remained determined to demonstrate that secular prophecy had run its course, and that his accession to the English throne was the peaceful fulfilment of British unification not only predicted by the likes of Merlin, Bede and Thomas the Rhymer, but also endorsed from French and Danish sources. A text, published in Edinburgh with royal approval in 1617 and printed in both Latin verse and Scots metre, gained notable British currency throughout the 1640s. For the prophecies favouring union and concerted action against the papal Antichrist could also be interpreted to uphold Covenanting claims against the absentee Stuart monarch to secure Scottish deliverance from dependence on England, their recovery of Berwick-upon-Tweed (lost since the Wars of Independence) and the imposition of British unification from the north.[62]

The realignment of the Britannic perspective to serve the Royalist cause of Charles I led to the reissue of Thornborough's plea of 1604 for a composite British nation in 1641. At the same time, Thomas Heywood published his *Life of Merlin*, which allied secular prophecy to a chronological account of English history from Brut to Charles I. Thus, the accession of the Stuart dynasty in 1603 was not only the fulfilment of prophecy but also the laying to rest of English hegemonic claims over Scotland.[63] Ussher's contemporaneous work on biblical chronology had reputedly undermined the mythic line of Scottish kings, and in the process Buchanan's staunch advocacy of a contractual rather than an organic bond between monarchy and civil society.[64] But Buchanan's vibrant intellectual legacy was central to the Scottish formulation. Evident in the contractual interpretation of fundamental law favoured by the Scottish Estates in the negotiations for union that were terminated in 1607, this legacy resurfaced in the National Covenant of 1638, the centrepiece of Scottish providentialism in the mid-seventeenth century.[65]

Notwithstanding differences in polity between Episcopalianism and Presbyterianism, the Protestant doctrine of the Kirk of Scotland had remained staunchly Calvinist since the Reformation. The Arminian challenge, first aroused within the Dutch Reformed Kirk before spreading to the Church of England, had gained no foothold in Scotland before 1629. Arminianism accepted Calvinist orthodoxy with regard to original sin and justification by faith, but rejected its absolute belief in predestination which offered salvation only for the elect and eternal damnation for the reprobate. Hence, the Calvinist teaching that the grace of God was irresistible for the elect, who as the true believers could not fall from grace, was renounced in favour of universal atonement. This precept offered salvation to every individual prepared to repent of his or her sins. For the Arminian, therefore, the assurance of salvation was freely available for all believers but conditional on human endeavour. For the Calvinist, who believed in absolute and exclusive salvation for the elect, belief in free will was an unwarrantable limitation on the sovereignty of God. The Kirk, however, was concerned not only to promote the salvation of the elect but to identify the national interest with a dutiful dedication to the godly life. Doctrinal precepts, moreover, underwrote the international responsibilities of the Kirk, which retained a watching brief over the fate of Reformed Protestantism. This special concern was intensified by the course of the Counter-Reformation and the political alignments brought about by the Thirty Years War. For the alliance of militant Catholicism and Habsburg autocracy was ranged against and initially triumphant over Reformed interests within the Holy Roman Empire.[66]

Kirk-inspired fears of the Counter-Reformation, coupled to James I's decided preference for erastian Episcopalianism after 1603, prompted militant Presbyterians to band together locally in covenants. Banding together for the purposes of local government or political alliance was a socially established practice in Scotland that had been adopted specifically for religious purposes at the Reformation. Yet the description of a religious band as a covenant only gained common currency after 1590, as a result of the arrival from the continent of covenant or federal theology. In Scotland, as in New England, the idea of the covenant was popularly translated in the early seventeenth century not simply as an elaboration of God's compact with the elect, but as a means of revealing God's purposes towards his people.[67] At its most potent, the covenant could be interpreted as a divine band between God and the people of Scotland. Such a covenant had a comprehensive appeal for Scottish society as a whole, not just the political elite. Covenanting was still a minority activity for Presbyterians in the opening decades of the seventeenth century, however. After the exhortation from the Kirk's general assembly for a mutual band between ministers and their congregations in 1596, no national renewal occurred until 1638.[68]

In return for a guarantee that James I would attempt no further liturgical innovations, the Scottish Estates in 1621 had ratified the Five Articles, whose most controversial aspect was that all members of congregations were required to kneel when participating in communion. The ensuing reluctance of the bishops to publicise nonconformity by prosecution had enabled Presbyterian laity, with the connivance of sympathetic ministers, either to absent themselves from communion or to refrain from kneeling. A more radical development was the covert growth of praying societies, known as conventicles, which sought to sustain the purity of the Kirk by private meetings for collective devotion. By 1629, conventicling circuits established for preaching and administering nonconforming communions had spread from Edinburgh to Fife, to west-central and south-west Scotland and on into Ulster. In essence, conventiclers were a pressure group who acted as catalysts for rather than instigators of revolution. Collective as well as personal discipline was maintained by periodic fasting. Their militant sense of righteousness reinforced their assurance that they were God's elect on earth. However, their elitist image, not dissimilar to that of the Puritans in New England, exposed them to charges of separatism.[69]

For their part, the conventiclers were not convinced that the nobles, as leaders of the political nation disaffected with the authoritarian rule of Charles I, were intent on the pursuit of godliness. Nonetheless, the disaffected leadership came to appreciate the ideological advantage of such an association. For the conventiclers were foremost among nonconforming Presbyterians advocating communal banding in covenants as the alternative religious standard to liturgical innovations promoted imperiously by Charles I and the Arminian-inclined Archbishop of Canterbury, William Laud. The covenant of grace and works not only assured the righteous of their temporal as well as their spiritual calling, but affirmed the special relationship between God and Scotland whose people were heirs to ancient Israel as his covenanted nation. Thus, covenanting in Scotland was a tangible manifestation of the divine connection between God and the Scottish people. Covenanting adherence in Scotland was not so much a decisive cause of revolt against Charles I as a means of communicating symbolically a fundamental ideological message: that opposition to the royal prerogative in defence of religious and civil liberty was divinely warranted. By identifying their cause with the covenant of grace and works, the disaffected availed themselves of the seventeenth-century equivalent of liberationist theology, which found political expression first through the National Covenant for Scotland in 1638 and then through the Solemn League and Covenant for Britain in 1643.[70]

The act of covenanting provided the Scots with the political will to effect British revolution. No less potent, though lacking public endorsement from Presbyterian ministers, was the popular appeal of secular prophecy. A gentleman of Newcastle writing to a friend in London on 8 September 1640, when the north of England was occupied by the Covenanting Army at the conclusion of the Bishops' Wars, records the insolent discourse of the common Scottish soldiers. Not only did they routinely disparage the Royalist war effort and, indeed, the martial prowess of the English nation, but in their cups they justified their conquest as the fulfilment of prophecy. Particularly remarkable was their recitation of verses translated from Latin into Scots, attributed to Merlin and applied to the course of the Bishops' Wars, 'and they beleeve it noe lesse then Gospell'. These verses were in fact textual variants of the first in the series of *The Whole Prophecies* printed in Edinburgh and dedicated to King James of Great Britain in 1617. Especial weighting was given to the lines asserting that England faced forcible flattening, sudden death and ruination, having been betrayed from within as well as besieged by the Scots. Irish plotting and Welsh menaces were compounded by French hostility and Dutch alienation, which foretold greater griefs to come.[71]

Such prophesying underscored the commitment of the Covenanting movement to secure recognition from the crown and the English parliament of the political independence of Scotland, recognition attained by the Treaty of London in August 1641. Conversely, prophesying from the perspective of Merlin Caledonicus on reformation rather than conquest also facilitated the refashioning of the regal union into British confederation, the substance of the Solemn League and Covenant of 1643 that

found institutional expression through the Committee of Both Kingdoms from 1644 to 1646.[72] However, prophecy that foretold a return to
peace in the British Isles after the cathartic impact of war on all three
kingdoms instigated from the north could be utilised also from a Gothic
perspective: thus, the prospect of the English triumphing over internal
foes as well as external enemies justified the forcible conquest of Ireland
and the occupation of Scotland by Oliver Cromwell in 1650–51.[73]

The Gothic interpretation of providence and prophecy in England
had initially shared a common grounding in Calvinist orthodoxy with
the Britannic. Protestant polemicists through sermons and journals
viewed the repeated intervention of the Almighty as confirmation that
England was an elect nation. But the whole nation was not chosen for
salvation, thus the religious sense of nationhood fostered by providentialism and prophecy was discriminatory and ultimately divisive, with
transatlantic fault lines opening up from the 1620s between Puritans and
Arminians and from the 1640s between Presbyterianism and Independent Congregationalists.[74] God's providential frustration of the Spanish
Armada in 1588, of the Gunpowder Plot in 1605 and of the Spanish
match between the Infanta and Prince Charles in 1624 were translated
vernacularly into celebrations of national deliverance marked by bonfires, the ringing of church bells and public holidays. By the 1630s,
however, these celebrations against the satanic alliance of the Habsburgs
and the papacy were increasingly identified with Puritanism and the
preservation of Calvinist orthodoxy.[75] Although this stance can appear
xenophobic and insular, Calvinist orthodoxy had been sustained at the
Synod of Dort in 1618, held on the recommendation of James I and
attended by British clerics to counter the growth of Arminianism in and
from the United Provinces.[76] Nevertheless, with Charles I married to the
French Catholic Henrietta Maria in 1625, and with his endeavours to
distance himself from the northern European Protestant powers in
favour of a Habsburg rapprochement after 1632, Puritan apprehensions
were heightened rather than abated by the favour accorded to Arminianism by William Laud. As Archbishop of Canterbury from 1633, he
was more interested in a peaceful accommodation with the papacy than
with the perpetuation of militant antagonism towards Rome.[77]

Polarisation between Puritanism and Arminianism turned what had
been primarily a localised or regional festive culture into an English
political divide – in effect, a vernacular contention between the Britannic and the Gothic that predated the military divide of the civil wars.[78]
Undoubtedly, the Gothic perspective gained a particular momentum by

linking the dangers of Roman Catholicism towards England with the purportedly extensive massacres of Protestants in Ireland in 1641. The subsequent deposition of witnesses testified to the treacherous intent of the Irish rebels to reject English overlordship, whether exercised by Charles I or Parliament, and to establish their own monarchy with the full backing of the papacy. Deliverance from the popish plots and Irish designs on England engineered by the Catholic Confederates remained a recurrent theme of almanacs and other vernacular publications during the 1640s.[79]

Conversely, the Scots were viewed benignly, as military guarantors for the English parliament in its protection of laws and liberties against an authoritarian monarchy, a fraternal assistance that was consolidated by the Solemn League and Covenant in 1643. Over the next five years, however, the prospect of Presbyterian solidarity gave way before the rise of Oliver Cromwell and the Independents, the formation of the New Model Army and the failed Engagement between Charles I and conservative Covenanters. Although Cromwell remained supportive of the radical Covenanters who reasserted their political control in 1648, the trial and execution of Charles I and the attempted Scottish patriotic accommodation with Charles II as the covenanted King of Great Britain drove an irreparable breach between the Gothic and Scottish perspectives. Covenanters became as much enemies as the Irish Confederates. Accordingly, George Wither, the vernacular soothsayer and Puritan poet, who had originally fought against the Scottish Covenanters during the Bishops' Wars, signalled his move from Royalist sympathiser to Parliamentary stalwart in *Britain's Second Rembrancer* (1641). While he remained virulently anti-Irish, his attitudes towards the Scots were mollified by the Covenanters' support for the Parliamentary forces, in which he acquired the rank of major. Nonetheless, the internecine divisions between the English and the Welsh, the Scots and the Irish were likened to a discordant game of cards, presaging either the tearing asunder or the forcible reunification of all three kingdoms in *Prosopopoeia Britannica* (1648). A supporter of the regicide, Wither's call to the well-affected for public thanksgiving for the English republic's merciful deliverance from domestic and foreign tyrants was articulated in *The British Appeal* (1650), which lambasted both the bloody Irish and the acquisitive Scots (for their designs on the four northern English counties which they had occupied in 1640–41 and again from 1644 to 1647).[80]

Wither and, to a far greater extent, John Milton were proponents of the prophetic epic which bolstered the Gothic nature of the republican regime in England during the 1650s, a decade in which providence and prophecy not only shaped the political argument but inspired Oliver Cromwell and his closest associates to claim divine sanction for their conquest and incorporation of both Ireland and Scotland into first the Commonwealth and then the Protectorate from 1654. Indeed, John Milton claimed that the Commonwealth was the true heir to British loyalty originally vested in the Stuarts and then in the Solemn League and Covenant of 1643. The refusal of the Irish and the Scots to accept the regicide were manifestations of their selfish sectional interests that ran against the commonweal to which England alone remained providentially committed. The underhand behaviour of powerful factions in both countries disguised their violent intentions to undermine the English core of British loyalty. No matter their aggressive behaviour as conquerors, republican commentators were shielded from self-criticism by the godly reason with which the English under Cromwell had reconstructed themselves not just as a superior but as a chosen people.[81] Cromwell's close political associate and ambassador to Sweden, Bulstrode Whitelocke, personifies the polemical importance of further bolstering the Gothic standpoint with judicial astrology. Not only was the first English translation of Olaus Magnus dedicated to him in 1658,[82] but he was the assiduous patron of William Lilly, the most prolific and prosperous astrologer of the mid-seventeenth century, who initially published his revelations under the sobriquet Merlinus Anglicus Junior or, alternatively, England's Prophetical Merlin from 1644.

Lilly's extensive output, his vigorous engagement with Royalist rivals like Sir George Wharton and his close association with first Parliament and then the Commonwealth make him an immensely valuable political weathervane for the emergent dominance of the Gothic perspective by the late 1640s.[83] In 1644, Lilly attested his willingness to serve his country and promote unity between England, Scotland and Ireland. While England and Scotland had consolidated their union through Parliamentarians and Covenanters, he predicted Ireland would in time come in 'when the blood of the massacred English Protestants is restored'. He also informed the Covenanting movement in 1645 that 'some waspish Antagonists of that nation against Astrology' would not diminish his love for Scotland. By 1647, he asserted his confidence that Scotland would resist traitorous accommodations with the Royalists and continue to assist the Parliamentary forces against 'the inhumane' Irish Confederates. In the course of the Engagement between conservative Covenanters and Charles I, he dismissed 'those who plead Scottish civility or call them Brethren' as an affront to Parliament. At the same time, he was still prepared to exonerate from blame the radical Covenanters opposed to the Engagement, whom he deemed honourable and lovable. In the aftermath of the regicide and the attempted patriotic accommodations with Charles II, he became an apologist for English republican hegemony over both Scotland and Ireland.[84]

While his capacity to predict the outcome of battles and the lifting of sieges enhanced his public reputation, Lilly's acclaimed powers of prognostication were expressed most notably in his interpretation of such prophecies as the White King, the Dreadful Deadman and the Lyon of the North. The first of these, who brought about British disunity and the invasion of England from Scotland, was identified with Charles I, articulating a fear within court circles that had sought unsuccessfully to dissuade the monarch from wearing white robes at his English coronation in 1625. His interpretation of the second prophecy paved the way for Oliver Cromwell as the restorer of order throughout the British Isles. By denying that Charles II was the Lyon of the North – an appellation also applied to Gustav II Adolph, the Swedish leader of the Protestant forces in the Thirty Years War at the outset of the 1630s – Lilly negated the restoration of the Stuarts through a patriotic accommodation with the Scots in 1650–51. However, he did leave the door open for the eventual Restoration of Charles II to all three kingdoms from the north, albeit he predicted this would happen in 1663 rather than in 1660.[85]

In the same way that Milton led the Gothic claims for providential authority in his anglocentric interpretation of Britain, Lilly had demonstrated the flexibility of prophecy when applied to a Gothic perspective on contemporary politics. The Restoration ostensibly marked a more sceptical approach to the impact of providence and prophecy, as evident in the reminiscences of the exiled Royalist Edward Hyde, who attributed rebellion primarily to natural causes, and in the religious exegesis of such displaced academics as John Rotheram, formerly of Oxford but writing from Barbados, to affirm that the age of miracles had passed. Nonetheless, a desire to judge men for their conduct in the revolutionary decades remained a political as well as a religious imperative.[86] For those contemporaries within, rather than detached from, the three kingdoms at the Restoration, the prevailing discourse remained that of providential triumphalism reinforced by biblical as well as secular prophecy. Thus, the Riders Almanacs, produced under the title of *The British Merlin*, moved seamlessly from a Gothic to a Britannic perspective between 1656 and 1661. Simultaneously, the restoration of the Stuart dynasty aligned

God's special providence, prophetic deliverance and historic legitimacy not only with the Britannic perspective, but also with the conclusion of the political convulsions that had divided the British Isles since the time of Brut.[87] Manifestly, the Restoration marked the final phase of the British Revolution. However, there was no need to look further back for its origins than the prerogative rule of Charles I, set within the transnational and transoceanic context of the Britannic empire.

2   The Britannic Empire, *c.*1629

The hopes of James I, if not for a perfect union, at least for political and commercial integration of England and Scotland, were terminated by a wrecking motion in the House of Commons in September 1607. Nonetheless, James was determined to demonstrate the sovereign independence of the three kingdoms under imperial monarchy. Accordingly, he promoted an international British agenda as manifest in foreign policy through espionage, embassies and military intervention in the Thirty Years War, a policy continued by his son Charles I on his accession in 1625. At the same time, the early Stuart's Britannic version of *ius imperium* gave territorial as well as ideological integrity to the unity of Scotland, England and Ireland as multiple kingdoms – a perspective which also sought to demonstrate the interdependence of the three kingdoms at home and abroad.[1] Thus, James implemented civilising projects designed to bring order throughout his exclusive Britannic empire – namely, the cross-border policing of the middle shires, the plantation of Ulster, and the military and legislative offensive against the West Highlands and Islands. The annexation of Orkney and Shetland was partly an extension of such a policy, but primarily the consolidation of the territorial waters around the British Isles into the Stuart's *ius imperium*. His projection of the Stuarts as the first composite British dynasty impacted significantly on colonial policy. While trading and colonial ventures were authorised separately from Scotland and England, the Britannic perception of empire was particularly suited to their endeavours to challenge, by acquisition and settlement, Spanish dominion in the New World.[2]

However, the Britannic perspective faced several obstacles. The rejection of full union meant that there was no formal British executive or legislature for all three kingdoms. The bedchambers of the early Stuarts did afford a measure of informal policy co-ordination, which ensured that neither early Stuart was uncounselled in British affairs.[3] The lack of a unified legal system required patents for honours to be issued separately for England, Ireland and Scotland which, in turn, inhibited the creation of a British nobility, notwithstanding the growing tendency of courtiers to hold titles in more than one kingdom. The English parliament manifested a continuing Gothic hostility to the use of the designation 'Great Britain' in its dealings with the crown.[4] Likewise, once political and commercial integration had been rejected, the Scottish Estates reverted to the practice of not using Great Britain. Nonetheless, the Scots were foremost amongst the peoples of the three kingdoms in accepting the British internationalism of their native dynasty. Scots played significant roles, overtly and covertly, in the military and diplomatic affairs concerted from the British court. Some Scots, as proponents of the Britannic empire, used the appellation 'Britanno-Scotus'. Others preferred the more ambivalent 'Scoto-Britannus', which sustained Scottish perceptions of aristocratic republicanism and confessional confederation.[5]

Britannic Monarchy

Intent on demonstrating his *ius imperium* by land and sea, James I was a monarch who preferred persuasion to coercion. The concept of kingship brought by James into England drew heavily on the notions of divine right that the King of Scots had ardently propagated to counter demands for Presbyterian autonomy within the Kirk or fractious nobles in the state. Simultaneously, divine right had been deployed to promote his claims to the English throne. In keeping with his successful exercise of kingship in Scotland, James determined upon the equitable management of constituent interests throughout his British dominions. Despite the rejection of political and commercial integration in 1607, personal forbearance, based on the distinction between the theoretically absolute powers of an imperial monarch and the empirical exercise of political entente, continued to shape his relationship with the English parliament. Thus, his parliamentary address of March 1610 distinguished between the absolute powers which served for law at the first establishment of monarchy and the present, settled state of a kingdom governed by its own fundamental laws and orders. In essence, James and the parliamentary upholders of common law did not disagree about the importance of constitutional consensus, but over the priorities for its achievement. Advocates of the Gothic perspective viewed the king's prerogative power as supplementary to statutes grounded in common law. James, however, claimed divine right to suspend or dispense with statutes whenever he deemed that particular circumstances warranted the

exercise of his prerogative powers. Notwithstanding subsequent observations on the omniscient impact of statute when implemented, James
never fully came to grips with the contractual limitations on monarchy
implicit in the English concept of parliamentary sovereignty.[6]

Nonetheless, his imperial standing not just in England but in all three
kingdoms was reinforced by the internationalism of his Britannic perspective. Not only was James I intent on fostering political stability at
home, but he also elevated Great Britain into the premier league of international diplomacy. He was instrumental in establishing the political
accord that prevented the territorial dismemberment of Russia to suit
the respective interests of Sweden, Poland and the English Muscovy
Company prior to the accession of the Romanov dynasty in 1613. His
sponsorship of international synods at Tonneins in 1614 and at Dort in
1618–19 marked him out as the undisputed leader of the Reformed or
Calvinist tradition and a creditable promoter of a united Protestant front
of Calvinists and Lutherans against Habsburg hegemony and the
Counter-Reformation. At the same time, his attempted diplomatic
symmetry through marriage alliances opened up the prospect of a pan-
European accommodation, if not the reunion of Christendom.[7]

Ten years after the marriage of his daughter Elizabeth to the influential German prince Frederick, the Elector Palatine, in 1613, James
attempted the betrothal of Charles, as Prince of Wales, to the Spanish
Infanta. In the interim, however, the Elector Palatine's efforts to secure
election as King of Bohemia and prevent the Austrian Habsburg arch-
duke, Ferdinand, becoming Holy Roman Emperor had been overturned.
Their dispute had instigated the European conflagration that became
known as the Thirty Years War from 1618. Within two years, Ferdinand
II, as the successful candidate for emperor, had annexed Bohemia as a
hereditary possession of the Austrian Habsburgs. His determination to
suppress Protestantism within his imperial estates led him to move
against the Palatinate, forcing Frederick and Elizabeth into exile in the
Dutch Netherlands. By 1621, the expiry of the 13-year truce between
the United Provinces and Spain faced Europe with the imminent realisation of Habsburg hegemony. The Spanish crown's obvious lack of
enthusiasm for a marriage alliance meant that James was increasingly
drawn by established family ties towards direct involvement in the Thirty
Years War in association with the United Provinces and France in an
anti-Habsburg alliance. However, while James had faced increasing
criticism in the English parliament and in the vernacular press for his
manifest failure to support either Elector Frederick or the Dutch, his

public pacifism had not prevented his covert military and financial support for the recovery of the Palatinate. Further pushed by his Lutheran brother-in-law, Christian IV of Denmark–Norway, whose territorial ambitions in northern Europe were threatened by the attachment of Poland–Lithuania to the Habsburg alliance, James stalled on making an irrevocable commitment to military intervention on the side of the elector and other Protestant princes. The anti-Habsburg coalition that was concluded at The Hague in December 1625 occurred nine months after his death.[8]

Notwithstanding his willingness to deploy force and, indeed, countenance the increase of covert British forces engaged in the Thirty Years War, James was not an exponent of absolutism. Nowhere in his British dominions did he endeavour to create a standing army, the essential feature of any absolute regime.[9] His preference for persuasion over coercion, allied to his belief in the providential nature of his imperial calling, led to his firm promotion of Episcopalianism through pulpit and polity in all three kingdoms. Calvinism, as received in Scotland at the Reformation, had stressed resistance to ungodly monarchy, a feature reinforced by Andrew Melville and his associates, whose vociferous claims for ecclesiastical autonomy had led to the first period of Presbyterianism in the Kirk during the 1590s. Accordingly, when the regal union was being effected, James was in the process of wresting control of the Kirk from the Melvilleans. This was accomplished initially by the insinuation of bishops into parliament as the restored clerical estate; then by their appointment as constant moderators of the regional synods, supported by episcopal adherents in the same capacity in the district presbyteries; and finally, by the full spiritual restoration and reconsecration of the Scottish episcopate by the English in 1610.

The royal prerogative was further deployed to fortify episcopal authority along Anglican lines by the creation of courts of high commission, which provided civil sanctions for ecclesiastical censures. Presbyterianism was not abolished, however. James had preferred to graft diocesan control onto the existing hierarchical system of church courts. The parliamentary ratification of the king's ecclesiastical policy in 1612 omitted any reference to the bishops being subject to censure by general assemblies, and their supreme legislative authority for the national affairs of the Kirk was not superseded. Thus, the liturgical innovations known as the Five Articles were introduced through a general assembly at Perth in 1618. The spirit of moderation and co-operation which characterised episcopal relationships with synods and presbyteries under the auspices of John Spottiswood as Archbishop of St Andrews was certainly strained but not sundered by their passage. For James had ensured their endorsement by the Scottish Estates in 1621 by his promise that there would be no further liturgical innovation that would push the Kirk towards congruity in worship with Anglicanism.[10]

At the same time as James was marginalising and dispersing the Melvilleans into internal or continental exile, he was overseeing a massive expansion of the nobility which gave the landed elite little grounds to make common cause with religious dissidents. By a parliamentary enactment of 1587, which had annexed the temporal property of the pre-Reformation church to the crown, James laid the foundation for his wholescale creation of temporal lordships primarily to reward gentry and burgesses drawn into royal service. Although an enactment of 1606 restored the temporalities of the Scottish bishops, temporal lordships created from secularised monastic property remained the most important avenue of elevation into the peerage, the crown in Scotland being notably more generous in this respect than the Tudors in England and Ireland. Having secured the temporalities and made prescriptive claims on the teinds (tithes) as the traditional spirituality of the Kirk, the landed elite was by no means receptive to Melvillean claims for teind redistribution to augment ministers' stipends, increase educational provision and enhance poor relief and other pious uses.[11]

In England, not only was there no apparent threat to the landed interest from clerical endeavours to reverse the dissolution of the monasteries, but there was also no tradition of reformation in defiance of the monarchy. Notwithstanding his failure to reconcile the Anglican establishment at Hampton Court to Puritanism in 1604, James was determined to deflect criticisms of his conduct as a godly prince by staunchly upholding Calvinism as received in England at the Reformation and moderated in the wake of the Synod of Dort in favour of hypothetical universalism. Whereas Presbyterians and Puritans relied on the preaching of the word to convey the exclusive message of salvation for the elect, the Anglican universalists sought to stress the inclusive nature of the church through communal participation in the sacraments and rituals of public worship. In emphasising the importance of grace but not denying election, Anglicanism, under the direction of George Abbot as Archbishop of Canterbury, did not compromise with Arminianism. Nonetheless, Dort had signalled potential divisions within the Church of England, especially the danger of polarity between Puritanism and Arminianism, if the uniquely Anglican perspective of hypothetical universalism could not be sustained. Accordingly, James would rather Puritans decamp for Ireland or the Americas than remain a divisive influence within England.[12]

In Ireland, Protestantism remained on the defensive, having failed to make appreciable inroads among the native Irish and the Old English beyond the Pale. Indeed, residual missionary inclinations among the episcopate were more than held in check by the religious and cultural dynamicism of the Counter-Reformation in Ireland.[13] At the same time, the secularisation of church property was no more a reversible process than in England or Scotland. Under the leadership of James Ussher as Archbishop of Armagh, the episcopate in Ireland was acutely conscious of the need to shore up solidarity among Protestants in the wake of plantation. Accordingly, the first national convocation of the Church of Ireland, which met simultaneously with the Irish parliament, issued 104 confessional articles in 1615 that were markedly more Calvinist than the 39 articles that had prevailed in the Church of England since the Reformation. Nonetheless, the Church of Ireland remained a dependency, not an entity autonomous from the Church of England. Although the Protestant episcopate was inclined to allow a discreet measure of accommodation on matters of polity and worship to both English Puritans and Scottish Presbyterians, such discretion was also practised by English and Scottish bishops under James I. However, no court of high commission operated to contain nonconformity within the Church of Ireland until 1636. Both the Puritans and the Presbyterians decanted into Ireland retained dissident elements that maintained sectarian links both within the island and with the British mainland.[14]

Britannic leniency towards nonconformity in general and Puritanism in particular was a feature of the public furore surrounding the collapse of the Spanish match in 1624. When Prince Charles and the royal favourite, George Villiers, Marquis (later Duke) of Buckingham, appeared to be stoking up resentment towards Spain in the English parliament, their disruptive militancy chimed in with the demands of Puritan polemicists for war against the Habsburgs in support of the Dutch Republic and the restoration of Elector Frederick and his 'Winter Queen' to the Palatinate.[15] That James, simultaneously, adopted a more relaxed, if not benign, approach to Arminianism was a clear sign that he was losing his political touch in his dotage, a tendency particularly attested by his handling of Scottish affairs.

The last years of James's reign witnessed a marked decline in his responsiveness to the political nation. The landed classes became increasingly disillusioned with absentee kingship, especially as James had reneged on his promise at the regal union that he would return to Scotland every three years. He did so only once – in 1617. At the same time, he instigated the beginnings of teind redistribution. In 1620, he attempted to circumvent parliament by having a convention of the nobility vote supply, and when this manoeuvre was rejected he introduced a new, extraordinary tax on annualrents (interest payments and annuities) for the assent of all the Scottish Estates in 1621. This tax, which was supplementary to the ordinary tax on land, was to be levied over the next four years, ostensibly to support British military engagement in the Thirty Years War. As all creditors and borrowers were required to submit bi-annual inventories of monies loaned, regular inquiries were instituted into the financial competence of landowners as estate managers. Simultaneously, the tax on annualrents acted as a disincentive to the working of capital and was disliked even more by the mercantile community, already growing restless with the readiness of James to grant patents and monopolies to courtiers and speculators.

Common cause among disaffected nobles, gentry and burgesses was enhanced by the packaged passage of all Five Articles in 1621 to prevent this liturgical programme being compromised by its most contentious issue, kneeling at communion. This issue, which was the touchstone for Presbyterian nonconformity, reconnected political and religious dissent in Scotland. The promulgation of the Five Articles through parliament galvanised a new generation of radicals within the ministry, most notably Alexander Henderson and David Dickson, who had hitherto acquiesced in erastian Episcopalianism. This radicalism found favourable reception with nobles such as John Leslie, 6th Earl of Rothes, whose continuing disquiet with the last years of James spilled over into Charles I's reign. The parliament of 1621 also precipitated a loss of confidence within the governmental framework of absentee kingship. Nonetheless, there was no immediate prospect of the collapse of Britannic monarchy in, or precipitated from, Scotland.[16]

Despite tensions created by the prominent influx of Scots to the British court following the regal union, neither a dominant Scottish presence nor the resultant English antagonism was sustained throughout the reign of James I. For Scotland, the dominant feature of monarchy by 1629 was absenteeism. Charles, who had belatedly departed for England as an infant in 1604, did not return to Scotland until 1633. On the one hand, absenteeism undoubtedly added to the mystique of Britannic monarchy, which stood above faction and the familiar readiness of prominent Scottish politicians to criticise royal policies. On the other hand, absenteeism, compounded by the more mannered English practice of adulation and flattery from favourites and their clients, fuelled fears that Scotland, like Ireland, would be reduced to a province.[17] Notwithstanding the rather intemperate statement of Charles I in 1625, 'that the welfare of England is inseparable from [that of] Scotland', he like his father was intent on promoting the Stuarts internationally as a British dynasty. Both furthered the Britannic perspective of the Stuarts – not the process of anglicisation[18] – through foreign, frontier and colonial policies.

Foreign Policy

Treaties of war and peace, and marriage alliances – whether projected ones, like the Spanish match, or those that were accomplished, like that with France for the marriage of Henrietta Maria to Charles I – were contracted on behalf of the crown of Great Britain and Ireland, not of England – a pattern maintained from the regal union and only broken by the emergence of the Covenanting movement. In terms of diplomatic accreditation, the early Stuarts preferred to represent both Scotland and England as kings of Great Britain when addressing and being addressed by such monarchs as Christian IV of Denmark–Norway, Gustav II Adolph and Queen Kristina of Sweden, and the Romanov tsars of Russia; likewise the nobility and elective kings of Poland, the cities of the Hanseatic League and the Germanic princes within the Holy Roman Empire. In the absence of a British peerage, the honours system of both countries was deployed to reward diplomats. Thus, Sir James Hay, the Scot who also headed the espionage service under James I, was ennobled in England first as Viscount Doncaster, then as Earl of Carlisle. Charles I awarded Scottish titles to English career diplomats such as Walter Aston, who was created Lord Forfar.[19]

With respect to the actual conduct of diplomatic affairs, James I had rationalised his ambassadorial service. Scots were accorded primacy in Scandinavia and northern Europe, while Russia and the rest of Europe remained the leading but not the sole preserve of English diplomats – a division of labour Charles I sustained until the emergence of the Covenanting movement.[20] Scottish diplomats such as Sir Robert Anstruther and his half-brother Sir John Spens were given formative roles in Scandinavia and the Baltic, where the Scottish crown had hitherto exercised a distinctive influence and enjoyed diplomatic relations no less cordial than those accorded to the English. Anstruther continued as the foremost British diplomat in the region after the accession of Charles, overseeing British military intervention in support of Christian IV of Denmark–Norway. Building upon his good standing with the Hanseatic League, Charles later gave Anstruther the key responsibility of negotiating with the Germanic princes at the close of 1632, when British backing for Swedish intervention in the Thirty Years War had been checked by the death of Gustav II Adolph at Lutzen that September. British intervention in support of the Swedish king had been brokered effectively between Anstruther and Spens, who also acted for Denmark and Sweden respectively in their diplomatic dealings with the Stuarts. In effect, the early Stuarts were not only redeploying Scottish diplomatic expertise, but were tapping into the emergence of specialist diplomats with an intellectual or military background in northern Europe. Reliance on networking by professional diplomats, which came to supersede but not to replace traditional embassies commissioned for specific tasks and negotiations, was a product of the Thirty Years War and the peculiar position of Sweden. For the Vasa dynasty was still striving for international recognition and was intent not only on breaking free from Danish dominance in Scandinavia but also on making territorial claims around the Baltic that were grounded in Gothic historiography.[21]

However, there was a difference in practice between formal documents in Latin attesting to British diplomacy and diplomatic exchanges conducted in the vernacular, where there was a cavalier interchange between the use of 'Great Britain' and 'England'. In part, this interchange was embedded within diplomatic treaties. The Spanish match was to be confirmed by the English parliament but toleration was to be offered to Roman Catholics in all the Stuart dominions. Henrietta Maria's marriage contract specified toleration for her fellow Catholics from France at the court and its environs in England. Buckingham was more inclined to refer to England than to Great Britain and Anstruther, when acting for the Danes, occasionally referred to English diplomatic concerns. He was even addressed by Spens in March 1621 as the 'Lord Ambassador from the King's Ma[jes]tie of England' – albeit he was drawing the attention of his half-brother to his own return to Scotland while on Swedish service. In turn, letters exhorting recruitment into Danish service, while often referring to Charles I as King of England and to his English Privy Council as the British Senate, always referred to officials and institutions such as the Privy Council north of the border as distinctively Scottish. The deployment of the term 'Anglo-Britannus'

by the veteran naval commander Charles Howard, 1st Earl of Nottingham, when petitioning Christian IV for the liberation of a suspect pirate
in October 1616, appears to have been a rather isolated usage which
certainly did not survive the reign of James I.[22]

Nonetheless, James Hay, as Viscount Doncaster, consistently reported
on British affairs when serving as ambassador at large at Brussels in
the Spanish Netherlands, at the imperial court in Salzburg and at The
Hague in the United Provinces in 1619–20. During this period (as later
on diplomatic service as the Earl of Carlisle), he accredited legations in
the service of the British king and practically deployed fellow Scots as
British agents when running the espionage service. Thus, after the most
powerful clan chief and foremost Scottish noble, Archibald Campbell,
7th Earl of Argyll, had fled into exile in the Spanish Netherlands during
1618, his continental stay of almost a decade was monitored by a British
espionage network controlled by Doncaster. Argyll, who had overstretched himself financially in pursuing British influence at court, had
come under sustained political attack in Scotland following the revelation of his conversion to Roman Catholicism, which he had concealed
since his second marriage, to Anna Cornwallis, a noted English recusant, in 1610. In the early years of his exile he became involved in the
émigré intrigues of the native Irish earls defeated in the Nine Years War
and their Scottish allies among the ClanDonald South in Kintyre and
Islay, exiled after rebelling against James I in 1615. Argyll, who had actually suppressed the rebellion of the ClanDonald South, was soon
detached from these intrigues, which were designed to facilitate a possible Spanish invasion of Ulster reinforced by support from the clans on
the Scottish side of the North Channel. Argyll was primarily concerned
with British rehabilitation rather than Gaelic adventurism, a rehabilitation that commenced in 1622 when he was licensed to recruit forces from
all three kingdoms into Habsburg service to complement the intended
Spanish match. His regiment, which included the first contingents of
Scots in Habsburg service, served to decant potentially troublesome
elements from both sides of the North Channel. Following Charles I's
declaration of war against Spain, Argyll gave up his command in the
Army of Flanders to secure acceptance at the British court.[23]

From an anglocentric perspective, the main focus of early Stuart
foreign policy appears to have been the political divisions occasioned by
support for Spain or the United Provinces. These divisions were not only
evident between the crown and the English parliament, but also served
to differentiate the factions advising on foreign policy at court.[24] Scottish

polemicists were to the fore in shaping this debate in British directions. Thus, Thomas Scott, the Anglo-Scot stridently sympathetic to the Dutch, took it upon himself to petition the English parliament in the name of Scottish ministers against the machinations of the papacy and Spain. At the same time, he sought to warn 'the British nation' in the aftermath of the Spanish match that it was a clandestine alliance of the papacy and the Habsburgs that was subverting the capacity of the German princes to aid in the restitution of the Palatinate.[25] Three years later, Peter Hay of Naughton 'in North-Britane' warned his fellow Scots of their need to wake up to the fearful dangers that threatened Great Britain from Spanish ambitions, particularly their deceitful skills 'to fish in drumblie waters'. While counselling Charles to exercise patience to win over all his subjects in a godly commonwealth, he was insistent that this was not the time for Scots to contest domestic issues with the king when the pressing British question was 'the preservation of the State'.[26]

For James Maxwell of Little Airds in Dumfriesshire, the threat to Protestantism was superseded by the threat to Christendom, a threat posed not by Spain but by the Turk. As a passionate advocate of British union and imperial monarchy, he urged a resolution of European differences. Having questioned the right of the Elector Palatine to the Bohemian crown, he even took up a post in Castile as historiographer royal to Philip IV of Spain. In calling from an apocalyptic perspective for a restored Constantine empire and, if necessary, a British Middle East, Maxwell was echoing the poetic message for the reintegration of Europe originally conveyed to Prince Henry by Sir William Alexander of Menstrie, the influential courtier and colonial undertaker who became Secretary of State for Scottish Affairs under Charles I. Patrick Gordon from Huntly in Aberdeenshire, using the unlikely vehicle of an epic poem celebrating the martial achievements of Robert the Bruce during the Wars of Independence in the fourteenth century, urged Prince Charles to fulfil the prophetic expansion of the imperial destiny of the Stuarts beyond the Danube, the Nile and even the Euphrates, to the Ganges.[27] However fanciful their notions, there was a clear realisation that an expansive empire was predicated on two practicalities. The first was the requirement for British forces; the second was the need to mobilise the martial culture of Scotland, traditionally associated with the clans but endemic throughout the Highlands and Lowlands, in the service of the Britannic empire.

Notwithstanding rival Spanish and Dutch alignments in the English parliament and at court, the main theatre of European war at the accession of Charles I was Germany. The most distinctive and most overt British military intervention in Danish then Swedish service was effected by the Scottish-dominated Stuart diplomatic corps in northern Europe. However, the formation of British forces in the service of the Stuarts actually predated the Thirty Years War. A British expeditionary force was first raised from English and Scottish forces redeployed from Dutch service when James decided to back the respective claims of the Electors of Brandenburg and Palatine over those of the Austrian Habsburgs to the duchies of Julich and Cleeves in 1609–10. On the outbreak of the Kalmar War in 1611, another British force was raised to assist the Danes against the Swedes. However, as Christian IV was aggressively resistant to peace negotiations, James condoned separate freelance recruitment in Scotland to assist the Swedes. Ironically, this latter recruitment was co-ordinated by Sir James Spens, then acting as both the British ambassador to Sweden and the general of all British troops in Sweden. No fighting took place between British and Scottish forces prior to the eventual conclusion of peace in 1613.[28]

When the Bohemian situation imploded in 1618, James authorised the separate levying of Scottish, English and British forces. Colonel John Seton raised the first contingent from the Scottish brigade in Dutch service, Sir Horace Vere recruited a regiment in England, while Sir Andrew Gray, a Scot already serving in Bohemia, returned to raise a British force in both Scotland and England in 1620. It was this latter mobilisation that led John Taylor, the water poet, to compose *An English-mans Love to Bohemia* as a valedictory address 'to all the noble Souldiers that goe from great Britaine to that honourable Expedition'. Taylor, who had accompanied James I when he returned to Scotland in 1617, extolled not only the accomplishments of Gray as colonel, but also the unification of the martial cultures. The English battle glories ranged from the Hundred Years War against France to the Tudor campaigns in Ireland, whereas those of the Scots were traced through the Wars of Independence and subsequent Crusades, conveniently glossing over the 'auld alliance' that usually pitted the Scots against the English. All past differences were now put aside, and the recent service of both the English and the Scots in the Dutch revolt against Spain was now to be consolidated in the service of the Winter Queen as a worthy undertaking that would 'immortalize our Britaines name'.[29]

When further contingents were mobilised under the German adventurer Count Ernst von Mansfeld in 1624–5, the regiments took on a distinctive British flavour, with English forces being added to the Scottish troops raised by Colonel Gray. Although he was assigned the command of an English regiment, Viscount Doncaster ensured that all his leading officers were Scots. While Mansfeld's forces won German recognition as a British expeditionary force, their patent lack of success in recovering the Palatinate was attributed by the Scots to English ineptitude. Such attitudes militated against the creation of a unified command to fight for Charles I against France and Spain, even though contingents from Ireland, led by planters but including displaced natives, joined the expeditionary forces. Scots were reluctant participants in the British contingent commanded by the Scottish courtier William Douglas, 6th Earl of Morton, that was dispatched by Buckingham to relieve the Huguenots in La Rochelle after Charles I opened hostilities with France in 1626. Concerns for co-religionists were subordinated to apprehensions about losing favoured nation status in the wine trade. The French had been sufficiently mindful of the 'auld alliance' to set at liberty the 60 Scottish ships among the 120 British vessels impounded while loading claret at Bordeaux. Other major European powers were also prepared to exercise positive discrimination in order to unravel the British packaging of the Stuarts. When Charles I declared war on Spain in 1625, the Spaniards reciprocated against the three kingdoms – yet freedom of trade was maintained with the Scots and the Irish, 'as they coloured not English goods'.[30]

Apprehensions about a unified command structure were, in part, resolved by placing British forces raised for Danish service under the command of the Scottish courtier Robert Maxwell, 1st Earl of Nithsdale, in 1627 and those for Swedish service, four years later, under another Scottish courtier, James Hamilton, 3rd Marquess of Hamilton. However, Scottish freelance recruitment for Swedish service had already commenced in 1629 under Sir James Spens, whom Gustav II Adolph had confirmed as commander of the British forces while he was serving as Swedish ambassador to the King of Great Britain. Freelance Scottish recruitment continued once Hamilton's expeditionary force had failed to make any significant impression after 15 months in the German theatre. A key element of this latter recruitment was that the Scottish troops were to remain distinctive units within the Swedish army, as was already the practice in the French and Dutch armies. They were not mingled in with all other forces as had happened under Danish service, and, where integrated with other British forces, their command structure was predominantly Scottish.[31]

Scots composed over 50 per cent of the 100,000 troops raised from the three kingdoms to fight in the anti-Habsburg forces, a preponderance reinforced by the overwhelming dominance of Scots among the career officers. Over 90 per cent of around 3000 identifiable officers from the British Isles were Scottish.[32] At a time when confessionalism was becoming a significant recruiting factor throughout Europe, Scottish motivation – beyond traditional ties of the 'auld alliance' with France – was overwhelmingly in favour of Protestantism. Accordingly, Scottish forces in Scandinavian service were deemed reliable *hjaelptrupper* (help troops), not simply *lejetrupper* (mercenaries). Nonetheless, prominent Scottish Catholics such as Colonel Gray and the Earl of Nithsdale commanded British expeditionary forces. Their participation also demonstrates the widespread British commitment, first flagged up by Taylor, the water poet, to the restoration of Elizabeth Stuart and her family to the Palatinate. The Winter Queen assiduously cultivated the support of Scottish troops serving both within and beyond the British expeditionary forces. Notwithstanding his less than glorious assistance to the Swedish forces in 1631–2, the Marquess of Hamilton became the confidant of, if not the unofficial ambassador to, Elizabeth of Bohemia and broker for the recruitment of troops on her behalf from the British Isles. As is evident from contemporaneous pronouncements by the Kirk in favour of their Calvinist and other Reformed brethren in the Palatinate and Bohemia, from the vernacular press circulating within Scotland and from letters home from Scottish soldiers serving abroad, the restoration of the Stuart princess became the touchstone of Scottish engagement in the Thirty Years War.[33]

Scottish commanders in the imperial armies were also supportive of this Stuart restoration. Colonel Henry Bruce, though a committed Catholic, gave up his imperial command to join the British forces in 1620. He could no longer reconcile his employment by Ferdinand II with his desire to serve the Winter Queen, a sentiment that was also influential in the subsequent drift of Scottish troops away from service in the Spanish Netherlands and Poland towards Sweden. Walter Leslie of Balquhain in Aberdeenshire, though a Protestant, was created a count in the Holy Roman Empire for his involvement in the assassination of General Albrecht von Wallenstein at the behest of the emperor in 1634. After the Peace of Prague in 1635, which reconciled Catholic and Lutheran forces within Germany, Count Leslie laboured in vain to bring about a Stuart–Austrian Habsburg alliance to reclaim the Palatinate. Irish Catholic officers such Colonel John Butler also expressed sentiments supportive of the Winter Queen. While serving with the Habsburg forces in the Spanish Netherlands in 1631, Butler recanted his previous service for Poland–Lithuania against the Swedes, since Gustav II Adolph was now furthering the service of the king's sister.[34]

Like the Scots, the Irish had a vigorous martial culture and a penchant for freelance recruitment, usually in the service of the Habsburgs and potentially threatening to Britannic monarchy.[35] However, reported Habsburg backing in 1625 for the placing of Ireland under Spanish control and the deposition of Charles I as King of Scots was no more than Gaelic posturing by the native Irish earls exiled from Ulster. This posturing was fanned by Randal MacDonnell, 1st Earl of Antrim, claimant to the chiefship of the ClanDonald South and pretender to the lordship of the Isles, which had been forfeited by his clan forebears at the end of the fifteenth century.[36] Antrim, a political gadfly with extremely limited backing among the other Scottish branches of the ClanDonald, was indulging in the recreation of Gaelic solidarity across the North Channel that had been overtaken by rival perceptions of British state formation. On the Irish side, vernacular discourse was conducted primarily within the framework of faith and motherland to unite the native Irish and the Old English as *Éireannaigh*. The Scottish Gaels, now separated by the course of the Reformation as well as the North Channel, were cultivating the term *Albannaich* to further national cohesion between Highlander and Lowlander. Thus, the regimental history written by Colonel Robert Munro, a member of the clan elite of the Munros of Foulis in Cromarty, celebrated the achievements of Protestant Scottish forces primarily in Swedish service during the 1630s.[37] Indeed, the Irish threat with Habsburg backing did not materialise until 1640, two years after the Scottish *hjaelptrupper* had returned from Sweden and the German theatre to support the Covenanting revolution against Charles I.

Frontier Policy

The impact of the Britannic empire on frontier policy has been a neglected facet in introverted Scottish perspectives of state formation, which have been founded on three highly questionable assumptions: firstly, that the military and legislative programme pursued by the early Stuarts after 1603 was essentially a continuation of a centralising programme pursued before the regal union; secondly, that clans and families not directly engaging with Scottish central government cannot be deemed Scottish; and thirdly, that central government in Edinburgh was the sole arbiter of the process of civility propagated as the rationale for the crown's frontier policy.[38]

Although the Britannic agenda of the imperial monarchy was to produce markedly differing reactions within the three kingdoms, the regal union made possible concerted executive action in London, Dublin and Edinburgh which led to the implementation of four projects to civilise frontier areas – on the Anglo-Scottish borders, in Ulster, on the adjacent western seaboard in the Highlands and Western Isles, and in the Northern Isles of Orkney and Shetland. This frontier programme – to re-channel disruptive energies into productive settlement, to reorientate estate management commercially and to inculcate both social and religious reformation – was implemented with the assistance of the Royal Navy around all three kingdoms and with the support of the episcopate in all frontier dioceses.[39] At the same time, the 'de facto' role of chiefs and heads of families as local governors required Scottish central government to seek pragmatic working accommodations. Clan elites ostracised and, indeed, victimised by Scottish central government before 1603 could subsequently win political favour at the British court. Despite repeated endeavours to conform to the requirements from Edinburgh to demilitarise, give surety for their good conduct and insure their landed titles by avoiding rent arrears, successive Mackintosh chiefs of the Clan-Chattan fell prey to the territorial acquisitiveness of the noble house of Huntly. This acquisitiveness was checked, not by central government, but by the protection afforded to the Mackintosh chiefs by Archibald, 7th Earl of Argyll and chief of ClanCampbell, which enabled them to sustain their Gaelic cultural identity and, simultaneously, present themselves as orderly and loyal subjects of the crown by 1609. As a result of this political clientage, Sir Lachlan Mackintosh of Dunnachton, until his untimely death in 1622, combined his role as chief of ClanChattan with that of gentleman of the bedchamber and companion to Prince Charles.[40] The records of central government should not be deemed a reliable indicator of the situation within frontier localities. The political counsellors at Edinburgh were as adept at playing down continuous disruptions on the Anglo-Scottish borders as in overstating the impact of disorderly elements within the ClanDonald and their associates. The retention of Gaelic as against Scottish or Irish priorities on either side of the North Channel was not shared by all the clans on the western seaboard, far less those in the central, eastern and northern Highlands.[41]

As a first step in civilising the frontiers, the borders of Scotland and England became the middle shires of Britain. The main problem in this region had been the riding families, or reiving clans. In return for their ready deployment as political muscle, they had enjoyed the protection of powerful Scottish and English nobles. Long before the regal union, however, noble houses on both sides of the border had come to recognise the political, social and economic advantages of supporting their respective crowns in maintaining order. Reiving activities were subject not only to punitive but also to preventative measures. Set-piece dauntings, when the respective crowns separately mobilised military expeditions to overawe and hang incorrigible reivers, were expensive and rare. More usual, though less commemorated in Border ballads, were commissions of summary justice given to nobles to discipline reivers by fire and sword. Preventative measures tended to concentrate on making heads of families accountable for their followers in the same way that landlords were held responsible for the conduct of their tenantry. These sureties, which could be exacted comprehensively by the imposition of a general band, also carried fiscal sanctions. The most glaring weakness of the punitive measures was the capacity of riding families to flit across Scottish and English jurisdictions at will. This weakness was seemingly remedied in 1605 by the establishment of a conjoint Border police commission of five Scottish and five English judicial officers, led in the field by Sir William Cranston and directed from Edinburgh by George Home, 1st Earl of Dunbar, the effective manager of Scottish government in the wake of regal union, who shuttled regularly to court to co-ordinate British policy. Cross-border policing was declared a pronounced success within four years, yet the general band had to be reimposed in 1612. Border disturbances were a continuous, if localised, feature over the next three decades.[42]

Indeed, leading Border families availed themselves of indigenous political muscle in July 1626 in order to disrupt the endeavours of Scottish councillors to carry out directives from Charles I to establish prerogative courts and restructure central government. After Dunbar's death in 1611, there would appear to have been little co-ordination in policing between the Scottish Privy Council at Edinburgh and the English Council of the North at York. Indeed, the Council for Wales and the Marches was still concerned with demilitarisation along the controverted boundary during the 1630s. Despite a century of assimilation, Welshmen were still inclined to appear in 'harnesse or privie Coats' – that is, chain-mail waistcoats – when attending fairs, markets and even church services. That the Borders were partially pacified can be attributed less to reformed cultural attitudes than to the selective removal of disruptive elements by migration, either episodically through military service overseas or permanently as colonists in Ireland.[43]

The plantation of Ulster, as the showpiece British endeavour of the Stuart's frontier policy, was not formally launched until 1610, when the forfeited estates of the exiled Gaelic lords were contracted to undertakers and planters drawn from both England and Scotland. Although this was propagated as a British endeavour, the satellite relationship of Ireland was affirmed by the contractual emphasis on English common law as the determining influence in local government, estate management and conveyancing. In effect, Ulster was following the precedent set by the substantial colonisation of Munster from southern England in the 1580s, which continued as a distinctly English venture leavened by some Welsh settlers into the 1630s. The plantation of Connacht, which commenced in the Leitrim in 1619–20 as exemplary settlements among the native Irish, was a British venture that developed as an Ulster overspill through appropriation and selective leasing policies that worked to the detriment of Gaelic landholders.

Prior to the flight of the Irish earls of Tyrone and Tyrconnell, British settlements had actually commenced on escheated lands in the east of the province in 1606. Two Scottish adventurers had come to an arrangement that pre-empted the forfeiture of another Gaelic lord. Following a tripartite partition in which Conn O'Neill retained a third of his estates in County Down, Scottish migrants were encouraged by James Hamilton (subsequently Viscount Clandeboye) and William Montgomery of Braidstone (subsequently Viscount Ards) to settle in East Ulster. The paramount need to promote economic recovery after decades of continuous warfare ensured that there was limited displacement of the native Irish beyond the ranks of the landed classes. A minority, but not an insubstantial, stake in the Ulster plantation was allocated to Irishmen on condition that they adopted English agrarian practices and abandoned customary exactions from their tenantry. Randal MacDonnell of the Glens, the Gaelic lord ennobled as Viscount Dunluce in 1618, became a planter in East Ulster. Notwithstanding his Roman Catholicism, the future Earl of Antrim was noted for his diligence in recruiting Protestant farmers from Lowland Scotland, partly to evade crippling fines for recusancy, but primarily to further his commercial approach to estate management. The Scottish Catholic recusant James Hamilton, 1st Earl of Abercorn, took his Irish title as Viscount Strabane from his plantation in West Ulster. Their participation in the showpiece endeavour of frontier policy suggests the inclusion as much as the marginalisation of Ireland in the Britannic empire.[44]

It should not be presumed, however, that English and Scottish adventurers were uniformly enthusiastic about British plantation as a civilised undertaking. The City of London had to be continuously cajoled and reminded of their British obligations as undertakers for the planting of County Derry and the commercial development of Londonderry. Scottish undertakers and planters were able to capitalise on growing domestic prosperity which, in turn, attracted settlers of considerably higher calibre than the disruptive elements distilled from the Borders and other frontier areas. For it was only by the prior acquisition of funds in Scotland that settlers were provided with the necessary stake to develop the devastated tracts of Ulster. While the need for venture capital gave an undoubted advantage to migrants from commercially developed areas, planting by Scots in Ulster should not be regarded as the preserve of Lowlanders. Indeed, the conditions for British undertakers that were issued in 1610 specified inland Scottish as well as English planters. As borne out by the muster-rolls for the 1630s, Gaelic-speaking tenants in Ulster were neither exclusively Irish nor exclusively migrants displaced from the western seaboard as a result of the crown's associated policy of civilising Scottish Gaeldom. The imposition of punitive tariffs on grain imports by the Scottish Privy Council during the 1620s adversely affected the profitability of farming in Ulster and tangibly reduced immigration. But two bad harvests in successive years in 1635–6 brought a renewed flood of emigrants, mainly from north of the Tay. By the outbreak of the Covenanting movement, Scottish settlers in the province amounted to no less than a third and probably nearer to half of the 100,000 reputed immigrants.[45]

Notwithstanding the numbers migrating from Scotland, the efficacy of frontier policy in planting Ulster as a permanent wedge between the Scottish and the Irish Gaels must be scrutinised sceptically. The accompanying polemical rhetoric, which castigated the Gael for barbarity and incivility, cannot be dissociated from projected financial gains to the Scottish and English Exchequers. These gains, which proved more fictitious than factual, tended to be written by speculators rather than planters. In reality, the Stuart dynasty lacked the political commitment as well as the financial resources to effect the wholesale transformation of frontier society within Gaeldom. The process of civilising in all frontier regions relied on initiatives taken by leading local landowners to commercialise estate management at the expense of the customary practices and relationships consolidated by kinship and local association. Marketing of produce and labour took priority over the redistribution of surpluses through feasting and feuding.[46]

Moreover, concerted British action did not require a uniform policy for 'civilising' the Gael, albeit the screening of suitable colonists for Ulster was among the supplementary duties bestowed on the judicial commission charged to 'civilise' the western seaboard of Scottish Gaeldom in 1608. The two leading commissioners were Andrew Stewart, Lord Ochiltree, who had prior experience on the judicial commission for the Borders and subsequently became a colonial undertaker in Ulster, and Andrew Knox, Bishop of the Isles, who came to hold the Ulster diocese of Raphoe in conjunction with that of the Isles from 1611 to 1618. The initial aversion of chiefs and leading clan gentry to collaborate with Lord Ochiltree and Bishop Knox was usually remedied after brief spells of imprisonment in the Lowlands. Despite a shared cultural heritage, Gaelic society in Scotland had differed socially and legally from that in Ireland since the middle ages and religiously since the Reformation. Whereas clanship can be deemed a product of feudalism, kinship and local association, Gaelic society in Ireland lacked a corresponding feudal dimension. The loss of landed title by the clan elite, which threatened their clans' continuity of settlement on their ancestral territories, served as an established check to rebellion not commonplace among the Irish Gaels. Roman Catholicism, which was largely revived through Franciscan missions from Ireland and inroads by Jesuits and secular clergy based in landed households on the Lowland peripheries, posed no substantive threat to the gradual spread of Protestantism throughout Scotland following the Reformation in 1560.[47]

Regal priorities differed critically with respect to civilising influences. James I regarded Ulster as a province which, until planted with colonists, was not an acceptable part of his Britannic dominions. Scottish Gaeldom was held not to require such drastic surgery. In *Basilikon Doron*, he first drew a distinction between the virtually irredeemable islanders and the redeemable Highlanders. James VI subsequently demarcated the western seaboard of Scottish Gaeldom as an 'almost rotten and decayed' member of the body politic which was, nonetheless, capable of recovery through the inculcation of 'civilitie, obedyence and religioun' among the clans. The Scottish Privy Council also exerted a moderating influence by playing on the extravagance and impracticality of plantations along Ulster lines in Scotland – a case strengthened by the repeated failure of adventurers from Fife (including the future diplomat Sir John Spens of Wormiston) to establish a plantation on the island of Lewis in the teeth of clan hostility between 1598 and 1609. No less significantly, the prospect of a more fertile area for plantation in Ulster reinforced Lowland reluctance to participate in, or finance, the successive military expeditions required to uproot the clans of the western seaboard.[48]

Accordingly, the essence of frontier policy within Scottish Gaeldom was not to promote expropriation but primarily to expedite the pace at which the clan elite on the western seaboard would become assimilated into Scottish landed society. Only three clans, debilitated by internal dissension among their chiefs and leading gentry, were expropriated between 1607 and 1625 – namely, the MacDonalds of Kintyre and Islay (the ClanDonald South), the MacLeods of Lewis and the MacIains of Ardnamurchan. A fourth, the ClanGregor, was dispersed and outlawed. The Statutes of Iona of 1609, reissued piecemeal in the wake of the abortive rising of ClanDonald South in 1615, professed to educate the clan elite about their responsibilities as members of the Scottish landed classes, not to denigrate their status. Thus, the legislative programme concentrated on the redundancy of the *buannachan*, the military cadre who had served seasonally as 'redshanks' during the opposition of the native Irish to Tudor hegemony; on the commercial reorientation of customary relationships within the clans; and on the imposition of bands of surety to hold the clan elite accountable for the conduct of their followers. However, the redeployment of the *buannachan* in order to promote more commercialised estate management was but a gradual accomplishment, as is evident from the upsurge of banditry in maritime districts between 1609 and 1615 and occasional lapses into piracy by island clans during the 1620s and 1630s. A partial remedy was provided by the recruitment of clansmen as well as Borderers for military service abroad during the Thirty Years War.

At the same time, central government's insistence on annual accountability led chiefs and leading clan gentry to make prolonged and expensive stays in the Lowlands. Their accumulating debts severely strained and, in some cases, outstripped their financial resources despite increased rents. These debts were notably exploited by the acquisitive house of Argyll to expand the landed influence of the ClanCampbell, an influence already augmented by their role as leading instigators of and agents for selective military expropriation. In the process, the vernacular poetry of the Scottish Gael, like the strictures of their Irish counterparts against conquest and colonisation, afforded a uniquely forceful means of protest against the political, social and commercial ramifications resulting from intrusive British influences after 1603. Nevertheless, James I had clearly pointed the way for political advancement in Scotland and Ireland through acceptance of his Britannic vocabulary. The house of Argyll was to the fore from 1607 in using the term 'North British' for Scotland and 'British' for settlers in Ulster. The British influence at court of Archibald Campbell, the 7th earl, had been cultivated from 1604 by Richard Burke, 4th Earl of Clanricarde, the head of the prominent Old English family, later an acclaimed if absentee governor of Galway who later opposed the plantation of Connacht.[49]

The annexation of Orkney and Shetland between 1611 and 1614 was partly an extension of frontier policy in that culturally distinctive Norse customs were eradicated in favour of the standardised administration of law throughout Scotland. There was undoubted imperial symmetry in the imposition of Scots law over the Northern Isles to complement the imposition of English common law throughout Ulster. Simultaneously, a social and cultural reformation was promoted, persuasively through the influence of James Law as Bishop of Orkney and coercively by the for-feiture and subsequent execution of Patrick Stewart, Earl of Orkney. This racketeer had paid as little regard to the directives of the crown as the expropriated Gaelic elite in Scotland and Ireland. Control over Orkney and Shetland also opened up the prospect of British collaboration to compete effectively with Dutch dominance of the herring fishing in the North Sea. The Stuart dynasty remained acutely conscious of the finan-cial potential from an industry which commenced annually off Orkney and Shetland in June and continued along the Scottish and English coasts until late January. Although the Northern Isles were not formally planted, migrations from fishing communities in Fife and along the Moray Firth helped assert Scottish control over commercial outposts in the North Sea hitherto regarded as the preserve of the Dutch and the Hanse.[50]

However, there was a wider imperial reason for annexing islands mort-gaged to Scotland by the Danish–Norwegian crown in the mid-fifteenth century. The consolidation of the territorial waters around the British Isles into the Stuart's imperial dominions served as a practical rebuttal to the claims for *mare liberum* articulated by the Dutch jurist Grotius in 1609. These claims for open access, though primarily directed against the Spanish in the East and West Indies, had North Sea ramifications. Ten years earlier, John Dee, as naval adviser to Elizabeth Tudor, had advocated national security and imperial expansion based on exclusive maritime dominance, which not only termed all territorial waters the

'British Seas' but also laid claims to the Atlantic waters from Florida to Greenland and into the Arctic. Rather than have recourse to untutored civil law compilations to justify closed seas, James I preferred to rely on two Scottish jurists, William Wellwood and Craig of Riccarton, to sustain his intellectual case for *mare clausum* around his Britannic empire.[51] Although he reached an accommodation with his brother-in-law not to resurrect Danish territorial claims on the Northern Isles, Christian IV remained as concerned about the unlicensed fishing by the English off Greenland and by the Scots off the Faroes as he was about the unchecked piracy of the Dunkirkers from the North Sea to the Bay of Biscay.[52]

Christian IV was to use his diplomatic accord with the Habsburgs in 1629–30 as an opportunity to claim exclusive jurisdiction over fishing in the north-eastern Atlantic and to license access of English and Scottish whaling ventures to Greenland and Arctic waters. Ostensibly to control piracy, Christian covertly agreed to provide Spain with a base in the Northern Isles from which they could pursue economic warfare at the expense of the Dutch herring fleet.[53] At the same time, he had his historiographer royal, Pontanus, prepare an overt refutation of the Britannic case for *mare clausum* on the grounds that the 'British Seas' were not the internationally recognised waters around the British Isles, merely the channel between England and France. Charles, unlike his father, preferred to rely on English lawyers, most notably Sir John Boroughs and John Selden, to uphold his *ius imperium* to the seas surrounding the British Isles. There were two representational difficulties for what was essentially a Gothic defence of empire. All maps accompanying the texts of Camden and Speed, as those by Blaeu and other Dutch cartographers, confined the 'British Seas' to the waters of the Channel. Only the *Carta Marina* of Olaus Magnus in 1539 upheld this description of the territorial waters off England and Scotland. Contemporaneous English maps were Dutch engraved, with the result that Dutch ships were depicted as sailing freely around the British Isles on open rather than closed seas![54]

Colonial Policy

Since the Americas were 'beyond the line' of international regulation in the first half of the seventeenth century, colonial policy was especially amenable to the promotion of British endeavours.[55] As evidenced by the plantation of Ulster, the monarchical concept of the British empire was readily exportable and notably geared to entrepreneurship and exploitation of native peoples. Entrepreneurship in the Americas took priority over the evangelisation that featured in Spanish and French colonial endeavours. While the planting of the gospel was undoubtedly as important as the planting of the soil in New England, the cure of souls became secondary to the cure of sugar in the Caribbean, and the mysteries of transubstantiation could not claim precedence over the intricacies of the tobacco trade in the Chesapeake. Exploitation ranged from the pressurised, if not enforced, indentured service of migrants with few resources from the British Isles to the expulsion of native Americans and their enslavement along with negroes rudely shipped from Africa. Promotional propaganda notwithstanding, the British imperial mission to civilise was founded not on religious revelation, reformation or uniformity but on commercial opportunity, opportunism and indebtedness tempered by sectarian toleration in the Americas.[56]

Whereas the martial cultures of Scotland and Ireland were particularly attracted to military service on the European continent, the more developed mercantile culture of England was the dominant ethos of the American colonies. The Irish were hardly more than ancillary participants in plantation projects on their own island. Nevertheless, the extent of their violent victimisation, summary expropriation and enforced cultural assimilation under the early Stuarts is prone to exaggeration when compared to their past treatment under the Tudors. In a colonial context, the exploitation of the Irish pales in comparison to the discriminatory treatment handed out to native Americans, the Carib Indians and African slaves. At the same time, the role of the Irish as exploiters in the Americas has tended to be underplayed. There is considerably less equivocation about the Scots, who tend to feature among the exploiters rather than the exploited. However, the Scots were less engaged as planters in Ulster and the Americas than as soldiers on the continent. Although at least 30,000 Scots were involved in the plantation of Ulster, military service in the Thirty Years War involved considerably greater numbers of Scots. Indeed, for both Scottish and English planters, settlement in Ulster served more as a barrier than as a bridge to further British colonial engagement in the Americas. Only the English plantations in Munster, where around 25,000 migrants had settled, seem to have encouraged further migration to the Americas, migration that reinforced English dominance of colonial engagement from the three kingdoms.[57]

By 1629, less than 10,000 people had left the British Isles for the American colonies, around a third of the British population then settled in Ulster. However, migration to the American colonies increased exponentially, with at least 80,000 leaving during the next decade. The vast majority of these American colonists came from England, principally from East Anglia and the Home Counties via London, from the West Country via Bristol and from the north-west via Liverpool. There was nothing to preclude departing ships from calling into ports such as Cork and Galway on the west coast of Ireland to take on additional travellers as well as supplies. Moreover London, the largest city in Europe, with a population well in excess of 300,000 at this juncture, was the principal port of departure for colonial migrants from all over the British Isles. Indeed, London was becoming the British, not just the English, metropolis with an established expertise for mercantile adventuring throughout the European continent, including Muscovy, Turkey and the Levant, that was combined with privateering in the West and East Indies. The establishment of the East India Company in 1600 and that of the African Company in 1618 were essentially the diversification as well as the continuation of this expertise.[58] The initial endeavours of James to support a supplementary Scottish Company trading through Muscovy to the East Indies in 1617 had more to do with the unfulfilled quest for a northwest passage than with any serious endeavour to challenge the monopoly of the London merchant houses. Indeed, when reaffirming the monopoly of the East India Company in 1632, Charles I specified that although the Company operated under English law, its trade was to be conducted exclusively through London. Its merchant adventurers had the sole right to license ships and crews, factors and soldiers, with no reservation that they must be English. Scots adventurers in the service of the East India Company since the reign of James I continued to be in receipt of pensions paid through an agent in Scotland prior to the emergence of the Covenanting movement.[59]

While the American colonies were very much a secondary focus of London merchant adventurers, the changing economic climate in the aftermath of the regal union made them an increasingly attractive option for new joint-stock investments that attracted courtiers and the landed classes. European inflation, occasioned primarily by the influx of gold and silver from Spanish and Portuguese colonies in the New World, brought about price rises which in England had stimulated a growth of manufacturing, particularly textiles, during the sixteenth century. This expansion in commercial activity in England, which was able to absorb both a growth in population and the release of rural labour following enclosure and the intensification of agriculture, stood in marked contrast to Scotland and Ireland, which required considerable emigration to sustain social stability. However, the Dutch revolt against Spain disrupted English textile markets in the Netherlands. While the silting up of the Scheldt confirmed the replacement of Antwerp by Amsterdam as the major European trading entrepôt, English sales of heavy woollen and linen fabrics continued to lose out to the new, lighter draperies from Flemish and Dutch looms. At the same time an international shortage of bullion, already apparent in 1603, had become critical by 1625, when the supply of gold and silver from the New World was irreversibly on a downward spiral.

Trading ventures to the East Indies, far from producing new outlets for English textiles and other manufactured products, led to an influx of more sophisticated Asian manufactures along with peppers and spices. Although re-exported through London companies trading to the continent, Muscovy, Turkey and the Levant, imported Asian goods had become a drain on bullion that was only partially relieved by the search for gold and silver in Africa. The creation of American colonies, initially through companies for the plantation of Virginia (1606), Newfoundland (1610), Bermuda (the Summer Isles, 1611) and New England (1620), was vital to the process of import substitution, that is, the securing of alternative supplies of fish, furs, timber, tar and pitch, which had hitherto been purchased expensively in European markets. The prospect of new mineral resources for copper and iron, as for tobacco and later for sugar, were not realised until the initial plantation companies were on the point of being abandoned. Crucially, however, joint-stock ventures were moderated to encourage relatively small-scale investors as well as the mercantile and political elite, as was especially evident in the refounding of the Virginia Company in 1624. Again there was no restriction to English investors only as the Stuart dominions in the Americas were expanded to include Barbados and other Leeward Islands in the Caribbean.[60]

At the same time, the debasement and clipping of coin warranted by German princes from the outbreak of the Thirty Years War had ushered in a period of hyper-inflation throughout the Holy Roman Empire which pushed back the attainment of price stability throughout Europe. As price rises continued to spiral upwards as the supply of bullion necessary to underwrite credit transactions began to dwindle, employment prospects, especially those in the manufacturing districts of England, were jeopardised. Since Puritanism was also strong in manufacturing districts yet on the defensive from the growth of Arminianism within the

Anglican hierarchy, New England became particularly attractive to ministers and entrepreneurial gentry. Thus, John Winthrop from the Stour Valley in Sussex, who had previously flirted with an Irish plantation, became a joint founder of the Massachusetts Bay Company in 1629. He was a prime mover in community migrations by Puritan families from East Anglia to New England who hoped to recreate both a godly and an economically stable commonwealth there. This aspiration was seemingly furthered by the spread of Puritan colonies into Connecticut, Rhode Island and New Haven and the consolidation of Bermuda over the next decade. Notwithstanding the association of English Parliamentarians and Puritans, which gave a Gothic character to these colonial developments, the New England pattern was not typical for the Stuart's American dominions. Nor, given the separatist tendencies of Puritans, was their emigration particularly welcomed by British opponents of the Arminian tendencies within the Church of England. Thus, the Scottish Presbyterian cleric Robert Baillie, though sympathising with their desire to escape 'from the yoke of Episcopal persecution', was concerned that their radical disregard for a structured polity in the church could be re-exported back across the Atlantic 'to be dangerous to the rest of the world'.[61]

The bulk of British migration to the colonies was not to New England, but to Virginia around the Chesapeake and to Barbados and the Leeward Islands, where there was a demand for the entrepreneurship and wage labour associated with English manufacturing and the prospect of settlements for those denied land by English enclosures. Prospects of religious toleration tied to commerce proved as attractive to Roman Catholics as to Puritans, as is evident from the foundation of Maryland in 1634 by Cecil Calvert, Lord Baltimore, whose family's initial attempts at colonialism had been in the less congenial climes of Newfoundland. Moreover, the Gothic alliance of English Parliamentarians and Puritans was no guarantee of godly colonies, as was particularly evident from the fate of the Providence Island Company, which was founded in 1630 but dissolved after little more than a decade. The settlers' predilection for privateering in the Caribbean provoked the Spanish to reassert their claims to sovereignty. Nor were these colonial endeavours strictly demarcated in terms of the movement of people and capital. The landless migrated between Caribbean and mainland colonies in search of better prospects and less hostile environments for family settlement. Conversely, the settler elite invested in diverse colonial companies in Virginia and Bermuda as well as New

England, and dispersed their families from mainland colonies to more lucrative ventures in Barbados and the Leeward Islands.[62]

The foundations of the Stuart's dominions in the Americas were neither an exclusive English endeavour nor sustainable as such. Nor were Scots and Irish engaged solely with colonialism as indentured servants, military auxiliaries or in the professions. The Irish were notably involved with English adventurers in the forlorn search for colonies in the Amazon and were reputed to dominate settlement in Montserrat in the Leeward Islands. Colvin's Case of 1608 had accorded common nationality to all those born within Scotland and England since the accomplishment of regal union. Nonetheless, the abandonment of political and commercial integration had meant that no access to English markets or colonial ventures was freely afforded or guaranteed to Scottish domiciles. Although Scottish merchants were no longer considered aliens from Christmas 1604, English customs officials remained reluctant to admit their exemption from the discriminatory tariffs imposed on imported merchandise. While Scottish settlers in Ulster were eventually recognised as naturalised Irishmen in 1632, the Scots carrying trade to and from Ireland remained subject to discriminatory tariffs. The colonial situation proved somewhat more accommodating. Domicile restrictions were difficult to police given that Scottish courtiers had bases in both countries, Scottish merchant houses opened up in London, and those travelling from Scotland to the colonies frequently passed through English ports. Moreover, the Scots regarded themselves as independent but collaborative players in empire and without the cultural baggage of colonial dependency attributed to the Irish.[63]

Although some consideration was given at the British court to the transportation of disruptive Scottish elements to Virginia, the Scottish Privy Council deemed the further removal of troublemakers from the Anglo-Scottish borders unnecessary and gave no support to Episcopal proposals to banish Presbyterian nonconformists in 1618. Notwithstanding this initial rejection of servitor colonialism, Scottish entrepreneurial interests were prepared to countenance British collaboration to consolidate the development of the Newfoundland fisheries from 1620. However, within both governmental and entrepreneurial circles there was a declared preference for an identifiable Scottish venture to expand the colonial dominions of the Stuart monarchy. In 1621, Sir William Alexander of Menstrie, who originally planned to develop a plantation he had secured from the Newfoundland Company, proposed a scheme for a New Scotland in the Canadian Maritimes. English colonies in

Virginia and New England were still pioneering ventures and no meaningful English presence had yet been established in the Caribbean.
Hence, Scottish ambitions were portrayed as no less legitimate than the
endeavours of other European countries in the bid to develop New
Spain, New France or the New Netherlands.

Indeed, under Alexander of Menstrie's proposal, New England was
to be complemented by a New Scotland to bolster the British cause
against the French, especially in their settlement of North America
designated Acadia. Moreover, a Canadian colony offered the remunerative prospect of channelling Scottish migration away from northern
Europe, especially Poland–Lithuania, to exploit the reputedly abundant
sources of timber, fish and furs – the latter commodity offering notably
lucrative prospects from the sale of beaver pelts in European markets.
At the same time, New Scotland offered a distinctive British alternative
to Ulster in which Scots law would be utilised to implement and direct
plantations. The British undertaking in Ulster had offered the induce-
ment of baronetcies under English patent, so Canadian undertakers
were invited to purchase the title of baronet under Scottish patent. Sales
of title, which were initially intended to realise a limited income (around
£16,667) to the crown from Scottish gentry, were never fully subscribed
despite the admission of English, Irish and even French gentry as
baronets of Nova Scotia from 1629. Sales of title, nonetheless, did
demonstrate the commitment of the Britannic monarchy to the capital-
ising of colonial projects, albeit the Nova Scotian venture remained
chronically underfunded. No less vital, and in marked contrast to Ulster,
were the logistical difficulties of elongated supply lines in supporting
initial settlement.[64]

The first exploratory venture sent out by Sir William Alexander in
1622 had to take refuge with the Newfoundland fisheries. Obliged to
subcontract the settlement of Cape Breton Island, renamed New
Galloway, to the Scottish laird Sir John Gordon of Lochinvar, Alexander of Menstrie was able to tap into colonial expertise from Ulster when
the second expeditionary fleet set sail under the command of his son
William in the spring of 1628. By the following year, in a third venture
that embarked from the Kentish Downs, William had brought a new
cohort of settlers which, in terms of personnel and pioneering intent,
was effectively more British than Scottish. Reinforced settlements were
established at the former French mainland base of Port Royal and at
Port aux Balemes in Cape Breton. However, the viability of the Scottish
venture was undermined by a rival English project led by two London-

based Scottish entrepreneurs, David and James Kirk, who were intent on capturing Quebec from the French as well as exploiting the commercial potential of the Maritimes. The displaced French were also determined to retain their foothold in Acadia.

While internal British rivalries were partially resolved by the formation of the English and Scottish Company to trade on the St Lawrence River, Nova Scotia remained vulnerable to French military and diplomatic pressure. The Cape Breton settlement was soon overrun by the French, while the continuance of that at Port Royal was jeopardised by the commencement of peace negotiations to resolve Charles I's differences with Louis XIII in 1629. The French were insistent not only that they should reclaim Quebec but that the Scots should vacate Port Royal, which they viewed as having been settled by conquest in time of war. The requirement for the Scots to vacate was a non-negotiable point of honour for the French to which Charles eventually assented in 1632. Notwithstanding their committed participation in the Britannic empire, the interests of Scottish entrepreneurs were thus deemed expendable when their commercial aspirations conflicted with the needs of international diplomacy.[65]

Charles I offered ostensible pledges of support for Nova Scotia, signalled by Alexander of Menstrie becoming Viscount Stirling in 1630 and his further elevation to Earl of Stirling two years later, when he was compensated with the right to mint copper coinage for Scotland to the value of £10,000 sterling. However, the enforced vacation of Port Royal served as a disincentive to further plantation. Stirling's intimate association with the court's imposition of administrative and economic uniformity throughout the British Isles, as well as the currency debasement that resulted from his copper coinage, meant that there was no political will within Scotland to sustain his Canadian undertaking, a situation that stood in marked contrast to the English Puritan drive to populate New England during the 1630s. Stirling received further colonial recognition in 1635, when he was accorded a compensatory interest in New England, where Maine bordered the Maritimes with Long Island as a somewhat distant appendage. More importantly, Stirling's personal involvement in both New England and Nova Scotia continued to promote British association in colonial councils, Stirling being regarded as a key player in facilitating inter-colonial trade with Virginia. He was an experienced associate of English and Scottish courtiers promoting plantations along the Piscataqua River in New England to secure that initially established by the Scottish adventurer David Thomas as undertaker for settlers from the English West Country in the mid-1620s. Nevertheless, neither Stirling nor his family sought direct involvement in further colonial ventures in the Americas.[66] His son William did return to profitable adventuring in Africa with the Scottish Guinea Company of 1634, which was essentially a London-based venture licensed to trade as far south as Angola. Two voyages brought back sufficient gold and silver for Charles to strike a new Scottish coinage celebrating imperial monarchy in 1637, ironically in the midst of the Scottish rioting that presaged the emergence of the Covenanting movement![67]

Despite its effective abandonment by 1634, the proprietorial model under which Alexander of Menstrie had colonised Nova Scotia became the favoured means for promoting colonies beyond Virginia and Massachusetts. Thus, Barbados and the Leeward Islands were assigned under the proprietary control of the Earl of Carlisle from 1629. Although these Caribbean colonies were certainly English in terms of government, the character of their settlement can be viewed as British. Carlisle ran his colonial undertakings in a similar manner to his military participation, as Viscount Doncaster, in the British expeditionary forces of 1624–5. His principal factor was his Scottish kinsman Peter Hay of Haystoun. Scots also featured in the London merchant syndicate favoured with leases for the best land in Barbados. The designation of a Scotland district on that island suggests that place names related as much to settlers' backgrounds as to geographic features.[68] Furthermore, the ill-fated Canadian venture stimulated trading developments from the Scottish western seaboard to the American colonies. From the 1630s, ships from Ayr and Glasgow directly re-exported tobacco through the Baltic Sound. East coast ports such as Aberdeen and Dundee were also becoming involved in the Chesapeake trade two decades before the official opening up of English colonial trade to the Scots in the 1650s. Nova Scotia thus served to redirect Scottish entrepreneurial endeavours westwards to diversify, but not to replace, the eastward trade to continental Europe and Scandinavia.[69]

Political Reconfiguration

In terms of active participation from all three kingdoms, the Scots were to the fore in driving the imperial Britannic project of the early Stuarts. Not only did Scots feature willingly and proactively in foreign, frontier and colonial policies, but the Scottish Estates successively voted extraordinary taxation to support British involvement in the Thirty Years War

in 1621, 1625, 1630 and 1633. However, the regal union had a different domestic resonance as both Scotland and Ireland became progres
sively disaffected as a result of the attempted imposition of uniformity
that resulted from Charles I's metropolitan interpretation of his British
ius imperium after 1629. Contemporaneous military engagement on the
continent led to the formation of Scottish and Irish brigades that were
readily placed to return to oppose this narrowing of the Britannic perspective during the 1630s. Colonial migration to the Americas, however,
promoted stability in England by relieving both economic and religious
pressures and, simultaneously, by offering up the prospect of enhanced
customs revenues to the crown from an expanding colonial trade. Certainly, two of the regicides executed in 1662, Hugh Peters and Sir Henry
Vane the younger, had accumulated political experience in New England
after their migration in 1635 which they subsequently used to enhance
the Puritan cause in England. Peters, who had served as a nonconforming minister to the English mercantile community in Rotterdam, spent
six controversial years in New England before returning as an advocate
of Independency in the English church and becoming chaplain to Oliver
Cromwell. Vane the younger, though he only stayed for two years, served
a turbulent term as governor of the Massachusetts Bay Company prior
to becoming a stalwart for Independency within the English parliament.
While their colonial experience deepened their radical, sectarian commitment, it neither instigated nor directly contributed to revolution in
any way comparable to the returning soldiers in Scotland and Ireland.[70]

Whereas the Irish were primarily intent on redefining the constitutional status of their island as an English dependency, the Scots were
committed to the political reconfiguration of the British Isles. The
Scottish soldiers in Swedish service had been nurtured in a military and
diplomatic environment created by Sir James Spens that favoured the
distinctive concept of Scoto-Britannus. During his training at the
Huguenot Academy in Sedan, the irenicist John Durie had come under
the tutelage of his kinsman Andrew Melville, the Presbyterian critic of
the Britannic empire who had been exiled to France in 1622 after eleven
years of imprisonment in the Tower of London. However, it was only
after serving as secretary to Spens in 1628 that Durie adopted the
designation Scoto-Britannus in the course of his peregrinations around
northern Europe to promote confessional confederation among
Calvinists and Lutherans in the 1630s. Although his protracted discussions with Swedish Lutheran clergy at Uppsala proved fruitless, the
Swedish Chancellor, Axel Oxenstierna, supported his endeavours. Durie

left with official commendation for his peace-making efforts and for his intellectual supporters in 'the British Churches', notably the academics in the Faculties of Divinity at King's and Marischall Colleges who became known as the Aberdeen Doctors. His departure from Sweden in May 1638 presaged the return of the Scottish *hjaelptrupper* to assist the Covenanting movement and the resurrection of the Scoto-Britannus in a domestic context.[71] However, this designation, as indeed the international standing of the Aberdeen Doctors, carried little weight domestically. For the Scots were militantly opposed to what had become in effect, if not in name, Anglo-Britannic monarchy under Charles I. The Covenanting movement was intent not on a peaceful accommodation, but on a godly redefinition of the political agenda. Permanent checks were to be imposed on the prerogative rule in Kirk and state. Regal union was to be replaced by federative union.

The much travelled William Lithgow offered several key indicators for political reconfiguration when commenting on the siege of Breda successfully conducted by Henry, Prince of Orange, at the expense of the Spanish Army of Flanders from July to October 1637. Particularly commended were the martial vigour and technical expertise of the Scottish forces in Dutch service under the command of James Livingstone, Lord Almond (later 1st Earl of Callendar). Their endeavours were deemed complementary to those 'valiant Scottish Worthies' who had fought in anti-Habsburg forces during the Thirty Years War, especially those in Swedish service commanded by General Alexander Leslie. Both Leslie and Almond were to become lynchpins of the Covenanting Army. The presence of Louis Frederick, the new Elector Palatine, as an observer was cited approvingly. Indeed, Lithgow travelled to The Hague after the liberation of Breda to pay his personal respects to Elizabeth of Bohemia. Lithgow also noted that the entourage of the Elector Palatine included two English nobles, Robert Rich, 2nd Earl of Warwick, and Spencer Compton, 2nd Earl of Northampton. The former, with extensive colonial experience as an undertaker and privateer, was a disaffected courtier sympathetic to Puritanism who became a Parliamentary mainstay. The latter remained an ardent supporter of the domestic if not the foreign policies of Charles I and was to give his life for the Royalist cause in 1643. Where Warwick was to embrace the Scottish Covenanters as allies, Northampton remained an implacable opponent of their incursions into England. Both, however, supported the summoning of Parliament for the resolution of constitutional issues in the wake of the Bishops' Wars. Lithgow was not enamoured of Dutch materialism and he warned the unwary 'Britannian or Hybernian' of purgative perils in Dutch seaports. Nevertheless, he deemed their federative government, in terms of politics, providence and intelligence, as excelling 'all the Common-wealths of the world'.[72]

3 The Prerogative Rule of Charles I, 1629–1638

After the outbreak of the Thirty Years War in 1618, English apprehensions were primarily focused on issues of prerogative, property and conformity. For the Stuarts succeeded in aggravating rather than solving difficulties inherited from the Tudors relating to parliamentary privilege, finance and religious dissent. That Westminster had exclusive rights to vote supply for foreign and domestic policy was an erroneous Gothic assertion, which was effectively silenced when Charles I summarily dissolved parliament in 1629.[1] Plantation had not facilitated the political management of Ireland. The Irish situation was not hopeless, however. The Old English had opened direct negotiations with Charles I in 1626, taking advantage of his need for money to fight his wars with France and Spain and, simultaneously, to sustain British military intervention in the Thirty Years War. In return for financial supply from Ireland, Charles was prepared to support a detailed programme of social and legal reforms that would uphold stability in landownership. Existing plantations were to be confirmed, and an end to further appropriation of Irish estates in Munster, Connacht and Ulster was promised. A more relaxed approach to penal laws against Roman Catholics was also hinted at. Although a delegation of British planters and Irish landowners went to London in 1628, these concessions, known as the 'Graces', were to remain largely unfulfilled. Nevertheless, they continued to be desired as confirmation of Ireland's independent standing within the Stuart dominions.[2]

Scotland was the least amenable of the three kingdoms to management from the court. Antipathies aroused by a regressive fiscal policy and liturgical innovations that challenged the received Reformed tradition were aggravated by the prospect of wholesale appropriation of Scottish estates through an ill-conceived and ineptly executed Revocation Scheme. The studied neglect of Charles I to arrange his coronation in his 'ancient and native kingdom' further fuelled Scottish antagonism. Indeed, by 1629 the Britannic perspective was facing a more committed challenge from the Scottish than from either the Gothic or the Irish – a situation that is seriously underplayed by the anglocentric tendency to describe the 1630s as the period of the 'personal rule'.[3] Whereas Charles was to rule without calling an English parliament for another 11 years, he was obliged to summon a coronation parliament in Scotland, which was actually preceded by a Convention of the Scottish Estates in 1630. One year later, the Irish parliament met in three sessions that continued into 1635.[4] Within a British context, therefore, the key feature of the 1630s was not the personal rule of Charles I but his reliance on the royal prerogative to enforce his will over all three kingdoms. The prerogative rule also occasioned the Scottish paradox: the Scots, who had been foremost in upholding James I's projection of Britannic monarchy through foreign, frontier and colonial policies, became the first to revolt against the reprogramming of Britannic monarchy by Charles I.

Monarchy Reprogrammed

Although he was energetically intent on changing the style, pace and direction of Britannic monarchy, Charles exhibited three patent and ultimately crucial weaknesses from the outset of his reign. Firstly, he was incapable of acknowledging that political manoeuvring within constitutional assemblies was not necessarily intended to obstruct or reverse royal initiatives. Secondly, and despite an express directive to the contrary from his father in 1620 when he was heir apparent,[5] Charles consistently pushed his prerogative to the limit without convincingly demonstrating the present necessity for authoritarian rule. Thirdly, Charles tended to view criticism, however informed, as subversive and even seditious. His life centred on the court where he promoted a dignified formality, patronised the arts to cultivate an image of benign kingship, and ordered life minutely in the royal household. The idealised representation of the Britannic court as heaven on earth was articulated in the masque *Coelum Britannicum*, devised by Inigo Jones in 1637. Yet Charles had systematically distanced himself from the public practice of kingship by limiting the right to personally petition the king, by withdrawing from ceremonials and displays outside the court, and by attempting to prevent his subjects from requesting the exercise of his power to heal, notably by touching for scrofula, known as 'the King's evil'. Charles was not impervious to criticism and he was certainly a capable political propagandist. Nonetheless, he preferred to rule by proclamation rather than acclamation, by private counsel rather than by parliamentary consensus and by judicial decree rather than due process. In effect, he was a micro-manager of limited intellect and contestable probity in politics. He consistently claimed, from his accession in 1625 until his execution in 1649, that he had acted uprightly according to his own conscience.[6]

Charles's unavailing sense of injured righteousness cannot convincingly be explained in terms of a lack of good counsel with respect to England by 1629. Certainly the attack on Buckingham in the English parliament of 1626, which also rejected the king's request for a fiscal benevolence, indicated an escalation of dissent from his father's reign. Sir John Elliot and Sir Dudley Digges were committed to the Tower for using seditious words in the attempted impeachment of Buckingham. However, Charles's determination to resort to taxes raised on the strength of his prerogative rather than through parliamentary supply, such as the forced loan of 1626–7, was indicative of selective counselling that favoured the king as being answerable only to God. In turn, Charles became more focused on compelling compliance rather than on seeking consent in the wake of Buckingham's assassination in 1628. The mobilisation of British expeditionary forces had instigated debates over compulsory billeting and recourse to martial law, especially the need of English localities to supply Scottish and Irish troops. Notwithstanding the justices of the King's Bench having upheld imprisonment by royal command, Charles was accused by John Selden, as both an attorney and a parliamentarian, of attempting to falsify the judicial record in the Five Knights' Case, which was provoked by the forced loan. Charles, it was claimed, sought a precedent for discretionary imprisonment without prior charges. The ensuing Petition of Right was promulgated by the Commons in opposition to billeting, martial law, forced loans and arbitrary imprisonment. It drew on precedents that ranged from the right to due process for any accused freeman, enshrined in the Magna Carta of 1215, to the need for parliamentary consent to taxation, loans and impositions as authorised by both Edward I and Edward III in the fourteenth century. In essence, the Petition was as much a Gothic declaration against martial law as an attempt to secure legal mechanisms for the protection of individual English rights and liberties.[7]

Advocacy of the supremacy of the common law and parliamentary statute attracted considerable support in the Commons and served to radicalise Members of Parliament like the hitherto acquiescent John Pym. Conversely, Charles could defend his recourse to martial law from a Britannic perspective. Current hostilities against France and Spain, together with preparations to support the military incursions of

Christian IV in northern Europe, constituted a state of war which justified his suspension of impediments in common law and parliamentary statute to the imposition of billeting, forced loans and even ship money as a national rather than a coastal levy. This perspective was upheld by the Lords and, indeed, won over former parliamentary activists like Sir Dudley Digges and Thomas Wentworth, the future Earl of Strafford. The Petition of Right was approved in the Lords, where it was not viewed as a threat to the king's authority to imprison without charge for reasons of state. When confronted with a renewed challenge to royal authority in the Commons that ranged from the collection of customs dues to religious innovations without parliamentary consent in 1629, Charles jailed nine protest leaders (including Sir John Elliot again) in order to vindicate his prerogative power to imprison. Although he did not deny them remedy at common law as prescribed in the Petition of Right, the Gothic case for a stated cause of arrest under *habeas corpus* went by default. Parliament having been dissolved on 10 March, the Commons was left powerless to defend its privilege of free speech after Charles accused Elliot and his eight associates of sedition for physically coercing the Speaker to delay the adjournment of the House.[8]

Loyalty and obedience, which were the imperatives for advancement at court, became the necessary requirements of Charles's prerogative rule after his dissolution of the English parliament. Although he had notably expanded the membership of his English Privy Council from his father's reign, doubts about its competence, consistency and energy, as well as the inadequate statutory basis for its wide range of executive responsibilities which had already surfaced in the 1620s, were consolidated in the 1630s. Rather than entrust key decisions to his full council, Charles's authoritarian approach to government led him increasingly to rely on an inner core of trusted advisers, headed by William Laud as Bishop of London, and from 1633 as Archbishop of Canterbury, and by Francis, Lord Cottington. Wentworth, who cut his administrative teeth as Lord President of the Council of the North from 1628, was gradually admitted to this inner circle after his appointment as Lord-Deputy for Ireland in 1632.[9] However, his usual absence from court required his assiduous cultivation of influential correspondents among leading officials and counsellors and his judicious recruitment of clients who included writers of newsletters as well as courtiers. Simultaneously, Wentworth firmly, and at times vindictively, closed down the Irish lines of communication to court which councillors in Dublin had used against his predecessor as lord-deputy, Henry Cary, 1st Viscount Falkland.[10]

In Scotland, the problem of inadequate counselling was compounded by Charles's exclusion of English councillors from interfering in affairs that he deemed his own special preserve. In the reported wisdom of Edward Hyde (later Earl of Clarendon), Scotland was rarely given a passing thought at court where external interest was focused primarily on Germany, Poland and all other parts of Europe.[11] Although the attitudes of English courtiers to Scottish affairs for most of the 1630s may well have varied from peripheral involvement to downright indifference, Britannic monarchy was confronted by a problem of intelligence gathering that was rooted essentially in political economy. James I had failed to maintain control over the rates at which foreign coin was allowed to circulate within Scotland after 1619. England had no comparable experience of foreign dollars circulating at rates far in excess of equivalent native coin. The Scottish Mint encountered particular difficulty in acquiring and transporting gold to Scotland. Notwithstanding the standardisation of Scots money at a twelfth of the value of sterling in 1603, the gold coin of the common monarchy was actually circulating at rates 30–40 per cent above its prescribed value by 1629. In effect, while the official exchange rate of Scots to English money remained at 12 : 1, the actual exchange of gold coin in the London markets pushed up this rate to 16 : 1, a major disincentive for Scottish nobles and gentry to attend the court. Such unfavourable rates made no small contribution to the growing isolation of the court from the political nation in Scotland – a situation which Charles I failed to comprehend, far less to correct.[12]

That the structural difficulties confronting Britannic monarchy in Scotland appeared less critical than the clash between Charles I and the parliament in England can be attributed to the energetic commitment expended in shuttle diplomacy by William Graham, 7th Earl of Menteith. As lord president of the Scottish Privy Council, he revived effective liaison between Scotland and the court from 1628 until his dismissal from office in 1633. Menteith's energy ensured that royal government in Scotland continued to function despite growing unrest over Revocation and ongoing taxation, which had surfaced at the Convention of Estates in July 1630. Menteith welded the majority of councillors, bishops, courtiers and officials then attending into a cohesive court party which backed his resolve to debate only the relevance, not the substance, of contentious aspects of the Revocation Scheme raised by the nobility and itemised grievances from the gentry over the conduct of central and local government. Once assent had been given to the renewal of ordinary and extraordinary taxation for four years, all proposals to redress grievances and improve government were deferred to the consideration of the coronation parliament. His rise to become the most influential politician in Scotland had aroused resentment among the all-but-eclipsed old guard of Jacobean officials, however. Menteith neglected to maintain good relations with them as with the Earl of Stirling, secretary at court for Scottish affairs.

Lack of prudence, notably his questioning of the Scottish pedigree of the Stuarts when in his cups, triggered Menteith's downfall and eventual withdrawal from public life in 1633. The failure of Charles to maintain Menteith in office beyond his coronation parliament demonstrated his manifest lack of understanding about the importance of political management. His capacity to govern Scotland for the rest of his personal rule certainly suffered from his failure to find a successor willing to undertake a similar style of shuttle diplomacy on behalf of the absentee monarch. But to contend that Menteith's fall from grace transformed the character of Scottish politics, paving the way for revolution, is to overstate the case.[13]

Menteith's political eclipse aggravated rather than instigated the growing estrangement between leading officials and the court, particularly as Charles moved to protect a leading Scottish courtier who simultaneously faced charges of treason. In the spring of 1631, James, Marquess of Hamilton, was accused of being the prime mover in a conspiracy to imprison the king and the young Prince Charles, cloister the queen and execute the leading royal advisers in England and Scotland. Reputedly, this was to be accomplished by the British expeditionary forces Hamilton had recruited to fight with Gustav II Adolph of Sweden. His leading accuser was James Stewart, Lord Ochiltree, a former colonial adventurer in Nova Scotia and now a courtier much given to malicious gossip who had sought to play on Hamilton's position as the leading claimant to the Scottish throne beyond the royal house. In contrast to the Menteith affair, Charles was able to keep investigations into this case within the confines of the court. Hamilton was duly pronounced innocent but Ochiltree was despatched to Scotland to face an indictment for treason. Charges had still not been pressed in the summer of 1633 when a royal warrant confirmed that Ochiltree was sentenced to life imprisonment in Blackness Castle on the Firth of Forth. Charles's subsequent delegation of Scottish affairs to Hamilton meant that shuttle diplomacy no longer complemented the assiduous cultivation of British clientage by leading Scottish officials in Edinburgh. At the same time, the managerial credibility of the court was not helped by Hamilton's manifest preference for a policy of benign neglect north of the border, a policy tantamount to the pursuit of quiescent provincialism. In contrast to Wentworth in Ireland, Hamilton continued to tolerate the practice of councillors in Edinburgh lobbying the court directly and diversely.[14]

Charles was primarily responsible for cutting himself off from his one supportive source of external counselling. His uncle Christian IV of Denmark–Norway, with whom he had been in regular contact as Prince of Great Britain since 1616, was a noted, if grandiose, exponent of imperial monarchy in northern Europe. From the beginning of the Thirty Years War, Christian IV had expanded his watching brief over British affairs. He assiduously cultivated contacts among the political elite in all three kingdoms rather than relying on despatches from court. After Archbishop Abbot had delivered the objections of both Houses of the English parliament to the Spanish match in March 1624, the English primate informed Christian that its sundering had been greeted with universal incredulity and exhilaration throughout the British Isles. Christian was supplied with a copy of James I's parliamentary address complaining about the lack of support given to him by the Lords and Commons; about his continuing concerns that Ireland remained a back door for a hostile foreign invasion; and about his pressing need for supplies to finance his diplomatic endeavours in support of the Palatinate and to build up military reinforcements, especially for the Royal Navy. In what was to prove his valedictory address, James had affirmed 'that as I am not ambitious of any other man, goods or lands, so I desire not to brooke a furrow of land in England, Scotland and Ireland without the restitution of the Palatinate'. James also hinted at an ongoing financial commitment to the King of Denmark–Norway that signified his shift towards the overt intervention of British expeditionary forces in opposition to the Habsburgs.[15]

When Charles translated this hint into a formal commitment, Christian IV was particularly concerned about the reliability of Buckingham. Six months after the marriage contracted between Charles I and Princess Henrietta Maria of France in June 1625, Buckingham had provided Christian with an extensive postscript commentating on the detailed implementation of the Hague Convention. However, as Charles was compromising his capacity to assist the Danes and the Dutch by threatening war with Spain and France, Christian was distrustful of Buckingham. He advised Charles to dispense with his services in March 1626. Following the parliamentary attack on the duke, however, Christian encouraged Charles to leave little scope for discussion on criticisms of royal policy. Buckingham had been largely rehabilitated in the eyes of Christian for his sterling endeavours to co-ordinate the raising of expeditionary forces throughout the British Isles. This rehabilitation was supported by testimony from the royal muster-master in Scotland, Alexander Lindsay, Lord Spynie, an experienced campaigner, who oversaw the recruitment of forces for service with the Danes not only within Scotland but among Scottish forces already serving on the continent. Spynie, however, also informed Christian that Charles I was facing internal difficulties in the prosecution of his Revocation Scheme which, by threatening to undermine landed title, was viewed as detrimental to the Scottish nobility.[16]

Once Charles was committed to armed intervention in support of Christian IV, his relationship with his uncle changed dramatically. In part, this was because Christian's military endeavours had effectively collapsed by January 1629, when he was obliged to sue for peace with Emperor Ferdinand II at Lübeck. Their personal relationship primarily deteriorated over Charles's failure to honour the financial commitments made by both himself and his father. Having agreed to expeditionary financing that had accumulated to £247,000 by June 1628, he found that military intervention in the Thirty Years War proved a major contributor to the financial debts that were encumbering Britannic monarchy. Another decade was to elapse before this capital payment and accumulating interest to the Danish king were met in full. Accordingly, Charles I was to be deprived of the informal counsel and advice of Christian IV for much of the 1630s.[17]

Fiscal Opportunism

The financial difficulties that damaged relations with Christian IV were part of a more deep-seated problem afflicting Britannic monarchy, namely its inability to live off the revenues ordinarily available to the crown. These difficulties were compounded by the outbreak of the Thirty Years War and made particularly potent by the authoritarianism and fiscal opportunism of Charles I. At the same time, the attempts of the early Stuarts to broaden the basis of royal revenue in all three kingdoms show the Britannic nature of their fiscal priorities, whereas the national concerns of the English parliament, which contributed around a quarter of those revenues, remained firmly Gothic.

As a result of the Bate's Case of 1606, James I had successfully upheld his prerogative powers to impose duties for the regulation of commerce within his dominions. But this was given the Gothic spin that the king could levy impositions at will. Accordingly, the English parliament was moved to reject the Grand Contract offered by James in 1610, in which he surrendered incidental sources of ordinary revenue – such as wardships and purveyances – and even offered to forgo any further impositions without parliamentary consent in return for an annual subsidy of £200,000. Subsidies primarily fell on landed income derived from seasonal rents whose monetary value was more vulnerable to inflation than income routinely accumulated through trade and commerce. Though not immune from inflation, the crown, through its powers of patronage and prerogative, was considerably better placed to protect its revenue base than the men of property who composed the Lords and the Commons.

James had undoubtedly overcompensated for the parsimonious regime that had operated in the last years of Elizabeth Tudor, and the seemingly disproportionate number of Scots aggravated vernacular perceptions about the lavish and wasteful expenditure at the early Stuart court. Despite his spendthrift reputation and his manifest inability to fashion a stable and lasting financial settlement in England, James did not bankrupt Britannic monarchy. His recourse to his prerogative powers to facilitate financial liquidity was as much an issue of political economy as of constitutional controversy.[18] Household costs were expediently laid off as charges to courtiers and other parties, but not without a political cost to the monarchy. The provision of goods to the crown as purveyance was transacted at the king's price, which was usually well below the market price. Where money was offered in place of goods, compositions were exacted to ensure that rates of commutation for purveyances preserved price differentials in favour of the crown. Favoured courtiers were awarded wardships, which enabled them to profit from the revenues of a landed estate during the minority of the heir. Above all, courtiers and their clients were also awarded patents and monopolies, the exclusive licence to work and market select commodities.

Ostensibly designed to raise the quality of native manufactures and promote alternatives to imports, monopolies too often led to an additional sales tax on existing products.[19] Although monopolies and patents could impact adversely on royal revenues derived from imports and exports, this was again offset by farming contracts for customs and imposts to consortia of merchants, usually through the cities of London, Dublin and Edinburgh for England, Ireland and Scotland respectively. Such farming, however, encouraged the early Stuarts to look to future revenues to finance government rather than seek to balance actual income against current expenditure. As the crown had a deserved reputation for poor repayment of debts, sources of credit were not easily forthcoming, even within the city of London where loans were mortgaged to Britannic requirements that the city plant Londonderry in Ulster. When Charles I sought to liquidate extensive debts and simultaneously secure a further loan from the city in 1627, he surrendered a substantive body of crown lands worth about £350,000. In the process of surrendering the crown's last major saleable body of lands in England, he critically compromised his stock of secured assets essential to secure further loans. Borrowing on continental markets was expensive with little mileage in offering royal patronage as collateral, as Charles discovered in 1626 when he was unable to pawn his crown jewels in Amsterdam. His financial credibility was further undermined when he made no effort to arrest the bankruptcy of his principal continental creditor, Philip Burlamachi, by 1633. Routine costs of government had often to be borne by leading officials whose understandable inclination to recoup their expenditure from the readiest available royal revenues raised doubts about their probity which, in turn, further tarnished vernacular perceptions about the probity of royal government. Conversely, when these same leading officials faced cutbacks in their fees and pensions, in England in 1629–31 and again in 1637–8 and in the interim in Scotland in 1634–5, their political will to sustain Britannic monarchy in the face of personal harassment diminished markedly.[20]

The crown also laid off the costs of defending England by land and sea. The requirement that all able-bodied men between the ages of 16 and 60 attend an annual muster in each county had been effectively commuted under Elizabeth Tudor into elite corps of trained bands raised and equipped at the expense of the able-bodied not required for service. Naval defences had been entrusted principally to privateering, again at no cost to the crown. However, changes in methods of warfare were making these measures increasingly redundant. The technological shift in favour of guns and artillery increased both the capacity and the cost of infantry over cavalry. The gradual recourse to broadsides for naval engagements required the construction of specialised warships rather than a reliance on merchant ships that could be converted for privateering. James had borne the cost of the initial British expeditionary forces to the continent in 1610–12 and again in 1618 from his ordinary resources. However, the escalation of the Thirty Years War and mounting political pressure to restore the Winter Queen and her husband to the Palatinate required extraordinary subsidies by 1621. Already over £1 million in debt, James estimated that the costs of direct British intervention would be around £1 million for every year of engagement. Notwithstanding his padding of costs to recover royal finances, James's projections were both in tune with the changing manner of waging war and Britannic in scope. The Commons, wedded to Gothic perceptions of expenditure and a touching belief in the efficacy of privateering, offered less than £300,000 as an annual subsidy. The Scottish Estates, through a land tax and a tax on the working of money (annualrents), offered the prospect of raising around £600,000 Scots (£50,000 sterling) over four years. This proportionally more generous offer was actually renewed for another four years by the Estates in 1625, when the Commons broke with convention and refused to award the customs dues known as tonnage and poundage to Charles I for life. Reluctant to set precedents that would further justify impositions for life, the Commons even failed to ratify tonnage and poundage for a year and were not prepared to offer more than £120,000 as subsidies towards meeting the £720,000 already committed by Britannic monarchy to war and diplomacy.[21]

Charles sought to counter such truculence not only by asserting his prerogative right to exact tonnage and poundage, but also by claiming the subsidies lost by his dissolution of parliament as a benevolence. The increased offer from the Commons of a subsidy of £200,000 in 1626 continued to fall far short of his continental commitments, which were now augmented by his declarations of war against France and Spain. Accordingly, he imposed a forced loan in lieu of subsidies after a further dissolution of parliament. In 1627, he had 68 prominent landowners jailed for non-payment under martial law. The Commons' presentation of the Petition of Right in 1628 was not sweetened by the offer of £280,000 in subsidies, especially as Irish landowners in association with British planters were prepared to pay £120,000 towards the ever-escalating military budget on the unfulfilled promise of the Graces. Although suing for peace with France and Spain in 1629 was a vital contribution to cutting costs, Britannic monarchy had expended over £2 million on war and diplomacy during the 1620s. Charles was close to £1.5 million in debt when he dissolved the English parliament that same year. Although he was able to scale down his military, if not his financial, commitments to Christian IV, he was not quit of formal military engagement in the Thirty Years War until the death of Gustav II Adolph in 1632. While he continued to exact tonnage and poundage in England, the only parliamentary source of supply was the renewal of the land tax and tax on annualrents voted by the Scottish Estates in 1630. The prospects of another £50,000 sterling over four years made no more than a marginal dent in the financial deficit under which Britannic monarchy was operating under Charles I.[22]

The king's preference for fiscal expedients authorised by his prerogative rather than inadequate subsidies voted by the English parliament undoubtedly raised issues of trust about motives and intentions. Concerns over breaches of trust were not the sole preserve of the Commons, however.[23] Indeed, the Commons was compromising the capacity of Charles to fulfil his Britannic commitments. The royal chaplain, Roger Maynwaring, provoked Gothic outrage when he argued in sermons at court published in 1627 that the paying of fiscal dues was a religious obligation not open to challenge by constitutional assemblies. The requirement of supply for 'the pressing Necessities of State' was not exclusively English, but was of Britannic significance 'for the Safety and Protection of his Maiesties Kingdoms, Territories and Dominions'. Accordingly, those refusing to comply with fiscal directives should be accounted recusants in the temporal sense, in the same way that religious dissidents refusing to comply with the penal laws upholding the established Church of England were recusants in the spiritual sense.[24] Such encouragement by anti-Calvinists for the payment of benevolences and forced loans undoubtedly furthered the identification of Puritan and parliamentary interests by 1629.[25]

In Scotland, notwithstanding the relative generosity of the taxation renewed by conventions of the Estates in 1625 and 1630, the premeditated endeavours of Charles to shift fiscal obligations away from parliamentary supply to benevolences was firmly rejected. In placing Scotland on a war footing, ostensibly for defensive purposes, from 1625, Charles I had asserted that the recurrent cost of maintaining British fortifications against Habsburg invasion could better be met from additional imposts on coal rather than by taxation. Not only would these imposts be determined at court rather than be voted by the Scottish Estates, but the cost differential which markedly favoured Scottish over English coal in the lucrative Dutch market would be critically eroded. Faced with such a threat to Scotland's major source of foreign currency, the Scottish Privy Council reaffirmed the rejection of additional imposts by the Scottish Estates in 1625 and blocked renewed proposals from court in 1626 and 1627. This obstructive action, the first sustained questioning of the good faith of Charles I by the political elite in any of the three kingdoms, reflected Scottish concerns that the Britannic perspective of the Stuarts was becoming distinctively anglocentric. This direction was first signalled in Scotland by the new monarch's promotion, solely on the strength of his prerogative, of social and administrative uniformity through his ill-conceived, technically complex and financially unproductive Revocation Scheme. Launched covertly in 1625 and not given parliamentary ratification until 1633, the Scheme generated a climate of distrust throughout the political nation.[26]

A Revocation of Principle?

Traditionally, Scotland had adhered to the notions of virtue and pedigree necessary to constitute nobility that prevailed throughout Europe. By the outset of Charles I's reign, however, Scotland had come into line with England in defining the nobility as the peerage, those who held titles ranging from lord to duke, as distinct from the lairds or gentry whose ranks varied from the untitled to knights baronet.[27] Nonetheless, Scotland retained a distinctive system of landholding based on feudal conveyancing. Thus, those who held land heritably from the crown in freehold differentiated between the land they held and worked directly as property and the land they conveyed to other landowners by heritable feus over which they retained superiority. Although the consent of their superiors was mandatory, heritable feuars also engaged in subinfeudation to reward kinsmen and local associates, or to recompense creditors through mortgages which secured loans against rents. Thus, despite the distinction between nobles and gentry that was shared with England, nobles and gentry were not exclusively freeholders in Scotland. Indeed, Scottish lords and lairds usually held significant amounts of land as feuars as well as as freeholders, a pattern consolidated by the secularisation of church property in the sixteenth century. The distinction between non-titled freeholders and feuars cannot be equated with that between the shire and the parish gentry.

There were other significant differences in terms of judicial and ecclesiastical privileges. In England there was a clear demarcation between central and local government, the latter being run in the counties by commissions of the peace and sheriff courts supervised by judges of assize on regional circuits. Although James VI had attempted to align Scottish and English local and regional government prior to the regal union, heritable jurisdictions still prevailed at regional and local level in Scotland at the accession of Charles I. A barony, granted to some but not all freeholders, conveyed the right of private estate management and the power to mutilate thieves and hang murderers caught red-handed. A regality, granted to some but not all nobles, ceded extensive public rights to try civil and criminal cases similar to those exercised by sheriffs and judges on circuit as justice-ayres.[28]

The secularisation of church property had also augmented the legal and prescriptive rights to teinds (tithes) exercised by nobles and gentry. Traditionally, a few barons had exercised the right of lay patrons in parishes where they held the right to nominate the minister and under-write his stipend. The massive creation of temporal lordships by James VI had enabled their holders to acquire the titularship of teinds in parishes where they exercised the right of ecclesiastical patronage. Within every parish, the lay patron or titular controlled the teinds of other landowners, designated ecclesiastically as heritors. In parishes where control was vested in the lay patron, the heritors were usually feuars or, if freeholders, kinsmen and local associates. Where a temporal lordship was dispersed geographically and titularship was not exercised over a consolidated group of parishes, a considerable portion of heritors were neither bound to the titular as feudal superior nor even tied by kinship and local association. As a measure of appeasement, titulars farmed the collection of their parochial teinds to prominent local landowners designated as tacksmen. Since the rights of the titulars and tacksmen took priority over those of the heritors, the process of collecting crops designated as teind at harvest time was prone to fractious delays.[29]

Charles I was to demonstrate his complete lack of understanding of the feudal nature of Scottish landholding in his avowed claim that the Revocation Scheme would emancipate the gentry through surrender of superiorities, abolition of heritable jurisdictions and teind redistribution. Who was to be emancipated was unclear. If it was the lairds in their capacity as feuars and heritors, why discriminate against lords in the same situation? Conversely, if all feuars were to become freeholders and if all heritors were to own their own teinds, how was the surrendering of superiorities and the redistribution of teinds to be financed? What compensation was to be offered for the abolition of heritable jurisdictions? Teind redistribution was also promoted as a way of augmenting ministers' stipends and increasing the provision of churches, schools and hospitals. Such redistribution for pious uses would limit the amount of teinds that heritors could retain for their own use and thus was effectively a permanent alienation of their resources no less than those of the titulars and lay patrons. Teind redistribution also threatened an increase in direct taxation, as Charles was claiming an annuity from the teinds for the permanent benefit of the crown. This claim, regarded as far from honourable even within official circles, demonstrated that Revocation was as much about fiscal opportunism as it was about social engineering.[30]

The grounds on which Charles sought to effect his Revocation Scheme were essentially spurious. On account of the minorities that had bedevilled Scottish kingship since the fourteenth century, it had become an accepted constitutional tenet that a sovereign, between his 21st and 25th years, could annul all grants of royal property, pensions and offices made by any regency government prior to his majority. No regency government had acted in Scotland for Charles I, who was in his 25th year at his accession. However, he was a minor when proclaimed Prince of Scotland in succession to his late brother Henry in 1612. Accordingly, Charles claimed a revocation as prince and maintained that the patrimony of the principality was indivisible from that of the crown. Since grants hurtful to the principality were generally inimical to the crown, he was entitled to a general revocation of all grants of property and revenue from the crown patrimony for an indeterminate duration. Charles discreetly served notice of his intent in October 1625 without reference to the Convention of Estates then sitting in Edinburgh. He remained impervious to the subsequent warning from his Scottish Treasurer, John Erskine, 7th Earl of Mar. If landed titles and jurisdiction could be revoked solely by the royal prerogative, no landowner could be sure of any inheritance within Scotland done 'be any of his Majesties predicessors sen King Fergus the First', from whom Charles was reputed to be 147th in succession.[31]

In a bid to allay mounting concerns as news of the Revocation Scheme leaked out from Edinburgh, Charles refined his Scheme in February and again in July 1626. He claimed to be following the immediate precedent of his father's revocation in 1587 and its associated act of annexation, which had incorporated teinds as spiritualities, as well as church lands as temporalities, within the crown patrimony. No reading of the act can support this contention. Its main purpose was to create the legal basis for the erection of temporal lordships as James VI established a landed resource to reward royal officials and counsellors. Despite specifying that the surrender of superiorities was to apply solely to kirklands, this still left over two-fifths of all Scottish estates liable to revocation. Indeed, over a quarter of the Scottish Privy Council, which Charles reconstituted with 48 members in March 1626, stood to be among the foremost victims of his Revocation Scheme. In order to enforce compliance from the temporal lords in particular and the political nation in general, Charles suspended his father's act of prescription of 1617. Under this act, the 13-year period for questioning heritable rights to property possessed continuously for 40 years was due to lapse in June 1630. Charles sought confirmation of his prerogative right to suspend the act from the College of Justice, as the supreme civil court in Scotland, in March 1630. In giving their assent, however, the senators of the College added the proviso that the suspension applied to property claimed by the crown as far back as 1455, but no further!

Notwithstanding the five-year delay in imposing a retrospective time limit on the surrender of superiorities, abolition of heritable jurisdictions and teind redistribution, one supplementary area of the Scheme did have a limit prescribed from the outset. This was 1540, a notional starting point for the reversal of feudal tenures, which has been repeated erroneously and consistently in British historiography as the starting point for the whole Revocation. The increasingly commercialised approach to estate management, reinforced by the secularisation of church property in the sixteenth century, had led to the regularisation of feu duties. The replacement of incidental reliefs arising from wardship, marriage and non-entry of heirs by annual monetary compositions known as taxed ward had enabled landowners to regularise their financial outgoings. The reversion of feudal tenures under taxed ward since 1540 was a blatant exercise of fiscal opportunism. In contrast to England, reliefs in Scotland were not set at definite rates but were scaled to current rentals. Unlike fixed compositions, reliefs tended to be adjusted for inflation whenever landlords raised rents. Once the estate of a freeholder had passed into royal custody during a minority, the reversion of taxed ward enabled the crown to raise as well as retain rents until the heir came of age. Furthermore, the king had the right to sell or gift the wardship and marriage of an heir, a right that was a potentially lucrative source of patronage.

The fiscal opportunism of Charles I was compounded by his promotion of Revocation as an aspect of prerogative rule. This was particularly evident in relation to three key processes for the implementation of his Scheme. In January 1627, he established the Commission for Surrenders and Teinds as a prerogative court empowered to offer compensation for surrendered superiorities and to quantify and cost teinds liable for redistribution. The Commission, which was initially scheduled to run for six months, lasted over a decade before being wound up in July 1637, just before rioting against religious innovations commenced in Edinburgh. As Charles I belatedly came to realise, its divisive operations and its increasing reliance on bishops for routine administration was second only to his Revocation in 'sowing seeds of sedition and discontent' in Scotland.[32] All executive decisions concerning the surrender of superiorities, the abolition of heritable jurisdictions and teind redistribution were determined solely by Charles. Redistribution in particular could not be effected until the teinds in every parish had been evaluated, a task whose technical complexity Charles wholly underestimated. In order to ensure the compliance of all titulars and lay patrons as teind sellers and heritors as teind buyers, Charles demanded that they, respectively and collectively, subscribe to a general submission, which was issued as a legal decreet from the court in January 1628. In effect, this promise to comply with rates of compensation and valuation that were still to be determined was a blank cheque for the king. Another legal decreet issued by Charles in September 1629 specified the rates of compensation for the surrender of superiorities, the rates at which teinds were to be quantified and costed for purchase by heritors, and restrictions on purchases to ensure adequate redistribution for pious uses.

There was no ringing endorsement for these measures at the Convention of Estates in July 1630. The gentry, attending as commissioners from the shires, led the call that the king be petitioned to take account of 'the great feare' aroused by his efforts to compel compliance with the Revocation Scheme. Charles had been prepared to license separate conventions for the gentry, burgesses and clergy, but not the nobility, to define their respective and antagonistic positions in 1627. But he remained reluctant to convene a plenary meeting of the Scottish Estates despite the continuing apprehensions of the nobility that the implementation of Revocation would result in 'irreperable ruin to an infinite number of families of all qualities in every region of the land'.[33]

The complex task of evaluating teinds was devolved to subcommissions operating within the civil bounds of every presbytery. Subcommissions included not only members of the national Commission for Surrenders and Teinds, but also co-opted gentry of local influence to expedite the actual process of valuation in every parish within the civil presbytery. Persuading sub-commissioners to serve in every presbytery was certainly not facilitated by the prospects of a technically exacting workload and anomalous as well as contentious valuations. Sub-commissions were authorised for 59 presbyteries in July 1628, but only 15 were operative in February 1629. Although every sub-commission was functioning by the end of that year, few bothered to submit regular reports of their diligence over the next five years. Instead of expediting valuations, the sub-commissions actively colluded with local vested interests to restrict the amount of teind redistributable for ministers' stipends, pious uses and the king's annuity. Collusion had become such a community enterprise that Charles censured the Commission for Surrenders and Teinds in July 1635 for its routine acceptance of parochial valuations in which the amount of teind eligible for redistribution had been diminished by as much as a third. The Commission admitted in December 1636 that teinds had not yet been valued in most parishes.[34]

Undoubtedly, social deference and a reluctance to become entangled in legal confrontations with obstructive titulars and lay patrons contributed to the widespread aversion among heritors to secure their own teinds by compulsory purchase. Few sales proceeded by voluntary agreement. Despite vociferous overtures from clergy intent on securing augmented stipends, ministers were more concerned to appease than to confront titulars, lay patrons and heritors. Indeed, ministers actually colluded in the deliberate undervaluing of teinds. Inaccurate and incomplete valuations particularly prejudiced the exaction of the king's annuity, which Charles had prescribed as commencing at the harvest of 1628. Annuity payments proved a negligible source of royal revenue.

Other aspects of Charles's Revocation Scheme were no more remunerative. In the case of superiorities and heritable jurisdictions, their respective surrender and abolition proved a financial drain on the crown, especially as the supplies voted in the Conventions of Estates in 1625 and 1630 were not readily available to meet the costs of compensation. Instead, the revenues raised from the taxes on land and annualrents were earmarked for British expeditionary forces on the continent, national defence and the maintenance of the Scottish civil establishment at court and in Edinburgh. By 1634, however, Charles had substantially increased his revenues, primarily through the auspices of John Stewart, 1st Earl of Traquair, who on the political eclipse of Menteith had established himself as the foremost Scottish-based administrator and second only to Hamilton in counselling the king on Scottish affairs. In July, William Dick of Braid, a leading Edinburgh merchant and financier, was induced to take over the farming of the imposts of wines, and three months later the customs; his cumulative annual payments of around £11,250 sterling brought in an additional £3250 to the Scottish Treasury. At the same time, the increase from four to six years in the taxes on land and annualrents awarded by the coronation parliament realised the equivalent of

£61,140 by August 1636. However, Charles still carried an accumulating deficit of £10,970 aggravated by the lavish expenses of his coronation visit.[35]

Charles was obliged to suspend payments of compensation negotiated for the abolition of heritable jurisdictions in October 1634. Only 11 temporal lords, less than a third of the total number, made any meaningful effort to negotiate with the crown. No more than five made a comprehensive surrender of superiorities. Instead of being annexed inalienably to the crown, they tended to be gifted to the church. Thus, superiority over their feuars was merely transferred, not terminated. Although nine nobles and four gentry contracted for the abolition of heritable jurisdictions, the crown's lack of ready cash led to payments by protracted instalment or the retention of regalities and other heritable offices under mortgage. In essence, local government remained a matter of hereditary private enterprise in Scotland. When Charles attempted to reinvigorate the peace commissions in September 1634 along English lines, the willingness of the gentry to serve as justices had been prejudiced by their onerous and politically thankless experience on the sub-commissions for the valuation of teinds. By July 1637, the Scottish Privy Council was prepared to admit, notwithstanding frequent citations of justices for negligence and dereliction of duty, that service on the peace commissions was effectively in disarray.[36]

Financial constraints compounded by local rioting had led to the prompt shelving of the least significant aspect of the Revocation Scheme, to reverse the conversion of feudal tenures since 1540. In the spring of 1628, Charles was induced to forgo reversing tenures in return for an evasion tax proposed by Sir Alexander Strachan of Thornton, a courtier of dubious repute. As part of a project rather optimistically promoted to treble the revenues available to the crown from feudal casualties, at least £2000 sterling was to be exacted annually in compositions from landlords who had defaulted on payments of reliefs or converted feudal tenures without royal approval. A further £19,667 was to be realised by compositions for unpaid feudal dues, escheated goods of outlaws, rent arrears, renegotiated titles and breaches of penal statutes.[37] Charles simultaneously reinvigorated the justice-ayres. Four geographically distinct circuit courts were to be operated by the senators of the College of Justice twice yearly to try all capital cases, all transgressions of penal statutes and to oversee the competence of local government officers. Plans to hold biannual circuits were never implemented, and rarely were the shires within each judicial circuit visited more than once over the next three years. The lack of specification in the formal indictment of offenders immediately proved contentious, for the indictments did not inform reputed offenders whether they faced capital charges or merely breaches of penal statutes. The justice-ayres were reminded in September 1629 that circuit courts were to be held at Strachan of Thornton's convenience. He was empowered to dispense with prosecutions and exact compositions for breaches of penal statutes, half of which he was to retain for his own profit. Such was the outcry from the localities that Thornton's patent was first suspended unilaterally by leading officials and then set aside in the wake of protests at the Convention of Estates in 1630. The circuit courts were also suspended. Their revival in 1631 proved no more than fitful.[38]

British Incongruity

The Revocation Scheme exposed the incongruities of promoting Britannic monarchy by royal prerogative. In terms of public reception, political ramifications and governmental experimentation, these incongruities had a profound British impact in paving the way for revolution against the prerogative rule of Charles I. His reputed intent to effect a thorough process of state reconstruction in England was actually tested and found wanting in Scotland.[39] Dissatisfaction with the scope and the implementation of the Revocation Scheme first lowered the threshold for violent resistance to monarchical decrees throughout the British Isles. The Privy Council in Edinburgh was subjected to armed lobbying on two occasions, in February 1627 and April 1629. In the interim, disorders were reported in several localities during the attempted valuation of teinds by sub-commissions, and the justice-ayres in all four judicial circuits encountered significant opposition until their operations ceased in 1631.

Furthermore, political discontent within the Scottish localities was becoming associated with the first systematic targeting of the bishops and their clerical associates for their promotion of prerogative rule in civil as well as ecclesiastical affairs. At the Convention of Estates in July 1630, John Elphinstone, Lord Balmerino, protested that bishops' exaction of an oath of conformity from all entrants to the ministry since 1626 lacked parliamentary warrant. A concerted constitutional attack on the episcopal role in church and state was prepared but, in the absence of a defined privilege of free speech in the Scottish Estates, prudently not delivered to the coronation parliament of 1633 by John Campbell, Lord Loudoun.[40]

Although he was not yet an implacable opponent of episcopacy, the peripatetic William Lithgow did publish a dire warning to Charles I in anticipation of the coronation parliament. His strictures against grievances and abuses stood in marked contrast to the contemporaneous eulogies the king received as 'the Britannic Sun' from the University of Oxford and as the heroic protector of Great Britain from Andrew Boyd, Bishop of Argyll.[41] Scotland remained an unconquered nation celebrated internationally for its martial culture, but its commonwealth was being undone for want of good government under Charles I. Notwithstanding Lithgow's eulogy for the noble houses of Scotland, the episodic migration of the landed elite to London, particularly for the funeral of James I in April 1625, constituted a drain on specie to the detriment of estate management as well as trade. Indeed, England was becoming a curse and London was robbing Scotland of its mercantile gain as nobles and gentry travelled to court. As a progressive alternative to Revocation for the regeneration of the country and the harmonising of British endeavours, Lithgow proposed a wholesale policy of Scottish plantation. Nobles and gentry should foreswear attendance at court and divert their energies towards the improvement of their estates by enclosures, drainage, parks, long leases and low rents such as their counterparts were implementing in England and Ireland and the Earl of Stirling was promoting in Nova Scotia.[42]

Rather than accept constructive criticism, Charles resorted to managerial overkill with respect to the composition, agenda and proceedings of the coronation parliament in June 1633. He transcended similar techniques used by his father to secure the passage of the Five Articles of Perth and the taxes on land and annualrents in 1621. All those seeking to be excused from the coronation parliament, including four of the five Englishmen who held Scottish honours but no Scottish estates, were encouraged to place their proxies at the disposal of the court. As an additional encouragement, 54 gentry were dubbed knights and 9 created peers, while 10 existing peers were elevated in rank during the seven weeks of the coronation visit. But Charles's award of honours was conditional on the beneficiaries supporting his legislative programme. The Committee of Articles was the most crucial vehicle for management once the parliament commenced on 20 June. The bishops were the lynchpins for royal control over the Committee's membership. As added surety, Charles decreed that the Chancellor, John Hay, 1st Earl of Kinnoul, should preside over the Committee, on which eight other officers of state sat and voted.[43] During the eight days in which the Committee met to compile the full legislative programme, all separate conventions of Estates were banned. A meeting of the gentry to draw up a remedial programme for royal government was interrupted and dispersed. Despite the support of sympathetic nobles, a petition from nonconforming clergy was suppressed, as was a supplication by commissioners from the shires and burghs attacking the agenda rumoured to have been drawn up by the Committee of Articles as inimical 'both to Kirk and countrey'.[44]

Only one day was set aside for the plenary approval of the legislative programme. The composite agenda of 168 measures was presented for acceptance or rejection as a whole, with no distinction for voting purposes observed between public enactments and private bills. Votes were collected at random, not recorded systematically from each Estate. Debate was not encouraged. Charles attended in person to reproach dissenters and note their names. The block passage of legislation was further secured by dubious tallying. The Earl of Rothes challenged the result favouring the court but retracted on being threatened with prosecution for treason. Public rumour soon reversed the final outcome on the grounds that the tally of individual votes cast by persons actually present went against the court. Rothes, Balmerino and Loudoun, as leaders of the disaffected, were not yet prepared to criticise the crown directly. However, Charles's reliance on bishops to secure control of the Committee of Articles, to enforce rigorous vetting of the composite agenda and to collude in voting practices enabled the disaffected in each Estate to concert their protests against parliamentary direction 'by the Episcopall and courte faction'.[45]

Indeed, a distinctive Scottish critique of Britannic monarchy emerged in the aftermath of the coronation parliament when William Haig, a former crown solicitor, penned a Supplication to justify the conduct of the disaffected element in voting against the block passage of the legislative programme. Reputedly endorsed by 35 out of the 45 peers who attended, Haig's Supplication criticised Charles I for not being as attuned to Scottish sensibilities as his father, for seeking both Revocation and relatively high taxation, for favouring parasitic influences at court, and for his toleration of 'Poperie and Arminianism'. Above all, the lack of constitutional limitations on his prerogative gave rise to 'a generall feare of some innovations intended in essential points of religion'.[46] Arminianism was more a perceived than an actual threat to the Calvinist orthodoxy of the Kirk. Its emotive association with Catholicism was intended primarily to highlight the danger to the Kirk from the wholesale importation of the religious standards currently in favour at court.

William Laud's stage management of Charles I's coronation ceremonial on 18 July 1633 had brought home to Scottish Calvinists that the court rather than Rome posed the immediate threat to their Reformed tradition. John Spottiswood, Archbishop of St Andrews, and the five other Scottish bishops officiating had worn rochets, a practice unwitnessed since the Reformation; the same applied to their seeming deference to the altar and crucifix when conducting divine service.

The most contentious piece of legislation in 1633 was the reaffirmation of the enactment of 1606 acknowledging the royal prerogative in church and state in association with that of 1609 empowering James I to prescribe the apparel of all legal officers as well as clergy. Thus, Charles was claiming that the right to regulate apparel – conceded personally to, but never exercised by, his father – was vested inherently in the crown. Charles further ensured that the relatively innocuous issue of clerical dress remained a matter of constitutional controversy when he ordered the wearing of 'whytes' by the clergy from October. Bishops were to continue wearing the rochets worn at the coronation ceremony when attending affairs of state or officiating in the church. Notice was duly served that a British drive for religious uniformity would be unstinting when Charles accompanied this directive with a further order that daily prayers in the Chapel Royal, the cathedrals and the universities were to be conducted according to the English liturgy, until some course be taken to devise a Scottish complement to the Book of Common Prayer.[47]

These observances were in keeping with the pastoral orders issued by Archbishop Abbot that associated clerical dress with liturgical standards and the promotion of conformity in England. They were given added bite, however, with Laud's translation from the bishopric of London to the archbishopric of Canterbury in September, especially when news leaked through to Scotland about his clampdown on nonconformity in England and his threatened dissolution of the churches of foreign nations. Established in London since the 1540s, they were viewed as bastions of the Reformed tradition as received and now under considerable threat in continental Europe.[48] Scottish Presbyterians, committed assuredly to the attainment of a godly commonwealth through the preaching of the word, inspired prayer and disciplined religious observance, remained wary of being called Puritans by their Episcopalian opponents, not least because of the schismatic tendencies associated with that label in England. Nonetheless, they were increasingly prepared to make common cause as pastors in their steadfast opposition to Catholicism and Arminianism as to prelacy and profanity.[49]

Nonconformity was further politicised in Scotland by the reconstitution of the Court of High Commission in October 1634, with sweeping powers to impose civil censures for ecclesiastical transgressions. Although it exercised considerable restraint in attempting to get militant Presbyterians to recognise its jurisdiction, episcopal dominance of its proceedings and demarcation disputes with the Scottish Privy Council coupled fears for Presbyterianism with antipathy to the bishops. These fears were, in turn, fuelled by incongruous rumours.[50] Sir William Brereton, the English traveller and future Parliamentarian commander, gleaned from conversations with disaffected gentry and ministers in Edinburgh during June 1635 that 48 abbeys and priories were to be restored to the clergy. The potential restoration of all temporal lordships not in episcopal hands at the outset of the Revocation Scheme was of momentous political significance, for restored abbots and priors, once allied with bishops, would compose a substantial phalanx for the court that would facilitate a royal stranglehold over future parliamentary proceedings. The veteran administrator and temporal lord Thomas Hamilton, 1st Earl of Haddington, had warned the court that same month that public rumours were now equating the progress of the Revocation Scheme with the reversal of the Scottish Reformation. No less damaging was the corrosive effect of adverse publicity. The printing of all major proclamations concerning Revocation meant that criticisms of Charles's prerogative rule would not be confined to Scotland: 'Englishmen can read them and understand Scots'.[51]

'Thorough'

Antipathy to the episcopate was further fuelled by the determination of Archbishop Laud to promote Scottish acolytes, such as John Maxwell, Bishop of Ross, and Thomas Sydserf, Bishop of Galloway, who were charged with the pursuit of 'thorough' north of the border. Although he was not the author of the Book of Orders instituted in England in 1631, Laud was determined to ensure greater efficiency, probity and uniformity in royal government throughout the British Isles. His sponsorship for the Book's comprehensive regulatory supervision of local government initiated a decade of unremitting pressure on the justices of the peace in the English shires. In supporting the renewal of the Scottish peace commissions according to the English model in 1634, Laud intended that Scotland should serve as an experimental area to correct English malfunctions – most notably, the declining commitment of the gentry to serve as justices or submit regular reports of their diligence to the Privy Council. The appointment of Scottish clergy as justices duly provided a precedent for his drafting of Anglican priests onto the English peace commissions to expedite the rating and collection of ship money – the most contentious, yet also the most remunerative, imposition of Charles's prerogative rule in England.[52]

Laud's advocacy of 'thorough' had already been anticipated by Charles I in his efforts to restructure local government in association with his Revocation Scheme. Thus, his prescription of June 1628 that the justice-ayres were to oversee the competence of local government mirrored his deployment of judges of assize in England. The functioning of the justice-ayres had been compromised by Thornton's financial speculations. Nevertheless, his administrative patent had provided a precedent for Charles's attempts to finance his prerogative rule in England through resort to fiscal opportunism after 1629.

Much to the consternation of English landowners, Charles used the Court of Wards under the direction of Lord Cottington to treble his income from feudal casualties. His imposition of fines on landowners of substance for failing to present themselves for a knighthood at his English coronation realised £174,000. Oliver Cromwell was among the miscreants who paid up in 1632. Fiscal opportunism as much as antiquarianism was evident in his associated campaign to fine landowners up to £20,000 for encroachments on the ancient boundaries of royal forests. But Charles's penchant for imposing large fines on prominent landowners and then cutting them back to more moderate compositions proved politically counterproductive. At the same time, his licensing of speculators to deforest the woodlands in the south-west, drive through enclosures in the Midlands, drain the fens in East Anglia and deregulate the expansion of London provoked localised unrest beyond the ranks of the political elite. Manifestly, fiscal opportunism took priority over resource management. The hostmen of Newcastle, having been fined £16,444 and charged an annual imposition of £2000 in 1624, were obliged to pay a further fine of £22,000 in 1630 to maintain their monopoly on the coal trade from the Tyne. Increased revenues generated through customs, particularly from an expanding colonial trade, rather than fiscal opportunism were primarily responsible for the increase in royal income in England from £750,000 in 1629 to around £1 million by 1635, and a corresponding drop in royal debts from £2 million to £1 million. Fines and compositions were occasional sources of revenue whereas ship money, targeted to bring in over £200,000 annually, offered the prospect of wiping out royal debts within five years.[53]

Charles extended the levy of ship money from the coastal shires to all of England in 1635. His justification was the creation of a royal navy capable of upholding his *ius imperium* over the British seas, especially in the Channel where piracy had assumed a massive and disruptive presence to the detriment of trade and commerce. Turks from Algiers had joined the Dunkirkers as perennial predators. Charles's declaration of a state of emergency was Britannic, but the burden of coastal defence fell solely on England. Similar declarations at the outset of his reign had been occasioned by actual wars with Spain and France in which Scotland and Ireland had been included as participants and contributors. Whereas these wars had diverted British expeditionary forces from relieving the Palatinate, Charles's decision to concentrate on building up his naval resources negated any further military endeavour to restore the son of the Winter Queen to his land-locked electorate. Notwithstanding the localised resistance of prominent nobles sympathetic to Puritanism, such as the Earl of Warwick in Essex and William Fiennes, 1st Viscount Saye & Sele, in the shires of Gloucester, Oxford and Lincoln, there was no systematic opposition to the initial levies of ship money throughout England. Those for 1636, 1637 and 1638 all realised around £200,000, notwithstanding complaints of inequitable rating favouring the more affluent and demarcation disputes between town and country and hundreds and parishes in and across most English counties. Even where sheriffs, as in Rutland and Suffolk, objected to directives compelling their listing of those defaulting or refusing to pay ship money, private lobbying of the English Privy Council took precedence over active collusion of the kind already evident in Scotland to negate the Revocation Scheme.[54]

A Gothic critique on the lack of parliamentary warrant for ship money was first suggested in 1636 by William Prynne, the Puritan polemicist who had been debarred from practising law, publicly pilloried, mutilated about the ears and incarcerated in the Tower for injudicious drama reviews. Prynne's criticisms, which were first circulated covertly in manuscript, contended that the levying of ship money was directly contrary to the fundamental laws and liberties of England. However, the substance of his published complaints drew on grievances accumulated from the processes of assessment and collection over the next five years. Monies raised through tonnage and poundage were deemed sufficient to meet current emergencies. A levy in the absence of war was without precedent. Compulsory expansion throughout England effectively imposed a double penalty on non-coastal counties required to sponsor trained bands. The 27 ships actually built fell below the 45 prescribed not only in terms of numbers, but also in their size and effectiveness. The rates at which the king was demanding provisions for his fleet was too high in relation to comparable exactions from 1625 to 1629. No compensation was offered for damages incurred through piracy. Prynne's alleged illegalities, injustices, abuses and grievances were brought into public debate as a result of the king's prosecution of John Hampden for non-payment of ship money in Buckinghamshire in November 1637. A more focused Gothic critique was able to draw on the minority position of the five judges out of the twelve on the King's Bench who dissented from the principal finding issued in June 1638, that the king, on the strength of his prerogative, had the sole right to declare a state of emergency and how government was to be conducted for the duration. In particular, Justice Croke affirmed that there was no precedent for a subject's goods to be taken in lieu of ship money by either statute law or common law: 'We are Judges and are to Judge according to Laws, and not according to State Policy and Conveniency'.[55]

In seeking to bring a test case against ship money, Hampden was supported by other noted Puritans, such as his leading counsel, Oliver St John, together with John Pym, Robert, Earl of Warwick, and William, Viscount Saye & Sele. Although all were involved in the Providence Island Company, their colonial affiliations served as much to provide a retreat from England as an agency for resistance to the prerogative rule. Their Gothic critique, prepared but not released as a petition at the outset of 1637, drew heavily on Prynne's initial attack on ship money.[56] The groundswell against ship money in the wake of the Hampden Case was certainly assisted by the increasing identification of Puritanism with opposition to Arminianism and the intolerant conformity enforced by Archbishop Laud. Yet the growth of covert Puritan associations along the lines of Scottish conventicles was primarily for mutual support rather than for political networking against Charles I.

The first call on the king to summon a parliament and abandon ship money came in December 1637 from Henry Davers, 1st Earl of Danby, a courtier, not a Puritan activist. Indeed, the organisation of a cohesive constitutional case against ship money had to await the outbreak of the Bishops' Wars in Scotland, which was also marked by a dramatic rise in non-payment, with over a third of the money levied for 1639 uncollected. The king having failed to secure supply from the Short Parliament of April 1640, the subsequent invasion of England by the Scottish Covenanters occasioned the breakdown not only of payments of ship money, but also of local government in England and Wales.[57] In this situation, three years after the formulation of the Scottish case against Britannic monarchy, the Puritan lawyer Henry Parker felt sufficiently secure to articulate a Gothic case which contended that Charles I had maintained a prerogative rule 'as destroys all other law and is incompatible with popular liberty'. Like the Scottish Covenanters, he identified the bishops as the principal opponents of the constitutional assemblies necessary to check the tyrannical inclinations of the king.[58]

First identified in Scotland in the wake of the coronation visit and made manifest in England by the ship money controversy, the explicit association of Arminianism with 'thorough' and its implicit association with threats to property and constitutional assemblies became starkly apparent in Ireland under Wentworth. Encouraged by such Irish polemicists as John Cusacke, who upheld the prerogative power of the crown to run Ireland as a colony, Wentworth was intent on moving beyond the Tudor conquest of Ireland as a dependent kingdom under the common law and parliamentary statute. His governing remit, however, was not to create a provincial model for absolutism, but to expand the resources available to Britannic monarchy through prerogative rule with or without constitutional consensus. Ireland was to become a net contributor rather than a perennial drain on the royal coffers. His seven-year stint as lord-deputy demonstrably borrowed from Scottish precedents concerning revocation and fiscal opportunism: for his true purpose, which was endorsed by Archbishop Laud and his principal acolyte in Ireland, James Bramhall, Bishop of Derry, was to reclaim crown lands and reverse the secularisation of church lands. Exemplary and remunerative plantations were to be promoted simultaneously with the secure establishment of Episcopalianism along not just Anglican, but Arminian, lines. Indeed, Ireland would become a laboratory not so much for anglicisation or even ecclesiastical congruence as for British improvement, which was to be achieved on the one hand through plantation and land reclamation and on the other by the inculcation of order and seemliness in religious observance. In effect, Wentworth was adding an English religious dimension to the Scottish commercialisation of estate management advocated by William Lithgow. Ireland was to become a productive dependency, not an underdeveloped colony of Britannic monarchy.[59]

However, the incongruities in this policy were soon evident. Went-worth's use of the Court of Ward and Liveries to augment royal revenues and his putative deployment of a commission for defective titles to effect a landed revocation for the benefit of crown and church destabilised the plantations as well as native Irish and Old English landowners. His willingness to restore three-quarters of confiscated land on the payment of compositions was further tempered by his intent to require subscription to the Anglican Oath of Supremacy, not just to an oath of allegiance to Britannic monarchy. This requirement was anathema not only to Irish Catholics but also to Scottish Presbyterians and other nonconforming planters. The imminent threat of destabilisation, coupled to the king's protracted failure to have the Graces endorsed by statute, surfaced during the parliament summoned at Dublin in July 1634. Unlike Charles I, Wentworth was not distrustful of parliaments so long as a clear demarcation was made between grants of supply to the crown and redress of grievances by royal favour.

In contrast to the truncated proceedings in the Scottish coronation parliament, the Irish parliament met over three sessions varying from three weeks to three months before its dissolution in April 1635. The noted generosity of James I in granting peerages, the solid phalanx of bishops and the willingness of non-resident Irish lords to grant their proxies in support of the court ensured that Wentworth had firm control of the Lords. Nonetheless, the Protestant majority of planters and office-holders in the Commons – nominally 143 out of the 256 members from the counties and boroughs – was notably fragile given the disaffection of a grouping of 20 to 30 members associated with the Earl of Cork, who was alienated by Wentworth's intent to revoke lay titles to church lands. Poyning's Law (of 1494) had stipulated that no bill could be introduced into either the Lords or the Commons in the Irish parliament without prior approval from the king and Privy Council in England. An amendment in 1557 had excluded the drafting of bills in England but allowed appeals from the Irish parliament to the crown. Although unenthusiastic about this latter aspect, Wentworth interpreted the statute as vesting the initiative for framing legislation with the lord-deputy and the Irish Privy Council. Accordingly, he was confident of a compliant parliament.

This confidence was not dented by the brief first session, which processed his bill for defective titles and granted six subsidies amounting to £120,000, loans, gifts and other voluntary contributions having realised £310,000 over the past two years. Although there was no more than limited sparring on their confirmation, the Graces became the central issue when the second session of parliament commenced in November after a three-month recess. If Wentworth had conceded statutory recognition for all 51 Graces, not only his administration but also the prerogative rule in Ireland would have been circumscribed. His plans to scrutinise defective titles would have had to be shelved along with his resolve for the wholesale plantation of Connacht. In the event, only two Graces directly relating to the plantation of Connacht were refused. No more than ten were given statutory recognition, albeit the Old and New English in Leinster and the British planters in Ulster were beneficiaries. The taking of the Oath of Allegiance was one of the 16 Graces that were to continue at the king's pleasure, while the remainder were left variously to the discretion of the lord-deputy, the judiciary and the episcopate. Wentworth temporarily lost control of the parliament following a backlash in the Commons led by Sir Piers Crosby, a Protestant Irish planter in Munster and Ulster and a landowner in Galway under threat from Wentworth's schemes for Connacht. Although Wentworth remained wary of further parliamentary disruption, collaboration between the Catholic Irish and disaffected Protestant planters was not sustained into the third session other than to negate a bill restricting imports of gunpowder. The main legislative achievement of this session was to ratify the new Canons prescribed for the Church of Ireland by the convocation of the Protestant clergy, which had sat in tandem with the Irish parliament.[60]

Promotion of religious uniformity in Ireland served as an exemplary warning for Scots opposed to the liturgical innovations hinted at by Charles in October 1633. Despite a valiant rearguard action fought by Archbishop Ussher to uphold Calvinist orthodoxy as defined in the Irish Articles of 1615, the Irish Convocation was moved by Bishop Bramhall, backed up by Laud and Wentworth, towards the aggressive imposition of religious uniformity which left little room for national diversity. The reversal in the prevailing British practice of minimal conformity and godly acquiescence, first signposted by the Irish Canons, which moved Anglicanism along distinctly Arminian lines, was particularly unfavourable to Scottish Presbyterians who had taken refuge in the Ulster plantations. Indeed, the resultant clampdown on nonconformity was accompanied by a distinctive Scotophobia among the principal protagonists of the Irish Canons as an improvement on current English practice.[61] The small, but zealous, vanguard of Scottish Presbyterians composed less than a tenth of the Protestant ministry in Ulster. Their vulnerability to a concerted attack by Irish and Scottish bishops was demonstrated by the suspension of Robert Blair and John Livingstone in 1631, for participating in revivalist meetings organised as conventicling communions on both sides of the North Channel. This vanguard was acutely exposed by the Episcopalian offensive co-ordinated by Laud and Bramhall in the wake of the passage of the Irish Canons. Not only were Blair and Livingstone excommunicated, but their Presbyterian associates were deposed for nonconformity. Along with prominent conventiclers from both Ulster and Scotland, they decided to seek release 'from the bondage of prelates'. In September 1636, around 140 nonconformists embarked from Ulster for New England. Although their ship neared Newfoundland, tempestuous weather forced their return to Scotland by November – a reversal interpreted as divine intervention. God had made evident 'that it was not his will that they should glorify him in America, he having work for them at home'.[62]

The return of the conventiclers to Scotland rather than Ireland was indicative of the better prospects for terminating the prerogative rule in the former. The promotion of 'thorough' in regulating government, landed title and, above all, religious polity and observance was conceived at court and promoted by Wentworth, Laud and the Canterburian bishops as imperial rationalising on behalf of Britannic monarchy. However, 'thorough' was received in Ireland, as in Scotland, as unwarranted anglicising and unwanted provincialising. The Irish response, though less muted than that of the English to ship money, was nonetheless sectarian and exclusive, even though Wentworth by his vindictiveness towards political opponents and by his venality as a land grabber in Munster, Connacht and Ulster had alienated the Protestant planters as well as the Catholic Irish. Geoffrey Keating's formulation of the Irish standpoint, which was concluded during Wentworth's governorship, brought together the native Irish and the Old English under a confessional rubric. As Wentworth's opponents at court were well aware by 1635, when they supported Sir Piers Crosby's endeavours to move the Irish brigades from Spanish into French service, the Irish Catholics had ready-made forces which the disaffected could summon home to their assistance. This awareness certainly facilitated the successful attempts led by the Old English absentee Ulrick Burke, 5th Earl of Clanricarde, to negate Wentworth's plans for the wholescale plantation of Connacht. Nonetheless, the exemption of the Clanricarde estates in Galway from plantation was only conceded after the outbreak of the Bishops' Wars.

The Irish formulation, however, excluded not only the New English and British planters but also Protestants among the native Irish, such as

Sir Piers Crosby, and, more substantially, among the Old English, such as James Butler, 12th Earl (later Marquess and Duke) of Ormond. No alternative Gothic formulation emerged in Ireland to unite interests alienated by Britannic monarchy. Wentworth's instrumental role in May 1635, in having the London guilds fined £70,000 and deprived of their extensive estates in and around Londonderry to his ultimate benefit, did contribute to the city's backing for the summoning of the English parliament in November 1640.[63] However, London was immediately responsive to the demands of the Scottish Covenanters that had been formulated on the basis of a national consensus opposed to the authoritarian promotion of uniformity in the state no less than in the church. This consensus, moreover, was reinforced by the potent message from Ulster that the leading agents of Britannic monarchy no longer trusted the Scots.

Britannic No More

The national consensus within Scotland was first stimulated by the outcry against Charles I's scheme for a common fishing. This initiative, on as grandiose a scale as ship money and likewise fashioned according to English mercantilist aspirations, was intended to open a window of opportunity into Scottish territorial waters at the expense of the native fishing industry as much as of the Dutch fleet. At the same time, the common fishing, as a confederation of self-financing provincial associations regulated by a council of prominent adventurers from all three kingdoms, was modelled on the corporate structure of the College of Herring Fishing that met yearly to regulate the operations of the Dutch fleet.

On being presented with this proposal in 1630, the Scottish Estates could assert no more than a watching brief over negotiations at court between commissioners appointed by the Scottish Privy Council and their English counterparts, who were exclusively courtiers and officials appointed by and answerable only to Charles. Determined to promote the common fishing to sustain the king's claim to sovereignty around the British Isles, the English commissioners were prepared to rely on the king's prerogative to secure the associated British adventurers unrestricted and exclusive access to inshore as well as deep-sea fishing off the Scottish coasts. While reluctantly accepting the implementation of the common fishing, the Scottish Privy Council vigorously rebuffed its Britannic promotion. The suppression of the name of Scotland in all authorising warrants was found to be particularly prejudicial. Especially confusing was the generic use of 'the name of great Britane altho ther be no unioun as yit with England'. The Council thus articulated widespread concerns that the common fishing was the thin edge of a wedge designed to relegate Scotland to the provincial status of Ireland. Indeed, Irish interests were not represented directly at the negotiations, but were encompassed within the remit of the English commissioners, who exhibited little concern for their advancement.[64]

The lack of Scottish commitment to the common fishing was especially notable in the ongoing forum for discussions on economic policy established by the Privy Council. Plenary sessions involved not only leading royal burghs but also the Committee of Review established by the Convention of Estates in 1630, whose membership included Rothes, Loudoun and Balmerino. These sessions, which were initiated at Perth in September 1631 and continued at Edinburgh in October 1632, were accompanied by a vigorous propaganda campaign that equated the vitality of the native fishing industry with the national interest. Since the prime fishing grounds around the British Isles were off the Scottish coasts, the plenary sessions tapped into a general antipathy to English adventurers being conceded any greater privileges than Dutch, French or Spanish fishermen. No attempt was made to amend or reject the charter of incorporation for the associated adventurers drawn up at court after two years' negotiation by the commissioners for both kingdoms. Nevertheless, the contents of the charter did afford specific guidance on the imposition of constitutional checks on Britannic monarchy. For Charles had insisted that the crown must ratify all ordinances passed by the governing council to ensure that they be not derogatory 'to the statutes, Laws, Liberties or acts of parliament of his Majesties kingdoms'. In turn, the governing council was to review the decisions of the provincial associations to ensure that they be not repugnant 'to the lawes, acts of parliament nor statutes of his Majesties kingdomes'. This emphasis on safeguards against contrariness resurfaced as an integral component of the National Covenant of 1638. The Scottish perspective made common cause with the Gothic on the proviso that these safeguards should be subject to the oversight of constitutional assemblies.[65]

In the event, no more than three provincial associations were formed, all headed by leading English officials. These associations were on the brink of bankruptcy by August 1638, 17 months after their fishing activities around the Western Isles had been abandoned following systematic disruption by inhospitable landlords and clan chiefs. Sporadic preying by piratical Dunkirkers as well as Dutch warships also took its toll. The ship money fleet was powerless to intervene. The Scottish Privy Council made no effort to hold landlords and chiefs to account, nor to implement the licensing of foreign fleets once Charles decided that his *ius imperium* could best be served by fines and compositions rather than by naval broadsides.[66]

The main political legacy of the common fishing was the continuance, on the initiative of the lay members of the Scottish Privy Council, of the plenary sessions on economic policy. Restraining imports of foreign dollars and augmenting stocks of native coin, with minimum disruption to the country's commerce, was duly recommended in January 1633. Having proscribed all discussion on the coinage in the coronation parliament, Charles was obliged to devalue the country's silver coin not once but twice in 1636 in a despairing attempt to check the excessive circulation of foreign dollars in Scotland. His invitation for a renewal of plenary discussions in June 1637 was negated by the national consensus building up in favour of active resistance to religious innovations.[67]

In the interim, the national consensus emerging through the plenary sessions of councillors, parliamentarians and burgesses had prevented Charles from reactivating the appointment of Lord Spynie in May 1634 as muster-master and colonel of the trained bands in Scotland. This initiative, which was a blatant attempt to import the English practice of financing an elite militia, would have created a standing army at no cost to the monarchy. Mobilising against the imposition of tariff reform, which would erode the cost advantage Scottish goods enjoyed in continental markets, did lead to a further significant concession in December 1636. Charles agreed, against the wishes of the Canterburian bishops, that tariffs on the export of Scottish staple products should not be increased from 5 to 7 per cent of their rated value. A similar exemption was granted to the Scottish carrying trade, and the increase in tariffs for the droving of livestock was restricted to 1 per cent. However, Charles was already inflicting considerable damage on the country's main currency earner, the export trade in coal and salt.

Having increased taxes on English coals, Charles decreed that the custom on bulk exports from Scotland should be doubled in February 1634. Not only did this reduce the Scottish cost advantage from nine- to fivefold over English coal in the lucrative Dutch markets, but the greater risk of piracy by Dunkirkers on the longer sea voyage to the Firth of Forth induced Dutch convoys to switch back to the coal depots on the River Tyne from the summer of 1635. Traquair reported that the export trade in both coal and salt had undergone 'very great decay' by October 1637. Indeed, the latter had been severely damaged by Charles's licensing of associations in both Scotland and England for the production and wholesale distribution of salt throughout the British Isles by April 1636. However, the proposed Scottish association was subordinated to the English, with a strict quota imposed on bulk exports to England and tariffs equalised between both countries. Having been 'so much opposed and crossed be ye Inglische', there was little scope left for redirecting exports of salt from Dutch to English markets by January 1637.[68]

Economic recession was thus court induced and provoked fears about endemic social disorder. Widespread redundancies among the native workforce coincided with the spread of plague from England and followed on from two years of agricultural dearth during 1635–6. However, the manufacturing of political disorder was already on the Scottish agenda as a result of the trial of Lord Balmerino for concealing, condoning and revising Haig's Supplication. Archbishop Spottiswood, spurred on by the Canterburian bishops, was instrumental in bringing the petition to the attention of the court in May 1634. They were also the prime players in the investigative commission established in July which tied Balmerino to the publication and distribution of what Charles had determined was a 'scandalous and seditious lybell'. The bishops were especially vehement in seeking a treasonable indictment when Balmerino was arraigned before a judicial commission presided over by William Hay, 10th Earl of Errol, in December. After this commission had determined that the charges of leasing-making – stirring up enmity between the king and his subjects by false and malicious writing – were relevant, they attempted to influence the final selection of the assize of 15 laymen drawn from the 45 nobles and gentry summoned to Edinburgh to determine the extent of Balmerino's guilt. Their intrusive behaviour not only aggravated tensions within the Scottish Privy Council but also alienated moderate opinion among nobles and gentry not yet aligned with the disaffected parliamentarians.

Following the eventual impanelling of the assize in March 1635, the conduct of the final proceedings was marked by elements of legal chicanery as well as farce. Notwithstanding the objections of the defence counsel, Strachan of Thornton was not obliged to stand down. Traquair was elected to preside over the deliberations of the assize even though he had served on the investigative committee that had formulated the treasonable charges. On his casting vote, Balmerino was found guilty on only one charge, that of failing to reveal that the Supplication's author was William Haig, now safely ensconced in the United Provinces. William Keith, 6th Earl Marischal, subsequently claimed that he had been filed in favour of a conviction because he was asleep when the vote to acquit was taken. The threat of political reprisals moved Traquair to go to court to persuade Charles that although the guilty verdict was just, the execution of Balmerino would be impolitic. Ironically, his most influential supporter was Archbishop Laud, who looked to English precedent in deciding that the imposition of the death penalty by such a narrow margin was inequitable. However, the full pardon granted to Balmerino in June could not undo the crucial damage his trial had inflicted on Britannic monarchy. From its initial session in December 1634 until its conclusion in March 1635, the trial was held against a continuous backdrop of public and private prayer meetings for the comfort of Balmerino, reinforced by tumultuous petitioning and political agitation. Indeed, the trial marked a decisive shift away from reform and towards revolution in exposing Charles's lack of effective forces of coercion and persuasion in Scotland.[69]

The prerogative rule in Scotland was not just parlous but close to paralysis. The groundswell of disaffection in the country was accompanied by the steady erosion of political will within the Scottish Privy Council to take concerted action on behalf of Charles I. The demonstrable polarity between the bishops and the lay councillors was exploited by Traquair to project himself as the main check to the political ambitions of the Canterburians. However, Traquair's strategy depended upon his retention of substantial support from the middle ground in Scottish politics. This support could no longer be guaranteed in the wake of Balmerino's trial. Antipathy to the appointment of the aged Spottiswood as chancellor in December 1634, the first bishop to hold the office since the Reformation, and the aggressive posturing of the Canterburians persuaded discontented lay officials to give covert counselling to the disaffected parliamentarians. In effect, the bishops were politically isolated, and, simultaneously, public disillusionment spread about the capacity of the Privy Council to prevent Scotland being treated as a province. By the time Charles's plans for liturgical innovation were clarified, by the autumn of 1635, the divisions within his Scottish administration stood in stark contrast to the cohesiveness of the disaffected parliamentarians in defence of the national interest.[70]

Although Laud never challenged Hamilton's paramount responsibility at court for managing civil affairs, he was prepared to defer only to the king in the conduct of ecclesiastical affairs in Scotland. He positively encouraged the bishops to seek his clientage and channel all their correspondence to court through him. He demanded and was given editorial control over the Book of Canons and the prayer book Charles planned to meet the want of uniformity in discipline and worship between Scotland and the other two kingdoms. Notwithstanding Laud's claims to be upholding Reformed tradition, charges from the Calvinist mainstream in both Scotland and England that the king and the Archbishop of Canterbury were innovators in the pursuit of religious uniformity were irrefutable. Intended as a shift along Anglican lines in favour of sacerdotalism and Arminianism, liturgical innovations were received in Scotland as little better than a divisive sacramental exercise to insinuate Catholicism, a deliberate subterfuge by a Romanised court in conjunction with 'popishlie affected Bishops'.[71] The conviction of Scottish Calvinists that direct action was necessary to resist the undermining of the entire Reformed tradition of the Kirk and counteract the operations of ungodly monarchy in the state led to premeditated rioting in 1637 and the issue of the National Covenant in 1638.

4 Covenants and Confederations, 1638–1643

When Charles I authorised liturgical innovations for Scotland, he initiated a direct attack on established Calvinist orthodoxy that was symbolised by the precedence he and Archbishop Laud accorded to the placing of the altar for observance of the sacraments over the pulpit for the preaching of the word. This attack had revolutionary potential in Scotland, where preaching had been reckoned the chief part of divine service since the Reformation and where the sacramental practices associated with Arminianism were widely linked with popery. Laud personally had no intention of insinuating Roman Catholicism throughout the king's dominions. He consistently deplored the fashionable Catholicism of the court clique associated with Queen Henrietta Maria. He was notably resistant to their lobbying of the papacy for a cardinal's hat for George Con, an expatriate Scot within the Vatican bureaucracy who had arrived at court as papal envoy to the queen in 1636. Nonetheless, Laud and his Canterburians made no public effort to dispel vernacular identification of liturgical innovations with popish practices. Their crucial error was their failure to realise that liturgical innovations could not be isolated from a political setting that was patently inhospitable. Contemporary accusations of popery against Laud, which were damaging because of the close association of Protestantism and patriotism in England, were made the more heinous in Scotland by the imposition of sacerdotalism as a provincial exercise. The Canterburians were castigated as the 'English faction'.[1]

The Scottish version of the Book of Canons was duly published in Aberdeen at the outset of 1636. It gave no commitment to general assemblies as the supreme national court in the Kirk. All clergy and laity who refused to acknowledge the royal supremacy in ecclesiastical affairs, episcopal government unfettered by presbyteries or future liturgical innovations faced excommunication. The Scottish version of the prayer book, which as the Service Book incurred public odium, was not actually published in Edinburgh until April 1637. Its proposed liturgical innovations had accommodated Scottish sensibilities. Lessons from the Apocrypha in the English Book of Common Prayer were removed because of scriptural unsoundness. However, the 15 months that elapsed between the publication of the two books afforded the disaffected ample time to mount a concerted attack. As both books were introduced by royal missives and without plenary consultation, they were deemed unconstitutional. They were both held to suborn the received Reformed tradition. The association of religious uniformity with 'thorough' led liturgical innovation to be viewed as a step too far in the relegation of Scotland from a kingdom to a province. The deliberate targeting of the malicious influence of Laud allowed the disaffected to portray themselves as the defenders of the national interest without launching an outright attack on Charles I.[2]

The rioting that greeted attempted readings from the Service Book in Edinburgh on 23 July, and in Glasgow on 10 August, presaged a 'crisis by monthly instalments' that culminated in the issue of the National Covenant as the Scottish manifesto on 28 February 1638. Another five months were to elapse before a committee for Scottish affairs was instituted at court. Having delayed almost a year from the first riots in coming to terms with the Scottish situation, the court remained reactive as the Covenanters sustained their revolutionary momentum throughout the British Isles.[3] When Prince Charles Louis, the claimant to the Palatinate, had visited the court in 1635–7, the masques and other entertainments presented in his honour had expressed polite criticisms not only of a pro-Habsburg foreign policy, but also of prerogative rule without recourse to an English parliament. Facing constitutional breakdown and civil war precipitated in and exported from Scotland, it was no longer feasible for the court to ring-fence vernacular expressions of dissent, notwithstanding a reflex tightening of censorship and the comforting promotion of the masque *Britannia Triumphans* by Inigo Jones in January 1638. Indeed, after Richard Braithwaite's satiric play *Mercurius Britannicus* first appeared in London, its script, overtly critical of ship money, gained wide circulation in England during 1641.[4]

Scottish Revolutionary

The influx of Ulster nonconformists to the south-west of Scotland, which coincided with the imposition of the Scottish Canons, served to harden the resolve of conventiclers to resist further liturgical innovations as laid out in the Service Book. Despite the vehemence of their language towards the bishops as prelates and their conviction that the political nation should atone for past sins and oppose the promotion of religious uniformity, the conventiclers were catalysts for rather than instigators of revolution. In essence, they were a pressure group organised covertly throughout the Lowlands by 1637. Their disciplined nature enabled the disaffected leadership of Rothes, Loudoun and Balmerino to organise resistance discreetly, although they were ever wary of attracting official surveillance from too close association with conventiclers. The leadership appreciated the ideological value of the conventiclers' godly intent on reforming an errant Kirk whose present corruption was attributable 'to our breach of the covenant, contempt of the Gospel and our defection from the truth'. For their part, conventiclers such as Samuel Rutherford cautioned against political confrontation in the name of religion: 'I am not of that mind, that tumults of arms is the way to put Christ on his throne.' Nonetheless, conventiclers had been charged to prepare for the coming of Christ, 'The Great Messenger of the Covenant', prior to the publication of the Service Book. The subsequent rioting in Scotland's two principal cities merely appeared spontaneous.[5]

The purveying of apocalyptic visions was secondary to selective briefings of sympathetic nobles and gentry to write personally to lay councillors for the suspension of liturgical innovations. The decision of the Privy Council on 24 August to take no further action either to apprehend rioters or to mandate the use of the Service Book until the court was fully appraised of the critical state of Scottish affairs caused the disaffected leadership to broaden their strategy of resistance. Orderly lobbying in Edinburgh by nobles, gentry, burgesses and ministers, reinforced by 68 standardised, but not stereotyped, petitions from burghs, parishes and presbyteries, led to the synthesising of protests into the National Petition of 20 September, which called for an end to liturgical innovations. With no offer of constructive dialogue from the court, petitioning reinforced by mass lobbying was extended to attack prerogative courts and to reduce the authority of the bishops in Kirk and state. David Dickson, an Ayrshire minister sympathetic to conventicling, drafted the National Supplication of 17 October, which first served public notice that the disaffected must suffer 'the ruin of our estates and fortunes' or endure divine retribution for 'breach of our covenant with God, and forsaking the way of true religione'. The disaffected leadership elevated their divine obligation to supplicate above their duty to obey royal proclamations to disperse. Their controlled militancy was underscored the next day. At the request of Traquair and other lay councillors, the disaffected leadership dispersed the mobbing of Bishop Sydserf of Galloway, a Canterburian and a noted prosecutor of conventiclers.[6]

Grass-roots petitioning and mass lobbying in Edinburgh were initially organised on an informal basis among the constituent Estates of the political nation. From November, however, co-ordination was directed effectively by the Tables of the nobles, gentry, burgesses and clergy. Each Estate formed a Table, with representatives from the other three joining the nobles to form a revolutionary executive that was constituted formally as the fifth Table at the outset of December. The fifth Table publicly acknowledged its leadership of a provisional government in the week before the National Covenant was promulgated. Archibald Johnston of Wariston, an Edinburgh lawyer of undoubted personal piety, also a conventicler zealously committed to the triumph of Presbyterianism, drew up this Scottish constitution. An insomniac of prodigious energy, Wariston had readily penned rebuttals to royal proclamations against the disaffected Tables, rebuttals that called for fundamental checks on the prerogative rule by drawing selectively on biblical sources, Roman law commentaries and parliamentary precedents. In pressing the need for free constituent assemblies to redress past and prevent future excesses of royal authoritarianism, he was assisted by Alexander Henderson. A minister from Fife with limited sympathy for conventicling, Henderson had masterminded the riots against the Service Book and co-ordinated clerical appeals from the pulpit for nationwide commitment to the Tables.[7]

The National Covenant was a revolutionary enterprise binding the Scottish people by social compact to justify and consolidate revolt against Britannic monarchy. Its moderate tenor, coupled with its conservative format and appeal to precedents, belied its radical intent. All four Tables having approved the finalised version before subscriptions commenced, its appearance of unanimity was not deceptive. The National Covenant deliberately maintained a studied ambiguity not just to attract support from all classes and from every locality, but primarily to avoid specific imputations of treason. The Scottish perspective was thus formalised by a written constitution that asserted the independence of a sovereign people under God and, in the process, gave force to Buchanan's anti-imperial, aristocratic republic.

The first part of the Covenant reiterated the Negative Confession of 1581 in association with a selective series of parliamentary enactments perpetrated to maintain the 'true religion and the King's Majesty'. Loyalty to the crown was conditional on its expunging idolatrous, superstitious and popish practices from the Kirk; protecting the purity of the

Reformed tradition; and upholding the rights of the Scots people to be governed according to the common laws of the realm as grounded in statute. Precedents for the removal of erroneous doctrines and prejudicial practices culminated with the collation and codification of the penal laws against Catholic recusants in 1609. The urgency of an uncompromising Protestant crusade to ward off the unabated threat from the Counter-Reformation was thus pressed. The attack on episcopacy was contained in the resolve of the Tables to sweep away all innovations, not just religious, which had threatened national independence and subjects' liberties since the regal union. Innovations prejudicial to parliamentary authority were deplored 'as this Realme could be no more a free Monarchy'.

The second part elaborated the concept of a twofold contract, which encapsulated the dual imperatives of covenanting by drawing on historical and political as well as biblical precepts. Opposition to prerogative rule by divine right was inspired by the ideological resistance to monarchy that emanated from the French Huguenots and, to a lesser extent, the Dutch Calvinists, and by the legacy of resistance to an ungodly monarch espoused by John Knox at the Reformation and rationalised in its aftermath by George Buchanan. The religious covenant was a tripartite compact between the king, the people and God to uphold religious purity in which the Israelites were replaced by the Scots in the role of chosen people. Whereas obedience to God was unconditional and irresistible, the people's obligations to the king were limited and conditional. If the king betrayed his people by ungodly acts, the people had a positive duty to resist. Operating within the framework of this religious covenant was a constitutional contract between the king on the one hand and the people on the other, for the maintenance of good and lawful government and a just political order. If the king failed to uphold the fundamental laws and liberties of the kingdom or sought to subvert his subjects' privileges or Estates, the people were entitled to take appropriate remedial action. Final determination of all religious and civil issues was to be left to general assemblies and parliaments free from the censorious royal management evident during the coronation visit. The intention of the fifth Table was not just to secure the redress of pressing grievances, but to effect permanent checks on Britannic monarchy to safeguard the religious and constitutional imperatives of covenanting.[8]

The third and most revolutionary part of the Covenant was the oath of allegiance and mutual association. Subscribers were required to swear that they would 'stand to the defence of our dread Soveraigne, the Kings

Majesty, his Person and Authority, in the defence and preservation of the foresaid true Religion, Liberties and Lawes of the Kingdome'. This commitment was conditional. Loyalty was reserved for a covenanted king. Insofar as he accepted the religious and constitutional imperatives of the National Covenant, the king was to be defended. There was no necessary incompatibility in promising to defend royal authority while simultaneously promoting policies contrary to the professed interests of Charles I. Resistance to Charles I was in the long-term interests of monarchy and people if the kingdom was to be restored to godly rule. Within a broader European perspective, the propagation of this distinction by the fifth Table avoided recourse to republicanism. However, the people's right of resistance to an ungodly monarch did not vindicate any attempt by a private citizen to assassinate Charles I as a tyrant. Charles was the legitimate Stuart, not a usurper. Instead, the revolutionary oath upheld the corporate right of the people to resist a lawful king who threatened to become tyrannical. Such resistance was to be exercised by the natural leaders of society, not the nobles exclusively but the Tables as the corporate embodiment of the inferior magistrates imbued with civic virtue. The oath required the subscribers to recognise the Tables as the divinely warranted custodians of the national interest.[9]

As well as equipping the Tables with the rhetoric of defiance, the National Covenant provided the political will to effect revolution. In the week following its issue in Edinburgh, copies of the Covenant were prepared for subscription in all leading towns and cities, universities and rural parishes. Initially, subscription was to be confined to communicants. But, carried along by popular enthusiasm and concerted propaganda spearheaded by Alexander Henderson, stress was laid on covenanting as the manifestation of the willingness, the holiness and the multiplication of the Scots as the chosen people. The practice was changed. Communion became available only to the covenanted. Such implacable resolve left little scope for neutrality. Earthly vengeance as well as divine retribution awaited those not moved to covenant with God.[10]

In the nine months that followed the promulgation of the National Covenant, the Tables negotiated free constitutional assemblies and organised a fighting fund based on a voluntary land tax. Negotiations, primarily with the Marquess of Hamilton, who was dispatched from court as king's commissioner in May, were conducted against a background of mass lobbying at the behest of the Tables who were able to mobilise tens of thousands. No more than 300 Royalist adherents met

Hamilton when he arrived in June, by which time the lay councillors were broadly in sympathy with the Covenanters. The refusal of the Tables, particularly that of the gentry, to compromise on the National Covenant obliged Hamilton to return to court twice, in July and August, before conceding unconditionally that a general assembly would be summoned at Glasgow in November. In the interim, covenanting ideologues faced a formidable intellectual challenge from the six Aberdeen Doctors. Not only did they stand out against subscription to the National Covenant, but they also maintained that any resort to arms against the lawful prince was on no account warranted. In public debates with Henderson and Dickson, they argued convincingly that neither episcopal government nor the Five Articles were inimical to the Reformed tradition, nor were they necessarily abjured by the Negative Confession of 1581.[11]

However, the Aberdeen Doctors were not convinced they had sufficient political backing for an episcopal counter-attack at the Glasgow Assembly. Their defence of Episcopalianism did, however, inspire Hamilton to formulate a tangible alternative to the National Covenant. The Negative Confession of 1581 was associated with a bond of 1589 designed specifically to counter Roman Catholicism that generally committed subscribers to help the king withstand internal as well as foreign foes. When this King's Covenant was presented for subscription to the Privy Council on 22 September 1638, the same day that the summons was issued for the Glasgow Assembly, Hamilton sought to discredit the Covenanting movement throughout the British Isles. Leading Covenanters were named in the commissions for collecting subscriptions. However, the King's Covenant neither regained the political initiative for the Britannic cause nor expedited the formation of a cohesive Royalist party.[12] The most positive responses came from the north-east and the central Highlands, where George Gordon, 2nd Marquess of Huntly, and his associates were not averse to coercion. An initial degree of success in west, central and eastern Scotland, as in the Borders, was largely confined to the respective domains of the king's commissioner and prominent councillors. Covenanters actively opposed subscription in the south-west, Fife and the Lothians.

Intimidation notwithstanding, Britannic prospects were dealt a debilitating blow at the beginning of November. Sir Thomas Hope of Craighall, the lord advocate, made public his opinion, endorsed by four senators of the College of Justice, that episcopal government was both illegal and inconsistent with the Negative Confession – an opinion that accorded with the radical interpretation favoured by the fifth Table. The Covenanting leadership seized the opportunity to switch tack. Subscription to the King's Covenant was no longer prejudicial but complementary to the National Covenant. Subscribers to both were committed to the repudiation of episcopacy, the Five Articles and liturgical innovations. Glasgow had been selected as the venue for the general assembly on the grounds that the city's proximity to Hamilton's principal domain would allow him to bring his considerable landed influence into play against the Tables. He had miscalculated. His formidable mother, Anna Cunningham, the dowager marchioness and a committed Covenanter, exercised political and financial control over his estates. Though obliged to move from Edinburgh, the Tables effectively controlled the composition, remit and proceedings of the Glasgow Assembly in a more rigorous manner than Charles I had managed his coronation parliament.[13]

The presbyteries were the managerial key to the general assembly. Once the fifth Table had made known their intention that the assembly should be composed primarily of clerical and lay commissioners from presbyteries, members of the Tables serving in kirk sessions as parochial elders were intruded onto presbyteries as ruling elders in August and September. Indeed, the elections for commissioners from the presbyteries – as from royal burghs – tended to conform to guidelines circulated by the fifth Table in the month before the Glasgow Assembly was formally summoned. The electoral process in most presbyteries was loaded in favour of the Covenanters. Ministers who favoured episcopacy tended to be either absent, under threat of removal, suspended or disqualified. In 39 out of the 62 designated presbyteries, the guidelines of the Tables were followed by October: an overwhelming commitment to a Presbyterian reformation was achieved from the 39 burghs.[14]

By summoning all nobles who had subscribed to the National Covenant, by having four gentry from every presbytery accompany the commissioners as assessors, and by likewise reinforcing each burgh with from two to six assessors, the fifth Table ensured that the Glasgow Assembly was effectively a plenary meeting of the Tables. Proceedings were conducted in an intimidatory atmosphere. Charges cataloguing the personal and pastoral failings of the bishops were submitted from the presbyteries by members of the Tables not chosen as commissioners. The Covenanting leadership successfully promoted the selection of Henderson as moderator and Johnston of Wariston as clerk. Control over proceedings was further enhanced by Covenanting dominance in the membership of the committees for preparing and transacting business.

The bishops, who had prudently absented themselves, had lodged a declaration against the usurped authority of the Tables in controlling the composition and remit of the assembly. As this was not read until six days after the assembly had begun, its content was rendered meaningless. The assembly's response, asserting its right to try the bishops on 28 November, prompted a walkout by Hamilton. Next day, his command to dissolve was upstaged by the assembly continuing to sit – the first open act of constitutional defiance of the prerogative rule. The assembly proceeded to sweep all vestiges of episcopacy, the Court of High Commission, the Five Articles and other liturgical innovations out of the Kirk before dissolving itself on 20 December.

Although the Glasgow Assembly had effected a Presbyterian reformation, it made no claims to clerical autonomy. Certainly, the prohibition on ministers exercising civil office had widespread constitutional ramifications, notably the abolition of the clerical Estate in parliament (duly effected in June 1640). However, provision was also made for commissioners not to sit in, but to represent the interests of the Kirk to, the next parliament. This committee served as a precedent for the Commission of the Kirk established in 1641 as a pressure group for the general assembly on parliament. With its composition made up of committed Presbyterian ministers led by Henderson supported by the elder sons of peers not eligible for parliament and gentry not chosen to represent the shires in the forthcoming parliament, the committee was designed to replace the clerical Table, now effectively redundant. The assembly's final enactment asserted the inherent right of the Kirk to warrant general assemblies at least once a year and designated the next for Edinburgh in July 1639. This abrogation of the right to appoint time and place constituted a second, blatant attack on the royal prerogative. War became inevitable.[15]

The Thirty Years War: the British Theatre

The replacement of Episcopalianism by Presbyterianism through constitutional defiance caused the armed conflict between Charles I and the Covenanting movement of 1639–40 to become known as the Bishops' Wars. Charles's patent incapacity to defeat Covenanting forces in two successive campaigns obliged him to accept permanent checks on the royal prerogative in Kirk and state. He was also obliged to recognise that adherence to the National Covenant, not acquiescence in the dictates of Britannic monarchy, was the vital prerequisite for the exercise of political power in Scotland. The Scottish resistance to Charles I had a European, not just a Britannic, significance, however. Whereas contemporaneous revolts in Portugal and Catalonia against a centralising Spanish monarchy were protesting about the costs of continuing engagement in the Thirty Years War, the Covenanting movement brought this European war to the British Isles. In essence, the Bishops' Wars constituted its British theatre.

Prior to the Bishops' Wars, Charles had been prepared to assist Spain against the Dutch with Irish troops and English ships, ostensibly to secure the restoration of his nephew Charles Louis to the Palatinate. In return for landing facilities for troops in transit through the Channel, the Spaniards became Charles's best hope of securing external assistance against the Covenanters. However, the Dutch Admiral Tromp decisively defeated the Spanish fleet in the Downs in the autumn of 1639, with the ship money fleet powerless to intervene. This defeat demonstrated that Charles was of limited assistance to the Habsburgs. It also ensured that the Covenanters continued to be supplied with men and munitions through Holland and Zealand.[16] Indeed, the Covenanting movement drew on diplomatic, military and material support from the reconstituted anti-Habsburg alliance of France, Sweden and the United Provinces that had continued the Thirty Years War in the aftermath of the Peace of Prague in 1635.

The British ramifications of the Covenanters' revolutionary agenda were monitored closely through newsletter, parliamentary journal and diplomatic memo by the troubled Spaniards, the wary Danes and the pragmatic French as well as by the supportive Swedes and the Dutch.[17] The Covenanters had established their own Dutch press prior to the outbreak of the Bishops' Wars in 1639, when they rather than the court of Charles I were the first to receive embassies openly from Sweden and Denmark as well as covertly from France.[18] Cardinal Armand-Jean de Richelieu sent Abbé Chambre, alias Thomas Chambers, a Scottish Jesuit, who first made contact with the disaffected leadership in the autumn of 1637 under the guise of boosting recruitment for the Scottish regiment which had been in French service since 1633. Rewarded by becoming Richelieu's almoner, Chambers returned to Scotland to report on Covenanting affairs prior to the Bishops' Wars. Despite his religious affiliations, the Covenanters expediently used him as their chief contact with Richelieu during 1640, when Chambers became the unofficial Scottish ambassador to the French court. French liaison with Sweden during the British theatre of the Thirty Years War was maintained through Grotius, the celebrated Dutch jurist in exile, who then served as the Swedish ambassador to France.[19]

These international dealings of the Covenanting movement provide a wider context for the ubiquitous fears of popish plotting that had featured in the insular political life of all three kingdoms since the beginning of the Thirty Years War.[20] Their build-up of arms during the summer of 1638 and their overtures to France at the outset of the Bishops' Wars laid the basis for suspicions at court that the Scots' betrayal of Charles I was part of a popish plot. Conversely, the Covenanters' well-founded apprehensions that Charles I was attempting to mobilise Habsburg as well as Danish support fuelled rumours of further popish plotting not only to undermine their movement, but also to obviate the summoning of an English parliament. Ireland also proved the testing ground for the veracity of these rumours, with a black propaganda campaign directed by Wentworth against the Covenanting movement being reciprocated in kind. John Corbet, an expatriate Scottish cleric based in Ireland following his deposition for opposing the National Covenant, issued an epistle which claimed not only that the Covenanting oath of allegiance was Jesuitical, but also that the movement was a conspiracy inspired by Jesuits. This was met by an oblique Covenanting disclaimer which conveyed papal apprehensions that the movement's assault on absolute monarchy and prelacy would be extended to England and concluded with a purported curial endorsement that constitutionalism must be crushed in both countries.[21]

While Wentworth was still concentrating on ensuring that forces recruited from Ireland for Spanish service should be under reliable commanders, Covenanting intelligence from the continent was reporting the imminent release of Irish forces from Spanish service to effect further rebellion against Charles I.[22] Although the release of Irish forces for this purpose was delayed by two years, it can be viewed as belated Spanish intervention in the British theatre which, in turn, further fuelled fears of popish plotting that consolidated the alliance of Scottish Covenanters with English Parliamentarians. However, the immediate threat of external intervention in 1639 came from neither the French nor the Spanish but from Sweden, which gave unstinting diplomatic, military and material support to the Covenanting movement. Chancellor Axel Oxenstierna, deeply concerned that the growing rapprochement between Charles I and the Habsburgs would inflame the perennial antipathies of Denmark–Norway and Poland–Lithuania, was notably receptive to Covenanting pleas for assistance made by Alexander Leslie, a field-marshal and 30-year veteran in Swedish service. Having returned in a private capacity to Scotland following the promulgation of the National Covenant, Leslie had been won over by his kinsman John, Earl of Rothes. Although Leslie, a longstanding associate and correspondent of Hamilton, had attended the marquess when he first returned to Scotland to negotiate with the Covenanters in June 1638, his commitment to Covenanting imperatives in church and state was communicated that same month to Oxenstierna. The failure to secure the services of Leslie was indisputably the most culpable charge that can be laid against Hamilton in his inept dealings as king's commissioner.[23] For Leslie returned to Sweden in July to secure political and military backing from the Swedish state council, backing that was achieved after debates on the British situation in the Riksråd in August.

Leslie arrived back in Scotland equipped with arms and ammunition as a retirement present from Swedish service. He was ready to take charge of the Covenanting army in advance of the Glasgow Assembly, although news of his homecoming was not made public until the outset of 1639. Leslie was undoubtedly the prime mover in securing not only his own release but that of leading Scottish officers in Swedish and Dutch service, most notably the foremost military tactician, Colonel Robert Munro, and the artillery genius Colonel Alexander (Dear Sandy) Hamilton. By maintaining a regular correspondence with Oxenstierna, he paved the way for the further release of Scottish officers such as Colonel David Leslie from Swedish service in advance of the second Bishops' War, their release also being rewarded with munitions. Diplomatic backing for the Covenanting invasion of England was announced during the Covenanting embassy to Sweden of another military veteran, Colonel John Cochrane, in July–August 1640, when the Riksråd authorised further supplies of munitions and copper via Holland.[24]

However, Swedish sympathies for the Covenanting movement could not guarantee the passage of soldiers, arms and ammunition through the Baltic Sound and across the North Sea. This covert movement also involved the active collusion of the Scottish diaspora, notably the mercantile communities in Gothenburg, Danzig, Amsterdam and Campvere as well as naval officers in both Danish and Swedish service. Diplomats from the Covenanting movement also worked to counter the family ties of Christian IV by encouraging him to mediate during the Bishops' Wars, overtures that his nephew Charles rejected in both 1639 and 1640. At the same time, the apparent willingness of Charles to pawn Orkney and Shetland in return for Danish support against the Scots was no more realistic than the addition of Newcastle to this equation in return for aid against the English Parliamentarians in 1642. Effectively neutralised by Covenanting diplomacy, by Covenanting control over the Northern Isles and by the openness of the north-east of England to occupation in 1640–41, Christian IV opted to allow the passage of arms and ammunition to all three kingdoms – so long as English, Scottish and Irish procurers paid higher tolls, particularly exorbitant in the case of saltpetre, through the Sound.[25]

The monumental significance of formal Swedish backing has in part been disguised by the shipments of men, arms and ammunition through the Hanse ports of Hamburg, Bremen and Lübeck as well as from the United Provinces. However, Hamilton was becoming wary of Swedish involvement as early as June 1638. Notwithstanding the stop on Scottish trade imposed by Charles I at the outset of the Bishops' Wars, the Covenanters' continuing ability to gain supplies from Sweden was noted apprehensively in England during the Short Parliament of April 1640.[26]

In the meantime, the fifth Table, as the Covenanting executive, had restructured the movement's links with the localities. Restructuring, actually based on a blueprint drawn up by the Glasgow Assembly, was underway by January 1639, when Scotland was placed on a war footing. The gentry were to the fore in establishing committees of war within the shires to liaise with and carry out directives from Edinburgh. Each committee of war had a permanent convener, in order to levy, equip and train troops; to assess and collect a compulsory contribution based on landed and commercial rents; and to encourage commitment to the cause in every presbytery and parish. The immediate purpose of the Covenanting leadership in centrally reorientating local government was the mobilising and provisioning of a national army. Every able-bodied man between 16 and 60 was eligible for military service and every shire committee of war was expected to raise and maintain at least one regiment of foot and a troop of cavalry. The shire regiments of foot were organised into quarterly brigades of eight to ten regiments. Sufficient cavalry were mobilised in every shire to form at least one regiment from each quarter. Regional mobilisation facilitated the formation of a Covenanting vanguard, selected from the ablest men in the shires, to resist invasion by land or sea and quell Royalist discontent within Scotland. Recruitment for the shire levies, though less rigorous than selection for the vanguard, was based on conscription; the landed class were preferred as volunteers for the cavalry after their enlistment as fighting men. The returning veterans from the continental theatres of the

Thirty Years War provided a professional backbone for the Covenanting army. They filled every alternate position of command among commissioned and non-commissioned officers, albeit the colonel of each regiment 'may be some nobleman or gentleman of quality'. All artillery officers, gunners and engineers were also veterans, as were the mustermasters recruited by the shire committees of war to pass on the basic skills of drilling and exercising with muskets and pikes.[27]

The returning veterans ensured that the Covenanters adopted the main advances in the methodology of warfare pioneered by the Dutch and carried on by the Swedes. The development of rapid-fire musketry, the linear phalanxing of pikemen by musketeers and heavy artillery, and the deployment of cavalry troops supported by mobile field artillery on the flanks improved the manoeuvrability of battle formations. The vulnerability of unwieldy infantry regiments to close-quarter skirmishing was simultaneously minimised. The Covenanting army not only conformed to the most innovatory continental practices of warfare. Armed service was regarded as a national endeavour that was reinforced by ecclesiastical as well as military discipline. Logistical difficulties did hinder the efficient mobilising of levies, supplies and funds from the shires during the First Bishops' War. Desertions from the armed forces were continuous. Nonetheless, the relative efficiency of restructured local government was attested by the military supremacy the Covenanting army consistently enjoyed in the field. The Britannic or Royalist forces relied predominantly on family obligation and political clientage to raise forces to supplement the trained bands from the English shires. Usually a third more troops were on active service for the Covenanting cause. Wentworth's raising of Irish levies remained no more than a potential threat to Covenanting supremacy during the Second Bishops' War.[28]

The Covenanting movement was faced with engagements on four fronts during the first campaign in 1639. Antrim's threatened invasion of the western seaboard failed to materialise and Hamilton's naval assault on the east coast proved no more than a fitful stop to trade. However, the Marquess of Huntly, his son James, Lord Aboyne, and those associated with the house of Gordon maintained a five-month resistance in the north-east that was not quashed until the Covenanters concluded the Pacification of Berwick. The troops that Charles marched to the Anglo-Scottish border in June were outnumbered and underfunded. The truce suspended hostilities and prevented bloodshed. During the second campaign of 1640, the Covenanters were obliged to maintain not only an invasion force in England, but also a home guard capable of rapid movement from the north-east to the south-west of Scotland. The switch from defence to offence being justified by reported Royalist mobilisation in England and Ireland, the Covenanting army crossed the Tweed and routed the Royalist forces at Newburn on 28 August. As the English commanders of the Royalist forces recognised, the supremacy of the Covenanting army was not just numerical. The Covenanting movement was second only to the Swedish crown in possessing a standing army conscripted for national service and sustained by centralised government – a development which anticipated the emergence of the New Model Army of the English Parliamentarians by six years and which was never achieved by the Confederation of Irish Catholics during the 1640s.[29]

Exemplary Radicalism

In the course of the Bishops' Wars the Tables, as the revolutionary embodiment of the Covenanting movement, accomplished by persuasion and coercion a thorough transformation of government within Scotland. Their radicalism was evident in the centralising of government in oligarchic, rather than aristocratic, hands. Committees of nobles, gentry and burgesses with clerical reinforcement by pulpit and pen imposed unprecedented demands on the Scottish localities for ideological conformity, financial supply and military recruitment. In turn, the Covenanting movement served as a radical exemplar for terminating the prerogative rule of Charles I in England and Ireland.[30]

In addition to the military advantages gained from Leslie's command, returning veterans and restructuring according to the Swedish model, the Covenanting movement benefited hugely in political terms from its acquisition of Archibald Campbell, 8th Earl (later Marquess) of Argyll. Ostensibly won over by the eloquence of Johnston of Wariston when serving as counsellor to Hamilton during the Glasgow Assembly, Argyll (while still Lord Lorne) had been fortifying his estates on the western seaboard and drawing up plans for a war committee for Argyllshire during the summer of 1638. His immediate stimulus was the need to counter the posturing of the Earl of Antrim, who was attempting to use the anticipated political breakdown between the court and the Covenanting movement to press his claims to the ancestral lands of the ClanDonald South in Kintyre and Islay. Indeed, Lorne had recently thwarted the plans of his impecunious father, the 7th Earl of Argyll, and his spendthrift half-brother James, Lord Kintyre, to sell the Scottish landmass closest to Ireland to Antrim. Lorne, though a committed Presbyterian, had made no overt declaration for the Covenanting movement until the death of his estranged father at court. The 8th Earl shared with Wentworth an abiding distrust of Antrim. The lord-deputy was content to expose the lack of substance in Antrim's self-serving proposals to use the impending Bishops' Wars to his territorial advantage. However, the 8th Earl was resolved that the pursuit of war to achieve the public ends of the Covenanting movement would also serve the private interests of the house of Argyll both defensively on the western seaboard and offensively in facilitating Campbell expansionism in northern Scotland. Nonetheless, the 8th Earl was more than an acquisitive magnate. He was a consummate statesman whose strategic importance to the Covenanting movement was recognised by the sustained but fruitless endeavours of Wentworth to reclaim him for Britannic monarchy. Likewise, Hamilton had perceptively warned the court as he prepared to leave the Glasgow Assembly that Argyll must be watched above all other Scottish politicians, 'for it feares me he will proufe the dangerousest man in this state'.[31]

Initially in the wake of the Glasgow Assembly, Argyll sought publicly to appear as a broker between the court and the Covenanting leadership while privately steering the centralised restructuring of the Tables and placing Scotland on a war footing. Prior to the advent of war, he assumed the position of political prominence in Covenanting affairs that he was to hold throughout the 1640s. He sustained this position by his judicious support of leading ideologues and financial facilitators. Simultaneously, he assiduously cultivated like-minded radical politicians within Scotland, such as his kinsman John Campbell, Lord Loudoun, who had been to the fore in opposing the prerogative rule during the 1630s. He furthered a British agenda by diligently courting influential contacts within the city of London and among disaffected English nobles and gentry. By the conclusion of the Bishops' Wars, he was recognised by those favouring the recall of the English parliament as the 'foremost man of business' in Scotland. Within the radical mainstream of the Covenanting movement, he was the moving spirit who 'rules all the rest' in promoting a revolutionary programme that advocated the federative reconfiguration of regal union and the necessity of defeating Charles I in the field. Indeed, by both institutionalising and exporting revolution, the Covenanters sought to promote concentric British loyalties, a characteristic personified by Argyll as clan chief, Scottish magnate and British statesman.[32]

In the eyes of Argyll, limited monarchy remained a non-negotiable, constitutional imperative. Under his leadership, the radical mainstream interpreted the role of the political Estates as not just to participate in but to control central government. The political Estates were the trustees of the national interest on behalf of the people. The king was merely the trustee of the political Estates, who executed their power to make law. The course of the Bishops' Wars of 1639–40 provided a practical demonstration of the power that held monarchy to account. According to Samuel Rutherford, the Tables were obliged to hold the crown to the dual imperatives of the National Covenant in the interests of the monarchy, if not of Charles personally: that is, of the king *in abstracto* if not *in concreto*.[33] This power to hold to account was maintained consistently by the radical mainstream to justify resistance in both the First and Second Bishops' Wars. In the spring of 1639, ministers advocated recourse to arms from the pulpit following precepts drawn up by Alexander Henderson. An essential distinction was maintained. On the one hand, subjects rising or standing out against law and reason that they might be free from their obedience to their king were not justified in their actions. On the other hand, the Scottish people, 'holding fast their alledgence to their soveraine and in all humilitie supplicating for Religioun and justice', were obliged, used 'to defend themselves against extreame violence and oppression bringing utter ruin and desolation upon the kirk and kingdome, upon themselves and their posteritie'. These arguments, used to defend Scotland in 1639, were reiterated in 1640 to vindicate the Covenanting army's invasion of England, now portrayed as an offensive posture for defensive purposes.[34]

Under the terms of the Pacification of Berwick, Charles had assented to a general assembly in Edinburgh, which duly endorsed the programme of its predecessor in Glasgow by solemnly renouncing episcopacy in August 1639. However, the parliament that was summoned for the resolution of civil affairs in September did not follow the script prescribed by the Tables. Traquair, who had replaced the demoralised Hamilton as king's commissioner in Scotland, was intent on frustrating radical initiatives to limit the royal prerogative by focusing debate on procedural deliberations. Itemised programmes from the gentry and burgesses for the redress of constitutional, economic and administrative grievances arising from the prerogative rule were held up for seven weeks in a Committee of Articles shorn of clerical commissioners but including such prominent Royalist sympathisers as Huntly. Proceedings reached an impasse by mid-November. The Tables sought to enhance the constitutional supremacy of parliament by emphasising the Estates' right to determine their own proceedings. While enthusiasm for radical reform was by no means universal, Traquair was unable to heal divisions, particularly evident among the nobility, to the king's advantage. At the instigation of Charles I, parliament was prorogued for seven months to afford him time to mobilise sufficient forces in England and Ireland. In the interim, the Tables, meeting as a general convention in March 1640, levied the first national tax on behalf of the Covenanting movement, which bound the political nation to pay a tenth of landed and commercial rents according to valuations commenced in burghs and presbyteries during 1639. The raising of standing regiments was also authorised to intimidate refractory taxpayers and offer employment for the veterans of the Thirty Years War retained since the Pacification of Berwick. The fifth Table was reconstituted as a Committee of Estates with a permanent rather than an occasional membership that rejected Charles's attempt to further prorogue the Scottish parliament summoned for Edinburgh at the outset of July.[35]

The Estates declared themselves to be a legally constituted assembly and Traquair was removed as king's commissioner. Having validated past proceedings of the Tables, the Estates proceeded to carry out a constitutional revolution, which demonstrated their political vitality. The clerical Estate in parliament was abolished and the gentry, in recognition of their stalwart service on the Tables, had their voting powers effectively doubled. Instead of one composite vote being cast for each shire, gentry summoned as shire commissioners were accorded the same individual voting rights as those enjoyed by nobles and burgesses. Subscription to the National Covenant was made compulsory for all holding public office. The Committee of Articles was declared an optional procedure and, if deployed, was to be elected by and answerable to the reconstituted three Estates. A Triennial Act specified that parliament should meet every three years regardless of a royal summons. Ostensibly on account of the imminent danger of invasion by Royalist forces, a Committee of Estates was constituted formally with comprehensive powers to govern the whole kingdom. The Committee, which consisted of 40 members drawn from the nobility, gentry and burgesses, was split into two sections. Equal numbers of each Estate either remained in Edinburgh to sustain central government or accompanied the army, whose movements were not restricted to Scotland – a clear indication that the Covenanters were to take the war against Britannic monarchy into England.[36]

The establishment of the Committee of Estates represented a classical, if corporate, alternative to the vesting of executive power in a monarch who was patently untrustworthy, palpably reluctant to make lasting concessions and resolutely intent on reversing all constraints on the royal prerogative. Accompanying legislation would suggest that the Covenanting leadership was intent upon legitimising not only its past but also its future exercise of executive power. Restructured local government was reinforced as the principal agency for the nationwide imposition of ideological conformity, financial supply and military recruitment. In addition to ratifying the exaction of the tenth by the shire committees of war, a compulsory loan of a twentieth of valued rents was imposed to meet the anticipated shortfall in borrowing required to cover expenditure in the First Bishops' War and the increased payments and allowances to the Covenanting army for the Second. The scope of treason was extended to cover all who advised or assisted policies destructive of the Covenanting movement. Waging war on behalf of the Covenanting movement became patriotic; waging war against it was treasonable.[37]

Having equipped themselves with the ways and means to export revolution, the Covenanting army followed up the rout at Newburn by moving vigorously into the counties of Northumberland and Durham. Newcastle was occupied by 30 August. Covenanting control of the coal supply to London pressurised Charles I into suing for peace. Having weakened his position in the north of England by his tactless handling of loyal supporters such as Henry, Lord Clifford (subsequently 6th Earl of Cumberland), in the First Bishops' War, Charles failed to capitalise on strong antipathies towards the Scots in Yorkshire when mobilising for the Second Bishops' War. Indeed, the county gentry petitioned Charles to consider the wider impact of his Scottish policies, and some were sympathetic to the disaffected groundswell that had commenced in the south for the recall of parliament. At the same time, news of the reported abuses by Royalist forces assembled in Yorkshire had discouraged further recruitment and fostered localism in counties such as Hertford and Essex, where the trained bands would not be drawn to the Thames for fear of being shipped north. Those mobilised in Norfolk and Cambridge turned against their officers.

From their issue of articles of war on 10 August until negotiations for a cessation of arms commenced at Ripon in Yorkshire on 2 October, the Covenanting leadership proactively encouraged support not only from the parliamentary inclined nobles and gentry in England, but also from the city of London, frequently the butt of criticism at court for its reluctance to finance the Royalist army.[38] As well as justifying their move to an offensive posture to maintain the movement's constitutional gains within Scotland, the Covenanting leadership promised that their army would observe strict military discipline in England pending the conclusion of a settlement. To this end, the removal of the negotiations to London and the recall of the English parliament were deemed indispensable. The Covenanting movement was thus able to assert and retain the political initiative in Britain from the outset of the peace negotiations.[39]

The revolutionary significance of the impact of the Covenanting army on the constitutional crisis engulfing Britannic monarchy still tends to be underestimated, notwithstanding a growing appreciation of the trigger effect the emergence of the movement in Scotland had in provoking rebellion and civil war in Ireland and England.[40] The Scottish revolt was undoubtedly not the cause of confrontation between crown and parliament in England or between Catholic Confederates, British planters and Britannic monarchy in Ireland. But only the presence of the Covenanting army in the north of England obliged Charles to summon parliament after an 11-year lapse. Only the security afforded by the Covenanting army allowed the English disaffected sufficient scope to press for constitutional checks on monarchy, which both safeguarded and revived the Gothic tradition of parliamentary sovereignty. The Covenanting movement provided not just military security but a constitutional model for revolt. A Triennial Act and an act continuing the current assembly enabled the 'Long Parliament' to resist dissolution by royal fiat and, in the longer term, secure control over the apparatus of government in church and state. Ultimately, the Scottish example justified recourse to arms in England by the Parliamentarians in 1642. Conversely, the pressure to redress grievances generated by the 'Long Parliament' meant that Charles was amenable to buying off the Scots to concentrate on English problems prior to the outbreak of the Irish rebellion in October 1641, where again the Catholic Confederates justified their recourse to arms by following the Scottish example.[41]

Gothic Revivalism

The political revival of the Gothic tradition in England was certainly due in part to the nationwide desire for the parliamentary redress of grievances arising from Charles I's prerogative rule. But it was primarily due to external stimuli. The pressures generated by the Covenanting movement had an audience well beyond the political nation in that pamphlets upholding the Scottish perspective and published in Edinburgh, Glasgow, Amsterdam and Leiden were smuggled through mercantile, military and Puritan networks to be read by the general public in England.[42] Growing concerns were also being expressed well beyond the confines of the court and the city of London about Ireland as an English political dependency. The 'Short Parliament' in the spring of 1640, which witnessed the first stirrings of the Gothic revival, was actually preceded by an Irish parliament on 16 March, where Wentworth, now ennobled as the Earl of Strafford but absent at the outset of proceedings, had his parliamentary priorities accomplished within a week. Supply was voted first, and rather than progress to discussing grievances, the Irish parliament, with the full knowledge of the English Privy Council, then effectively declared war against the Scottish Covenanters. With considerable satisfaction, Strafford reported how much the Irish MPs 'abhor and detest the Scotch Covenanters' and how ready they were 'to assist the King in the reducing of them by Force to the Obedience and Loyalty of Subjects'. By requesting four rather than six subsidies, Strafford gained consent to mobilise 8000 troops for deployment against the Covenanting movement – albeit the amount to be realised as subsidies was rated at £120,000 by the parliament when it resumed briefly in June, not the £200,000 he had anticipated.[43]

The 'Short Parliament' that commenced on 13 April was not so accommodating to Charles I. John Pym took up the theme of parliamentary liberties and privileges in the Commons by calling for the redress of religious and secular grievances before voting supply. He was particularly vexed about papists being admitted to places of trust and power in public or civic life and by recent innovations within the Church of England 'to prepare us for Poperie'. The associated discouragement to Protestant orthodoxy through ecclesiastical courts was questioning not only episcopal but royal authority. With regard to civil government, he appealed to the common law title 'on Extravagancie' to castigate impositions and the whole range of fiscally opportune measures that had characterised the prerogative rule in England. Commencing with tonnage and poundage, restraints for knighthood and monopolies before citing ship money, these and like impositions which had benefited their farmers more than the royal coffers were deemed to have pressed upon individual consciences 'and all bonds between the prerogative and Libertie broken'. On 4 May, Charles offered the prospect but not the promise of relief from ship money in return for 12 subsidies to meet his anticipated costs of £100,000 per month to renew war against the Covenanting movement. The Commons having failed to meet the agreed deadline for a response and thus demonstrated their lack of trust in Charles, the king promptly dissolved parliament on the following day.[44]

The reluctance of both king and parliament to make concessions was compounded by the detention of the four Scottish commissioners who had been negotiating in good faith at court since the outset of 1640. The grounds for their detention, two days before the 'Short Parliament' commenced, was the revelation of a letter drafted, but never delivered, to the French court which justified recourse to arms by the Covenanting movement and upheld free constitutional assemblies to prevent Scotland becoming 'a conquered province, as Ireland, under subjection to England'. There was certainly no intent to renounce the Stuart monarchy, nor were the Covenanters contemplating the transfer of their allegiance to France – an option exercised by the Catalans at the outset of 1641 after their revolt against the Spanish monarchy. However, the letter allowed Charles to taunt the Scottish commissioners as to whether they came to negotiate 'as ambassadors or as subjects'. Lord Loudoun, as the leading Scottish commissioner as well as a signatory to the letter, was incarcerated in the Tower of London for two months. This heavy-handed gesture served as a precedent for the detention and interrogation of the king's leading opponents in both Lords and Commons during the 'Short Parliament'.[45]

Notwithstanding its peremptory dissolution, the 'Short Parliament' had afforded a public platform for the first airing of English grievances, for communication between the disaffected in the Lords and the Commons, and for expressions of solidarity with the Scots. The convocation of the clergy that met in tandem with the 'Short Parliament' was not dissolved, however. The convocation had not only voted subsidies to the king, but was continued in order to promulgate a series of canons to uphold conformity and conserve the Anglican establishment without ruling out further Laudian reprogramming of the Church of England. By the publication of these canons in June, London had become the scene of disturbances that targeted Laud's official residence at Lambeth House. The mobilising of the trained bands of Kent, Surrey, Sussex, Essex and Middlesex to deal with indisciplined soldiers affiliated to the Royalist army proved ineffective. Concerns were expressed at court that further disturbances were likely in Norfolk and in the clothier districts in the West Country, with Wiltshire being in particular need of pacification. Indeed, General James King, a Scot who had actually returned from Swedish service to support Britannic monarchy, was dispatched to Hamburg in July to recruit veterans of the Thirty Years War. Should their services against the Covenanters not be required, they were to be deployed in England 'to bridle and bring under the stubborne disposisons of the Comons of this Kingdom'.[46]

In the six months that elapsed between the dissolution of the 'Short' and the summoning of the 'Long' Parliament (which continued to the Restoration), closer liaison was achieved between the Covenanters and the English disaffected. John Clotworthy, the Ulster planter sympathetic to conventicling by Puritans and Presbyterians, actually instigated this liaison on a British basis. Clotworthy, who was also an investor in the Londonderry Company and brother-in-law of John Pym, visited Edinburgh in the summer of 1638 where he conversed and subsequently corresponded with Johnston of Wariston. He went on to sit in both Irish and English parliaments during 1640. Formal contacts between the opponents of the prerogative rule in Scotland and England, authorised initially by the Covenanting leadership in February 1639, were stepped up following reports that English noblemen were reluctant to support the king's invasion during the First Bishops' War. The two most secure conduits for these contacts would appear to have been Robert Greville, Lord Brooke, and William, Viscount Saye & Sele, whose son Nathaniel Fiennes was among a group of Englishmen attending the general assembly and parliaments in Edinburgh that autumn. At this juncture, Scotland could still be seen as an alternative to America for English disaffected wishing to remove themselves from the prerogative rule.[47]

However, an appreciation of the superiority of the Covenanting army led to a growing awareness of the prospects for deliverance within England. On the promptings of Wariston and Loudoun, Thomas, Lord Saville, unilaterally invited the Covenanters into England on behalf of the disaffected English nobility prior to the outbreak of the Second Bishops' War. His unauthorised letter served as a handy justification for the Covenanters' recourse to an offensive posture. Nonetheless, Covenanting demands that the English parliament be recalled to participate in the peace negotiations that commenced at Ripon in October before transferring to London in December 1640 harmonised with a supplication in the name of 12 peers headed by Francis Russell, 4th Earl of Bedford. The supplication, which was submitted to Charles I on 28 August, also requested the immediate recall of parliament to conclude a settlement with the Scots as well as resolve indigenous grievances. Of the five main grounds for recall, the first four – the wasting of revenues on war, innovations in religion, deployment of popish recusants and the mischievous bringing in of predominantly Catholic Irish forces – were held in common with the Covenanters. The fifth and final ground was ship money. Redress through parliament was also justified in the Gothic tract issued by John Selden extolling the power of the peers and commons meeting as the great council 'to preserve a just interest to the Commonwealth'.[48]

Charles was obliged to treat with the Covenanting movement after a council of peers, summoned to York on 24 September, affirmed that continuing English support for Britannic monarchy could no longer be relied upon. Once Charles had issued writs summoning a parliament at Westminster on 3 November, the council of peers assumed responsibility for the English side of the negotiations, from which Charles I was excluded at the insistence of the Covenanting leadership. This responsibility was retained by the Lords under the leadership of John Digby, 1st Earl of Bristol, until the peace negotiations were eventually brought to a conclusion in August 1641. Having agreed not to advance beyond the River Tees, the Committee of Estates with the Covenanting army secured a daily allowance of £850 sterling, which was apportioned weekly from Northumberland and Durham as well as Newcastle. Having already agreed to lend the king £200,000 for the upkeep of the Royalist army, the English peers, not Charles, underwrote this daily allowance pending a full settlement of reparations in the forthcoming 'Long Parliament'. Such action certainly supports a baronial reading of the descent towards civil war in England.[49]

In his opening address on 3 November, Charles I expressed the hope that parliament, under the guidance of the Lords, would see off the demands of the Covenanters, whom he continued to view as traitors. Playing on the complaints made from Berwick to Yorkshire about occupation by the Covenanting army, he desired that parliament sustain his army and prevent its disbanding until the conclusion of the treaty. In return, he was prepared to satisfy grievances, anticipating that parliament would seek no more than moderate measures of reform in church and state.[50] However, while the Commons were supportive of the need to prevent demobilised troops preying on the English localities, there was no prospect of MPs voting sufficient funds to enable the king to resume the Bishops' Wars. The Commons were not constrained by baronial networks of clients, friends and relatives and were more receptive than the Lords to external influences from Scotland and Ireland on religious policy and the prosecution of those counsellors principally responsible for sustaining prerogative rule.

The Covenanting executive with the army sent eight commissioners (including Loudoun, Wariston and Henderson) to represent the Scottish perspective during negotiations for the treaty in London; they were subsequently joined by three more commissioners, with Argyll as a supernumerary. Their presence was complemented by 13 commissioners from the Irish parliament, whose third session of 1640 had resumed on 1 October and overlapped with the first week of the 'Long Parliament'. Clotworthy and Richard, Earl of Cork, were also at hand to assist in the prosecution of Strafford, a pursuit in which the Scottish and Irish commissioners were united. His handling of the plantations, particularly his continuing threat to Connacht and his profiteering from the winding up of the Londonderry Company, had aroused the ire of the Irish parliament and made them see him as a major grievance requiring judicial redress. At the same time, Strafford was demonised by the Covenanters for his imposition of the notorious 'black oath' on Scottish settlers during the First Bishops' War.[51]

The proclamation authorising this oath on 29 May 1639 had actually been welcomed by leading Scottish planters in Ulster such as Viscount Clandeboye, who were keen to rid themselves of aspersions of being disloyal subjects. The oath followed closely that which Charles had attempted to impose on Scottish sojourners and traders in England and Wales from February and had demanded from March as a test of the fidelity of those troops engaged against the Covenanting army. However, the oath was effectively a loyalty test which demonstrated that the Ulster Scots, regardless of their Covenanting affiliations, were not trusted at court and were not regarded as equal partners in the Britannic projects of the Stuart monarchy. Strafford was unconcerned that the 'black oath' served to drive some settlers back to Scotland. Conversely, his heavy-handed action, coupled to his recruitment of Irish Catholics into the army he was building up for Charles in anticipation of the Second Bishops' War, had forced those settlers who remained to identify with the Covenanting movement in order to preserve their plantations. Strafford's persistent advocacy of war caused him to be identified as 'chief incendiary' in the eyes of the Covenanting movement, which was intent on judicial redress by September 1640.[52]

Notwithstanding the Irish and Scottish targeting of Strafford and Covenanting pressures to cement the peace treaty by the abolition of episcopacy, anglocentric historiography has continued to focus on the opportunity provided for the airing of local and regional grievances on a national platform. Certainly, the clamour to redress grievances released pent-up concerns in the country over the centralised running of England from the court.[53] However, the most incisive rebuttal of Charles I's intemperate opening address came in a petition presented to the Commons by Isaac Pennington on behalf of the city of London on 11 December. This 'root and branch petition', which sandwiched a composite secular grievance against fiscal opportunism (including the exaction of ship money) between a plethora of religious complaints, not only attacked Arminianism and the Laudian reprogramming of the Church of England, but also called for the abolition of episcopacy. This latter call, which conformed to the radical agenda of the Covenanting movement, was endorsed by the Scottish commissioners on 24 February 1641 and eventually emerged as a parliamentary bill on 10 May, albeit with the emphasis more on the replacement than on the abolition of episcopacy. Attempts to exclude the bishops from parliament, which foundered in the Lords on 8 June, led to a more radical call to abolish episcopacy root and branch, which passed its first reading in the Commons on 27 June but proved too divisive to effect. This assault on the religious establishment in England was not linked to a Covenanting agenda, however. Reform was not necessarily going to stop at the replacement of Episcopalianism with Presbyterianism, even in an erastian format. In turn, religion, in terms of the defence of Anglicanism, became a defining issue for those prepared to seek an accommodation rather than confrontation with Charles I over the next 12 months.[54]

However, to claim this as the defining issue of Royalism is an anglo-centric assertion which pays little respect to those already prepared to rally round the banner of Britannic monarchy during the Bishops' Wars, notably Catholics as well as courtiers and Episcopalians in all three kingdoms.[55] It is also to underestimate the anti-Scottish sentiment among English Parliamentarians that continued to shape political alignments well after the Royalists were defeated in civil war.[56] Moreover, the issue of religion should not be seen as the sole cause of polarity. The pro-Scottish faction, led initially in the Lords by Bedford and in the Commons by Pym, was concerned with a thorough reformation in church and state to achieve a godly commonwealth. Accordingly, the Covenanting leadership had designated them 'the Commonwealth's men' by May 1641.[57] In contrast to the radical grouping that was prepared to contemplate fundamental restructuring inspired by the Covenanting example, the members of the pro-Anglican, anti-Scottish faction have been described as 'constitutional Royalists'. With Edward Sackville, 4th Earl of Dorset, prominent in the Lords and Edward Hyde (the future Earl of Clarendon) among the more vociferous supporters in the Commons, these people laid stress on the rule of law and the search for a moderate church settlement.[58] In Scotland, the Tables had effectively and cohesively taken over the apparatus of government with a common commitment to Presbyterianism and limited monarchy. In England, however, the detention or flight of leading councillors had left the effective levers of government in the hands of the two rival, but far from homogeneous, factions in the 'Long Parliament', who were not always consistent in either their conservatism or their radicalism.

The position of the 'constitutional Royalists' had already been anticipated in Scotland by the conservative grouping within the Covenanting movement which formed around James Graham, 5th Earl (later 1st Marquess) of Montrose, after the Pacification of Berwick in 1639. Montrose advocated the maintenance of a constitutional equilibrium in which parliament would be a safeguard, not a permanent check on the monarchy. Montrose and his associates covertly signed the Cumbernauld Band in August 1640 in protest at the Covenanting decision to invade England, which was attributed not so much to the settled will of the radical mainstream led by Argyll as to 'the particular and indirect practiking of a few'. However, Montrose's overriding ambition and consuming jealousy left him exposed to the superior political manoeuvrings of Argyll. By the beginning of the peace negotiations at Ripon, Montrose was virtually isolated in Scotland. Unable to carry the support of influential fellow Banders such as Lord Almond, the Covenanting lieutenant-general formerly in Dutch service, Montrose and his small circle of relatives and intimates were imprisoned as plotters in May 1641.[59] At the same time, the seeming willingness of Charles I to indulge disaffected elements within his disengaged army who were plotting to secure the release of Strafford from captivity raised the substantive issue of trust, which became the polarising issue within the 'Long Parliament'. Those inclined to seek an accommodation were prepared to place their faith in Royalism, notwithstanding the king's subsequent involvement in a second army plot in June; in the 'Incident' at the Scottish Estates in October; and in the attempted arrest of Pym and four radical associates in the Commons in January 1642.[60] Those who differed came to believe, like Argyll in Scotland, that Charles had to be defeated in war.

For those distrustful of monarchy, the issue of how sovereignty was exercised reinvigorated the Gothic perspective. In turn, this perspective developed a distinctive Puritan spin as the defenders of Anglicanism rallied to Charles I. The Gothic emphasis on the supremacy of the English parliament was notably evident in a three kingdoms context during the trial of Strafford, which compounded the polarisation evident in the first session of the 'Long Parliament'. The Gothic ramifications were picked up by Erik Rosenkrantz, then a junior Danish legate, who either kept or commissioned an English diary covering events in the opening session. Undoubtedly influenced by Christian IV's support for the recall of the English parliament in the interests of accommodation, Rosenkrantz offered a contemporaneous international perspective of concern to a Scottish Covenanter or an Irish Catholic no less than an English Parliamentarian. Although Rosenkrantz noted the implementation, workings and recommendations of committees for general grievances on such issues as ship money in the Commons, his main concern was the treasonable charges pressed against Strafford in the Lords. These charges, which were instigated by the commissioners from the Scottish Covenanters, led first to Strafford's impeachment, then to his attainder, and eventually to his execution on 12 May. Simultaneously, the judicial proceedings demonstrated unequivocally to Rosenkrantz that Ireland was a subordinate kingdom. Although Strafford was an Englishman, the majority of evidence gathered against him concerned his conduct as lord-deputy of Ireland. Yet he was tried theatrically at Westminster Hall rather than before the Irish parliament for having subverted 'the Fundamentall lawes of the Kingdome of England and Ireland'. Simultaneously, Rosenkrantz reported votes of supply in the Commons as secondary to the fractious negotiations for peace and reparations which the commissioners for the Scottish Covenanters were conducting with the English Parliamentarians and Charles I.[61]

The 'Long Parliament' was initially receptive to Covenanting claims for reparations. On 6 February 1641, the English negotiators offered £300,000 sterling – that is, more than half the sum claimed for reparation (£514,128), but less than two-fifths of the Covenanters' estimated accumulated expenditure (£785,628) during the Bishops' Wars. The willingness of the Committee of Estates accompanying the army to accept this settlement was compromised when an advance instalment of £80,000 promised as 'brotherly assistance' failed to materialise and, simultaneously, the cess money exacted for daily maintenance fell seriously in arrears. However, the Scottish commissioners felt sufficiently emboldened by 25 May to demand equality of treatment with the English and the Irish in conducting free trade throughout the Stuart dominions, securing access to colonial commerce and gaining admission to mercantile companies. Moreover, the Scots no less than the English and Irish were to benefit from the lobbying of Christian IV by king and parliament for a reduction in the exorbitant tolls in the Baltic Sound.[62]

Notwithstanding these aspects of political economy, their main thrust was to strengthen the bond of union between England and Scotland professed since the first sustained appeal to British public opinion in the prelude to the Bishops' Wars. Unity in religion and uniformity in church government was secondary to securing a lasting alliance through a defensive and offensive league between the two kingdoms – that is, by confederation, not by incorporating parliamentary union. In effect, the organic discourse promoting imperial monarchy throughout the Stuart's dominions was now replaced by a contractual discourse that advocated constitutional limitations on monarchy. The Scottish perspective, when allied to the Gothic, would effect, not aristocratic republicanism, but covenanted confederalism. Nevertheless, the English negotiators were extremely wary of Scottish pressures to import Presbyterianism. As a Gothic counter, they maintained that the English parliament would decide on the nature of the Church of England. It was not fitting for ambassadors of foreign princes, far less commissioners who were also subjects of Charles I, 'to insist upon anything distinctive to government settled and established'. The only institutional innovation agreed upon was the appointment of parliamentary commissioners in both kingdoms, charged to keep the peace and redress any breaches in the intervals between parliaments. In ratifying the Treaty of London on 7 August 1641, the English parliament reserved its right to determine the nature of the English Reformation, but duly conceded that the waging of war and the stopping of trade within the king's dominions required parliamentary approval in both countries. The right of the Irish parliament to wage war was subsumed within the remit of the English parliament. In marked contrast to the Irish situation, the sovereign and independent power of the Scottish Estates as a 'free parliament' was formally recognised. The prompt bestowal of royal assent three days later, as Charles I prepared to depart for Scotland, seemingly laid to rest the spectre of provincialism which had haunted the nation since the regal union.[63]

The Covenanters were not exclusively concerned with such a bipartisan British approach, however. At the same time as the Scottish commissioners were presenting their proposals for union to their English counterparts, the Committee of Estates in Edinburgh was actively, but fruitlessly, promoting a tripartite confederation that would involve the

Estates General of the United Provinces. Once the Treaty of London had been concluded, the commander of the Scottish forces, General Alexander Leslie, initiated repeated, but unrequited, approaches to Oxenstierna, the Swedish Regent, for an alternative confederation involving Sweden, the Scottish Covenanters and the English Parliamentarians. This prospect won the ready endorsement of John Durie, the apostle of confessional confederation.[64]

As is evident from his entanglement in a second army plot to intimidate the 'Long Parliament' on the withdrawal of the Scottish forces from England, Charles had assented to the Treaty of London primarily in the hope of detaching the Covenanting movement from its alliance with the English Parliamentarians. This mission was forlorn. Despite its mandate having technically expired with the summoning of the Scottish parliament for 15 July 1641, the Committee of Estates continued to control proceedings on behalf of the radical mainstream. Although Montrose was offered a judicial hearing before the Scottish Estates on 24 August, the remit as well as the composition of the reconvened parliament was purposely ordered to prevent an alliance of conservative Covenanters with the pragmatic Royalists. This latter grouping, led by Hamilton, was prepared, with the tacit consent of Charles I, to subscribe to the National Covenant in order to attend the Scottish Estates. In turn, its action in Scotland anticipated the pragmatic association of erstwhile courtiers such as the Earl of Holland with the Parliamentarians in the course of 1642. Hamilton and Holland had a long track record of support for the restoration of the Palatinate to the family of the Winter Queen. Such support was a particularly defining feature of the Commonwealth grouping associated with Pym as, above all, with the Covenanting movement, which accorded an honoured place to Elector Louis Frederick when he accompanied Charles I to Scotland to attend the reconvened parliament. Indeed, mobilising military support for the restoration of the elector was given a serious hearing, not least because it allowed the Covenanters to retain a military presence within Scotland rather than disband all their forces. Meanwhile, Charles was encouraged to play golf rather than attend the Scottish Estates.[65]

The king's limited capacity to influence parliamentary proceedings was exposed when he appeared to condone the tumultuous lobbying of parliament on 12 October. 'The Incident', the rumoured assassination of Argyll and Hamilton as a prelude to the public rupture of the Scottish Estates by an armed force sympathetic to Montrose and reinforced by disgruntled war veterans, was forestalled by the flight of the intended victims from Edinburgh. Charles interpreted this action and the arrest of the reputed ringleaders as a personal affront. His insistence upon a public investigation to embarrass the Covenanting leadership as well as his former favourite hastened the political rapport between Covenanters and pragmatic Royalists that obliged Charles to accept the constitutional dictates of the radical mainstream.[66] The Scottish Estates secured an effective veto over the executive and judiciary when Charles gave a binding commitment that officers of state, Privy Councillors and judges would henceforth be chosen with the advice and consent of the Scottish Estates. Charles was thus obliged to accept permanent restrictions on the royal prerogative that fulfilled his own prophecy, in the spring of 1638, that the triumph of the Covenanting movement would leave him no more power than the Doge of Venice. The apparent compromise with pragmatic Royalists being appointed to the reconstituted Privy Council was no more than a cosmetic exercise. Although the Committee of Estates was not formally resuscitated, its past executive role was not only approved but continued on 16 November through the creation of interval committees – that is, diverse financial, ecclesiastical, diplomatic and judicial committees that were to endure, if necessary, until the next parliamentary session scheduled for 1644.[67]

Irish Confederates

In the meantime, the menacing presence of an armed Catholic force under Sir Phelim O'Neill brought the Irish perspective to the centre stage of British politics following the outbreak of rebellion in Ulster on 22 October 1641. Six days later, Charles had conveyed news of the Irish rebellion to the Scottish Estates, along with an invitation for armed intervention by the Covenanters to protect the plantations. The Covenanting leadership was not prepared to intervene without the consent of the English parliament; nevertheless, the Irish rebellion afforded a more plausible excuse than the restoration of the Palatinate for the retention and, indeed, the escalation of their military forces. The Scottish Estates duly offered the services of 10,000 troops to the 'Long Parliament' on 2 November. Charles's attempts to secure the commitment of Covenanting forces without waiting for the consent of the English parliament, in blatant disregard of the Treaty of London, used up his last reserves of political goodwill in Scotland. Indiscriminate reports of the 'cruel outrages of the Irish rebels' and the 'pitiful estate of the British in Ireland' afforded Charles the excuse to return to England on 17 November, to secure parliamentary backing for armed intervention. His demonstrable untrustworthiness on the Irish issue accelerated the descent to civil war in England. Simultaneously, the Irish revolt was fuelled by the blatant Gothic insensitivity of the 'Long Parliament'.[68]

Economic recession following a run of poor harvests from 1636, the pace of commercial reorientation of estate management and the growing indebtedness of native Irish landowners such as Sir Phelim O'Neill certainly contributed to the rapid spread of rebellion within and beyond Ulster. Although Old English sympathisers in the Pale failed to seize Dublin Castle on 23 October, the insurrection had spread to Connacht by November and to Munster by December – albeit the full extent of rebellion was not apparent until the following spring. Despite appealing to Covenanting precedents for their recourse to arms, the rebels had no coherent constitutional programme to implement prior to the landed elite and the clergy imposing a confederal governmental structure in May 1642. The resultant Catholic Confederation was designed to legitimise rebellion, restrain the excesses of reprisals against Protestant settlers and bring about a measure of political stability among the factional interests that together constituted the Irish interest. The reversal of plantations, though of particular significance to the native Irish, was secondary to the implementation of the Graces, which would have stopped plantation and offered the security for Catholicism which Strafford had been intent on undermining.

On the Protestant side, which was manifestly in a state of shock and awe at the pace of rebellion, there was no clear British solidarity. Although Scottish and English settlers shared an aversion to Catholicism, their more immediate concerns were directed against the implementation of 'thorough' and the political influence of the bishops, particularly the Laudians, in the Church of Ireland, who were viewed during Strafford's trial as 'the very canker of the commonwealth'. On the outbreak of rebellion, Irish fears of Covenanting military prowess meant initially that Scottish settlers were subject to relatively fewer reprisals and depredations than English ones. In turn, the English clergy in Dublin, who compiled grossly exaggerated depositions on the extent of atrocities against the Protestant plantations, differentiated between Scottish, Irish and Welsh victims and tended to use the word 'British' to describe settlers born in England. The term 'British' became a synonym for the English interest in Ireland.[69]

The royal promise to implement the Graces, which Charles I revitalised in March 1641, took on added force with the execution of

Strafford two months later. The predominantly Catholic army raised in Ireland by the former lord-deputy was leaderless and restless, a condition which aggravated fears in Scotland and England that it could be deployed in the plotting associated with Charles I. In the event, the one plot of substance owed more to continental than British links and involved the belated return of veterans in Spanish service, such as Owen Roe O'Neill, to consolidate the rebellion fomented by the native Irish in Ulster. The capacity of the native Irish to reach out to the Old English was facilitated not just by their Catholicism, but by their joint determination to prevent direct rule by the English parliament. Accordingly, the Irish perspective as first articulated by Geoffrey Keating advocated loyalty to the crown to resolve factional and territorial differences and to prevent Ireland becoming a parliamentary dependency. On the one hand, the sweeping away of such prerogative courts as Star Chamber and High Commission by the 'Long Parliament' in July 1641, like the abolition of ship money and other aspects of fiscal opportunism in August, was indicative of a radical legislative programme. On the other hand, this programme can be viewed as a Gothic assertion of parliamentary supremacy and centralised government that carried a direct threat to the continuance of distinctive and customary practices that did not conform to the English common law. The removal of Star Chamber, for instance, terminated the Council for Wales and the Marches. At considerable inconvenience and enhanced expense, litigants were required to travel to Westminster rather than Ludlow in pursuit of justice dispensed through the medium of English rather than Welsh.[70]

While not immediately facing absorption along Welsh lines, Irish fears of becoming further dependent on England were not ameliorated by the negotiations for the Treaty of London. The Scottish commissioners not only insisted that the English parliament sanction the king's future raising of forces in England and Ireland, but wanted the Irish parliament to ratify its acceptance of this dependency. This standpoint was supported by such Commonwealthmen as Simonds D'Ewes, who were intent on enforcing the dependency of the Irish upon the English parliament in order to limit monarchical power in England. The mood in the Irish parliament, whose resumption coincided with the execution of Strafford, was markedly different from the session at the beginning of 1641, which had supported the pre-trial proceedings against him in England. Taking its lead from Patrick Darcy, an Old English lawyer, the Irish parliament was intent on asserting its legislative privileges to impose permanent checks on the exercise of executive power through Dublin and to secure direct access to the monarchy at court. Although Ireland was to be governed by the common law and general customs of England, all statutes were to be made and approved by the Irish parliament. The annexation of Ireland to the English crown was accepted; the subordination of the Irish to the English parliament was not. This doctrine commanded majority support in the Irish Commons and was subsequently endorsed by the Confederate Catholics. Nevertheless, Irish opposition should not be overstated as a principled parliamentary critique of arbitrary rule in which nationalist voices in Ireland replicated the country interest in England.[71]

In essence, both the native Irish and the Old English were not opposed to the prerogative powers of monarchy so much as to the pretensions of the English parliament to legislate for Ireland. They had become increasingly alarmed not just at the prospect of the full panoply of the penal laws being deployed against recusancy, but at the language of extirpation used by Pym and his associates in relation to Catholicism. In particular, confederal unity with Scotland offered the prospect of reducing Ireland to the profession of Protestantism as the true religion, for which the abolition of episcopacy as advocated vociferously by Clotworthy in Ulster was but the first step. Clotworthy was also to the fore in promoting through the 'Long Parliament' the Adventurers Act of March 1642, which duly tied the recovery of Ireland to thorough plantation. This combination of speculative and religious interests attracted considerable support from the Protestant elite in Ireland, most notably the Earl of Cork, as from London merchants and English Parliamentarians. At the same time, the popular enthusiasm to subscribe funds for recovery owed much to the parliamentary lobbying of Henry Jones, Dean of Kilmore, and other Protestant clergymen who had survived and magnified the atrocities committed by barbaric Irish rebels. Simultaneously, emotive demands that parliament redress Irish atrocities broadened the appeal of a Gothic perspective which was determined to uphold English supremacy over Ireland.[72]

Although the adventurer scheme did not exclude Scottish subscribers, the Covenanting leadership had already made a distinctive response. With the return of impoverished refugees from Ulster, the burden of supporting widows and orphans became a national concern which was supported by voluntary subscription from February and troop mobilisation from March 1642, under Major-General Robert Munro. Although Munro exercised overall command of the forces already raised among the settlers in Ulster, which included Scottish as well as English commanders, published missives from the latter to the Gothic interest in the Commons reported the factual and providential success of the English army in the spring and summer of 1642. No attempt was made to talk about joint British endeavours to secure redress for Protestant settlers.[73]

Notwithstanding the marked but by no means cohesive hostility of English Parliamentarians and Scottish Covenanters, the Irish Catholics were reluctant rebels. Their ideological standpoint in favour of autonomy under the Stuarts made them anxious for reconciliation with Charles I. When the Confederation of Irish Catholics was established at Kilkenny in May 1642, Ireland was proclaimed to have the same freedom as that enjoyed by the subjects of the Stuart monarchy in both England and Scotland and 'commonly all kingdoms subject to any monarch'. As the Scottish Covenanters had done through the Treaty of London, the Irish Confederates were seeking to negotiate from a position of strength. Despite a similar rhetoric of resistance, however, the Confederate perspective was notably different. Their oath of association pledged allegiance to Charles I and their promise to act in his defence made no distinction between his person and his office – a theme reiterated by their official seal, which affirmed unconditional loyalty to God, king and country. When the Confederates held their first general assembly at Kilkenny five months later, they elected a supreme council of 24 members, six from each province. Although 12 were supposed to sit permanently between assemblies in the manner of the Committee of Estates, the unicameral assembly increasingly circumscribed the executive's scope for independent action. In effect, the Irish Catholics never developed centralised agencies of government and their cause remained that of a confederation of provincial associations riven by faction, under-financed yet militarily capable by land and sea.[74]

Apart from its structural weaknesses, the Confederation's objective of negotiating a treaty was undermined by the prolongation of civil war in Ireland for over a decade. More immediately, the outbreak of the Irish rebellion refocused political debate in England on the trustworthiness of Charles I. By 8 November 1641, Pym had moved the Commons to take responsibility for suppressing the Irish rebellion, a decision communicated to the Covenanting leadership as well as to the king. Prior to Charles I's return to London from Scotland, the Commons drew up and debated the Grand Remonstrance which had been in preparation by Pym and his associates ever since the opening of the 'Long Parliament' as an indictment of prerogative rule. This contentious petition, which secured only a narrow majority in the House, was duly presented to

Charles on 1 December. Again there was a clear attempt to draw on Scottish precedent by demanding that the king should only employ and retain officials, councillors and judges with the approval of parliament. At the same time, Scottish influence on the religious establishment was to be diluted by referring all issues of doctrine, worship and discipline to a synod of divines drawn from the other Protestant communities of Europe as well as England. The justification for such remedial action was to counter the malignant and popishly inclined counsels that had instigated the Bishops' Wars and facilitated the Irish rebellion 'and bloody massacre of your people'. While Charles prioritised the defence of Anglicanism, London was becoming more averse to royal interference in city government and, simultaneously, less stable a political centre, with rioting occurring at Whitehall and Westminster. Large numbers of unemployed soldiers and gentlemen adventurers were available for further plotting against parliament under the guise of seeking service overseas, especially in Ireland. Charles sought to pre-empt radical action in parliament by attempting to arrest Pym and four of his close associates in the Commons on 4 January 1642. Forewarned, the five MPs escaped. The king having lost face as well as political credibility, he abandoned the capital to parliamentary control six days later.

Over the next nine months, parliament in London and the court at York contested control over the English forces to be raised for the suppression of the Irish rebellion. All other issues became peripheral. Thus, the hitherto contentious removal of the bishops from the Lords was passed with royal approval in February. By 5 March, both the Commons and the Lords had agreed on the Militia Ordinance, which put the raising and command, as well as the supply, of forces, whether they were sent to Ireland or not, under parliamentary control. Hull, which was well stocked with arms from the Bishops' Wars, was placed under the charge of Sir John Hotham, who refused to grant Charles access to the city without parliamentary approval in April. Hostilities were initially opened through a propaganda war. On 26 May, the 'Long Parliament' drew up the Remonstrance on Hull, a Gothic defence of liberty and property based on a general appeal to parliamentary precedents that the king was the trustee for, not the absolute proprietor of, the kingdom of England. This trusteeship ought to be managed jointly with the advice of the Lords and the Commons. It was the king who had separated himself from parliament and threatened the peace and safety of the kingdom. The offence of treason required to be reinterpreted, therefore. In terms of breaching trust, acting against the interests of the kingdom carried greater weight than acting against the person of the king. On 1 June, the 'Long Parliament' published the Nineteen Propositions with the intention of dictating peace. Charles's executive and judiciary must be subject to parliamentary approval. He was also to consent to the reform of the Church of England by an international synod and obliged to accept the Militia Ordinance. At the same time, a rapport between Gothic and Scottish perspectives was suggested by the 17th ordinance, which encouraged the king to enter a confessional confederation with the United Provinces and 'other neighbouring princes and states of the Protestant religion'.[75]

On 6 June, the 'Long Parliament' specifically differentiated between the person of the king and the office of monarchy, claiming that the latter could be exercised by parliament as the supreme judiciary and the great council of the realm. The trained bands and militia were now at the disposal of the 'Long Parliament' for its own defence, not just for the suppression of the Irish rebellion. Henry Parker provided a further Gothic gloss in claiming that Charles I, having first deserted, was now prepared by force of arms to invade his general council. Charles was reputedly more solicitous of the interests of the Irish Confederates than of the many Protestants murdered daily by their hands. His issuing of commissions of array to shire and borough constituencies was 'as illegal and vexatious' as past levies of ship money and served to portray those serving in the Lords and Commons as worse rebels than the Irish. While he advocated a truce until the Irish rebellion had been suppressed, Parker saw the need for a British resolution. It was better that 'the State of Scotland were intreated to mediate and adjudicate' than that civil war should break out in England.[76]

Charles, however, was primarily concerned to reposition Britannic monarchy to make Royalism a cause worth fighting for. Accordingly, he responded to the Nineteen Propositions on 18 June, not by stressing his royal prerogative but by arguing for constitutional equilibrium through a 'regulated monarchy' respectful of, but not subordinated to, the counsel, judicial powers and financial supply of the Lords and the Commons. The tilting of this equilibrium in favour of parliament in general and the Commons in particular would unleash 'turbulent spirits' that threatened chaos in church and state. Indeed, Charles gave a potent rallying cry that proved effective in drawing support from both Houses of parliament, albeit the immediate English response to the raising of the royal standard at Nottingham on 22 August was rather muted. Nonetheless, the Royalist appeal was not confined to England. Montrose was drawn to the cause on his release from captivity in Scotland. Ormond, as the Royalist commander in Ireland, was stirred from the lethargy that had pragmatically afflicted him during the Bishops' Wars. Moreover, parliament also proved an able recruiter for Charles by its arbitrary levying of forced loans to assist the Commonwealth and its insistence on 6 September that the charges of war must be borne from the estates of those voted delinquent but not yet tried by both Houses.[77]

British Confederation

At the outset of the civil war, the Parliamentary cause had two distinct military advantages. The Royal Navy placed its trust in the Earl of Warwick and deserted the king; accordingly, the overseas aid from Christian IV continued to be anticipated rather than delivered. London supplied recruits by the thousand, the ready money to secure arms and ammunition and the customs gleaned from global commerce. Nevertheless, the initial advantage in the field lay with Charles, who mobilised support through commissions of array, supplemented by individual summons to the landed elite, in the north, the south-west and Wales. The reluctance of the Parliamentary forces, in contrast to the Scottish Covenanters, to seek outright victory meant that Charles won the day at Edgehill in Warwickshire on 23 October 1642. Although Charles moved his headquarters from York to Oxford, where he established an alternative parliament as well as his court, he was unable to mount a frontal assault on London. His forces, particularly the cavalry led by Prince Rupert, the younger brother of the Elector Louis Frederick, gained a bad press for their 'barbarous cruelty', reminiscent of the Irish rebels, in the Midlands during the spring of 1643.[78] By this juncture, the Parliamentary forces had regrouped into regional associations in the Midlands, East Anglia and the West Country. In the process a further Scottish precedent was deployed: the commissions of peace in the constituent shires were turned into committees of war. Finances were also overhauled to pay these forces. An act passed in March to raise £4 million in two instalments by December supplemented the weekly assessment imposed on shires under Parliamentary control from February. To counteract adverse publicity from levies on landed property, an ordinance of July instituted a new impost, effectively an excise tax, on imports.[79]

Acutely conscious that a substantive majority of the Lords and a significant minority of the Commons had become Royalists, Pym was instrumental in pushing for a military and religious alliance with the

Scottish Covenanters that opened up the prospect of confederal and confessional union. In order to revitalise Britannic monarchy, prevent further recourse to war within the British Isles and resolve the Irish situation through closer association with England, Henry Parker was arguing for a confederal executive or 'general junto' drawn equally from the three kingdoms. However, negotiations, which had actually commenced in September 1642 following formal Covenanting overtures to mediate from May, when the king was threatening to visit Ireland, took almost 11 months to come to fruition. The main stumbling block was not the hesitancy in the 'Long Parliament' about another round of Scottish assistance, but the regrouping of the pragmatic Royalists under Hamilton within the Scottish Privy Council, which since its reconstitution in November 1641 had remained susceptible to overtures from the king.[80]

With majority backing from the nobility, on 20 December Hamilton persuaded the Privy Council to publish a letter from the king justifying his stance towards the Parliamentarians, but not the declaration of the latter espousing religious unity and uniformity in church government. However, Argyll drew on overwhelming support from the gentry and burgesses, who constituted the inbuilt radical majority on the Council. The Parliamentarians' letter was published on 10 January 1643. Moreover, the Privy Council was not the only agency for the discussion of issues of war and peace in Scotland. As clearly demonstrated by the Covenanting decision to intervene in Ireland, initiative lay with the committee for conserving the Treaty of London, an exclusively radical body dominated by Argyll and his associates who retained contact with their English counterparts, effectively Pym's confederates. Simultaneously, the Committee for Common Burdens, which the radicals also controlled, managed the financing, equipping and levying of the Covenanting army of intervention. At a joint meeting of the Privy Council, the conservators of the peace and the Committee for Common Burdens on 12 May 1643, Argyll and his associates pressed successfully for a Convention of Estates to be summoned as an effective substitute for the parliament which Charles I was resolutely refusing to call. As Hamilton regretfully informed the court, the institutional dominance of the radical mainstream had resulted in the firm resolution of the Scottish Covenanters 'to be actors and no longer spectators in the English civil war'.[81]

Ostensibly required to supply the Covenanting army in Ireland and review the arrears of the brotherly assistance due under the Treaty of London, the Convention was managed adroitly by the radical mainstream from 22 June to 28 August. Papers recovered fortuitously from the Earl of Antrim following his capture in Ulster by the Covenanting army implicated prominent Scottish Royalists including Montrose. Two Catholic nobles, Nithsdale and Aboyne, were duly indicted for fomenting insurrection at home, while an Irish Catholic force was brought across to assist the king against the English Parliamentarians. On 19 August the general assembly, summoned to coincide with the Convention and over which Henderson presided, accepted an invitation from the 'Long Parliament' to observe, advise and direct discussions on the Presbyterian reformation of the Church of England. Suitably conditioned, the Convention on 26 August cemented a formal alliance with commissioners from the English parliament, led by Sir Henry Vane junior, for armed assistance to the Parliamentarians on the basis of the Solemn League and Covenant.[82]

This alliance, drawn up by Wariston and Henderson, affirmed that the Covenanting movement was in the driving seat in British revolutionary politics. Ireland was included within the remit of the Solemn League and Covenant, but only at the insistence of the English commissioners, the Scots being reluctant to accord equal standing to a satellite kingdom whose dominant confession was Roman Catholic. Notwithstanding that the political incompatibilities between the Scottish and the Gothic perspectives soon magnified, the Covenanting leadership was certainly determined to effect a federative, not a federalist,[83] reconfiguration of the three kingdoms. In effect, the Solemn League represented an extension of confessional confederation to achieve common spiritual and material aims while maintaining distinctive national structures in church and state. Confederal union was to replace regal union. In terms of ecumenical congruence, the Solemn League and Covenant was propagated as the necessary application of the covenant of works to that of grace in order to achieve religious reformation in all three kingdoms. In terms of political congruence, the power to hold the crown to account, if necessary by force, was exported from Scotland in clause three, which incorporated the Covenanting oath of allegiance and mutual association, 'That the world may bear witnesse with our consciences our Loyalty, and that we have no thought or intentions to diminish he Majesty's just power and greatnesse'.[84]

The Protestant Estates had reinvigorated confederation for confessional and constitutional purposes in early modern Europe firstly in Moravia, Austria and Hungary against imperial power in 1608, then in Bohemia, Moravia, Silesia and the two Lusatias against territorial integration in 1619. The association of a solemn league with a perpetual confederacy had been explicitly laid out in the incorporating articles of the United Colonies of New England, subscribed by four Puritan plantations for common defence against the Dutch, the French and the Indians, in May 1643 – three months before the Anglo-Scottish treaty. Despite a common tradition of providential banding by English Puritans and Scottish Presbyterians, any ideological connection between the confederal formulations for New England and Britain was purely coincidental.[85] Confessional confederation, however, was tainted by the polemical association of confederacy with conspiracy once the Irish rebels constituted themselves federatively at Kilkenny in 1642. Among British Protestants, the political and confessional aspirations of the Irish Catholics were deemed clandestine and nefarious. Confederation as a legitimate association was deliberately confused with confederacy as an illicit conspiracy. This polemical interchange of confederation and confederacy subsequently bedevilled Covenanting endeavours, under the radical leadership of Argyll, to reconfigure British politics.[86]

5 The Wars for the Three Kingdoms, 1644–1651

The Solemn League and Covenant signposted a British confederal commitment to war not just between but for the three kingdoms. In terms of the awkward relationships between England, Scotland and Ireland in the seventeenth century, the treaty was of fundamental significance in consummating 'the Scottish moment' – the brief period from 1638 to 1645 when the Stuart's ancient and native kingdom set the political agenda within the British Isles. Although the export of Covenanting ideology from Scotland was characterised by the language of religious revelation, negotiations had been founded primarily on political pragmatism and military experience, a combination initially welcomed by pro-Parliamentary polemicists like the journalist Marchmont Nedham, in his first edition of *Mercurius Britanicus* in August 1643.[1] The treaty was no less welcome to polemicists like Edward Bowles as the effective counter to an untrustworthy king who had been continuously plotting against the 'Long Parliament' since its inception; who had been seeking Habsburg aid from Flanders; and who had recently reached an accommodation with the Irish Confederates. The alliance with the Scots, which was endorsed by the Protestants of Zealand, was 'a seasonable engagement'.[2]

Indeed, Charles I's immediate response to the Solemn League and Covenant was to conclude his negotiations for a 12-month truce with the Irish Confederates on 15 September 1643. This truce opened up the prospect of importing Irish troops to aid the Royalist cause in England. The Earl of Loudoun, who had become chancellor on the Scottish Estates securing an effective veto over the executive and judiciary in 1641, issued a stinging rebuke to Charles I on 19 October. In response to letters from the king accusing the Covenanters of disobedience and slighting his prerogative, Loudoun asserted that the Solemn League and Covenant had been implemented, after 'mature deliberation', through a Convention of Estates. This political assembly had lacked neither constitutional warrant nor royal authority, since 'proclamations and citations given out by any of the king's judicatories are by law and inviolable united in the king's name and therefore warranted by the king'. Placing the kingdom of Scotland on a defensive footing was further justified by the recent cessation of hostilities between the Royalists and the Confederates in Ireland. For the Confederates, who had massacred many Protestants there, were now authorised to secure arms and ammunitions not only in the Stuart dominions, but in all kingdoms allied to the Stuart monarchy in order to prosecute all the king's Protestant subjects not prepared to embrace their peace with the Royalists. These subjects included Scottish Covenanters and English Presbyterians. The restoration of the Committee of Estates as the Scottish executive reinforced this rebuke. Authorised on 26 August, the same day that the Solemn League was issued, the Committee's primary task was to oversee preparations for military assistance to the English Parliamentarians. Having reconstituted shire committees of war, the central committee was divided into two sections by 1 December, one to remain in Edinburgh, the other to accompany the army into England. Loudoun and Argyll dominated the respective sections, with the Earl of Leven confirmed as the supreme commander of the Covenanting army.[3]

However, the immediate political price of armed Covenanting intervention coupled to compulsory subscription to the Solemn League throughout the British Isles was the spread of civil war from England and Ireland to Scotland. Within 12 months of the Solemn League being promulgated, there were Royalist, Parliamentary and Covenanting armies operating in England; Royalist, Confederate, Covenanting and Parliamentary armies disputing Ireland; and a Royalist army reinforced by Confederates contesting Scotland with the Covenanters. Within eight years, Scotland, like Ireland, was to be conquered by revamped Parliamentary forces under Oliver Cromwell. Gothic triumphalism would vanquish Royalists, Confederates and Covenanters alike.

Covenanted Britain

Although the Scots had stated their military intent by reoccupying Berwick-upon-Tweed on 20 September, another four months were to elapse before the Covenanting army began its push into England on 19 January 1644. The prospects of Scottish intervention were particularly welcomed by both Presbyterians, who had been campaigning since 1642 for unity in religion and uniformity in church government, and Independents, who supported a thorough reformation of the Church of

England with more emphasis on congregational autonomy than a Presbyterian hierarchy of courts. Stephen Marshall and Philip Nye, as the respective representatives of these interests, had accompanied the English Parliamentary commissioners who negotiated the Solemn League and Covenant. Both had attended the general assembly which ran in tandem with the Convention of Estates, and both concurred about the fundamental importance of the Covenant to Scotland, 'the whole body of the Nation looking upon it as the cause of God'. Both saw the Solemn League as the arm of the Lord being extended to England. Nye subsequently commended the Covenanting oath of allegiance to the Westminster Assembly of Divines as worthy not only of the three kingdoms, but 'of all the Kingdoms of the world'. His Independent colleague Jeremiah Burroughs asserted that Scotland, as a chosen nation, was 'united the most firmly under heaven, we may truly call it a Philadelphia'. England should rejoice to have the Scots 'in a near Union with us', and he strongly urged the Parliamentary treasury at the London Guildhall to advance £100,000 to facilitate Covenanting intervention. St John, as the solicitor-general for England, had taken up this theme of financial obligation in October 1643. The 'Long Parliament' had failed to supply the Covenanting army in Ireland for the past 14 months, and starvation had only been fended off by the Scottish Estates supplying £80,000 from its hard-pressed resources. A significant portion of the brotherly assistance promised by the Treaty of London still remained unpaid. Covenanting intervention opened up the twin prospects of assuring a Parliamentary victory and speeding up the sequestration of Royalist estates to meet the cost of war.

The other politician in whom the Covenanters placed particular trust was Sir Henry Vane the younger. He reported to the city of London that the Scots were so sensible of the dangers to religion if the Parliamentary cause should fail that they were ready to break through all military and financial difficulties in return for the advance of £100,000. In the formal terms negotiated for Covenanting intervention in November, the Scots accepted this advance which was to be discounted against the first monthly allowance for the 21,000 troops brought over the border. However, they also insisted that no pacification or peace treaty should be made by either kingdom, through their parliaments or armies, 'without the mutuall advice and consent of both Kingdoms'.[4] Further recognition of the importance of the Covenanters to the Parliamentary war effort was afforded by the use of the term 'British', not just 'English', to describe the forces raised among the planters to resist the Irish

Confederates. The supply of these British forces, as of the distinctive Scottish Covenanting army in Ulster, remained problematic, however. The Parliamentary treasury juggled with funds raised specifically for the Irish campaigns through subscription to the Adventurers Act of 1642. In a less discriminatory manner, fines imposed on Royalists and others deemed notorious delinquents were used to pay for the British and Scottish armies in Ireland as well as the Parliamentary forces in England.[5]

The reconvened Convention of Estates issued a declaration on behalf of both kingdoms on 6 January 1644 which was ratified by the 'Long Parliament' 13 days later and which vindicated joint action against the Royalists. Deemed 'the Popish, Prelaticall, and Malignant party', which had trampled under foot religion, laws and liberties in the three kingdoms, the Royalists were to be held to account for the 'troubles and sufferings' of Scotland, the 'desolation of Ireland' and the 'many unnatural Tragedies' in England. Confident that they were fighting a godly war, the Covenanters and Parliamentarians were intent on the preservation of the Church of Christ 'and this whole Island from utter ruine and devastation'. Public warning was given that neutrality and indifference would not be tolerated. All common soldiers who acknowledged past errors in fighting with the Royalists were to be freely accepted into the Covenant. Those of the Scottish nation who had engaged with the Royalist cause in England were to be given the opportunity to confess their mistakes and take the Covenant by 1 March, otherwise they would be treated as 'desperate Malignants' and their estates sequestrated. Those who had deserted the Parliamentary cause in England, but were not yet reckoned among the prior authors of the civil war, were offered the same timely opportunity to be restored to favour through the Covenant, subject to discretionary fines being imposed on their estates. Those who refused pardon were to be forfeited. No indemnity was to be offered to three categories of delinquents who were to face the summary justice due to traitors: Catholic recusants involved in plotting against Protestantism in Scotland and England and in sustaining civil war to bring both kingdoms 'under the Power and Tyranny of the Pope'; all Irish rebels, including Protestant Royalists, who had come to England to fight against the Parliamentary forces; and principal counsellors, 'who have kindled and fomented the Fire of Division and Warre' between the king and the 'Long Parliament'. Their movable and heritable estates were to be forfeited to pay the public debts and common burdens of both kingdoms. In effect, the extension of treason to cover anti-Covenanting activities in Scotland from 1640 was now applied to England.[6]

Royalists committed to the defence of Episcopalianism, as a *de iure* establishment warranted by scripture, neither sought nor were offered an accommodation with the Solemn League and Covenant. Indeed, as the Covenant was viewed as a national endeavour in England as well as in Scotland, Royalists were not deemed to be of the same nation as those confederated in the Solemn League. Not only had they associated with the Irish rebels, but they had participated in forces which reputedly included 'many French, Dutch, Walloons, Spanish, Irish, Danish and Negroes'. On the one hand, all those refusing to subscribe the Solemn League and Covenant were threatened with fines for delinquency. On the other hand, punitive fines were partially offset by the willingness of Presbyterian apologists such as Stephen Marshall and Thomas Mockett to accommodate English consciences. While little truck was had with papists, separatists or those claiming neutrality to avoid military commitments beyond their own localities, every effort was made to encompass a range of beliefs from Anglicanism to Congregationalism, provided their adherents upheld the reform of the Church of England purged of the Laudian bishops. Presbyterianism remained the stated ideal, but not necessarily according to the Scottish model. Thus, John Egerton, 1st Earl of Bridgewater and former president of the Council of Wales and the Marches, subscribed the Solemn League and Covenant, with minimum Parliamentary pressure, in February 1644, even though he had no track record as a committed Presbyterian.[7]

Although its intervention did not enjoy the swift and spectacular success it had in the Second Bishops' War, the Covenanting army consolidated the turning of hostilities in favour of the Parliamentary forces. Hitherto, the Royalists had had the edge in fighting regional campaigns, especially in the north and south-west if less convincingly in the Midlands. However, they were unable to carry the day against the Earl of Essex at Newbury in Gloucestershire on 19 September, when victory would have ceded control of the Severn Valley. The king gained little advantage from the peace with the Confederates as the Parliamentarian Sir Thomas Fairfax rounded up the small contingents sent across the Irish Sea at Nantwich in Cheshire on 25 January. The Covenanters immediately made their presence felt throughout the north of England. However, their army was unable to take Newcastle until October 1644, after a siege lasting almost three months. The Parliamentarians, therefore, did not gain an immediate advantage from the freeing up of coal supplies from the Tyne, which had come under Royalist control through the military endeavours of William Cavendish, 1st Earl (later Duke) of

Newcastle. During the same period, the Royalists had continued to use Newcastle as a port of entry for arms and ammunition from Denmark and the Netherlands. In terms of set battles, the Covenanting army made little contribution to the Parliamentarian war effort after the combined victory at Marston Moor in Yorkshire on 2 July 1644. Its three-year stay in England led to no meaningful establishment of Presbyterianism within the Church of England in terms consistent with the Scottish interpretation of the Solemn League.

Accordingly, Covenanting intervention has tended to be written off in both English and Scottish historiography as a naïve and ultimately fruitless endeavour to shape the outcome of the civil war. The Scots demonstrated a limited capacity to control events and tended to become the tools, if not the playthings, of rival Parliamentary interests, originally called the peace and the war parties, who came to be labelled politically as the Presbyterians and the Independents respectively.[8] The Covenanting army has also been viewed as ancillary to the major English military narrative of the civil war that culminated in the creation of the New Model Army and its crushing victory over the Royalist forces at Naseby in Northamptonshire on 14 June 1645.[9] Indeed, the three-year presence of the Covenanting army in the north of England has been deemed particularly counter-productive as anti-Scottish sentiment even led to former Royalists siding with the Independents to bring about its removal in January 1647.[10]

However, the interests of the Covenanting movement were British, not just English, and were maintained with ideological consistency tempered by political pragmatism. This was recognised by accredited international diplomats from France and Sweden as well as from the United Provinces and Denmark. The Scottish Covenanters were also the driving force behind the implementation of the Committee of Both Kingdoms, which co-ordinated the war effort against the Royalists, and the centralised restructuring of the English shire committees to provide ideological as well as military and financial support for the New Model Army. The Covenanting army of intervention remained the largest in the field in Parliamentary service. Furthermore, Scotland effectively expanded its territorial bounds to an unprecedented extent through the Covenanting armies of occupation, south from the Tweed to the Tees and on to the Humber, and west from the Solway Firth to Lough Neagh. This expansion, which was the greatest by any army from the three kingdoms prior to the Cromwellian occupations of Ireland and Scotland in 1650–51, provoked genuine if unfounded fears of Scottish imperialism in both England and Ireland throughout the 1640s.[11]

The extensive territorial commitment of the Covenanting forces was conducted against a backdrop of civil war within Scotland and divisions within Covenanting ranks on whether to scale down in, or even withdraw from, England. An alternative field of engagement beckoned as Scottish Covenanters debated the revival of confederation with Sweden and military assistance to their former sponsors to facilitate the wresting of the provinces to the east of the Baltic Sound from Christian IV of Denmark. The acquisition of these provinces by Sweden would eradicate the tolls currently crippling Scottish trade to and from the Baltic.[12] Considerations of political economy as well as religious and military concerns influenced the strategic thinking of the Covenanting leadership, as is evident from their insistence that eight ships be deployed at Parliamentary expense to protect Scottish coastal waters. The presence of five of these on the east coast reflects an economic concern for North Sea and Baltic ventures, especially with regard to the piratical activities of the Dunkirkers, rather than a potential naval threat from Royalist forces. However, the Earl of Warwick, as naval commander, did not fulfil this commitment until the summer of 1644, and then only on the east coast. The west coast was left exposed to Dunkirkers operating from Ireland. In the interim, the Covenanters had added Newcastle and coal supplies on the Tyne to their acquisition of Berwick. With the outbreak of civil war in England, Scottish ships had been seized and detained in both towns 'without evidence of injury or provocation' in breach of the Treaty of London and to the detriment of Scottish trade. During the period of Covenanting intervention, however, both towns tended to be classified as Scottish as much as English in Scandinavian trading records.[13]

British Reconfiguration

The key features of Covenanting policy during the period of intervention in England were a demonstrable concern with confederal union, a pragmatic willingness to temper military force with peace negotiations and an international commitment to Protestantism not just Presbyterianism. The Scottish commissioners who arrived in London to liaise with the Lords and the Commons on 5 February 1644 were committed to the pursuit of war against the Royalists. But they did not rule out the brokering of a negotiated peace between the king and the 'Long Parliament' that would be consistent with the British aspirations of the Covenanting movement and the international standing of the Solemn League and Covenant. The Scottish commissioners were well aware that an embassy had been sent from the United Provinces to effect a meaningful reconciliation. At the same time, the Covenanting leadership in Edinburgh was intent on reinvigorating the 'auld alliance' with France. William Ker, 3rd Earl of Lothian, was despatched as ambassador to France in the spring of 1643, and a contingent of troops had earlier been sent to reinforce the Scottish forces (Garde Écossais) in French service under Argyll's errant half-brother James, Lord Kintyre (now Earl of Irvine). Scottish forces were also in demand for Swedish service. Hugh Mowatt, an expatriate Scottish agent in Sweden, was sent to Britain as ambassador to both the Scottish Estates and the English parliament. On his arrival in London he met with the Scottish commissioners before progressing in June to Edinburgh, where he received a warm welcome as Swedish ambassador but no promise of troops until affairs had been settled in England. His prioritising of Scottish interests caused a measure of dissent among the Parliamentary cohorts in London when he arrived to promote confederation in December. At the same time, the Covenanting leadership was monitoring Danish attempts to secure Scottish forces through an embassy despatched under Colonel John Henderson, another expatriate Scot with longstanding ties to the house of Argyll. Although the leaders were not receptive to the raising of forces for Danish service other than to decant Royalist sympathisers from Scotland, they took umbrage when the Parliamentarians incarcerated Henderson as he was passing through London in June 1645.[14]

The Scottish position, which was consistently maintained by the commissioners in London as well as by the leadership in Edinburgh and that with the army, was to effect the Solemn League and Covenant as a written constitution for Britain in the same way as the National Covenant had served for Scotland. The ideal was the permanent establishment of a covenanted Stuart monarchy. The Covenanters, whose common cause with the Parliamentarians undoubtedly suffered from the deaths of Pym, Hampden and Brooke in 1643, realised that Charles I had to be defeated for this to be effected. Thus, they differed from the peace grouping led by Edward, 2nd Earl of Manchester, Essex and Warwick in the Lords and by Denzil Holles, Bulstrode Whitelocke and, to a more equivocal extent, Sir William Waller in the Commons. This group pursued war as an honourable means to bring Charles to the negotiating table without necessarily requiring outright victory. The Covenanters shared the desire to win held by the war grouping around Algernon Percy, 10th Earl of

Northumberland, and Saye & Sele in the Lords and Vane junior, St John and especially Oliver Cromwell in the Commons. However, they were not content to accept the establishment of parliamentary supremacy, the Gothic alternative to a written constitution.[15]

The Covenanting leadership was not content that peace negotiations, which opened at Uxbridge in November 1644, should simply tighten up on the propositions that had failed to secure agreement at Oxford in February 1643. The Scottish commissioners certainly respected such English issues of mutual concern as control over the militia, executive and judiciary, effecting religious reformation, the removal of delinquent counsellors and the exemption of named 'malignants' from pardon. Notwithstanding the guiding role played by Henderson and his colleagues in the Westminster Assembly in promoting Presbyterianism, the commissioners were not primarily concerned with effecting religious uniformity according to a Scottish prescription.[16] In order to secure a lasting peace between the king and the 'Long Parliament', the commissioners were instructed to negotiate 'with greater latitude'. The Scottish Covenanters had three resolute concerns: the suppression of the Catholic Confederation in Ireland; meaningful British representation in both the royal household and the executive councils for all three kingdoms; and the opening up of colonial trade and mercantile adventuring as requested but never conceded during negotiations for the Treaty of London in 1641.

Accordingly, the Scottish commissioners were determined that funding for the Covenanting forces in Ireland should be regularised. In order to prevent bickering between the commands of the Scottish and British armies, overall command was to be clearly vested in General Leven and, under him, Robert Munro. All the British in Ireland were to be obliged to subscribe the Solemn League and Covenant. At the same time, they were insistent that Ireland should be included 'under the name of England in all the articles'. Discrimination against the Irish continued in the proposals for reciprocal rights to membership of executive councils. The Scots were deemed capable of exercising any office in England and Ireland, but only the English were so qualified in Scotland. No mention was made of Irish representation when the Scots claimed half, but were prepared to settle for a third, of all places of trust in the royal household to counter the impact of absentee monarchy which had been prejudicial to Scotland since 1603. The Covenanters were also determined that no Scottish peer should be held to account in England for transgressions in Scotland in the way that Strafford had been tried for his malpractices in Ireland. Hamilton, though elevated to a dukedom for his efforts to secure Covenanting support for Charles I in 1642–3, had actually been imprisoned by the king when he reported his inability to prevent the Covenanting intervention on the side of the English Parliamentarians. The Scottish commissioners complained that Hamilton was kept prisoner in England contrary to Scots law, which required all subjects who committed wrongs in Scotland to be tried there.[17]

The claims for reciprocity and parity in commercial benefits were directed more against Gothic than Irish interests, however. The Gothic predilection for an exclusively English rather than an inclusively British agenda had already been evident in appeals to the 'Long Parliament' to enforce English jurisdiction over the colonies of Britannic monarchy. These appeals were effected in November 1643, when Warwick was appointed governor of the colonies in America and the West Indies.[18] Scottish transoceanic, commercial aspirations followed on from the attainment of 'a sure peace' grounded upon a package of military and political resolutions. However, this Scottish package enjoyed no consolidated or unequivocal support from the Parliamentarians, nor was it attractive to the king. Charles I remained adamantly opposed to a covenanted monarchy or to making any meaningful concessions in England that would diminish his power to the level secured by the Covenanters in Scotland by 1641.

While 'constitutional Royalists' such as Edward, 4th Earl of Dorset, continued to argue for a negotiated settlement, Charles's resolve not to compromise was stiffened by support from Queen Henrietta Maria and George, Lord Digby, who had flirted with the 'constitutional Royalists' prior to the outbreak of civil war. Committed to the Stuart monarchy, the Covenanters had no real alternative to Charles I. Although the Winter Queen's eldest son was reported to have subscribed the Solemn League and Covenant while in the United Provinces in March 1644, the restoration of the Elector Charles Louis to the Palatinate appeared imminent with French help. His two younger brothers, Princes Rupert and Maurice, were tainted through their martial association with the Royalist cause. A regency government appeared out of the question as the queen stood solidly with Charles and both the Prince of Wales (the future Charles II) and James, Duke of York, enjoyed the protection of France and the United Provinces. Outright republicanism as advocated by Henry Marten remained a distinctly minority pursuit in England and was abhorrent in Scotland. Nonetheless, there were growing concerns within the Covenanting movement that the Parliamentary war grouping was becoming less committed to a Stuart monarchy when the peace negotiations at Uxbridge broke up in February 1645. These concerns were compounded by differences over the direction of hostilities, a task entrusted primarily but not exclusively to the Committee for Both Kingdoms.[19]

In strategic terms, British unity entailed convergence of public policy rather than institutional incorporation. However, the Committee of Both Kingdoms, the one British institution that did arise out of the Solemn League and Covenant, opened up the fault lines between the Gothic and the Scottish perspectives. The remit of the Committee, which operated from February 1644 until October 1646, was keenly debated at its instigation, was subject to periodic review with members and responsibilities added, and was the focus of rival antagonisms among the main players in the peace and war groupings. The Scottish commissioners, whose numbers were raised from four to 11 in July 1644, after five more MPs were added prior to Marston Moor, enjoyed a disproportionate and moderating presence. Johnston of Wariston usually managed Committee business. The Committee was viewed within Parliamentary circles as an executive committee. Seven members of the Lords and 14 from the Commons, together with the Scottish commissioners in London, composed its original membership. Final decisions on the making of war and peace were never ceded to the Committee, however. Meeting at Derby House in London, it was empowered to negotiate with foreign states as well as serving as an official channel for dealings between the Covenanters and the Parliamentarians. However, to effectively carry out its diplomatic functions and oversee the war effort by land and sea against not only the Royalists in England but also the Catholic Confederation in Ireland, the Committee would have needed to operate as a federal executive – a role the increasingly Gothic 'Long Parliament' was palpably not prepared to concede.[20]

For their part, the Covenanting leadership viewed the Committee as a co-ordinating confederal council, the prime but not the sole agency for preserving the interests of Scotland in the management of the affairs of both kingdoms. Its British roots lay with the Commission for the Conservators of the Peace established by the Treaty of London in 1641, which evolved into the Commission for Negotiating the Solemn League and Covenant on Behalf of the English Parliament and the Scottish Estates. The English and Scottish commissioners, reconstituted as the Committees for Both Kingdoms, had also facilitated the Scottish reoccupation of Berwick, on terms favourable to the continuing autonomy of the frontier town, in September 1644. English commissioners had subsequently been attached to the Covenanting army of intervention but were seemingly not accorded the equivalent degree of consultation within the Committee of Estates attending the army as was given to the Scottish commissioners in London. The English commissioners, especially those such as Sir William Armine and Richard Barwiss with northern connections, became the most vociferous critics to the 'Long Parliament' of the deleterious impact of the Scottish presence in the north of England. In the aftermath of Marston Moor, when the Covenanting army became increasingly reluctant to move away from the northern theatre as civil war broke out in Scotland, their vitriol became a feature of the anti-Scottish sentiment that was coming to characterise the war grouping.[21]

However, both war and peace groupings had been anxious to involve Scottish expertise in international relations following the establishment of the Committee of Both Kingdoms. In February 1644, the Parliamentarians had taken the initiative in inviting the Covenanters to appoint a Scottish agent to work with Matthew Strickland, their English agent in the United Provinces. Thomas Cunningham, the leading fundraiser and financial facilitator for the Covenanting movement, based at Campvere in Zeeland, was duly nominated the following month. His remit, as prescribed by the Committee of Estates at Edinburgh in May, was not only to promote the joint cause before the States General, but also to extend the Solemn League and Covenant to the Dutch Republic. Thus the prospect of reviving confessional confederation in defence of European Protestantism was undertaken as a joint endeavour for both kingdoms. The States General, however, preferred to maintain a mediating position between Charles I and his British opponents while continuing to license shipments of arms and ammunition to all sides.[22]

The Parliamentarians also took the initiative in seeking a joint undertaking to promote confessional confederation with Sweden in the wake of Mowatt's embassy. Whereas the Scots felt inhibited by the Solemn League and Covenant from concluding a bilateral treaty with Sweden, the English Parliamentarians were less scrupulous, even though the issue had been referred to the Committee of Both Kingdoms in January 1645. However, the pro-Scottish influence of Oxenstierna was waning in Swedish affairs as Queen Kristina had come of age and embarked upon her personal rule. The British envoy sent to Sweden in May, Colonel Christopher Potley, a veteran recently released from Swedish service, duly took advantage of this situation to promote a bilateral alliance with the English Parliamentarians that marginalised Scottish interests, even though his letter of accreditation sought that immunity from the Danish exaction of Sound tolls 'be Common to the British, with the Swedish merchants and shipps'.[23] In order to counter any revived inclination on the part of Christian IV to assist Charles I, who was now complaining that his opponents in Scotland and England were threatening to transfer power from an aristocracy to a democracy, Saye & Sele and Johnston of Wariston had written a letter of assurance to the Danish king in June 1645. International recognition for the political accord of Scottish Covenanters with English Parliamentarians was sought through the diplomatic projection of the Committee of Both Kingdoms as *Concilium Amborum Magnae Britanniae*. However, the 'Long Parliament' had only temporarily set aside its endeavours since December 1643 to take over the Sound toll negotiations without reference to the Covenanting leadership or Scottish interests. This endeavour was effectively achieved in March 1646, when Richard Jenkes was despatched unilaterally to Denmark, albeit the treaty for relief was not concluded until June 1647.[24]

The refocusing of the Gothic perspective, stimulated by Covenanting intervention in England, was particularly manifest in relation to party differences. The first hint that the Scots were becoming a polarising influence between the peace and war groupings came after the battle of Marston Moor in July 1644, which Cromwell acclaimed as a triumph for the English forces of godliness. The victory, which secured the north and fragmented the Royalist forces, could not have been achieved without the resolute military presence of the Covenanting army intent on engagement under Leven. In the short term, any potential fissure was covered up by the triumphant generals, Fairfax, Manchester and Leven, writing to the Committee of Both Kingdoms to affirm their commitment to the Solemn League and Covenant. They urged that both the Lords and the Commons 'take the building of ye house of God & settlement of church government unto their cheifest thoughts'. However, Essex's campaign in Cornwall and the West Country in July and August was characterised by ineptitude. The inconclusive second battle of Newbury on 27 October was marked by the indecisiveness of Manchester, who was also unable to sustain the siege of Donnington Castle, Gloucestershire, on 9 November. Cromwell resumed his offensive, which was directed particularly against Manchester and his Scottish second-in-command, Major-General Lawrence Crawford, whom he had subjected to occasional carping criticism in the wake of Marston Moor. The outcome of this bickering, which Cromwell broadened into an attack in the Commons on all generals inclined to the peace group-ing, was a decisive parliamentary debate in late November. In his response, Manchester attacked Cromwell as a radical intent on war, antipathetic to the Lords and contemptuous of the Westminster Assem-bly of Divines. Cromwell was reputedly disdainful of the Scottish Covenanters, against whom he 'would als soon draw his sword as against these who ar declared enemies to both kingdoms'.

The initial reaction of the Scottish commissioners was not to promote reconciliation but to contemplate, in association with Essex and the peace grouping, the indictment of Cromwell as an incendiary. However, as the Covenanting leadership were intent on fronting negotiations with the king at Uxbridge and also shared the concerns of the war grouping about the lack of professionalism among the Parliamentary forces, the Scottish commissioners endorsed the Self-Denying Ordinance promoted in the Commons on 9 December. This ordinance, which sought to prevent MPs from holding civil or military commands, was actually the revival of a motion brought to the Lords 12 months earlier, but it was now given teeth by the power struggle between the peace and war groupings.[25] The eventual passage of the Self-Denying Ordinance through both Houses in April 1645 paved the way for the creation of the New Model Army, under the direction of Sir Thomas Fairfax as commander-in-chief. Those commanders associated with the peace grouping – Essex, Manchester, Warwick and Sir William Waller – were purged, as were the Scottish officers serving with the Parliamentary forces. Cromwell alone among the principal protagonists was granted a temporary exemption, which was made permanent after the decisive victory attained by the New Model Army at Naseby in June. Cromwell brilliantly commanded the cavalry and proclaimed a further Gothic triumph of the godly English, now untainted by Covenanting assistance.

From an anglocentric perspective, the establishment of the New Model Army can be viewed as a conservative measure that restructured existing Parliamentary forces, introduced no new forms of supply and continued to be directed mainly by the Committee of Both Kingdoms among the executive committees. Its radical nature only emerged in 1647, as the 'Long Parliament' divided on issues of war in Ireland and peace in England.[26] From a British perspective, however, the New Model Army was perceived from the outset as a radical creation. Essentially it was a Gothic construct, being based on, but without acknowledging, the national armies created initially in Sweden then in Scotland as products of the Thirty Years War. Under Fairfax and Cromwell it was fashioned to attain an English victory for the Parliamentarians, not a British reconfiguration that would accommodate the Scots and the monarchy as envisaged by the Solemn League and Covenant.

In the same way that parliament served as a national forum for the exposition and resolution of provincial and local grievances, the New Model Army sought to eliminate the provincialism that had caused dissension among commanders and the localism that had provoked 'Clubmen' risings. Originally directed against the Royalist forces in Shropshire, Worcestershire and Herefordshire from January to March 1645, these risings, which represented grass-roots resistance to repeated demands for men, money and supplies, were directed against Parliamentary forces when they spread to Wiltshire, Dorset and Somerset in May and June. Occurring mainly in areas where control had been contested and where financial and military levies had been demanded by both sides, further risings in Berkshire, Sussex, Hampshire, South Wales and the Welsh Marches were duly suppressed by the New Model Army between September and November.[27]

The Scottish Covenanters had been particularly supportive of the greater centralising emphasis on government to supply the New Model Army as it envisaged this process would bring expeditious relief to their hard-pressed army of intervention. Unlike the Second Bishops' War, when the Covenanting forces instigated the occupation of northern England, Scottish intervention in the civil war in England came over a year after the war had begun and when territories had already been devastated. Accordingly, the Covenanting army never achieved the same productive relationships with the county committees as it had enjoyed in 1640–41. Advances on sums raised for its monthly maintenance made by the city of London were underwritten by the customs. However, these payments of monies raised from sequestrated rents, gifts and forced loans continued to be fitful.[28]

The Parliamentary revenue base expanded with the vanquishing of Royalist forces. At the same time, monthly assessments were collated expeditiously through York for the northern English counties and through London for the southern on the creation of the New Model Army. Nevertheless, the Covenanting forces continued to be denied ready access to the resources of the county committees or to their assessors, collectors and sequestrators. Moreover, direct funding from the excise also remained problematic, particularly after the 'Long Parliament' reduced the tariff on coal exported from the Tyne under Covenanting oversight, ostensibly to encourage more trading. The

Covenanting forces, reliant as much on supplies from Scotland, raised usually on credit, as from London or latterly York, were obliged to take free quarters or impose their own levies, which were usually higher than comparable Parliamentary exactions. Their fiscal demands provoked revolts in Cumberland and Westmorland and the Covenanters also faced down the threat of a Clubman uprising in Yorkshire in the aftermath of Naseby.[29] However, antipathies towards the Scottish army of intervention must also be balanced against a growing aversion to the military, financial and ideological demands for commitment made by the county committees and a continuing willingness in some parts of Yorkshire and the north to see the Covenanters as forces for deliverance from Royalism and for the godly reconfiguration of Britain.[30]

Confederal Disunion

The British commitment of the Scots was of vital significance in persuading the peers who felt particularly threatened by the anti-aristocratic thrust of Cromwell's criticisms to accept the Self-Denying Ordinance. Resentful of its attack on their traditional role of holding military command by land or sea, they were adamant that the New Model Army must be prepared to the satisfaction of the Committee of Both Kingdoms where the Scottish commissioners were expected to play a key role. Joint advice and direction must be maintained between Parliamentarians and Covenanters, as it was not deemed advisable to embark upon a radical reconstruction that had introduced 'so great a Change in the whole management of a war' without advising or consulting with the Scottish commissioners. Indeed, these apprehensions signalled the growing significance of party divisions that had been formulated in the course of the Uxbridge negotiations, the passage of the Self-Denying Ordinance and the establishment of the New Model Army. The peace grouping that dominated in the Lords became identified with the Presbyterians while the war grouping, which just held sway in the Commons, became the Independents. The key to these divisions, which emerged before victory over Charles I was assured, was not so much religious affiliations as political attitudes to continued Covenanting intervention in England, which was an issue that transcended territorial pressure groups.[31]

The Presbyterians led by Essex, though by no means wholly committed to a religious settlement in accord with Scottish practice and pressure, inclined towards the Covenanters to support their conservative desires for an accommodation with Charles I as part of the British recon-figuration. Accordingly, they ensured that the Solemn League and Covenant had to be subscribed by all officers in the New Model Army 20 days after their appointment was confirmed by the Lords and the Commons. The Independents, for whom Cromwell was becoming increasingly prominent, certainly sought a more pluralist, if not wholly tolerant, religious establishment in England. They took their inspiration from the Puritan communities in New England, the alternative centre for confessional confederation along anglocentric rather than the conti-nental lines advocated by the Scottish Covenanters. Notwithstanding this Puritan, transatlantic dimension, the essence of their radicalism was their political commitment to parliamentary supremacy buttressed by the New Model Army. The Independents were intent on redefining the Gothic perspective through outright victory rather than by an accom-modation with Charles I. The Scots were no longer deemed essential to this objective after Naseby. The Independents were able to insist that ordinary soldiers enlisted in the New Model Army should only 'take ye Covenant' at the discretion of both Houses of Parliament. English con-siderations were thus given priority over the British reconfiguration espoused by the Covenanters. Nonetheless the Scots, rather than any transient or nebulous middle grouping, had become the third-party interest in Parliamentary circles in the course of 1645, a position rein-forced by the continuing good relations the Covenanting movement enjoyed with the city of London.[32]

However, the resolve of the Scottish Covenanters that British recon-figuration should reach an accommodation with the Stuart monarchy suffered critically when Charles's secret correspondence regarding a negotiated peace was intercepted and published in the wake of Naseby. While Marchmont Nedham's vituperative commentary in *Mercurius Britanicus* was officially censured, the more measured revelations penned by Henry Parker and his associates laid bare the untrustworthiness of Charles I.[33] At the same time, the Covenanters were compromised by hints of secret negotiations conducted through their French agents with the regency government of Cardinal Mazarin that involved dealings with Royalists, including Queen Henrietta Maria. These negotiations, which had been ongoing prior to Uxbridge without reference to the Commit-tee of Both Kingdoms, led to the arrival of the French embassy of Jean de Montereul in London in July. Charged to negotiate primarily with the Covenanters and with Charles I, he met with the Scottish commission-ers before progressing to Scotland, where he explored the prospects for two eventualities: a tripartite accommodation between the Covenanters, the Presbyterians and the king and a military revival of the 'auld alliance' should the Scots go to war against the Parliamentarians. The latter eventuality seemed the more likely given the assertiveness of the Independents and the fears the Covenanters shared with the Presbyterians about the rise of a radical element knows as the 'Reformeirs', subsequently the Levellers, within the New Model Army. Montereul was also instrumental in seeking assurances that Charles I would be safe should he seek the protection of the Covenanting army, a situation that came to pass on 5 May 1646 when the king left Oxford to surrender to Leven's forces at Newark, two months after the formal capitulation of the Royalist forces in England at Stow-on-the-Wold, Gloucestershire.[34]

In addition to their covert diplomacy, the Scots were further open to charges of breaching their treaty obligations under the Solemn League by their preference to remain in the north and unilaterally establish garrisons between the Tees and Carlisle. Having conducted a lacklustre, short campaign along the Welsh marches in the summer of 1645, the Covenanting army remained resistant to overtures to venture south of the Humber until the civil war then raging in Scotland was resolved. The Covenanting leadership in Edinburgh concurred with the army command in seeking to prevent the Royalist forces in England joining up with those now active in Scotland. When they did eventually agree to participate in the siege of Newark-upon-Trent in November, the Committee of Estates insisted that General Leven be made supreme commander of the Covenanting and Parliamentary forces for a blockade that dragged on until May 1646. Their accord with the Presbyterians had enabled the Covenanting leadership to secure Scottish representation on the delegation sent from the Committee of Both Kingdoms to take stock of the war in Ireland in March 1645. Political distancing from the Independents led to Robert Munro being stripped of his overall command of the Scottish and British forces in Ireland. Further embroiled in controversy for the Covenanters' refusal to give up their Belfast garrison, the Scottish commissioners in London were effectively removed from executive discussions on Irish affairs by December. In the meantime, more provocation seemingly occurred in October, when the 'Long Parliament' opted for an erastian Presbyterian settlement in the Church of England.[35]

The efforts of the Scottish clerical commissioners to the Westminster Assembly of Divines had certainly been directed towards the replication in England of the relative autonomy enjoyed by the Scottish Kirk.

Robert Baillie was particularly articulate in expressing his disappointment about the malign influence of the Independents in parliament and
of sectaries within the New Model Army. Nevertheless, the Congregational influence exerted by Robert Nye and his associates in the
Westminster Assembly had been no more integral to the conduct of its
protracted proceedings than to the parliamentary attainder and execution of Archbishop Laud in January 1645. The Scots, in what they
viewed as the true spirit of confessional confederation, were prepared to
accept unreservedly the standards prescribed at Westminster for faith,
worship and even church government, though the familiar Scottish
terminology for presbyterian courts was replaced by the continental
preference for classical assemblies. However, the Scottish commissioners
and the Committee of Estates took a more pragmatic approach to the
erastian nature of English Presbyterianism as implemented by the 'Long
Parliament' in March 1646, when all church courts were subordinated
to parliament and their powers of ecclesiastical censure were strictly
limited. For the National Covenant of 1638 had affirmed that matters
of faith, worship and government in Scotland needed to be grounded in
parliamentary statutes. The committees of war established subsequently
in the Scottish shires had also not only carried out the civil sanctions
required for ecclesiastical transgressions, but had also determined the
ideological soundness of those suspected of being antipathetic to the
godliness of the Covenanting cause.[36]

Far more destructive to the common cause of Scottish Covenanters
and English Parliamentarians was their lack of agreement on negotiations with a patently untrustworthy king. Although the Scots had actively
been considering a further round of talks since the autumn of 1645, the
Lords and the Commons only seem to have given renewed impetus to
peace proposals at the beginning of 1646. The Scottish commissioners
were originally excluded from these discussions which commenced not
in the full Committee of Both Kingdoms but in a sub-committee and
resulted in the drawing up of terms that made an appearance in July as
the Newcastle Propositions. The king was then in Scottish custody, the
Covenanting army having withdrawn from Newark to Newcastle following his arrival at their camp in May. Throughout the protracted
process of negotiation the Scots remained reluctant to alter their standpoint at Uxbridge in 1644–5.

They took issue on three substantive and two subsidiary points of difference from the Parliamentary position. The Presbyterians had secured
agreement that the religious imperatives of the Solemn League and

Covenant would be sustained. However, the Scots, even though they were becoming reconciled to the replacement of episcopacy by erastian Presbyterianism in the Church of England, were unconvinced that any meaningful Parliamentary pressure would be exerted on Charles to take the Covenant. The Independents had insisted that the English militia as well as the executive and judiciary should come under parliamentary control for 20 years. The Scots did not regard control over the militia as solely an English issue. The effective exclusion of royal control for life was too long and a further disincentive to Charles to covenant. The issue of control over the forces in Ireland was in danger of going by default if the Parliamentarians took no account of Scottish interests. The current exclusion of Scots from discussions on Irish affairs was again viewed as a breach in the spirit of the Solemn League and contrary to the understanding upon which the Covenanting army had intervened in the English civil war. While there was little doubt that meaningful Scottish participation on the Committee of Both Kingdoms had run its course in relation to British affairs, the Covenanting leadership was insistent that the making of peace and war were common issues for Scotland and England. Accordingly, they sought the revival of the conservators of the peace established under the Treaty of London to act as a confederal council for Britain. Finally, the Scots were adamant that they must be meaningfully recompensed for their expenditure and their arrears of supply for maintaining their forces in both Ireland and England.[37]

Argyll, the driving force behind British confederation, had attempted to transcend divisions within and between Parliamentarians and Covenanters in a celebrated speech to the Grand Committee of Both Houses in June 1646. On the one side, English intransigence towards an accommodation with the Covenanters had grown now that the king was in Scottish custody. The Lords still exercised a restraining influence on the Scotophobia then rampant in the Commons, who maintained that the disposal of the king was a purely English, not a British, matter. Nonetheless, internal divisions between Presbyterians and Independents were a further complication, especially as the New Model Army inclined towards the latter in terms of restricting royal authority and promoting a controlled measure of religious toleration. On the other side, the Scottish Estates were increasingly restless about the continuing cost of military intervention in England and Ireland. Moreover, there were limited prospects for relief from excessive Sound tolls, the Covenanters having provided no substantive assistance to Sweden in its recent successful war against Denmark–Norway. Argyll was also experiencing increasing difficulty in holding together the radical Covenanting main-stream. The purging of public offices in the wake of the Scottish civil war had witnessed the emergence of a distinctive grouping of gentry and burgesses intent on the political exclusion of all nobles, their clients and associates tainted by association with Royalism. An act of proscription, which passed through the Scottish Estates in January, had imposed swingeing fines equivalent to as much as six years' rents on all those deemed delinquent or malignant. In these trying circumstances, Argyll steadfastly maintained the imperative of confederal action, while affirming that the move from regal to complete union remained a visionary ideal. The 'Long Parliament' should not negotiate unilaterally with Charles I and the Scottish armies in England and Ireland should be promptly supplied.[38]

Although the Covenanting leadership conceded reluctantly that the Newcastle Propositions should be presented without amendment to the king, his outright rejection of them left the Scots with the alternative of negotiating an honourable withdrawal from England or becoming embroiled in war with the Parliamentary forces. Nevertheless, their retention of the king until satisfactory recompense for past services had been agreed increased the ire of the Independents, detached the Presbyterians and led to a marked decline in support from their most steadfast constituency, the city of London. Siren voices in the 'Long Parliament' sought to deny the Covenanting army any recompense and were even pressing for reparations for the Scottish occupation of the north of England. Military commanders there, such as Sydenham Poyntz, were demanding the speedy withdrawal of the Covenanting army. In these circumstances, Loudoun maintained to the Grand Committee of Both Houses at the outset of October that the Covenanters had behaved with candour and integrity in their proceedings 'towards the King and our Brethren of England'. The Covenanting leadership, though wary of any toleration that threatened unity in religion, was determined that the disposal of the king should be effected by the joint advice and consent of both kingdoms, and that 'the Unity between the Kingdomes may be inviolably preserved'.[39]

Initiative in negotiating final terms for the withdrawal of the Covenanting army and the handing over of the king was taken by the Presbyterians, who saw a satisfactory resolution without recourse to the war threatened by the Independents as a means of consolidating their control over the 'Long Parliament'. The growing confidence and assertiveness of the Presbyterians was evident in the state funeral accorded to Essex on 22 October, the elaborate ceremonial commemorating a political prince as much as an aristocratic grandee.[40] Holles played a key role in securing £400,000 as compensation and getting the Covenanters to agree that this sum should be paid in two equal instalments, the first when the Covenanting army withdrew from England, the second to follow when funds became available. In effect, this was probably the first performance-related transfer between Scotland and England. Although the brothers de Bellièvre had been dispatched from France to mediate between the king and the 'Long Parliament' in July 1646, Charles remained as obstinate to French as to Scottish overtures to negotiate. Lingering hopes that he would realise the gravity of his situation and accept the Newcastle Propositions were dashed by a second refusal on 20 December. Hamilton, now freed from English captivity and restored to the Scottish Estates, attempted to delay giving up the king until firm assurances were given about his safety. However, Argyll had reasserted his control over the Scottish Estates, which resolved that an uncovenanted king should not be brought to Scotland. A vote on 16 January 1647 ensured that Charles was left at Newcastle, where he was duly handed over to the Parliamentarians 14 days later. The Covenanters had received no guarantees for his safety or for the future of the Stuart monarchy in England.[41]

Scotland Reclaimed, Ireland Lost?

In England, although they were steadily on the defensive after the Covenanting intervention at the beginning of 1644, the Royalists exercised effective and prolonged control of Cornwall, the West Country, Wales, the Welsh Marches and the western Midlands during the first phase of civil war. This control was manifest by sword, and by pen through such newsbooks as *Mercurius Aulicus*. In Ireland, while the Royalists under Ormond held Dublin throughout the rebellion until its surrender in the summer of 1647, the Catholic Confederates maintained the main brunt of opposition to the English Parliamentarians and the Scottish Covenanters. Paradoxically, in Scotland, the one kingdom where political control appeared to be unrivalled under the Covenanting movement from the close of the Bishops' Wars, the Royalists came closest to reclaiming it. This situation was brought about by the assistance afforded by the Catholic Confederates to the brilliant northern campaign mounted by Montrose in 1644–5, a campaign which mobilised clan hosts as well as a hitherto untapped polemical dynamic as expressed through poems and songs in vernacular Gaelic.[42]

At the cessation of hostilities agreed between the Royalists and the Confederates on 15 September 1643, the military advantage appeared to have swung in favour of the latter. The return in the summer of 1642 of both Owen Roe O'Neill and Thomas Preston, two veterans of the Spanish army of Flanders, had brought greater professionalism to the Catholic forces in Ulster and Leinster respectively. However, the Confederate preference for avoiding set battles had not prevented Ormond from securing Royalist enclaves in Leinster. Although supplies from the 'Long Parliament' had been severely curtailed by the outbreak of civil war in England, the combined Covenanting and British forces were entrenched in Ulster. Murrough O'Brien, Lord Inchiquinn, had made significant inroads against the Confederate forces in Munster led by Donagh McCarthy, Viscount Muskerry. Indeed, a military appraisal on the state of Ireland, seemingly commissioned for the English Parliamentarians at the cessation, was far from pessimistic about Protestant prospects. Although only Dublin and two other counties in Leinster were in Protestant hands, as against the eight dominated by the Confederation, one county was disputed and the Protestants had strongholds in three others. In Munster, the Protestants held no counties, but they contested control of two, and had strongholds in two of the four counties under Catholic control. In Connacht, the Protestants claimed to hold Roscommon and have strongholds in two of the three Catholic counties. In Ulster, Down was the only one of the five counties under undisputed Protestant control. The discounting of a controlling Catholic presence certainly underestimated the dominance of Confederate forces in Armagh and Monaghan. In sum, the Confederation had a controlling interest in 20 out of the 32 Irish counties. Accordingly, any claims for Ireland to be a 'free state' – that is, a state free from British rule – must take account of the fact that the Confederate writ was neither accepted nor unchallenged in over a third of counties in 1643 and never extended to the whole island prior to the dissolution of the Confederation six years later.[43]

The 12-month cessation also posed a strategic problem of conflicting interests for the Catholic Confederation that endured until 1649. The insular or Irish perspective required the pursuit of total victory before seeking an accommodation with the king to secure the Catholic recovery of all of Ireland. The alternative Royalist or Britannic perspective encouraged the Confederation to seek an expeditious settlement with the king and the release of Irish forces to counter the threat posed by the English Parliamentarians. A compromise between those positions was offered by the refusal of the Scottish and British forces to accept the cessation since it would lead to 'the destruction of all the Protestants & subversion of the British plantations'. A direct assault on Ulster was not entrusted to Owen Roe O'Neill, however, but to the far less capable James Tuchet, 3rd Earl of Castlehaven, who was intent on avoiding a battle in order to contain the Scottish and British forces. Lack of supplies and the favouring of Scottish over British forces in the allocation of quarters had produced internal tensions that had even led to a unilateral decision by the Scottish commanders to return three of their ten regiments to Scotland in February 1644. However, Robert Munro's counter-offensive, which carried the fight into Leinster, provided the cover necessary for the Covenanting army to take over Royalist garrisons, such as Belfast in Ulster. Reforged solidarity with the British forces was underscored by their resolute imposition of the Solemn League and Covenant on Ulster from the spring of 1644.

Simultaneously, Protestant forces in Munster, similarly moved by apprehensions that the Confederates were intent upon 'the extirpation of the British nation' and the Protestant religion, were encouraged to throw in their lot with the Parliamentary-backed British forces. In vain, the Confederate Catholics in Leinster and Munster issued a revised oath on 10 May offering landed security and religious toleration for the 'moderate, conformable Protestant', but not for Puritans, who would support their endeavours to recover the royal prerogative forcibly wrested from the king by the English Parliamentarians. Moreover, Inchiquinn had condemned the cessation by July and, having been denied the lord presidency of Munster by Charles I, returned to the field when given the same office by the 'Long Parliament'. In the meantime, Ormond's refusal to aid the Confederation in Ulster severely strained the prospects of converting the cessation into a lasting peace and denied Charles's hopes of meaningful reinforcements for his English campaign.[44]

Nevertheless, the second prong of the Confederate strategy, which was complementary to the assault on Ulster, was to pursue a Scottish rather than an English theatre of war. The defensive withdrawal of Covenanting forces from Ulster would also restrict further mobilisation of Scottish troops to aid both the English Parliamentarians and the British forces in Ulster. The main architect of this strategy was Randal MacDonnell, Earl of Antrim, who secured the support of both the king and the Supreme Council at Kilkenny to ship 2000 Irish troops to the western seaboard of Scotland under his charismatic kinsman Alasdair MacColla in June 1644. MacColla was charged to link up with Montrose, as the supreme Royalist commander in Scotland. While this was undoubtedly a far from disinterested scheme by Antrim to run the expeditionary force rebuffed by Strafford in 1639, only the logistical and financial support afforded by the Supreme Council made this endeavour feasible. MacColla, whose family had been evicted from Colonsay in the Inner Hebrides by Argyll during the First Bishops' War, had twice been thwarted in his attempts to recover the island, the last having been as recent as November 1643. Montrose, who had been operating inter-mittently on both sides of the border without any appreciable degree of military success in the spring of 1644, had operated independently of the guerrilla resistance being pursued disjointedly in north-east Scotland by the Marquess of Huntly. Irish intervention ensured the purposeful joining together of hitherto disparate Royalist forces in Scotland, which the Covenanting movement had not hitherto regarded as a serious threat.[45]

Although his relationship with the noble house of Huntly remained problematic throughout the Scottish civil war, Montrose provided the political credibility necessary to convince clans throughout the High-lands and Islands to come out for the Royalist cause. Notwithstanding MacColla's charismatic appeal as an epic hero of the Gael, his personal following, even within the branches of the ClanDonald on the western seaboard, was limited. His chequered record of commitment to the Roy-alists and the Confederates in Ireland occasioned antipathy rather than admiration in the Scottish Lowlands. The Royalist cause in Scotland, as elsewhere in the British Isles, was dependent primarily on family con-nections, a fact that accentuated the importance of clan hosts as terri-torial levies. Clan support for Charles I was essentially but not exclusively reactionary. Pragmatically, the clan were reacting against the centralised demands of the Covenanting movement for ideological, military and financial commitment; against the imposition of Presbyterianism; and against powerful magnates, most notably Argyll, whose public espousal of the Covenanting cause masked private territorial ambition. Princi-pled support was rooted in the traditional values of clanship that were projected nationally onto the political stage. As trustees for Scotland, the royal house of Stuart had a hereditary right to rule. In turn, Charles I's fight for his three kingdoms was just and righteous.

By mixing guerrilla warfare with pitched battles after they joined forces in August 1644, the Royalist commanders ran up a series of bloody victories which commenced at Tippermuir, Perthshire, on 1 September and culminated in the defeat of the Covenanting forces at Kilsyth, Stirlingshire, on 15 August 1645. The brilliance of their campaigning wholly outmanoeuvred and exposed the ineptitude of the Covenanting commanders, such as Argyll, who were originally charged with eradicating the Royalist threat in Scotland. Although troops withdrawn from England under David Leslie reasserted Covenanting dominance by defeating Montrose at Philiphaugh, Selkirkshire, on 13 September, the movement had retained no more than a minority commitment among the clans. The Royalist campaign, however, was scarred by the extensive devastation of territories in the southern and central Highlands and by the sacking of towns such as Aberdeen and Dundee. No tangible territorial acquisitions were made for the Royalists in the Lowlands. Certainly, widespread acquiescence in and resignation about the achievements of Montrose meant there was a good chance of his effecting Charles I's summoning of a parliament for Glasgow. However, the departure of MacColla and most of the clan levies after Kilsyth proved a critical loss. While Royalist commentators uncharitably attributed this departure to Montrose's refusal to let the clans sack Glasgow, MacColla was actually intent on fulfilling Antrim's commission to secure the western seaboard and maintain a bridgehead with Ireland.[46]

Nevertheless, the defeat at Philiphaugh led to the English ordinance of October 1644 for no quarter to the Irish being extended to Scotland. The Irish troops had provided the professional backbone for the Royalist forces in Scotland; they had also taken the lead in the sacking of Scottish towns. Irish soldiers and their camp followers were slaughtered, 'with such savage and inhumane crueltie, as nether Turke nor Scithean was ever hard to have done the lyke'. Even in Royalist eyes this conduct was partially justified by the total lack of compassion the Irish troops had exhibited in their ubiquitous killing of 'all they could be maister of, without any motion of pitie, or any consideration of humanity'.[47]

MacColla's maintenance of a bridgehead with Ireland did lead to his temporary reinforcement by Antrim in July 1646. However, Antrim's stay in Scotland was curtailed by instructions from Charles I, then in the custody of the Covenanting army in England, that the Royalist forces in Scotland should surrender. Nonetheless, MacColla continued to maintain his bridgehead for another 14 months in the forlorn hope that Antrim would be able to secure renewed assistance from the increasingly fractious and financially stretched Catholic Confederation. Although he defied Charles I, MacColla can be viewed as a more successful Royalist commander than Montrose, whose star waned on their parting. From his defeat at Philiphaugh until his departure into exile in September 1646, Montrose was a spent force in Scotland. His recruiting ability in the Lowlands was severely restricted by his close identification with the clans. His access to towns was barred by the spread of plague in the wake of the return of the avenging Covenanting army from England. His tetchy relationship with Huntly dissolved into acrimony and the Gordons reverted to their freelance campaigning, which continued sporadically until November 1647. While MacColla was not obliged to lay siege to large towns, his continuing waging of guerrilla warfare was distinctively less naïve and more constructive. MacColla had built up a ready reservoir of support among the clans opposed to the territorial ambitions of the ClanCampbell. His prolonged occupation of Kintyre and Islay continued to detract from Argyll's standing within the Covenanting movement.[48]

Although Royalist endeavours to reclaim Covenanted Scotland were effectively terminated at Philiphaugh, the Confederate intervention had reactivated tensions between the Scottish and British forces in Ulster. The longstanding concerns of the latter about discriminatory funding had not been resolved by the renewed endeavours of the Committee of Both Kingdoms to secure more regular supplies from the spring of 1644. The supplementary complaints of the British forces about inadequate protection afforded by the Parliamentarian navy under Warwick were compounded by the endeavours of the Covenanting leadership in Edinburgh and in London to have British as well as Scottish forces withdrawn from Ulster to resist Montrose.[49] Scottish territorial ambitions in Ulster were also questionable. The arrival of ten Covenanting regiments in May 1642 had provided the opportunity not only to retrench but also to consolidate Presbyterianism in Antrim and Down. While not every regiment had a kirk session on arrival, the ministers serving as chaplains along with leading officers serving as ruling elders had formed a presbytery of Ulster within a month. This presbytery gradually incorporated civilian congregations in parishes occupied by the army, provided the local ministers and gentry eligible for eldership purged themselves of past acceptance of the 'black oath'. A fresh injection of young ministers coupled to the licensed imposition of the Solemn League and Covenant in Ulster provided the impetus for the expansion of Presbyterianism into the counties of Derry, Donegal and Tyrone from the spring of 1644. Within Scotland, the Committee of Estates endorsed the special watching brief exercised by the Kirk over Ulster. In the spirit of confederation, this was also endorsed initially by the English parliament. Accordingly, the presbytery of Ulster served as ideological guardians of the Covenant against civil abuses by an army suffering from shortage of provision and pay and against sectaries, Anabaptists and other malign influences. Yet it was arguably as much out of respect for this confederal alliance as for the Britannic integrity of the *ius imperium* of Charles I that the occupying Covenanting army had made no attempt to impose its committee structure on Ulster, or even to annex the province pending fulfilment of English parliamentary promises for supply and brotherly assistance.[50]

The severity of the quartering and other exactions imposed on the Ulster population by the Covenanting forces distressed prominent Scottish planters, especially those such as James Hamilton, Viscount Clandeboye, who was suspected of past dealings with Strafford. Clandeboye actually appealed for relief over the heads of the Scottish commanders to the Covenanting leadership in Edinburgh, a route never seemingly attempted by those distressed by the Scottish forces in the northern counties of England. Notwithstanding tensions between the planters and the armed forces, there was a growing tendency to identify the interests of the Old and the New Scots rather than maintain British solidarity as supplies authorised from London became increasingly haphazard. By the summer of 1645, the Scottish army in Ulster consisted of around a quarter of the Covenanting forces contracted to the English Parliamentarians, but they were receiving no more than a seventh of supplies, whether as money or payments in kind. Nonetheless the Scottish forces were prepared to go on the offensive in Leinster to complement the British advance into Connacht. The decisive defeat of the Covenanting army by the forces of the Catholic Confederation at Benburb, County Tyrone, on 5 June 1646 not only stalled this offensive, but peremptorily ended the Covenanters' working accommodation with the Parliamentarians in Ireland six months before the Scottish forces withdrew from England. Indeed, this accommodation had been under threat since the appointment of the prominent Independent Philip Sidney, Viscount Lisle, as lord-lieutenant of Ireland in April. Simultaneously, genuine fears were emerging within the Covenanting movement that Ireland 'would bee lost' to England as the result of the Confederates' international machinations.[51]

At the same time as the Scots willingly and the English reluctantly were being integrated into the northern European, anti-Habsburg alliance, the Confederation of Irish Catholics won brief international recognition for their claim to be a 'free state' by their close association with the pro-Habsburg forces. On the one hand, the Confederates could draw on the long-established military, commercial and ecclesiastical networks maintained by the Irish diaspora to appeal primarily for financial assistance throughout the 1640s. The Confederates also gained militarily from the return of committed Catholic troops, especially from Spanish service, and confessionally from the disciplined inculcation of the Counter-Reformation by a clergy trained predominantly in continental seminaries. On the other hand, although the Confederation sent envoys to several European capitals and received diplomats in Kilkenny, these were rarely accredited since Ireland, notwithstanding the Catholic rebellion, still ranked at best as 'a third rate power'. Moreover, diplomatic missions, particularly after the arrival of the papal agent, Giovanni Battista Rinuccini, Bishop of Fermo, in October 1645, served to destabilise Confederate politics and negate prospects of a secure peace with the Royalists. Indeed, the diplomatic entanglements of the Confederates, further complicated by the determination of French agents to compete with rather than complement their Spanish and papal counterparts, were as much disruptive as supportive. Spain, overstretched in its continental commitments and contending with revolts in Portugal, Catalonia and Naples, viewed Catholic Ireland principally as a source of military recruits. France, which was intent on ensuring the major supply of Irish recruits into its forces, saw Ireland as an integral but also a component part in securing a British accommodation. Not only Confederate Catholics, but also conservative Scottish Covenanters and English Royalists, with or without Presbyterian assistance, were to be deployed to prevent the eclipse of the Stuart monarchy.

Only the papacy was committed unconditionally to no accommodation with Charles I without religious concessions. At the same time, the general willingness in Rome to see the war in Ireland purely as a religious struggle led to the forces of the Catholic Confederation being viewed as more ardent crusaders than they actually were. In terms of financial resources, the papacy probably had greater liquidity than any other European power. Unfortunately, the Vatican did not provide remotely adequate funding to match the personal zeal and commitment of Rinuccini as papal nuncio in Ireland. Prior to his departure in February 1649, the Catholic Confederation was effectively torn apart by French and papal factions. Although the Scottish Covenanters did release forces for Swedish, French and Dutch service, this never threatened to be debilitating, unlike the Spanish and French demands on the Irish Confederates.[52]

However, the granting of letters of marque and passports for commercial shipping by the continental agents of the Confederation both built up and sustained the naval resources at their disposal in the Irish Sea. The substantive presence of Dunkirker privateers was a major challenge to the Parliamentary navy, which tended to concentrate on preventing Royalist and Confederate forces being brought over to England rather than on securing unchallenged control of the territorial waters around the British Isles. By land as well as by sea, the Confederates built up sufficient forces that could more than hold their own against Scottish and English troops in Ireland, albeit they would only appear to have enjoyed numerical superiority in 1647, when the Parliamentary presence in Ireland was considerably affected by Leveller agitation in the New Model Army. However, their military capacity to sustain a standing army cannot be isolated from the state apparatus necessary for its support. Only in Ulster and Leinster was there a possibility of meaningfully servicing a standing army prior to the cessation of 1643. Thereafter, the fiscal basis for sustained support was lacking beyond Munster and south Leinster. By its nature, the Confederation was not given to a centralised structure, unlike the Scottish Covenanters from the outset of the Bishops' Wars and the English Parliamentarians from the creation of the New Model Army in 1645. Its provincial forces never controlled or secured supplies from the whole island, and areas of fiscal potential, such as Galway and Mayo in Connacht, remained largely untapped because of the intense factionalism occasioned by the peace process with the Royalists.[53]

The Confederates had entered negotiations with Ormond as custodians of the Irish perspective. They hoped to build upon the cessation of hostilities by securing a lasting treaty that would give Ireland autonomy and religious toleration under the Stuart monarchy. Negotiations, which were moved from Ireland to Oxford in November 1643, continued intermittently until they reached a conclusion in March 1646, promulgated as the first Ormond peace at the beginning of August. Conducted against the backdrop of the Uxbridge treating between the Royalists, the Scottish Covenanters and the English Parliamentarians, similar concerns were expressed with regard to religion, the militia and checks to executive power. The practice of Catholicism was to remain a prerogative grace rather than a constitutional right. The legislative independence of the Irish parliament was not secured. Nevertheless, there was a fair chance that the plantations in Connacht would be reversed. Above all, Charles came to consider the Confederates as allies rather than rebels. However, the Irish negotiations also had to contend with Lord Digby's support for Queen Henrietta Maria's endeavours to mobilise French support and, simultaneously, seek a private accommodation with the Confederates. The king's authorising of separate negotiations in Ireland by Edward Somerset, Earl of Glamorgan (later 2nd Marquess of Worcester), from June 1645 proved counter-productive. Ormond's negotiating position was undermined by the secret treaty the gormless Glamorgan negotiated with the Confederates in August, which offered 10,000 troops in return for complete toleration for Catholics and their retention of ecclesiastical property reoccupied since 1641. While this secret treaty appeared to offer English Royalists a vital lifeline in the aftermath of Naseby, both Charles I and Ormond were obliged to repudiate it when it was rewritten at the behest of Rinuccini in December. This second version prioritised full concession of religious and civil liberties to Catholics before troops were sent to England.[54]

Rinuccini's penchant for excommunicating all Confederates prepared to accept the Ormond peace, as later those in Munster who reached an accommodation with Inchiquinn in May 1648, emphatically polarised the cause of the Irish Catholics. Despite a tendency within Covenanting and Parliamentary circles to view this split as being between the Old English and the native Irish, this rather unsophisticated categorisation was certainly not shared by the vernacular Gaelic poets. Indeed, the splits within the Confederates appear to have mirrored those within the English Parliamentarians over peace and war. Like the Presbyterians, those pursuing peace were a conservative grouping headed by Viscount Muskerry and Richard Bellings, who sought toleration and landed security rather than the reversal of the plantations. Accordingly, they moved towards a Britannic perspective, particularly those who shared Ormond's ire that Rinuccini was steering the Confederation to throw off its allegiance to Charles I in favour of the papacy. This situation was viewed as no more tolerable to Charles than Philip IV of Spain having to contend with Catalonian endeavours to switch their allegiance to France. There had even been misplaced hopes that disgruntled Scottish forces in Ulster would be prepared to join this fledgling Royalist coalition prior to Benburb. The radicals supporting the papal nuncio, who included Maurice, Viscount Roche, and Dermot O'Brien, advocated the primacy of a military solution for the full restoration of a Catholic Ireland. In the same way that the Independents redefined the Gothic perspective with the withdrawal of the Scottish forces from England, so the radicals redefined the Irish perspective by their attempted removal of the island's Parliamentary and Covenanting forces. The prospects for a moderating, middling group under Nicholas Plunkett of Meath receded rapidly as the Confederation began to turn in on itself.[55]

By the autumn of 1647, the Ulster forces of Owen Roe O'Neill were looking south to aid the Rinuccini interest rather than pressing home the advantage gained over the Scottish forces in the north after Benburb. Moreover, the Confederate forces in Leinster were defeated on 8 August at Dungan's Hill, County Meath, by recently arrived Parliamentary forces under Michael Jones, who had taken up Ormond's offer to surrender Dublin. On 13 November, Inchiquinn defeated the Army of Munster at Knocknanuss, Co. Cork, where MacColla was a prominent casualty on the Confederate side. By the outset of 1648, the Irish phase of British revolutionary politics had become the first in the three kingdoms to implode. As part of a reinvigorated Britannic perspective being brokered by the French from Scotland as well as Ireland, the conservative Confederates under Muskerry made common cause with the Royalists under Ormond, the Presbyterian-inclined Parliamentary forces in Munster under Inchiquinn and the British forces in Ulster, from where the Scots were withdrawing gradually and gracelessly. At the same time, the redefined Irish perspective under Rinuccini was seeking an accommodation with the Independent-inclined Parliamentary forces in Leinster under Michael Jones and were looking to retain Scottish forces in Ulster. Internal rivalries within the Confederation served instead to allow Jones, backed by the former Royalist turned Parliamentarian commander George Monck, to push on into Ulster. The pendulum appeared to swing in favour of the Britannic over the Irish perspective when Ormond concluded a second peace on 17 January 1649, which conceded the free but not unconditional exercise of Catholicism and the retention of ecclesiastical property. Rinuccini left Ireland on 24 February. By this juncture, however, Irish affairs were no longer setting the agenda.[56]

The lord-lieutenancy exercised briefly but divisively by Viscount Lisle had more than hinted at a Gothic reappraisal of Ireland's constitutional relationship as a dependency of the English parliament, not the crown. This situation also carried the threat of the renewal of plantation as commended by Lisle's associate Sir John Temple. The centrality of Ireland to British revolutionary politics was reflected in the Committee for Irish Affairs, hitherto a sub-committee, taking over from the Committee of Both Kingdoms at Derby House in October 1646.

Clotworthy resurfaced as a leading ally of Holles. The Committee, however, proved a battleground for competing Presbyterian and Independent interests until the latter secured undisputed control with the help of the New Model Army in August 1647. Thereafter, the abbreviated Derby House Committee became a platform for Gothic triumphalism marked by the suppression of the Levellers, the defeat of the Engagers and the regicide – all key events which set the scene for the Cromwellian occupation of Ireland and Scotland in 1649–51.[57]

Gothic Triumphalism

With the transfer of Charles I from the Covenanters to the Parliamentarians and his lodging in Holmby Castle, Northamptonshire, political initiative appeared to pass to the Presbyterians, who were still committed to a negotiated peace. Retaining the support of the city of London, the Presbyterians flexed their muscles by having Viscount Lisle dismissed as lord-lieutenant of Ireland in March 1647. However, Holles and his associates overreached themselves on the Irish issue. Their determination to stand down most of the infantry units within the New Model Army other than those designated to assist the Parliamentary war effort in Ireland provoked a twin reaction in the country and the Army which ceded advantage to the Independents. Attempts to recover arrears of monthly maintenance while imposing a new levy to supply the troops in Ireland provoked a further round of grass-roots resistance in 14 counties as well as the city of London which were far more extensive than the Clubmen protests of 1645.[58] Simultaneously, extensive arrears of pay, a lack of indemnity for past acts of war and the Presbyterian mobilisation of disbanded troops of dubious provenance, 'the reformados', to reinforce the trained bands of London provoked agitation by both officers and soldiers in the New Model Army. On the instructions of Cromwell, Coronet George Joyce and his cavalry removed Charles I from Holmby at the beginning of June. Political discussions within the Army over the redress of grievances were broadened into the formulation of peace proposals in tandem with the Independents that were introduced to the Lords by Saye & Sele as the Heads of Proposals on 1 August. Collusive action was further evident when the New Model Army occupied London and intimidated the 'Long Parliament' five days later.[59]

The Heads of Proposals were probably the least restrictive terms offered to Charles I in England. Prominent Royalists were only to be barred from office for five years rather than for life, and the number of those denied an indemnity was reduced from 58 to seven. The king was to surrender control of the militia for ten rather than 20 years. The Triennial Act was to be replaced by biennial parliaments. Taking the Covenant was no longer to be compulsory. Independent congregations were to be tolerated outside an erastian Presbyterian structure, and Episcopalianism was even to be permitted, shorn of its coercive powers. While Charles was prepared to contemplate replacing the Privy Council with a Council of State, he was not prepared to compromise either on an episcopal establishment or on the militia. Negotiations were rendered redundant not only by the king's customary intransigence, but by an upsurge of agitation not restricted to the rank and file in the New Model Army. As a national institution, the Army had come to offer an alternative forum to parliament for articulate dissent and remedial programmes. An innovative, democratic polity for England marked the debates conducted at Putney from 28 October to 11 November 1647, when an uneasy truce was maintained with the Presbyterians and the city of London. The radical case, as specified in the Army's *Agreement of the People*, was led by Thomas Rainborow and John Wildman and drew on a 'Leveller' polemic that had begun with the much incarcerated John Lilburne in 1645. Colonel Henry Ireton, Cromwell's son-in-law, primarily presented the case for the officers and their Independent allies intent on maintaining unity.[60]

No less significant for British revolutionary politics was the radical challenge these debates presented to the prevailing Gothic perspective in the 'Long Parliament'. English liberty was not a continuous stream that had flowed since the incursion of the Anglo-Saxons, but was deemed by the Levellers to have been done away with by the Norman Conquest. The Gothic interpretation favoured by the Independents saw parliament as the supreme maintainer and the Army as the guardian of English religious and civil liberties. The Levellers sought a more proactive role for parliament, supported by the Army, to throw off the Norman yoke and meaningfully restore to all freeborn the religious and civil liberties undermined by both the monarchy and the propertied interest since 1066. Ireton, without doubting the integrity of his protagonists, stood by the social cohesion offered by the Gothic tradition of constitutional law, particularly as the Leveller emphasis on natural rather than civic rights appeared subversive of private property. The Levellers, however, stood neither for communism nor for unchecked individualism, but for the collective interests of the freeborn in a secular covenant of natural rights that promoted religious toleration. The confessional covenant of works and grace under which Puritans and Presbyterians required the limitation of monarchy was superseded. Sovereignty was vested in the people, not in parliament. Indeed, the people must be constantly vigilant lest government by the executive or the legislature encroach upon their natural rights and thereby break the true covenant to protect the people.[61]

Lauded historiographically as a radical point of departure from government by and for the propertied interest, there remained a critical gap between the process of Leveller agitation and the actual transformation of English government by written constitution. This gap contrasts notably with the Scottish moment when ideological policy was integrated into the political process.[62] The most immediate impact of the Leveller-inspired turmoil in the Army was the opportunity it afforded to Charles I to escape from Hampton Court and seek refuge in Carisbrooke Castle on the Isle of Wight. Having succeeded in ending the Putney Debates without a show of force, Fairfax moved swiftly to disperse the agitators. With the assistance of Cromwell, he crushed a belated effort at mutiny at Corkbrush Field, Ware, in mid-November. Nevertheless, Leveller influence within the New Model Army and on British revolutionary politics was by no means eradicated. The Levellers played an integral role in the pressure generated from within the Army to break off negotiations between the Parliamentarians and the king in January 1648, to secure the parliamentary prosecution of Charles I as 'that man of blood' from November, and to justify the subsequent regicide on 30 January 1649. The Levellers were also to the fore in protesting Cromwell's offensive endeavour to claim Ireland by conquest from May 1649.[63]

The Gothic threat to Ireland had particular ramifications in Scotland, where fears of sharing a provincial fate had revived a conservative element under Hamilton in the Scottish Estates during 1647. Although the Covenanting leadership had upheld the ideological consistency of their proceedings in England, their transfer of the king on top of radical endeavours to purge the conservatively inclined nobility in the wake of the Scottish civil war played into Hamilton's hands. While the Scottish commissioners who remained in London continued to be consulted on foreign and domestic matters relating to British revolutionary politics, John, Earl of Lauderdale, switched his allegiance from Argyll, as briefly did Loudoun on the prompting of Hamilton's brother William, Earl of Lanark. Lauderdale, Loudoun and Lanark covertly concluded the Engagement with Charles I in Carisbrooke Castle on 26 December 1647, to defend and restore the authority of Britannic monarchy.[64] The

Britannic Engagement, which came into force in 1648, was the first Scottish-instigated effort to promote incorporating union as prescribed by James VI and I in the wake of the regal union. Charles was not obliged by the Engagement to subscribe the Covenants. Ideological imperatives were further diluted by the stipulation that Presbyterianism would be imposed on England for a trial period of no more than three years. This effective abrogation of the Covenanters' power to hold monarchy to account through a 'tragicomediall' adventure was intolerable to the radicals, led by Argyll, who enjoyed the vociferous support of the commissioners for the Kirk now led by Robert Douglas since Henderson's death in late 1646. The Engagement, which effectively conceded that the Covenanters had lost the political initiative within the British Isles, represented a reactionary effort to reassert aristocratic dominance over Scotland and, simultaneously, promote a conservative resurgence in all three kingdoms.[65]

However, Scottish armed intervention in a renewed phase of civil war during 1648 only briefly raised the hopes of the English Royalists. The Engagers' invasion was not co-ordinated with localised resistance in Wales, Kent and Essex, nor with the brief Royalist resurgence on the border under Sir Marmaduke Langdale, nor with the naval mutiny in the Downs. French diplomatic brokerage notwithstanding, the Engagers did not make common cause with the Royalist coalition led by Ormond and Inchiquinn in Ireland, where the withdrawal of Covenanting forces under Sir George Munro hastened the demise of the armed Scottish presence in Ulster.[66] In England, where Marchmont Nedham reported the political transition through the pages of *Mercurius Pragmaticus*, the Britannic Engagement revived Scotophobia and the desire of the Independents to be quit of the Solemn League and Covenant. Although they had been intermittently suspected by the Independents and the Army for wishing to bring back Scottish forces during 1647, the Presbyterians remained aloof. Their residual commitment to the cause of both kingdoms took solace from the refusal of Argyll, Leven and David Leslie to participate in an expeditionary force that again began to unravel under Hamilton's uncertain military leadership.[67] The Engagers were soundly defeated by Cromwell at Preston, Lancashire, on 17 August. The New Model Army, supplemented by Independent militias in Leicester, Berkshire and Somerset vehemently opposed to a Britannic conservative resurgence, had effectively suppressed English dissent prior to the Engagers' invasion in July. Warwick had rallied the naval forces that had remained loyal to the Parliamentarians. Without supporting the

Engagers or blockading London, the mutineers were forced to seek shelter in the United Provinces by November.[68]

Scottish Royalists formerly allied to the Irish Confederates castigated the Britannic Engagement as a Tory endeavour. Conversely, conservative manipulation of the centralised committee structure to compel support led to a recurrence of petitioning on a scale unprecedented since 1637, against ungodly deviations from religious and constitutional fundamentals. The reaction of the conservative element was to extend the scope of treason for party advantage and impose martial law on recalcitrant localities. A grass-roots rising of the disaffected in the shires of Ayr and Lanark was vigorously suppressed at Mauchline Moor on 12 June 1648. However, once the news of Preston filtered back to Scotland, the radicals in western districts staged a successful revolt which commenced with the Whiggamore Raid on Edinburgh in September. Although Argyll and his supporters were checked temporarily at Stirling by Lanark, reinforced by the forces from Ireland under Munro, armed support from Oliver Cromwell, who had crossed the border to assist the Scottish radicals, persuaded the Engagers to give up the reins of government. Although Cromwell contemplated and many Scots feared a conquest, he was content to reinstall Argyll and the radicals in power with a renewed commitment to a policy of excluding political opponents from public office. While the Engagers were assured of their lives and property in return for disbanding their army, the rigorous application of the Act of Classes passed by the reconvened Scottish Estates in January 1649 entrenched schism within the movement.

The radical regime which came to power in Scotland at the outset of 1649 was committed to redressing the unremitting centralism that had been a feature of the Covenanting movement for the past 11 years and to a programme of social restructuring, including the imposition of the Revocation Scheme from below.[69] However, such radical programming was overtaken by news of the execution of Charles I on 30 January 1649. In England, as in Scotland, there had been an effective *coup d'état* by radical forces in late 1648. Although the 'Long Parliament' had effectively broken off negotiations with the Royalists at the outset of 1648, Presbyterians led by Holles had recommenced exploring the grounds for a settlement with Charles I in August. Negotiations, which dragged on until November under the guise of the Treaty of Newport, did mark a distinctive move away from the Heads of Proposals and back towards the Newcastle Propositions. The king was prepared to make concessions over the control of the militia and was willing to renew his concession to the Engagers for a trial period of three years for Presbyterianism in the Church of England. Nonetheless, the negotiations were unable to protect the king, now firmly imprisoned on the Isle of Wight, from increasingly assertive elements within the New Model Army, which occupied London on 2 December. Within four days, Colonel Thomas Pride had purged the 'Long Parliament': 317 MPs were arrested, excluded or walked out.[70]

The 'Rump Parliament' that was left, malleable to the control of Cromwell and the Independents, redefined English government in claiming that power was vested in the people and that the Commons represented supreme power. The Gothic perspective was thus redefined to ensure that the supremacy of the Commons overrode that of the monarchy or the Lords. Using this authority to establish a high court of justice on 6 January, Charles, who persisted with misplaced hopes for Ormond effecting a Royalist resurgence from Ireland, was brought to London and impeached as a tyrant, one implacably intent on 'the destruction of the fundamental laws and liberties' of England. After an eight-day trial from which the Lords was excluded, the king was sentenced to death on 27 January and duly executed three days later.[71]

News of the unilateral execution of Charles I was greeted with outrage in Scotland. Collaboration between the radical regimes in Edinburgh and London was sundered. The former's prompt proclamation of the Prince of Wales as Charles II on 5 February, not just as King of Scots but as King of Great Britain and Ireland, was a reassertion of the international identity of the house of Stuart within the context of confederal union. However, this proclamation and the subsequent opening up of negotiations in March with Charles, then in exile at Breda, to return as a covenanted monarch were also unilateral acts that in turn provoked profound indignation in England, where he was deemed King of Scots only.[72] Within a week of the regicide, the House of Lords and the monarchy had been abolished. Hamilton, whom Marchmont Nedham contended had a long pedigree as 'a fomentor of civil war', was duly executed for his leadership of the Britannic Engagement, albeit in his capacity as an English peer (Earl of Cambridge). With the Derby House Committee re-established as the Council of State from 13 February, the Gothic free state was proclaimed internationally on 14 May as the English Commonwealth (*Res Publica Anglicae*), untrammelled by any bilateral commitment to the Solemn League and Covenant which the Scots had breached by their Britannic Engagement.[73]

Cromwell's immediate priority, however, was not the correction of his errant former brethren in Scotland but the civilisation through conquest of Ireland, which was now regarded as a dependent state rather than a dependent kingdom. In the wake of the Leveller mutiny crushed at Burford, Oxfordshire, Cromwell conceded that the conquest of Ireland should not lead to the eradication of the native Irish or to their whole-sale confiscation. At his arrival, the Confederate forces allied to Ormond and Inchiquinn had driven the Confederate cohorts commanded by Owen Roe O'Neill deep into Ulster, where they met opposition from the Scottish troops under Sir George Munro, who had returned to Ireland after the failure of the Britannic Engagement. However, Munro's desultory attempts to support the Royalist coalition in Ulster only served to drive a further wedge between Scottish and English planters. George Monck, now firmly in command of the British forces in Ulster, concluded an expedient alliance with O'Neill for mutual support. Anticipation of Cromwell's invasion pushed Ormond back into Leinster and Inchiquinn into Munster. Eleven days before Cromwell landed near Dublin, Michael Jones decisively defeated Ormond at Rathmines on the Liffey on 2 August. Cromwell's brief but bloody campaign in Ireland was marked less by battles than by sieges, notably at Drogheda in September and at Wexford in October 1650, where his undoubted military brilliance was again tarnished by his penchant for the eradication of the ungodly. Notwithstanding a treaty between Ormond and O'Neill, Cromwellian forces had secured Ulster by the end of the year. In Munster, Inchiquinn's forces steadily mutinied and crossed over to join the troops led by his former Parliamentary associate Roger Boyle, Lord Broghill. By the time Cromwell left, in May 1650, Kilkenny had fallen and only the province of Connacht was offering substantial resistance, which took another three years to mop up. The conquest of Ireland was only effected after a massive injection of English troops and the licensing of almost 34,000 Irish soldiers to enter Spanish service.[74]

Although he did not leave Ireland for exile in France until December 1650, Ormond had effectively lost credibility among the Confederate forces by the death of O'Neill in November 1649. Nevertheless, Charles II continued to stall in his negotiations with the Scots in the vain hope that a Royalist coalition could be reforged in Ireland, with international support from Portugal, without his having to subscribe the Covenants. Indeed, the new monarch effectively sacrificed an attempt by Montrose to rekindle Royalist fortunes in Scotland with Scandinavian backing through the Orkney Isles in March 1650. Montrose met with no more success than the unco-ordinated guerrilla campaigns mounted by Royalists in the north of Scotland the previous year, which had led to the execution of Huntly, imprisoned in Edinburgh since his capture in late 1647. Montrose himself met a similar fate after his decisive defeat at Carbisdale in Sutherland on 27 April. Taken to Edinburgh, he was hanged in May. Charles, however, had not only compromised his credibility with Sweden and Denmark–Norway, but he had weakened the prospects of an inclusive patriotic accommodation between Covenanters and Royalists in Scotland.[75]

Having taken full advantage of the factional disarray among Royalists and Catholic Confederates to conquer Ireland, Cromwell was likewise able to exploit division within the Covenanting movement to effect the occupation of Scotland. The Cromwellian occupation of Scotland was undoubtedly facilitated by the fatal capacity of the Covenanters to snatch defeat from the jaws of victory at Dunbar, East Lothian, on 3 September 1650. Although the country was afflicted by endemic military and financial exhaustion, the Scottish predilection for ideological schism was unquenchable. The drive for radical purity in the wake of the Act of Classes had led to the internally damaging split between the Remonstrants (later the Protestors) and the Resolutioners. The Remonstrants, supported by Rutherford and Wariston, were certainly correct in deeming Charles II unreliable. Their insistence that their duty to support a covenanted king did not commit them unconditionally to a patently sinful Charles II was ideologically consistent with the Covenanting distinction between the person and the office of monarchy. But the Resolutioners, the radical majority led by Argyll and backed by Robert Douglas, claimed with equal validity to adhere to Covenanting principles. They countered with the curse of Meroz: that the pursuit of radical purity carried the danger of undefiled inactivity in the face of the external threat from Cromwell. The determination of the western association of radical Remonstrants to pursue their own campaign ceded Cromwell control of Scotland south of the Forth–Clyde by the close of 1650.[76]

Nonetheless, the patriotic accommodation of Resolutioners and former Royalists was consolidated in fundamentalist terms by the coronation of Charles II at Scone, Perthshire, as King of Great Britain and Ireland on 1 January 1651. Robert Douglas, who preached for two hours, reminded Charles II that his compulsory subscription of the Covenants was to deny absolutism, for 'total government is not upon a king'. The religious and constitutional imperatives of Covenanting were reaffirmed, the power to hold monarchy to account exercised by the political nation was endorsed and the vesting of the right of resistance in those who have power, 'as the estates of a land', was reasserted. The Act of Classes was eventually suspended to allow former Royalists to participate on the Committee of Estates, reconstituted as the Committee for Managing the Affairs of the Army at the outset of April. However, the erroneous British military strategy of the new king, who pushed for further Scottish intervention in England without assurances of support from Presbyterians and Royalists disaffected with the Commonwealth, came to grief at Worcester on 3 September 1651. Scottish independence was fatally undermined, albeit the Cromwellian occupation, already scarred by the sack of Dundee, took another 12 months to complete.[77]

6 Commonwealth and Protectorate, 1651–1660

In the wake of the regicide, Cromwell and his Independents and Army associates found themselves with a news management problem. Charles I's dignified refusal to become entangled in a show trial, his majestic bearing on the scaffold and his uncompromising support for Episcopalianism made him a martyr for Britannic monarchy. A cult of kingly sacrifice, based on the twin pillars of justice and piety, was soon developed through *Eikon Basilike*, the purported meditations of Charles I as he awaited execution, and later through the apologetic writings of the likes of Peter Heylyn, former chaplain to Archbishop Laud. News management was not just a domestic issue, since considerable international hostility was generated by the regicide.[1] The Emperor Alexia of Russia immediately cut off all trading relations with England through the Muscovy Company and sought concerted European action against the Commonwealth. France imposed a trade embargo and promised armed support. The States General of the United Provinces also offered prompt assistance to Charles II for his restoration. A group of Scottish Royalists assassinated Dr Isaac Dorislaus when he presented himself at The Hague in 1649 as agent for the Commonwealth. English Royalists also went unpunished when they assassinated Anthony Assam, the first emissary sent from the Commonwealth to Spain in 1650.[2] Commonwealth diplomats continued to face the very real threat of violence until well into the 1650s in the United Provinces, the Hanseatic towns and Scandinavia. Indeed, the Commonwealth underwent a siege mentality as newsletter writers came to appreciate that 'the English are become odious' on the continent. Grandiose plans for reprisals against the regicides never materialised, however.[3]

Charles II badly damaged his international credibility by his maladroit sacrificing of Montrose's expedition to Scotland in 1650. The failure of his patriotic accommodation with the Scots deprived him of any foreseeable prospect of power in the three kingdoms and made him a dependent pensioner rather than an independent player among European states. By the beginning of 1652, there appeared no real prospect of an internal resurgence to restore Britannic monarchy. Certainly, Cromwell's move against the Scots, which had led Fairfax to step down as commander of the New Model Army, received a mixed press in England, where hopes of British reconciliation were markedly receding in the wake of the regicide.[4] Among Presbyterians, especially among the metropolitan core for whom Covenanting was the foundation of political authority, Cromwell was portrayed as Strafford's heir in his weakening of Protestant solidarity, constitutional government and international resistance to Spanish hegemony in Europe and the Americas.[5] Among Independents, however, the defeat of the Scots was vital to the establishment of a free state and represented the ultimate British phase of Gothic triumphalism over Royalists, Presbyterians and Levellers. Their alliance with the Army found executive expression through the Council of State, which demonstrated that it was not in thrall to the 'Rump Parliament' by overseeing the military campaigns for the occupation of Ireland and Scotland, by organising a massive expansion of the Commonwealth navy and by conducting war with the Dutch.[6]

The establishment of the Commonwealth, based on the New Model Army and the fiscal resources of the 'Rump Parliament' which was dominated by the Independents, had two further advantages. Firstly, the creation of this military–fiscal state was reinforced by a mission to explain it at home and abroad carried out principally by two accomplished Latin scholars, John Thurloe and John Milton. They deployed their respective diplomatic and polemical skills in the service of the Commonwealth, 'and in a manner suitable to the ancient Glory of the English Nation'.[7] Secondly, the rival perspectives to the Gothic were in disarray. The Britannic was virtually subliminal. The Scottish was caught up in the introspection of the Protestor–Resolutioner controversy that dominated the Kirk. This acerbic schism prevented the calling of a general assembly during the 1650s and confirmed the sundering of the radical mainstream that had been a feature of the Covenanting movement in the 1640s. Vigorous contesting of the flame of ideological purity left both sides impervious to pleas for toleration. The Irish perspective was embroiled in the land issue. Removal from and relocation within Ireland became a pronounced feature of the 1650s as the renewal of plantations sought to consolidate the English, not the British, interest there. Irish landowners concentrated on survival strategies rather than political resistance.[8]

A Gothic Engagement

The emergence of the New Model Army in England had not only marked a shift away from reliance on provincial forces, but also constituted a key moment in the establishment of an assertive English national consciousness among the rank and file as well as the officers. This sense of identity was enhanced through the conquest of Ireland and Scotland, conquests necessitated by the refusal of both kingdoms to accept the creation of an English republic through regicide. The Irish were viewed as uncivilised and deluded, but neither subhuman nor beyond redemption. The Scots were chided as misled, even false, brethren who had strayed from the path of godliness through the uniting of Covenanters and Royalists in a patriotic accommodation to support Charles II. Indeed, a sense of English superiority seems to have pervaded the New Model Army, particularly as officers and soldiers viewed themselves as freeborn Englishmen who shared a common heritage of rights and liberties. Although some in the Army considered that England was not fully settled as a republic, the quashing of Leveller mutinies meant that there were few dissenting English voices to conquest in Ireland and Scotland. Under occupation, the Scots experienced greater leniency, though the Irish were rarely condemned as barbarous or treacherous prior to the brutalising impact of the guerrilla war. Thus, their political resistance to occupation was negated as the predatory activities of rapparees, the bandit groups defamed as Tories. The Scots Gaels, like their Irish counterparts, were to be the butt of ethnically debasing polemic. Royalist clans which refused to accept subjugation were also deemed Tories. They were smeared by association with predatory bands of caterans who had thrown over the social constraints of clanship, and with moss-troopers, former cavalrymen from all over the British Isles who had taken refuge in the Highlands and supported themselves by racketeering.[9]

With the Cromwellian forces triumphant in all three kingdoms by the autumn of 1651, enforced union all round was marked first by the Commonwealth, then by the Protectorate of England, Scotland and Ireland from 1654. In essence, these were labels of convenience for the concentration of power that reasserted England's intrusive hegemony under the guise of republicanism. Marchmont Nedham became a ready apologist in *Mercurius Politicus*. The deliberate avoidance of the term 'Great Britain' denoted not only a chauvinistic disregard for traditional Scottish defences against English overlordship, but also an emphatic rejection of both the Stuart vision of empire and the confederal conception of a kingdom united by covenanting. In projecting an exclusive Englishness, Cromwell, both as the supreme military commander and as the foremost politician in the Council of State, went further than Elizabeth Tudor in pushing the frontiers of English hegemony to include all three kingdoms. Cromwell was acting in harmony with the Gothic spirit infusing the New Model Army, where, since its inception in 1645, officers and soldiers had made no appreciable attempt to publicise themselves as British.[10]

Nevertheless, the Covenanters' recognition of Charles II as King of Great Britain and Ireland was not without a transatlantic impact. Charles II was proclaimed as the rightful heir to all three kingdoms in Maryland, Virginia, the Summer Isles (Bermuda), Antigua and Barbados. A power struggle in the last of these between Royalists and Parliamentarians led to the governor of the Leeward Islands, William, Lord Willoughby of Parham, expediently recognising Charles II until Barbados was retaken for the Commonwealth by a fleet under the command of Sir George Ayscue in January 1652. This recovery paved the way for the Commonwealth's assertion of control over Virginia and Maryland. Transatlantic naval operations coincided with the reclamation of the Scillies, Man and the Channel Islands, where 340 troops, consisting of 'French, German, Danes, Switzers, Scots, Dutch, Irish, English and islanders' under the command of Sir George Carteret, were allowed free passage to Virginia 'or any other plantation in America'. The decanting of dissidents, which Cromwell had instigated in Wales in 1648 then extended to Ireland and Scotland in 1649–51, demonstrated the exclusive nature of Gothic supremacy. However, the American colonies were not written off as a dumping ground. They were to be made more productive by the supply, both voluntary and enforced, of indentured labour from the British Isles. Thus, political incorporation of Ireland and Scotland was but the first step in the Gothic realignment of all the Stuart dominions within the Commonwealth.[11]

Political realignment in both British and transatlantic contexts, however, exposed inherent tensions between an Army pursuing radical reform in the interests of a godly Commonwealth and the Independent-dominated 'Rump Parliament' intent on conserving the propertied interest and promoting political stability in the absence of monarchy. Cromwell's inclination to side with the former yet sympathise with the latter facilitated a decade of constitutional experimentation that clearly promoted English over Scottish and Irish interests.[12] The first meaningful test for the alliance of Army and Independents came with the promulgation of the oath of loyalty to the Commonwealth, the Gothic Engagement of 1649–51.

Designed initially as a test for office for those appointed to the Council of State in February 1649, the Gothic Engagement for England and Ireland required acceptance of the legitimacy of the regicide, the abolition of the Lords and the vesting of parliamentary sovereignty in the Commons. As the majority of the Council of State had scruples over the regicide, the oath was amended to the swearing of allegiance to the Commonwealth 'as it is now established, without a king or house of lords'. This revised oath was tendered first to the city of London in September, then to the Army in October, before being extended to all in public office prior to the requirement for universal adult subscription by January 1650. In the interim, Bulstrode Whitelocke was instrumental in persuading the 'Rump Parliament' that all law books, judicial processes and legal decisions should be in English, that Englishmen be no longer deprived of their Gothic birthright. The taking of the oath was intended to complement the sweeping away of Britannic symbols of office in central and local government and their replacement by the Gothic tokens of English identity. Thus the coinage, flags, arms, seals and civic maces of the Commonwealth, which projected the cross of St George with the Irish harp attached, emphasised the parliamentary supremacy of the 'Rump' over the territories of England and Ireland. This switch in iconography was not confined to state buildings in and around London, but extended to municipal corporations throughout the Commonwealth.[13] The imposition of the oath also reflected a siege mentality in the wake of the regicide. Thus, George Wither eulogised the sovereignty of the 'Parliament of the English Republike' as 'Keepers of the Liberties of England' and protectors of 'the true Christian Faith' within the bounds of the Commonwealth against domestic usurpers and foreign tyrants.[14]

With overwhelming support from the Army, the Gothic Engagement proved an effective means of purging political opponents from public office. But the oath of loyalty was an ineffective test for assuring loyalty to the Commonwealth or for wresting control of the pulpits from Presbyterians and other dissidents. Indeed, the oath confirmed the English talent for scrupling first evident in the calls for subscription to the Solemn League and Covenant of 1643. Its sparse wording allowed for five different positions. Those wholly committed to the Commonwealth gave their willing assent. Those not convinced of the legitimacy of the regicide but prepared to give *de facto* recognition to the Council of State acquiesced. Those who scrupled whether the oath of loyalty clashed with their Covenanting commitments were divided. Some were prepared to offer no more than passive resistance. Others were willing to pay the price of exclusion from public office rather than deny the Covenant. The final group consisted of those implacably opposed to the regicide regime. The Army and the Independents tended to compose the first two groups. The Presbyterians were spread over the second to fourth categories. Although the Royalists were most readily identifiable in the fifth cohort, a reluctance to undergo further sequestration or fiscal discrimination led to the more pragmatic making accommodations like the Presbyterians.[15]

Outright opposition to the Gothic Engagement was most evident in districts of traditional Royalist sympathy, notably in the West Country. The oath did lead to the purging of local government. This verged on the debilitating, if not in London, certainly in other municipalities, as in counties with a limited Independent presence, notably Cheshire and Bedfordshire. The denial of recourse to law for all refusing the Engagement gave teeth to purging. Although restricted to secular government, the taking of the oath had religious connotations, as evident from the objections of Presbyterian ministers in Lancashire and Shropshire to its acclaimed priority over Covenanting commitments. John Durie, the peacemaker, now permanently resident in England, was commissioned by the Council of State to produce tracts in favour of universal subscription prior to the oath being made compulsory, which served to reinforce the *de facto* and pragmatic acceptance of the Commonwealth. The imposition of the oath was complemented by the determination of the Council of State to devise a national religious settlement, particularly with respect to the provision of tithes to accredited ministers and preachers and to the establishment of commissions for the propagation of the gospel in Wales and the north – areas requiring enlightenment from past association with *de iure* Episcopalianism.[16]

These commissions were subsequently extended to New England, to contain sectarianism, and to Ireland, where preaching ministers were introduced not so much to redress Catholicism as to eradicate all vestiges of Episcopalianism and control Presbyterianism. The oath as applied in Dublin and the municipal corporations became effectively a test of who would work with, acquiesce in or not actively oppose the Cromwellian conquest. Given the past strength of the Confederation of Irish Catholics, the constituency for acceptance and acquiescence was proportionally smaller than in England. However, former Confederates were no less conscious than Royalists of the need to make pragmatic accommodations to safeguard their estates well before the final surrender of Irish forces at Cloughoughter, County Cavan, completed the Cromwellian conquest in April 1653. At the same time, the threat of civil sanctions, especially sequestration, was particularly vexing to the English in Ireland, such as Edward, 2nd Viscount (later 1st Earl) of Conway, a former commander of the British forces in Ulster, who had quit his commission in 1649 rather than serve in the Royalist coalition under Ormond. However, as he had not participated in the subsequent Cromwellian occupation, he constantly feared for the security of his estates in Warwickshire and Ulster during the lifetime of the 'Rump Parliament'. Indeed, the Gothic Engagement had compounded the draconian onset of the Cromwellian occupation and the expulsion of residual Covenanting forces and some ministers to Scotland. Ulster Presbyterians were obliged to resort to conventicling not only in houses but also in fields. In the process, they laid claim to be the original, suffering remnant of the godly Covenanters.[17]

Political Incorporation

The Gothic nature of the Commonwealth was manifest in the separate incorporations of Ireland and Scotland with England. This was not the creation of a triple alliance of equal states. There was no place for either Ireland or Scotland when the 'Keepers of the Liberties of England' authenticated the process of government throughout the British Isles. Moreover, this incorporative process lacked formal parliamentary warrant other than for two years between April 1657 and May 1659. With the cross of St Andrew added to the insignia of the Commonwealth, Scotland took precedence over Ireland – a status maintained throughout the negotiations for union that spilled over into the Protectorate. Notwithstanding Cromwell's personal vexation that Scotland remained attached to the exiled Stuart dynasty, the Gothic perspective was marked by a desire to reach an accommodation that would appease distinctive religious and civic traditions.[18]

Unlike Ireland, Scotland was not annexed to the Commonwealth. Consent was sought through the political directive known as the tender of incorporation. The 'Rump Parliament' despatched commissioners to Scotland headed by Oliver St John and Henry Vane junior on the civil side and Major-General John Lambert and Lieutenant-General George Monck on the military side in November 1651. Their remit to order and manage the affairs of Scotland included their acting as commissioners for propagating the gospel; their purging of central and local government; their management of forfeited and confiscated estates; and their imposition of an oath of loyalty that offered religious liberty in return for incorporation. On their arrival in Scotland in January 1652, the commissioners instructed the constituent shires and royal burghs to elect two deputies each to come to Dalkeith to give their assent to union prior to their formal subscription of the tender at Edinburgh by March.[19] The Scottish deputies were certainly not negotiating from a position of equality. Yet these proceedings were not simply the imposition of an English settlement.[20]

Notwithstanding the reassertion of old claims for English hegemony over Scotland, the English commissioners soon abandoned that aspect of their remit that required that the laws of England be put into execution in Scotland and in Wales and Ireland. No attempt was made to effect the proposal made by Francis Bacon in the wake of the regal union that English security was best assured by the assimilation of Scotland under the common law. Moreover, the authorisation granted to the Scottish deputies, as 'persons of integritie and good affection to the wealfaire and peace of this Island', allowed for a measure of latitude. Thus, the deputies for the shires of Argyll, Midlothian and Selkirk were instructed to 'treat, reason and debate, but not to conclude' until they reported back on their proceedings at Dalkeith. This reservation of final consent to union duly affected the formal subscription of the tender of incorporation at Edinburgh.[21]

Of the 31 Scottish shires, 28 sent deputies to assent to union at Dalkeith, but only 20 sent deputies to Edinburgh to subscribe the tender. No more than 15 deputies signed the commission for 21 deputies (14 from the shires, 7 from the burghs) to continue detailed negotiations at Westminster between October 1652 and April 1653. Of the 58 royal burghs, 44 sent deputies to Dalkeith but only 37 were represented at Edinburgh, where 34 deputies actually subscribed the tender. Only 25 signed the commission for the deputies to Westminster. In effect, less than half the shires and burghs fully subscribed the process of incorporation. Enthusiasm for Scottish incorporation into the Commonwealth was minimal. Albeit delayed by storms in reaching Edinburgh, the deputies for Orkney and Shetland were mandated to support incorporation. Recently annexed to the Scottish crown by James I, the Northern Isles were nonetheless insistent that Scottish law must be maintained within the union. Conversely, only three shires (Renfrew, Ayr and Kirkcudbright) and three burghs (Renfrew, Ayr and Irvine), which represented the western association of Protestors, made no effort to participate in the process. For the majority of Scottish deputies who complied, their position varied from *de facto* acceptance to conditional acquiescence that reserved prior commitment to the Covenants. The 21 deputies summoned to England for further negotiations did so only after express permission had been attained from the exiled Charles II. They were also mandated to pursue an equitable reduction and redistribution of 'the Common burtheins of the kingdome'. The public debts arising from the patriotic accommodation had been compounded by the fiscal demands of Cromwellian occupation.[22]

The 21 Scottish deputies who attended at Westminster were made initially to feel as much supplicants as negotiators in their dealings with the English committee on union with Scotland. This committee, which included most of the leading commissioners sent to Scotland in January 1652, was supplemented principally by Bulstrode Whitelocke and Sir Arthur Haselrig on the civil side and Lord General Cromwell and Major-General Thomas Harrison on the military. Although the Scots lacked the parity accorded them in negotiating the Solemn League and Covenant, no attempt was made to recognise Ireland as a separate entity, as the English commissioners had insisted in 1643. In the course of the negotiations the Scots duly gained a measure of recognition for their standing not as political clients from a dependent state but as junior partners in union. The desire of the deputies to form a standing committee for Scottish affairs was not conceded. Nevertheless, they did succeed in retaining Scots law 'untill a knowne law shall be established for governing Scotland and England united into one Commonwealth' – a situation unchanged by the advent of the Protectorate in 1654. They were not able to establish that 60 MPs in the reconstituted 'Rump Parliament' should represent Scotland. However, their argument that the proportion of Scottish MPs should not be based solely on the monthly assessment, or cess, but should take into account relative populations and their parochial distribution was given extensive consideration. The deputies' argument that proportional assessment should not be the sole basis for Scottish representation while England continued with a traditional electoral system that overrepresented Cornwall and underrepresented Hereford was accepted. Electoral standardisation throughout the Commonwealth followed. The end result was that Scotland, like Ireland, was to be represented by 30 MPs, a proportion determined by assessment and population.[23]

Although the proportional representation was now decided, the actual distribution of Scottish seats was not settled until June 1654, when the Scottish shires were grouped into 20 constituencies and the burghs into 10. There was also a similar delay in resolving associated issues on the extent of forfeitures and confiscations, stabilising the currency, purging local government and administrating justice without respect to heritable jurisdictions and sweeping away feudal dependencies. The delay can be attributed partly to the changing political climate, but mostly to the lack of Scottish commitment to the Commonwealth.

Tensions between the Army and the 'Rump Parliament' led to the replacement of the latter by the Nominated or 'Barebones Parliament' in April 1653, just after the Committee on Union had concluded business. Only two of the 21 deputies were among the five Scottish nominees to a parliament which only lasted nine months before further pressure from the Army led to Cromwell assuming executive power as Lord Protector. Although the union of Scotland and Ireland with England did receive legislative sanction under an ordinance of the Protectorate in April 1654, another three years were to elapse before the union was embedded in statute. Only 21 constituencies actually returned members to serve for Scotland in September 1654, of whom nine were non-Scottish military or civil administrators. The Scottish MPs were rigorously vetted to ensure not only their current loyalty to the Protectorate, but that their past political activity had not been tainted by subscription to the Britannic Engagement. While a full complement of 30 MPs was returned at the next election, in 1656, only 14 constituencies were actually represented by Scots. Following the death of Oliver Cromwell in 1658, the election to the parliament called by his son Richard in 1659 returned another full complement. Only ten were Scots, including the Marquess of Argyll, who managed to get himself elected for Aberdeenshire despite the endeavours of the occupying forces to ensure only the return of pliable placemen.[24]

Active collaboration with the Cromwellian regime, though marginally more evident in Scotland than in Ireland, was confined to a radical handful. They provided a minority Scottish presence on the Commission for the Administration of Justice, which replaced the English commissioners as the civil government of Scotland from April 1652, and, subsequently, on the devolved Scottish Council instituted under the Protectorate in May 1655. Sharing British apocalyptic visions of world reordering, some like Sir James Hope of Hopetoun sought Cromwellian backing to carry through the social restructuring instigated in the anti-aristocratic parliament of 1649. However, they became estranged by the occupying regime's ineffective implementation of the radical legislative programme truncated by the patriotic accommodation. Leading Protestors such as Johnston of Wariston were won over to the Protectorate. Nevertheless, the majority of this persuasion, and virtually all the Resolutioners, remained as opposed to the Protectorate as they had been to the Commonwealth, which they had resolutely refused to serve either as deputies or as MPs. Indeed, the Scottish deputies, prior to the conclusion of their negotiations in April 1653, had attested that there were several assemblies in Edinburgh and elsewhere in Scotland of disaffected persons who were intent on 'keeping off the hearts of the people of Scotland from this Union'.[25]

Disaffection, supported by ongoing guerrilla resistance among the clans, duly led to a Royalist rising initiated in August by William Cunningham, 4th Earl of Glencairn, a former participant in the Britannic Engagement. This rising, which soon spread to the north-east of Scotland, was joined by the son and heir of Montrose and by the son and heir of Argyll. The nomadic moss-troopers proved a highly mobile irritant to outlying garrisons without posing a serious threat to Cromwellian occupation. Their involvement in the Royalist rising gave no more than a political veneer to their predatory activities. At the behest of Charles II, another veteran of the Britannic Engagement, Lieutenant-General George Middleton, returned from continental exile in March 1654 to replace Glencairn as commander. Sir George Munro, the former commander of the Scottish forces in Ulster, again proved disruptive, occasioning a debilitating rift between Middleton and Glencairn by April. In the meantime, the considerably more adept General George Monck replaced Lambert as commander of the New Model Army in Scotland. Having defeated Middleton at Dalnaspidal in Perthshire by 20 July, he undertook systematic pillaging and burning in the Highlands to persuade the clans, who had formed the bedrock of the Royalist campaign, to sue for peace collectively and severally. Effectively isolated, Middleton became an itinerant refugee in the Highlands. He returned to exile in April 1655.[26]

The Royalist rising had not yet been suppressed when the ordinance for political incorporation was promulgated on 12 April 1654. Its associated programme for the governance of Scotland restricted outright confiscations to 24 landowners, with another 73 subject to rigorous fines. Commissions of the peace were to be reinvigorated in the shires and heritable jurisdictions and feudal dependencies were to be swept away.

This latter aspect won contemporaneous commendation when the Scottish Council, under the direction of Roger, Lord Broghill (later 1st Earl of Orrery), sought to implement reform in Kirk and state. Transferred from his duties in Ireland as lord president of Munster to provide the civil complement to Monck's military pacification by individual treaties with Highland chiefs and Lowland landlords, Broghill was a talented conciliator. But his brief administration from September 1655 until August 1656 was more about style than substance.[27] Not only did the Protestor–Resolutioner conflict remain intractable, but he discovered rather sooner than Charles I in the course of the Revocation Scheme that the wholescale abolition of heritable jurisdictions and feudal superiorities was time-consuming, technically complex and politically disruptive. Reform was focused on the proscription of military tenures and work services exacted as rents. Feudal superiority was retained through commercial tenures and was necessary for the payment of teinds to cover the stipends of accredited ministers, schooling and social welfare in the burghs as in rural parishes.

Moreover, heritable jurisdictions were discreetly continued in practice if not in name, a precedent having been set by the package of concessions negotiated by the Marquess of Argyll in 1652. From the outset of the Cromwellian accommodation, the chief of ClanCampbell and his associates in Argyllshire had sought to buy time to promote recovery from the devastations of civil war. Simultaneously, they were intent on restricting the number of Cromwellian garrisons and the amount of military quartering on the shire. Having successfully resorted to arms in August to secure a favourable revision of terms by October, Argyll was allowed to exercise his extensive heritable jurisdiction without specific mention of his regalian or palatine powers. He was accorded a cess rebate for Argyllshire on condition that he agree to live peaceably and quietly and use his influence among his followers to the same end. Indeed, this accord, which was not dissimilar to the discreetly revived jurisdiction of the County and Duchy of Lancaster in October 1653, became the subsequent model for Monck's accords with chiefs and landlords liable to rigorous but discriminatory fines for past resistance to Cromwellian occupation. The main thrust of this policy, as pursued from 1655, was the conditional retention of landed interests and feudal privileges. Fiscal rebates were tied to punitive sureties for future good conduct. Even within the Highlands, the emphasis was on containment. Notwithstanding the forcible enlistment of moss-troopers and caterans for military service overseas, banditry remained an endemic problem in

Lowland districts bordering on the Highlands. Accordingly, Lieutenant-Colonel Donald MacGregor, a civil war veteran, was commissioned to eradicate all predatory raiding. A monopoly of control over protection rackets was thus accorded to the acting chief of the ClanGregor. The MacGregors could now claim Cromwellian backing for their extortionate levying of blackmail to guard Lowland districts from the rustling of livestock by moss-troopers and Highland caterans.[28]

The Gothic Emperor

Political incorporation was not the only aspect of state formation that carried over from the Commonwealth to the Protectorate. War with the United Provinces, which began in May 1652 and was not resolved until April 1654, exposed antagonisms based essentially on political economy but aggravated by diplomatic slights and apocalyptic triumphalism. At the same time, the Dutch War no less than political incorporation broadened the anglocentric agenda by opening up the prospect of a federative union that survived the disruptive shift from the Commonwealth to the Protectorate. Indeed, even more than enforced union with Scotland and Ireland, the Dutch War was a key element in the revolutionary politics in which a Gothic assembly gave way to a Gothic emperor. The Council of State in tandem with the 'Rump Parliament' asserted dominion over the 'British seas', imposed Navigation Laws and refashioned a new model navy. The Protectorate under Oliver Cromwell pursued commercial confederation with confessional undertones of irenicism in Protestant Europe, launched a Western Design in the Americas and threatened to replace the Britannic Stuarts with a hegemonic English dynasty.[29]

Conceived essentially as a reaction to foreign trade embargoes and continued expressions of loyalty to the Stuarts in the American colonies as well as in Scotland, the first Navigation Act, in August 1650, was designed to ring-fence rather than liberalise English overseas trade. The second Navigation Act, in October 1651, freed up trade without threatening the dominance of the English merchant companies. But this act was primarily intended to assert English independence of the Dutch carrying trade within the context of transoceanic resistance to commercial dominance by any rival colonial power. It sought to ensure the more systematic deployment of English convoys. Foreign access to the English colonies in North America and the Caribbean was strictly licensed, not prohibited. This change in position can in part be attributed to the extensive building up of naval resources and the politicising of the navy into a force no less partisan than the New Model Army between 1649 and 1651. The Commonwealth's shipping resources effectively trebled through building, capture and purchase. Over 80 warships were in active service by 1653.[30]

At the same time, France and the United Provinces, the two major powers within closest striking distance of Britain, were engulfed by internal conflicts. In France, the rule of Cardinal Jules Mazarin was challenged by a series of convulsions between 1648 and 1653 known as the parliamentary, princely and religious *frondes*, which spread from the provinces to Paris, initially in reaction to the incessant centralist demands for fiscal innovations during the Thirty Years War. These convulsions were compounded by the religious tensions occasioned by Jansenism and Gallicanism within the French practice of Roman Catholicism, as by the continuing Protestant challenge posed by the Huguenots in and around Bordeaux. The reassertion of provincial power in the United Provinces was facilitated by the demise of the Stadholder, William II of Orange, and the decision of the States General to leave the post vacant in December 1650. Hopes were raised not just of godly amity but of a political league between the English and the Dutch republics that would consolidate Protestantism and reduce global commercial rivalry.[31]

In January 1651, the Council of State despatched Oliver St John and Walter Strickland as ambassadors to The Hague. Their embassy, which lasted three months, proved a major disappointment. Like the Scots at the making of the Solemn League and Covenant in 1643, the English overlooked the complexity of the interests with which they sought to ally. Holland, and to a lesser extent Zeeland, as the leading mercantile provinces, were sympathetic to a republican alliance. However, the other landward and frontier provinces remained attached to the house of Orange, which was closely allied by marriage to the Stuarts. Accordingly, there was a noted reluctance at The Hague to conclude an alliance with the Commonwealth while the patriotic accommodation in Scotland offered Charles II some prospect of a British restoration. The States General were prepared to countenance a federative union, but their standpoint was initially that of confessional confederation, which again raised the spectre of the Solemn League. The Dutch alternative, already negotiated successfully with the Danes in September 1649, was for a commercial confederation that built upon a common Protestantism yet accorded priority to economic interests. Because of this, the Dutch had secured favoured nation status as far as the Baltic Sound tolls were concerned.

The English, however, initially reacted against the supplanting of confessional by commercial politics. Having been obliged to resort to arms to resist the oppressions of the tyrannical Charles I, the security of their 'just and native liberties' through parliament had been secured by wondrous victories in battle. By such 'a Series of Providence in England, Ireland and Scotland, the Lord was pleased to blesse a poor handfull' who now ran the Commonwealth. The umbrage of both the Council of State and the 'Rump Parliament' against the Dutch revived past commercial grievances that stretched back to the massacre of Amboyna perpetrated against members of the English East India Company in 1623. The assassination of Dr Dorislaus in 1649 remained a festering political sore. English rivalry was further fuelled by Dutch assertiveness in maintaining their dominance of the herring fishing in the North Sea and their lack of regard for the sovereignty around the British Isles originally claimed by the Stuarts. The Gothic defence of *ius imperium* mounted by Charles I when promoting his common fishing in the 1630s was duly appropriated by the Commonwealth. *The Soveraignty of the British Seas* by Sir John Boroughs was reissued in 1651 and was followed up by Marchmont Nedham's translation of John Selden's *Mare Clausum* in 1652. In the interim, the conquest of Scotland, which gave greater credibility to the Commonwealth's claims for maritime sovereignty, had also raised public concerns about the relative failure of London merchants to exploit 'the inestimable richness of the British Seas'.[32]

Doubts about the Dutch preference for materialism over godliness, which had facilitated the passage of the second Navigation Act, were duly appeased by the progress of negotiations after the States General sent ambassadors to London in December 1651. A commercial treaty underpinned by a common Protestantism appeared to be on the brink of conclusion by April 1652. Similar negotiations were also begun with Danish ambassadors. The Commonwealth was offered the prospect of parity in Sound tolls with the United Provinces and international recognition of its right to license access to the English colonies in the Americas. However, tensions at sea over Dutch access to British coastal waters, especially to the English Channel, without due recognition of the Commonwealth's claimed maritime sovereignty led to a skirmish between the Dutch navy under Admiral Tromp and the English fleet under the command of Robert Blake in May. Given the mutual distrust evident in the vernacular press of both countries, the situation rapidly deteriorated into war. Cromwell, no less than such apocalyptic sects as the Fifth Monarchists, shared the widespread belief among active supporters of the Commonwealth that England, having conquered Ireland and Scotland, was on a divine path to glory. As a leading proponent of Anglo-Dutch union, Marchmont Nedham was to the fore in changing its classical terms from amity to conquest. Ireland had been subjugated as a conquered territory and Scotland had been pressed into an unequal league but allowed a measure of consent. Originally offered a federation of equals, the Dutch were now to be incorporated on similar terms to the Scots.[33]

Over the next two years, a series of naval engagements mainly in and around the English Channel decided the outcome of the war. The Commonwealth gained prompt recognition of its legitimacy from France, which had condoned privateering in the Channel and the Irish Sea in the wake of the regicide, after the navy destroyed the French fleet off Dunkirk in September. Thereafter, France concentrated on its ongoing war with Spain. However, the United Provinces firmed up its commercial confederation with Denmark–Norway for mutual support in October 1652. Not only were the Danish ambassadors recalled from London, but also Commonwealth shipping was impounded in Copenhagen. Trade through the Baltic Sound was all but closed to English and Scottish ships by 1653. By the time Blake and the ubiquitous Monck had won a decisive series of naval engagements that culminated in the English victory off Texel (Sheviningen) in late July 1653, the cost and direction of the war had brought down the 'Rump Parliament' and severely emasculated its 'Barebones' successor. The renewed emphasis on sequestrations to pay for the massive increase in the navy proved especially disruptive in the English counties and provoked acerbic litigation that continued into the Protectorate. Nevertheless, the eventual conclusion of a peace treaty with the United Provinces in April 1654 was hailed as a diplomatic triumph for Oliver Cromwell as Lord Protector.[34]

In effecting the replacement of the 'Rump' by the 'Barebones' Parliament in April 1653, Cromwell was supported by the Army leadership, which had become increasingly frustrated by the 'Rump's' failure to implement greater electoral accountability and promote religious pluralism throughout England and Wales. In moving towards a nominated parliament, as a staging post on the way to a more representative assembly that would include members from Scotland and Ireland, Cromwell was enthusiastically supported by officers with strong links to the sects, most notably by Major-General Thomas Harrison and the

Fifth Monarchists. In contending that the providential direction 'in this revolution of affairs' since the beginning of civil war now required that parliament itself be 'winnowed, sifted, and brought to a handful', Cromwell was undoubtedly bolstered by the Fifth Monarchist belief that the saints were called to rule. However, Cromwell was less concerned with apocalyptic triumphalism and not persuaded that the national interest, as articulated through the civil and religious liberties of England, should necessarily be subordinated to the attainment of the kingdom of the saints throughout and beyond the Commonwealth. In standing for the hegemonic interests of England, Cromwell remained a sceptical rather than an assured interpreter of God's will. While he listened attentively to diverse sectarian opinions from Quakers to Fifth Monarchists, he refused to ally himself with any belief that claimed both privileged authority and exclusivity in ordering affairs of state. The 'Barebones Parliament' proved itself particularly inept in its handling of peace negotiations with the Dutch, and displayed a noted preference for the public humiliation being advocated by Fifth Monarchist preachers in London rather than for an amicable treaty. Glencairn's rising in Scotland offered the prospect of a Royalist resurgence spreading to England, where propertied interests were becoming increasingly concerned about greater tax burdens. Accordingly, Cromwell was receptive to the manoeuvres of Major-General Lambert and his Army associates in December that the 'Barebones Parliament' should dissolve itself and hand over power to a Protectorate established by a written constitution.[35]

The Instrument of Government under which Cromwell assumed supreme power over England, Scotland and Ireland was published on 16 December 1653. In terms of constitutional precedent, the Instrument was closest to the Heads of Proposals promulgated as a result of Army pressure in August 1647, particularly with regard to electoral reform and seat redistribution in parliament. The Council of State, which was to act as an interval committee between parliaments as proposed in 1647, was continued from the Commonwealth but now subordinated to the executive power vested in the Lord Protector. Although Cromwell was ceded no formal veto over legislation unless the Instrument was directly infringed or challenged by parliament, he was accorded extensive prerogative powers to issue ordinances that had the force of law until ratified or rejected by the next parliament, which was not due to meet until September 1654. The making of peace and war was vested in Cromwell. He was also accorded financial responsibility for the maintenance of the civil and military establishment, free from parliamentary interference.

Thus, the Instrument was less conditional than the first written British constitution, the Solemn League and Covenant of 1643. No limitations were imposed on the Protectorate that would justify resistance in church or state. Indeed, the Instrument marked a return to the tradition of legislative supremacy being exercised through the partnership of the king and parliament, now adapted to the Protectorate and the Commons. The Instrument primarily limited parliamentary authority. Parliament was empowered to ratify and consent to laws and taxation, but not to initiate government or alter the prescribed constitution. Parliament was to approve government officials in England, Scotland and Ireland, but not in the Council of State, which advised and assisted the Protector. Nor did parliament control its own membership. Oversight of those returned at elections was vested in the Council of State, which had the power to exclude those who were not 'persons of known integrity'.[36]

The constitutional settlement promoted by the Instrument was tied less to limited than to balanced monarchy, as advocated by Montrose and his followers in Scotland and by the 'constitutional Royalists' in England during the 1640s. However, the Instrument could also be interpreted as the warranting of mixed monarchy, as advocated by such Royalist ideologues of non-resistance as Dudley Digges and subsequently rationalised scientifically, if starkly, by Thomas Hobbes, especially in his *Leviathan* (1651).[37] Although this work began with the hope of a Royalist restoration through Scotland and was concluded pessimistically following the defeat of Charles II at Worcester, its main contemporaneous influence was to herald and authenticate the providential rise of Oliver Cromwell as the Gothic *dux bellum*. For the shift from the Commonwealth to the Protectorate marked the emergence of Cromwell as the imperial war leader who exercised sovereign power over the Stuart's former British dominions. Thus, Cromwell could be personified as the protector of civil society from the disaster of civil war. Collectively and individually, rights of resistance were superseded by instincts of self-preservation. He was not just the classically virtuous defender of the Commonwealth, but a Gothic emperor respectful of but not submissive to civil agencies founded upon law and untrammelled by clerical constraints in the pursuit of a godly reformation.[38]

In the event, Cromwell used his prerogative powers of ordinance under the Instrument of Government to push through union with Scotland and Ireland and to conclude an honourable treaty with the Dutch. In the process, he rationalised English hegemonic conquest for which the Gothic precedent was Edward I in the late thirteenth and early fourteenth centuries and established England as a major European power through war. He thus transcended the British diplomatic endeavours of the early Stuarts that were not marked by successful intervention in the Thirty Years War. His determination to achieve an amicable resolution rather than an apocalyptically charged peace with the Dutch led him to promote commercial confederation, to which the United Provinces assented publicly by the Treaty of Westminster in April 1654. Only a private article covered Cromwell's insistence that the Prince of Orange should be permanently excluded from the office of Stadholder. The English Navigation Laws were effectively set aside. The Dutch recognised that the Lord Protector was not only the legitimate sovereign power in England, Scotland and Ireland, but that all international rights previously claimed by the Stuart monarchy had passed to the Protectorate. At the same time, commercial confederation was extended to resolve difficulties with Frederik III of Denmark–Norway, which ensured that English, Scottish and Irish shipping paid the same Sound tolls as the Dutch. Simultaneously, Cromwell secured a like accord with Queen Kristina of Sweden that Commonwealth diplomats had found elusive.[39]

Cromwell was not able to restrain Charles X of Sweden from declaring war against Poland–Lithuania in 1655. However, his refusal to participate in a war that not only rekindled trading and territorial rivalries in the Baltic but also threatened Protestant harmony with the Dutch and the Danes obliged the young king to renegotiate their treaty of commercial confederation in July 1656. Polish and Lithuanian resistance to the invasion of their commonwealth was proving unquenchable. The rights of English, Scottish and Irish ships to trade in the Baltic on equal terms with other European powers were confirmed. The Swedes guaranteed not to increase the commercial tolls levied in the Polish and Prussian ports under their control. In return, the Swedes were conceded free access for fishing in the coastal waters around the British Isles. Such was the standing Cromwell attained for England in northern Europe that Protectorate diplomats were viewed as key players, along with diplomats from France and the United Provinces, in brokering and maintaining peace between Sweden and Denmark–Norway following their renewal of war in 1658. England, no less than France and the United Provinces, was a guarantor of the peace attained by the Treaty of Roskilde whereby Denmark ceded its three provinces to the east of the Baltic Sound – namely, Halland, Blekinge and Skåne – to Sweden. [40]

Having resisted overtures to exploit the civil war occasioned by the *frondes* in France to secure an English bridgehead across the Channel with

Spanish assistance, Cromwell opted for a more pragmatic alliance with Cardinal Mazarin. However, negotiations which commenced in March 1654 were delayed for six months until suspicions of French involvement in Royalist plotting to assassinate Cromwell, to instigate risings in the West Country, the Midlands and the north of England and to reinvigorate guerrilla resistance in Ireland and Scotland proved unfounded. Rumours that Charles II, the Duke of York, Ormond and Inchiquinn planned an invasion of southern England carried no more substance. Nonetheless, Royalist plotting had led to overtures to such disaffected groups as Presbyterians excluded from parliament, religious sectaries and disgruntled soldiers and sailors. A rising in Wiltshire was easily suppressed. Its leader, Colonel John Penruddock, and his closest associates were duly executed in May for treason under an ordinance of doubtful legitimacy that strained the loyalty of the English judiciary. But the majority of insurgents were treated with relative leniency, albeit some were transported to Barbados as indentured servants. The plotting was also used by the Cromwellian regime to imprison Major-General Harrison and other Fifth Monarchists and Levellers opposed to the creation of the Protectorate. The cost of maintaining armies of occupation in Scotland and Ireland and shoring up forces to resist further Royalist plotting in England made a military engagement against France a financial liability, notwithstanding the attractiveness of securing a bridgehead through Dunkirk. An offensive against Spain, however, could sustain the military nature of the Protectorate without increasing existing fiscal burdens by siphoning silver and gold away from the Spanish treasure fleets in the Americas.[41]

Cromwell's imperial pretensions in the Americas were bellicose rather than pacific. Spain was beyond the remit of the confessional solidarity that had underwritten commercial confederation, had no Protestant minority like the French Huguenots and maintained a Catholic Inquisition. In the winter of 1655–6, he sent a naval expeditionary force to lay siege to the Spanish treasure routes from the Americas to Europe. The primary aim of his Western Design was to take over the Panama Isthmus and divert the silver and gold bullion into Protectorate coffers. At the same time, Hispaniola was to be seized to serve as a transit station. He was convinced that Puritan settlements in New England especially, together with the settlements in Virginia and the Summer Isles, should be relocated to establish an English interest in the West Indies that would serve as a barrier against the expansion of Spanish power.

John Milton was brought into play, effectively to recycle polemical arguments against the Dutch that had helped provoke the war of 1652–3. Thus, the Spanish sponsoring of political faction was deemed an insidious, even cancerous, influence on English politics since 1603, notably in hampering trading ventures to the West Indies. Vengeance was sought for the unprovoked attack on the English colony at Santa Cruz on Porto Rico in 1651, for the unpunished assassination of Ambassador Assam in 1650 and for the Spanish abrogation of the Puritan settlement in the Providence Islands a decade earlier. Papal authorisation of Spanish dominion in the New World was rejected. Planted colonies were the 'best Right of Possession in America'. However, a divided command structure between Admiral William Penn and General Robert Venables, inadequate provisioning for the Caribbean and greater Spanish resistance than expected in San Domingo made the assault on Hispaniola a military fiasco. The Puritans of New England were not inclined to become involved in the Western Design, nor to view privateering against Spanish shipping as a godly enterprise. Jamaica was taken as a consolation prize in 1655, but the capture of the Panama Isthmus was abandoned. Cromwell could no longer be confident of an unbroken series of providences continuing to bless the Protectorate, far less its Gothic emperor.[42]

Civic Virtue and Godly Discipline

Religion remained a problematic issue for Cromwell. The treaties of commercial confederation with the Dutch, the Danes and the Swedes were underpinned by a confessional harmony between Calvinists and Lutherans that echoed the peace-seeking endeavours of John Durie in the 1630s. Indeed, Cromwell reactivated Durie's continental mission to the Reformed Swiss cantons, to the Protestant princes, cities and academies in Germany and to the Netherlands prior to the Western Design. For three years Durie laboured energetically but fruitlessly to promote a united front against the Habsburgs and their Catholic allies through a comprehensive confessional confederation that would be endorsed by the Danish and Swedish monarchies.[43] Not only did agreement on religious fundamentals, most notably on a confession of faith, remain unattainable between Calvinists and Lutherans, but the pluralist state of religious belief and practice that the Protectorate inherited from the Commonwealth left little grounds for common agreement among English Protestants. By the time Durie returned to England in 1657, a broad consensus was emerging in favour of the Trinity, upholding the indivisibility of the Father, the Son and the Holy Ghost, and in opposition to toleration for papists, prelates and licentious sects. In effect, Roman Catholicism remained proscribed. Anglicanism stripped of Laudian sacerdotalism was not criminalised. An uneasy tolerance was afforded to new sects, such as the Quakers, who were initially noted more for their disruptive than their contemplative behaviour.[44]

Cromwell had used his prerogative powers to establish two religious commissions in March and August 1654, which consisted mainly of Independents assisted by Presbyterians and even some Baptists not inclined to separatism. The first, the 'Triers', operated centrally to accredit preachers and examine their suitability to hold benefices or lectureships. The second, the 'Ejectors', operated in each county to remove those deemed scandalous, ignorant or insufficient from their preaching ministries. However, the reform and redistribution of parliamentary membership under the Instrument of Government, which markedly favoured the shire gentry over the burgesses, introduced an element intent on demonstrating that parliament was the independent guardian of the propertied interest. Thus, while they shared with Cromwell and the Army a desire to preserve a broad, established Church of England, they were less convinced about tolerating a generous freedom of worship and association for the sects. On a more material level, they remained far from accommodating to any ordinance for the maintenance of accredited preachers that would require the public appropriation of tithes. When the first parliament of the Protectorate assembled on Sunday 3 September 1654, chosen deliberately to commemorate the victories at Dunbar and Worcester, Cromwell and the Army were intent on intimidation as well as self-glorification. Nonetheless, the parliamentarians were determined that the Instrument of Government should be subject to amendment, particularly with respect to Cromwell's control of the Army, his effective veto over constitutional change and his public income – he had been granted crown lands that remained unsold or not yet disposed of as a perquisite of royalty.[45]

Having dissolved parliament at the earliest opportunity in January 1655, Cromwell determined to reduce the military establishment. Simultaneously, the role of the Army in promoting a godly reformation was enhanced. The pursuit of doctrinal truth became secondary to the inculcation of civic virtue and godly discipline. Accordingly, England and Wales were divided up into cantons by October and 12 major-generals were appointed to suppress all vestiges of Royalist dissent. Virtue and godliness were to be constantly promoted, especially in London where all houses of ill repute and for gaming were to be suppressed. This manifestly Puritan agenda was made particularly unpalatable by the decimation tax, whereby the expenses of the major-generals were to be defrayed by a levy of 10 per cent on the estates of Royalists who had long been subjected to discriminatory fines and sequestrations.[46] Whereas the early Stuarts had relied more on clerical persuasion to effect their British *ius imperium* over all three kingdoms, the Cromwellian Gothic empire maintained English hegemony primarily by military coercion. Both fell short on the establishment of a political consensus through constitutional assemblies. Notwithstanding the Council of State authorising the exclusion of around 100 MPs before the second Protectorate parliament began on 17 September 1656, the majority of those who remained were deeply hostile to the major-generals and refused to ratify the decimation tax. As evident from their less than successful endeavours to influence the voting in borough elections, the credibility of the major-generals within the localities was exhausted. Their rule came to an abrupt end in January 1657.[47]

In the interim, Cromwell responded positively to a personal overture from the chief rabbi of Amsterdam, Manasseh ben Israel, asking him to accord Jews the right to reside and trade freely and to worship publicly in synagogues. The readmission of the Jews since their expulsion from England by royal decreet in 1290 had immediate financial attractions in facilitating the working of money to the advantage of the state and in providing political intelligence especially about Spanish global manoeuvres. Cromwell was particularly persuaded by prophetic considerations that the coming of Christ's kingdom would be preceded by the conversion of the Jews. The Lord Protector, however, overestimated the support for readmission within the Council of State meeting in plenary session in December 1656 to accommodate informed opinion from the judiciary, the universities, the City and religious denominations. Nevertheless, he used his prerogative powers to ensure that Jewish residency and worship, which became concentrated in London, would not be subject to penal laws. The mishandled Western Design provoked a more direct and sustained attack on the spiritual and material direction of the Protectorate.

A former political colleague, Sir Henry Vane junior, called for the creation of a new godly Commonwealth, which would curb Cromwell's political powers and ensure greater participation in government by those who put the public good above private gain. The Council of State would continue as the executive body but supreme authority would be vested in a representative assembly, which was to consist of freely elected members of proven integrity committed to godly discipline. A watching brief over the executive power could be exercised either by a single person of stature, such as Cromwell, or by a greater number at the assembly's discretion. This opened up the prospect of a return to the 'Rump Parliament' prior to the abolition of the Lords – a situation that actually resurfaced in 1659 after Richard Cromwell succeeded his father as Lord Protector, albeit Vane in the interim was imprisoned and obliged to recant. However, a more challenging material critique of the Protectorate emerged from the pen of a former companion to Charles I when the king was imprisoned in 1648. James Harrington's *The Commonwealth of Oceana* (1656) offered a powerful and penetrating counterpoint to the global expansionism that had characterised Cromwell's reign as Gothic emperor. Although this work was intellectually subversive, it contained no incitement to resistance. Harrington, unlike Vane, escaped public censure.[48]

Harrington was primarily concerned to redress the Gothic balance of the constitution to ensure stability and the rule of law, objectives he shared with Hobbes. Whereas the philosophical Hobbes had sought to vest sovereignty in monarchy in a way that was not wholly inconsistent with Cromwell as both an imperial and an imperious Lord Protector, Harrington's approach was historical and rooted in civic humanism. Accordingly, he favoured neither a monarchy, which could degenerate into tyranny, nor even a saintly aristocracy as promoted by Vane, which could become an entrenched oligarchy. He advocated a more democratic order that was to be achieved by the agrarian redistribution of property, not for the purposes of social levelling, but to promote a more egalitarian and virtuous Commonwealth.[49] Cromwell, to whom his book was dedicated, was not to be marginalised, however. His statesmanship was essential for the accomplishment of this transformation and to ensure that the principle of rotation rather than hereditary succession applied to office holding. Membership of the Council of State was to continue to be rotated rather than exercised by a self-perpetuating oligarchy as suggested by Vane. Parliament was to be revitalised as a bi-cameral assembly. A senate was to be elected from elite landowners capable of serving the Commonwealth as cavalry. A common assembly was to be elected by all landowners and freemen, but not servants. A third of the membership of each body was to be replaced annually. Cromwell was also expected to take the lead in concluding this new self-denying ordinance through the replacement of the standing army by an armed citizen militia that would include all proprietors whether they served as infantry or cavalry. Harrington's Commonwealth, which was to continue to incorporate Ireland and Scotland, would have required the dismantling of the military–fiscal state shoring up the Protectorate, for which there was no immediate prospect during Cromwell's lifetime. Harrington remained an active propagandist, arguing influentially for a reformed Commonwealth rather than a reconstituted Protectorate or a monarchical Restoration, as the regime of Richard Cromwell disintegrated in the course of 1659.[50]

Notwithstanding the political critiques of Vane and Harrington or the parliamentary rebuff to the rule of the major-generals, Cromwell's imperial standing was actually enhanced by the failure of another assassination plot involving Royalists and Levellers in January 1657. A parliamentary remonstrance, which became known as the Humble Petition and Advice, begged Cromwell to accept the crown of the three kingdoms. Over the next five months Cromwell agonised about this decision. While his acceptance of the kingship was strongly advocated both in the Council of State and in parliament, old comrades in the Army expressed considerable reservations. Cromwell himself claimed that providence had worked against not only the Stuart dynasty but also the royal title. At the same time, his apparent deferral to the wishes of the Army high command can be viewed as compensation for his acceptance of an amended Humble Petition and Advice from which the offer of kingship was removed and the dominance of civil government asserted. The new written constitution, as enunciated on 25 May and clarified on 6 June, gave Cromwell sole right to nominate his successor as Lord Protector and to nominate a new senate or 'Other House' as floated by Vane and Harrington, which was to act as a judicial check on the Commons. This was not a return to traditional mixed monarchy, however, as Cromwell was obliged to concede that the power of appointing and removing councillors rested ultimately with parliament. Limitations on his power did not extend to the disbanding of the standing forces, merely to specifying that parliamentary consent was required to meet expenditure in excess of £1 million annually for the army and navy and £300,000 for the civil establishment. Nevertheless, after Cromwell's death the office of commander-in-chief was to be separated from and subordinate to that of the Lord Protector.[51]

This new constitution had a short shelf life. During the adjournment of parliament from 26 June 1657 until 20 January 1658, nominations were completed for the 'Other House' and the members excluded in the previous September were offered readmission in return for an oath of loyalty to the Protectorate. However, the reassembled parliament could not muster sufficient support to ratify the new constitution. Particularly aggrieved by criticisms of the 'Other House' as his nominated assembly, Cromwell dissolved parliament on 4 February. As he succumbed to debilitating and ultimately fatal illness, he named his son Richard, rather than his son-in-law Colonel Charles Fleetwood, as his successor. This was not so much a gesture towards dynasticism as his prioritising of a civil over a military Lord Protector. Nevertheless, neither the Instrument of Government nor the Humble Petition and Advice had secured parliamentary ratification. When Cromwell died on 3 September 1658, his immediate legacy was a family power struggle that negated the constitution, threatened renewed civil war and paved the way for a Restoration of the Stuart monarchy just over 20 months later.[52]

Cromwell's enduring appeal was that of an epic English hero, the revolutionary war leader classically nuanced by the poet Andrew Marvell who, simultaneously, recognised his imperial standing.[53] On the one hand, Cromwell's greatness as a Gothic emperor was praised as personifying the national excellencies of England; on the other, his exclusive approach to politics and his belligerent pursuit of peace through war made him an emblematic figure of England's times of distraction during the 1640s and 1650s. As a godly soldier he was determined to be the servant of a God who demanded sacrifices and ruled by will rather than by law or covenant.[54] Although the portraits of him emphasise his Puritan austerity, Presbyterian as well as Royalist commentators in England certainly viewed the state funeral accorded to Cromwell on 22 September 1658 as noteworthy for its imperial ramifications as well as its sumptuousness.[55] The Scots offered a different perspective. Cromwell's exercise of supreme authority over the British Isles was described variously as tyrannical or like a sultan, recalling disparagingly the Turkish version of absolute monarchy castigated by Harrington. James Fraser, the Presbyterian minister of Wardlaw in Inverness-shire, when in London after Cromwell's death, claimed that his dissected body was found to be 'full of corruption and filth, but his name and his memory stank worse'. In Ireland, the vernacular poets were and remained no more moderate in their criticisms of a received conqueror and a perceived oppressor, particularly as the country in the 1650s resumed its role as a laboratory for political economy through renewed plantations.[56]

Redefining the National Interest

While myth and humanism, providence and prophecy shaped rival perspectives of Britain, the influences causing and shaping revolution from the 1630s to the 1650s were primarily those of sovereignty and confessionalism, the key defining features of the early modern world. However, the most enduring legacy and the most formative influence of the British revolution, which paved the way to modernity from the 1650s, was that of political economy. Thus, the debate on the national interest which characterised this decade was defined and conducted primarily in terms of the interaction between commerce and public policy with respect to England.[57] Given the Gothic hegemony of the 1650s, which tied economic prosperity to political incorporation, this debate affected the prospects for national survival in Scotland, and more especially in Ireland.

Under the early Stuarts, issues of political economy tended to be project based, notably with respect to such topics as plantations, colonies, fishing, coal and salt, monopolies and currency. However, a pathbreaking work by Gervaise Markham, which was augmented and republished on several occasions between 1631 and 1648, identified the household as the basic unit for the economic prosperity of Great Britain, which was to be achieved primarily by soil enrichment, livestock breeding and the making of orchards and gardens. This work on wealth accumulation drew empirically on evidence from Kent and, like the contemporaneous writings of William Lithgow for the regeneration of Scotland, saw plantations as the key to the productive working of land. Both finessed Harrington in arguing that agrarian redistribution was as much about labour and the diversification of the rural economy as about the acquisition of property. The Calvinist emphasis on the productive use of worldly wealth in secular callings and a vocational desire among the mercantile community to emulate the Dutch led to the publication of commercial information packs such as that by the London merchant Robert Lewes in 1638.[58]

After the summoning of the 'Long Parliament', issues of political economy were integral to the Scottish calls for confessional confederation. The Scots demanded not only reparations for the damage to their trade during the Bishops' Wars, but also free access to colonies and overseas plantations. The duty of the legislature to promote the revival of English trade, lower interest rates and sustain a sound currency instigated a brief public debate in 1640–41. The key contribution was made by Sir Ralph Maddison, whose clear statement of the theory of the balance of trade was to be reprinted more revealingly in 1655 as *Great Britain's Remembrancer* – a title hitherto reserved for providential sermons and prophetic utterances.[59] Calls to free up colonial trade, particularly to the East Indies, and promotional literature for the American colonies continued to feature throughout the 1640s, when London merchants became notably adept at remonstrating against the lack of trade and the decline in manufactures. However, the emphasis on economic discourse during the civil war was geared to securing an adequate revenue base for the rival armies in England rather than to shaping a mercantilist policy characterised by protectionism for manufactures, the acquisition of bullion, and differential tariffs to encourage exports and deter imports. Although the Scottish Covenanters remained keen to secure a commercial presence in the East and West Indies, their primary policy focus was agrarian, to develop and preserve plantations characterised by parks, dykes and enclosures.[60]

On the eve of the creation of the Commonwealth as a free state, Henry Parker issued a seminal work which tied judicial freedom to commercial freedom and, in the process, signposted the shift away from confessional to commercial confederation in English alliances with northern European powers. Henry Robinson tied the people's freedom and patriotism to the advancement of trade and navigation under the Commonwealth. Having called for the improvement of trade and the commercial incorporation of 'the whole strength of England' as the key to wealth creation, William Potter made a sophisticated material pitch for the efficient working of money through bills of exchange in 1651. He sought a proactive role for the 'Rump Parliament' in the promotion of mercantile enterprise as a national endeavour and the creation of a land bank to extend the credit basis for agricultural improvements and industrial diversity.[61] Thomas Violet, a London goldsmith, who was particularly concerned to prevent the export of gold and silver to finance trade to the East Indies and the Levant, endorsed the public expansion of credit facilities beyond those that the Dutch enjoyed through the Bank of Amsterdam, where loans were tied to monetary deposits. A proactive discourse on economy certainly contributed to the political conditioning in favour of the Navigation Acts of 1650–51 and the Anglo-Dutch War of 1652–4. Similar mercantilist conditioning was evident during the Protectorate, when supporters of the Western Design insisted upon the Spaniards' acceptance of free trade in the West Indies. But as Richard Baker pointed out in 1659, the main beneficiaries of the damaging war with Spain were not the London mercantile community, but the Dutch and other covert traders in the Americas.[62]

Lobbying for a proactive approach to political economy through land reclamation, fen drainage and plantations on the one hand, and through an increased volume of trade and shipping on the other, had an ulterior motive. Enhanced national prosperity would generate a greater revenue base for government and lessen the current fiscal burden through which the army and navy were sustained. Nevertheless, proactive policy making required public education on such topics as the balance of trade, the accumulation and retention of bullion, contract law, the accurate assessment and measurement of commodities and, above all, the working of money at home and abroad. This educational task became a feature of the Protectorate. Thus, John Marius offered a scientific explanation for the international use of bills of exchange, letters of credit and assigned securities in 1655.[63] Royalists no less than Independents and Presbyterians took heart from the consolidation of London as an international entrepôt, its success under the Gothic empire giving hope for further growth in the event of a Britannic restoration.

The proliferation of coffee houses for commercial and cultural exchange, newspaper adverts and the mass marketing of sheet music made the 1650s a critical decade for economic transformation. Merchant houses acting as private banks offered deposit accounts. Overseas commerce was no longer tied to corporations of merchant adventurers. The fruits of political economy were not confined to the metropolis. Overland communications expanded. Coach roads now extended well beyond the 30-mile radius of the capital that had been the case prior to the civil wars. Urban renewal throughout England was furthered through commercial exchanges and other public buildings for civic improvement. Manufacturing industries were diversifying away from an overdependence on woollens into ceramic wares. New mortgaging facilities to encourage estate improvements called for better techniques for surveying and assessing land, which were particularly relevant for the renewal of English plantations in Ireland.[64]

Issues of political economy sharply demarcated Ireland from Scotland as two satellite states. The Protectorate was notably supportive of Scottish landowners attempting internal plantations. Sir James Hope of Hopetoun, the Cromwellian collaborator with a proven track record as a metallurgist and mining entrepreneur, was committed to the exploitation of indigenous silver resources which would lessen the British dependence on imports from the Americas and even prevent a future

Hispaniola fiasco.[65] However, the Act for the Settling of Ireland, passed by the 'Rump Parliament' in August 1652, laid the basis for a punitive policy of land confiscation targeted against the Irish Confederates, Royalists, and those who had not actively assisted the Cromwellian conquest. This act, and supplementary legislation in the 'Barebones Parliament' in June 1653, effectively sought to compensate those subscribers to the adventurers' scheme of 1642, which had remained largely unfulfilled. Up to 35,000 officers and men engaged with the New Model Army in the conquest of Ireland were also due to be paid off. The military high command in Ireland was instructed to begin the surveying of forfeited estates. A map of Ireland was produced by John Woodhouse to identify areas already settled and those suitable for planting. Nevertheless, active encouragement for another round of plantations had to await a series of ordinances from the Lord Protector issued between June and September 1654, which clearly indicated that confiscation of land was directed against former Catholic Confederates. English Protestants in Munster were indemnified and those in other provinces were allowed to negotiate the fines they were to pay for past associations with Royalist endeavours or for their failure to support conquest.[66]

Empiricists such as the émigré intellectual Samuel Hartlib offered advice based on experimentation to make productive plantations through land reclamation and fen drainage that were applicable in both England and Ireland. However, the manner in which plantations were to be implemented was contested vigorously through the advocacy of Colonel Richard Lawrence for the adventurers and soldiers and of Vincent Gookin from Munster for the established British planters. Public policy favoured the transplantation of the native Irish out of Ulster, Leinster and Munster into Connacht, where their settlements would be corralled by colonies of soldiers along the Atlantic coast and the banks of the River Shannon to close the door on foreign intervention from Spain and France. Whereas Lawrence called for the wholesale transportation of the native Irish into a Catholic *laager*, Gookin preferred to transfer their landed elite only and to retain tenants and labourers in all four provinces to ensure productivity and economic diversity in a thoroughly planted Ireland. Gookin, like George Monck when he was the supreme Parliamentary commander in Ulster in 1648, was primarily concerned with the recovery and augmentation of existing plantations. Monck had favoured the British over the Scottish forces whenever divisions arose over the protection and conservation of landed property.[67]

Ireland was deemed not likely to be improved to the advantage and security of England, 'after so great an Expence of blood and Treasure' in its conquest, until fully inhabited with Protestants. In the event, there was only a limited transfer of the native Irish, landed elite and their families to Connacht. Colonel Henry Cromwell, the younger son of the Lord Protector, who was given overall command of the Army in Ireland in December 1654 – albeit another three years were to elapse before he became lord-deputy – took his lead from Monck in Scotland. He opted for a policy of partial accommodation rather than wholescale forfeiture. The principal beneficiaries of the new round of plantations were not the adventurers or the soldiers, but the existing planters, who were able to procure the allotments of the former and purchase the promissory notes or debentures of the latter. The majority of the intended beneficiaries of the new plantations were disinclined to settle permanently in Ireland. Fewer than expected numbers of new settlers and Protestant tenants arrived in Ulster, Leinster and Munster. The Scottish planters, Catholic as well as Protestant, largely managed to stay their ground.[68] Ultimately, landed security in Ireland depended as much on political connection and economic resourcefulness, particularly with regard to credit, as on ethnicity or confessionalism. Nevertheless, the renewed round of planting represented a Gothic consolidation of the English, not the British, interest in Ireland, an interest that began to gear up to defend its political and commercial ascendancy as the Protectorate began to implode and a Restoration of the Stuart monarchy became a distinct possibility.[69]

Military–Fiscal Implosion

A key feature of the implosion of the Protectorate was that any international or domestic audit of public policy included not only judicial and confessional concerns affecting sovereignty and godly rule. Issues of political economy – notably the restoration, preservation and advancement of free trade, commerce, manufacturing and fisheries – were also routinely cited.[70] No less significant were the financial pressures generated by the armies of occupation required to keep Ireland and Scotland quiescent. By December 1654, the cost of maintaining garrisons and troops in Scotland amounted to £282,675, of which only £45,000 was raised locally through cess. Another £40,000 was provided by diverting money from Ireland, but the bulk of the revenue raised (£137,260) was met by direct subvention from England. However, there remained a deficit of more than £60,415. England's marginal capacity to be self-sufficient as a military–fiscal state through a revenue base generated principally from cess, customs and excise was terminated by the Western Design, whose costs exceeded the cost of royal government throughout the 1630s and added a further £500,000 annually to naval expenditure. This situation was further compounded by Cromwell's estrangement from the mercantile interests in the city of London and by the reduction in cess required by the revised Humble Petition and Advice of May 1657, when the Protectorate admitted to running an annual deficit of around £500,000. Naval procurers had exhausted their credit and were obliged to purchase supplies with ready cash. Pay for the New Model Army was at least six months in arrears, and the situation was not improved by the raising of an additional 6000 troops to fight in Flanders following an alliance with France against Spain in March 1657. By April 1659, the accumulated public debts of the Protectorate exceeded £2.2 million.

The annual income generated from England (£1.5 million) only fell £30,500 short of domestic expenditure. But Scotland was generating only £143,653 and was running a deficit of £163,619, while Ireland was generating £207,790 with a deficit of £138,690. Occupation of its satellite states had entrenched the Protectorate in a financial mire. Its aggressive foreign policy ensured that it never recovered. By December 1659, Richard Cromwell was personally held accountable for an accumulated public debt now just under £2.2 million, which was reduced only by £706,492 from notified arrears for customs and excise. A parliamentary cash advance of £600,000, to be raised through cess, cut this notional deficit to £849,374. The other current sources of public revenue in England, Scotland and Ireland did not exceed £150,000. The only prospect of generating further supply was through recourse to the fiscal expedients for which Charles I had been roundly condemned during his prerogative rule. Fiscal exhaustion, in turn, made any assertion of dominance by the New Model Army in civil affairs less and less tenable.[71]

Richard Cromwell's uneasy relations with contending factions in the Council of State were manifest in his decision to summon a parliament in January 1659, based on the old franchise rather than that laid down at the outset of the Protectorate in 1654. The Commons was hostile to the retention of the 'Other House'. In April, the Council of Officers meeting at Wallingford House and led by Fleetwood and Lambert forced the new Protector to dissolve the parliament as implacably hostile to the Army. However, the New Model Army was not united and not beyond challenge from within. Junior officers, with the support of the rank and file, pressed for the recall of the 'Rump Parliament', which the generals duly dispersed in October. The Council of State was replaced by a Committee of Safety charged to settle the constitution without recourse to a monarch or lord protector or the House of Lords in a restored Commonwealth. However, the strains between the civil and military authorities in England in 1659, as in 1640, required resolution through military intervention from Scotland. General George Monck, whose loyalty to the Wallingford House group had been questionable since the summer, called at the beginning of November for a responsible return to parliamentary government. Having ensured the loyalty of the Scottish garrisons under his command and confined disaffected officers in Tantallon Castle, East Lothian, he took over Berwick-upon-Tweed. At the same time, the acknowledged presence of agents for the exiled Charles II in Scotland raised apprehensions in England about another invasion from the north. The 'Rump Parliament' was again restored through regimental pressure on the high command on 27 December as the Army prepared to mutiny in the north of England and rioting beset London.[72]

Having summoned a convention of shire and burgh commissioners to meet in Edinburgh on 15 November to secure the peace in Scotland, Monck called for the election of one noble or gentry from each shire to attend on him at Berwick on 12 December. Following pressure to mobilise the shire militias for his assistance, Monck issued a clarion call to the nobles and gentry on 7 January 1660, that he was prepared to move 'in behalf of the Nation of Scotland' that its inhabitants 'may enjoy ane equality with the Nation of England'. Monck duly commenced his long march south aided by former adherents of the patriotic accommodation who included a contingent from the Royalist clans, most notably from Lochaber, led by Ewen Cameron of Lochiel, who had been an instigator of guerilla resistance to the Cromwellian occupation. Ireland was not far behind Scotland in staging pre-emptive action against the Army's high command. The English interest in Ireland had regrouped in a military and civil alliance around two experienced politicians: Sir Charles Coote, the veteran Protestant planter and commander, and Lord Broghill, recently returned from Scotland. In December 1659, Coote had actually instigated the first military action against the restored Commonwealth outside England by staging a *coup d'état* that captured Dublin. The city was retained in defiance of the military high command as represented by Edmund Ludlow, as implacable an opponent of the now retired Henry Cromwell as Charles Fleetwood was of Protector Richard. A Convention of Estates summoned for 27 January 1660 continued in session for the next four months to ensure that a

Restoration of the monarchy took full account of the English interest in Ireland.[73]

On entering London at the beginning of February 1660, Monck was instrumental in forcing through the recall of the 'Long Parliament' through the readmission of members excluded since December 1648. The Army high command under Fleetwood and Lambert had been primarily concerned to refashion the Protectorate. However, a joint rearguard action was fought on behalf of a restored Commonwealth untainted by Covenanting, with Nedham, Vane junior and other adherents of 'the good old cause'. Others clamoured for a renewed patriotic accommodation between Royalists and Presbyterians such as had materialised in Scotland but not in England in 1649–51. Having now brought about the British equivalent, Monck was persuaded that the recalled 'Long Parliament' should dissolve itself and call fresh elections, which was promptly accomplished by 25 April. Three weeks earlier, at Monck's suggestion, Charles II had issued a renewed Declaration of Breda. A free pardon was offered to all who 'return to the loyalty and obedience of good subjects'. Military arrears would be paid in full. Land sales made since 1642 would be confirmed, a concession particularly relevant to the English interest in Ireland. A general toleration remained a possibility, not a commitment. The new English parliament, an overwhelmingly Royalist convention, duly voted on 8 May for the Restoration of the Stuarts.[74]

An exultant John Evelyn described the entrance of Charles II into London on his birthday, 29 May 1660, as a restoration 'that was never mentioned in any history, ancient or modern, since the return of the Jews from their Babylonish captivity'. However, the main significance of the Restoration was the matters not mentioned in the Declaration of Breda, most notably the nature of the constitutional settlements to be accomplished in the three kingdoms and whether British union would continue on the hegemonic terms attributable to the prowess and prudence of the English.[75] Ultimately, three decades of revolutionary politics had not determined the extent to which the Gothic, the Scottish and the Irish perspectives could be accommodated to the Britannic.

Conclusion: A Britannic Restoration?

The Restoration of Charles II produced constitutional settlements in all three kingdoms which revived the Stuarts' *ius imperium* but ruled out the confederal concept of Britain and Ireland united by covenanting. From an anglocentric perspective, the academic community at Oxford University reworked Britannic myth and legend to portray Charles II as the sole light of Great Britain. The Lords and Commons concurred in a less illuminating gesture on 22 May 1661, when the Solemn League and Covenant, the most distinctive Scottish contribution to the British Revolution, was burned by the common hangman at Westminster and removed from all public places of record and from all churches in England and Wales. Laments for the passing of the Solemn League were not confined to Scotland or to the Scottish settlers in Ulster, however. The occasional dissenting voice was raised in the parliamentary debate on burning. No attempt was made to deny that the Scottish predilection for covenanting had instigated the seditious, rebellious and factious war for the three kingdoms, which had resulted in the abolition of episcopacy as well as the execution of Charles I. However, it was also observed that the Restoration could not have been achieved without the participation of committed Covenanters as well as Royalists in the patriotic accommodation that Monck had effected from Scotland in the previous year.[1]

Apart from the monarchy, episcopacy and aristocracy were restored as the twin pillars of Stuart rule. Parliaments as they had operated at the outset of the reign of Charles I were restored in England, Scotland and Ireland. With regard to the initial promises made by Charles II in his Declaration of Breda in April 1660, the free pardon to loyal subjects was not extended to the regicides, living or dead. Accordingly, the body of Cromwell was exhumed, hanged in its shroud and the skull impaled in Westminster Hall. The Marquess of Argyll became the most prominent victim among the revolutionary politicians who actually witnessed the Restoration. His trial, conviction and public beheading in Edinburgh in

227

May 1661, purportedly for his close association with Cromwell in the regicide, coincided with the public burning of the Solemn League in London. Military arrears were also paid off, if not in full, certainly in sufficient amounts to ensure stability through the peaceful disbanding of the Cromwellian forces and the substantive decommissioning of naval warships. The removal of Cromwellian garrisons took longer in Scotland and Ireland, however. Changes in landownership since 1642 were largely respected, with the significant exceptions that Charles II reclaimed the crown lands and the bishops were restored to their temporal estates in all three kingdoms. Recompense for forfeited and sequestered Royalists had particular force in Ireland, adding a new element to the consolidation of the English interest. Toleration remained a frustrated hope. Despite co-ordination from the court, the constitutional settlements in the three kingdoms took up to five years to conclude. Indeed, their differences were as important as their similarities, especially in assessing the extent to which the Restoration marked a return to Britannic monarchy as an organically inclusive construct.

In England, continuing fear of insurrection from below, fuelled by the abortive rising of Thomas Venner and the Fifth Monarchists in London during the winter of 1660, afforded considerable laxity for the recovery of prerogative powers within a balanced constitution. Thus, the Privy Council was restored as the king's executive agency of government. The Council was appropriately inclusive. Edward Hyde, created Earl of Clarendon, and the Earl of Southampton were the most prominent of the former 'constitutional royalists'. Ormond represented the former Royalist war effort. Denzil Holles and the Earl of Northumberland featured among former Parliamentarians. General Monck, elevated to the peerage as Duke of Albemarle, was foremost among a handful of former Cromwellians. His appointment as lord-lieutenant of Ireland instead of Ormond served to reassure the English interest during the protracted land settlement. At the same time, bridges built with the city of London were reinforced by permanent commissions of Trade and Plantations, which followed Cromwellian precedent by involving merchants as well as councillors as royal advisers.[2]

Parliament operated as the king's supreme legislature through the Lords and the Commons, whose membership, procedure and business reverted to the practices prevailing before the civil wars. The constitutional experimentation of the Commonwealth and the Protectorate was wholly disregarded. The restored Stuart monarchy was expected to observe traditional historical and constitutional boundaries. Charles II regained uncontested control of the militia and the judiciary as of central and local government. However, limitations on the monarchy were reaffirmed, most notably parliament's right to vote supply.[3] Anglicanism was restored to its establishment status within the Church of England, with sectarian dissent subject to discriminatory and draconian penal laws, named the Clarendon Code for their purported instigator. But there was no attempt to return to Laudian sacerdotalism at the expense of a broad communion of believers. Nevertheless, the defence of the restored erastian episcopacy, reinforced by the purity of Anglican tradition and untainted by popery, bolstered the anglocentric appropriation of Britain for Restoration England. The instigator of renewed claims for the spiritual and temporal supremacy of the English monarchy throughout the British Isles was William Prynne, who, after a career as a religious and political agitator, was reconciled to Anglicanism at the Restoration.[4]

Formally restored to independence in 1660, Scotland nonetheless continued to operate as a junior political partner, albeit with fuller participation of Scots in the process of government than in the 1650s. The Scottish Council at Whitehall, a devolved committee of the English Privy Council, initially marked Scotland's provincial standing while serving as a channel for the court to press for the constitutional settlement in Scotland to follow English practice. The abandonment of Presbyterianism, though not immediately required by Charles II, was due partly to the naivety of the Resolutioners as the major grouping in the Kirk in trusting negotiations to James Sharp and partly to this cleric's personal duplicity in securing himself the archbishopric of St Andrews in the restored episcopate. Nonetheless, the driving force behind this change to the religious establishment was the Scottish nobility led by former Britannic Engagers such as Middleton, Glencairn and, above all, Lauderdale. Their dominance in the revived Scottish Privy Council was fortified by unflinching support from the restored judiciary. Although Lauderdale was not the foremost political influence within Scotland at the outset of the Restoration, he soon turned the mendacity, venality and chicanery rampant throughout the regime to his personal advantage. His ascendancy, which was marked by the termination of the Scottish Council, led to his personal exercise of provincial government from 1667. Over the next decade, Scotland again served as a political laboratory. English fears that Lauderdale was using Scotland as a model for absolutism on the cheap were not groundless. Simultaneously, he exploited and exaggerated a climate of religious dissent in the Lowlands and social disorder in the Highlands to build up not only standing forces but a militia sustained by cess and empowered to quell unrest anywhere within the king's dominions.[5]

Scotland, however, also demonstrated the limits of Britannic conformity. The restoration of episcopacy led to the most sizeable element of Protestant dissent within the three kingdoms, which was led by militant Protestors and sustained by conventicles in house and field. Whereas the constitutional situation in England was effectively restored to that pertaining at the outset of the 'Long Parliament' in 1640–41, all vestiges of the Covenanting movement were swept away through the Act of Recissory in 1661. Scotland was returned to its constitutional standing at the coronation parliament of 1633. Although no effort was made to reimpose liturgical innovations, the oath of allegiance now mandatory for all officeholders replaced the imperative of covenanting with an unreserved commitment to the royal prerogative. The Restoration Settlement, initiated through the reconstituted Committee of Estates dissolved by Cromwell's forces in 1651, was ratified formally by the Scottish Estates in plenary session, with the bishops representing the clerical interest, by 1662, even though another year was to elapse before their full spiritual and temporal restoration. While former Royalists regained estates forfeited in the 1640s and 1650s, arrears of taxes due to the Covenanting movement were not written off. In effect, Scotland was recast as a military–fiscal state in debt, with nobles and gentry pressing for army commissions in order to benefit from a share of the stringent fines imposed on religious dissenters and disorderly clans.[6]

Scotland's constitutional standing was not so much approximate to that of England as realigned to that of Ireland, where a dependent parliament was restored. Like the Irish parliaments and the constitutional assemblies in the Caribbean colonies, the Scottish Estates in 1661 awarded Charles a substantive annuity (£40,000 sterling) for life, raised mainly through the excise. Such awards obviated the need for regular parliaments to vote supply. Scotland also became a training ground for the oppressive use of the armed forces, although the continuity of governors-general and in colonial administration has focused more attention on Ireland and the Stuarts' American dominions as military–fiscal dependencies.[7]

Ulster Presbyterians, like their Scottish brethren, were disadvantaged by the restoration of erastian episcopacy, which was also marked by successive outings of nonconformists and by the proscription of covenanting. Despite being tinged through distant association with the Blood Plot of old Cromwellians in and around Dublin during 1663, and despite Ulster featuring occasionally in the preaching circuit of Scottish field conventiclers, Presbyterianism in Ireland preferred to maintain a passive rather than a militant profile.

The Ulster Scots were fully cognisant that the constitutional settlement in Ireland was primarily directed at the consolidation of the English interest. Roger Boyle, the newly created Earl of Orrery and restored lord president of Munster, made clear to Ormond on 9 September 1661 that 'a true English Protestant Interest is ye Immoveable foundation' upon which the king intended to build the security of Ireland as well as England.[8] Accordingly, the land issue took clear precedence over the political and religious concerns that dominated the agenda in England and Scotland. The Acts of Settlement (1662) and of Explanation (1665) and, in the interim, the Irish Court of Claims established in 1663 were particularly concerned to ensure that former Royalists who had fought against the Catholic Confederates as well as the Cromwellian occupation were now recompensed for their past services. The Cromwellian confiscations of the 1650s were further adjusted to take account of 'innocent papists'. However, the Protestant establishment was not averse to recalling past approaches by the Catholic Confederates to Spain, France and the papacy to question the loyalty and suitability of Irish Catholics to hold political office, attain royal favour and inherit or acquire estates.[9]

In reality, restored Stuart rule over the multiple kingdoms represented a compromise between Britannic and Gothic perspectives. The Scottish and Irish perspectives were now subordinate but not subliminal. Amicable relations having been resumed between the Oldenburgs and the Stuarts in 1660, Frederik III's perplexities over the correct way to address Charles II were not helped by the latter's inconsistency. Thus, Charles II was addressed formally as both the 'King of Great Britain and Ireland' and as 'King of England, Scotland and Ireland'. Charles, in contrast to his father and grandfather, and subsequently to his brother, would seem to have preferred the latter formulation, which was inherited from the Commonwealth.[10] The inclusive Britannic perspective was highlighted by the Dutch academic Rutgerius Hermannides in his *Britannia Magna* of 1661, which nevertheless chronicled English hegemony over Scotland and Ireland. The exclusive Gothic perspective was articulated forcibly by the Swedish jurist Samuel von Pufendorf, who came to view England as a composite monarchy with Scottish and Irish dependencies. In Pufendorf's view, Charles II carried on the mantle of Cromwell in maintaining English greatness through dominion over the seas and the promotion of commerce.[11] John Ogilby, a Scot who made his reputation as a theatrical impresario in Ireland under Strafford, stage-managed the coronation of Charles II as King of England in 1661. Notwithstanding that Charles had already been crowned as the covenanted King of Great Britain and Ireland in Scotland on 1 January 1651, his English coronation went ahead on 23 April, St George's Day, to celebrate the desired end to revolutionary upheavals as much as the actual Stuart restoration. Triumphal arches built by the city of London celebrated Britannic monarchy by buttressing loyalty to the Stuarts with the commercial clout of the metropolis flanked by Edinburgh to the right and Dublin to the left. During the actual ceremonial, the interests of Scotland and Ireland were discreetly represented by the respective presences of Lauderdale and Ormond.[12]

Although the Restoration clearly marked a return to regal union, the resurgence of European mercantilism reawakened the debate on British state formation, which was now conducted primarily within the context of political economy rather than jurisprudence or confessionalism. The imposition of the Navigation Laws by the English parliament in 1660, 1663, 1667 and 1671, together with the rise of London to become a global entrepôt, facilitated a distinctively English, Gothic mercantilism in direct competition with the Dutch and the French that also impacted upon Scotland and Ireland. The English interest in Ireland was particularly aggrieved about the ban on importing Irish cattle into England that came into effect in 1667. Edward, Earl of Conway, and other Anglo-Irish landowners were to the fore in protesting against this discriminatory measure, which they held to undermine the Protestant ascendancy. Although Conway contemplated smuggling cattle through Wales as an expression of civil disobedience, he concentrated on securing alternative markets for salted carcasses of which the Royal Navy was the most prominent. At the same time, he diversified his estate management in Antrim through the intensive working of potash to facilitate the bleaching of cloth and the introduction of Walloons skilled in spinning and weaving to promote the manufacture of linen and wool. He also engaged with other English entrepreneurs to export timber to England from as far afield as County Wicklow. The complaints of the English interest were partially assuaged when Charles II issued a proclamation in February 1667 suspending the Navigation Acts insofar as they discouraged Irish trade with the American colonies and with allied powers in continental Europe. Simultaneously, imports of luxury goods continued to be prohibited as a drain on specie; other imports damaging to Irish manufacturing were also banned. The Duke of York, as Lord High Admiral for England and Ireland, was given responsibility for the licensing of trade to and from Irish ports.[13]

As Duke of York, James played a key public role in upholding a Britannic perspective. After the first imposition of the English Navigation Laws, Charles II had granted individual dispensations to Scottish entrepreneurs wishing to sustain sugar works in Glasgow and Edinburgh through trade to the Americas which were also broadened to cover trading ventures to Africa and Asia. However, James was instrumental in using the crown's acclaimed prerogative powers to suspend laws restricting Scottish no less than Irish participation in English overseas ventures. The pressing of Scots into service in the Royal Navy and the conscription of Scottish seamen to serve in the Second (1666–7) and Third (1672–4) Dutch Wars against their main commercial partner further encouraged a laxity in applying trading prohibitions. Having been awarded New York as a proprietary colony on its being wrested from the Dutch in 1664, James had been an assiduous and tolerant promoter of a durable Scottish and Dutch commercial network from 1673 that was based in Albany, named after his Scottish ducal title. His subsequent opening up of participation from all three kingdoms in the Hudson's Bay Company was reflected in the naming of the Bay's eastern shore as North and South Wales and its western shore as New Britain.[14]

The Duke of York also moderated the Gothic mercantilism that sought to secure the fishing resources around the British Isles for English benefit. The Company of the Royal Fishery of Great Britain and Ireland established in 1661, which drew upon the expertise of agents involved in the common fishing of Charles I, was a Thames-led initiative regulated by English common law. Having attracted criticism from the diarist Samuel Pepys that the money realised by lottery as well as public subscription proved more corrupting than remunerative, the company was remodelled in 1664. Its continuing operation was compromised by the existence of a separate Scottish initiative operating through provincial associations from 1661 that was recast in 1670 as the Royal Company for Fishery in Scotland. This venture, which stuttered on until 1690, remained distinct from and detrimental to the viability of the complementary Company of the Royal Fishery of England established under the duke's leadership in 1677. Regardless of any resolution on territorial waters claimed for Scotland or England respectively under Britannic monarchy, neither company could operate independently of Dutch fishing expertise.[15]

Whereas fishing, like colonialism, was part of the debate on national improvement through commerce in England, it was integral to the debate on national survival through entrepreneurship in Scotland. The Scots had certainly benefited from the prohibition on the import of Irish cattle into England in 1667, which they had consolidated with their own simultaneous ban on Irish imports. Thus, the droving of cattle and sheep from Scotland under licence had a clear run in English markets. Nevertheless, as the Scottish Privy Council's Committee of Inquiry into Trade realised in 1681 when calling for another round of protection, the Scots lacked the political muscle to make other mercantilist measures effective in the Restoration era.

Bilateral discussions on commerce and constitutional affairs tended to posit either closer political union or access to the claimed English colonies in the Americas and the Indies. Thus in both Ireland and Scotland overtures for union with England featured as central issues of political economy. Scotland, however, had no equivalent to Sir William Petty, who had cut his polemical teeth while a land surveyor during the Cromwellian confiscations in Ireland. Petty promoted union with England in order to facilitate social engineering, if not ethnic and cultural assimilation, through the transplantation of peoples. Proposals for commercial confederation issued from Scotland in 1664 and 1668 ran up against English fears about the competitive edge enjoyed by the Scottish carrying trade, the close Scottish trading links with the Dutch and, above all, the perceived Scottish threat to vested coal and salt interests in the north-east of England. Support for commercial union was also an important power play by Lauderdale to establish his supremacy at court as adviser on Scottish affairs. However, his promotion of political incorporation in 1668 and his subsequent wrecking of negotiations between commissioners for the English and Scottish parliaments two years later was an even more cynical ruse to cover up secret negotiations between Charles II and Louis XIV of France. Revived proposals for commercial confederation from England in 1674 never got off the drawing board as the Scots opted for colonial expansion, which remained a chimeric, if not an entirely fruitless, pursuit over the next two decades.

Notwithstanding the heroic endeavours of James, Duke of York, there was little political will either at the court of Charles II, in the English Privy Council or in the English parliament to sustain an inclusive Britannic agenda within the Stuart's dominions. The major outcome of the British Revolution of the mid-seventeenth century was the entrenchment of English hegemony over Scotland and Ireland. Hence, British state formation, stimulated by a further phase of revolutionary politics from 1689 to 1691 and driven primarily by considerations of political economy in 1706–7, had to be accomplished primarily on Gothic terms, at English rather than Scottish instigation, with the Irish sidelined by a Protestant ascendancy.[16]

Notes

Introduction: The British Problem

1. Cf. A. Fletcher & P. Roberts, eds, *Religion, Culture and Society in Early Modern Britain* (Cambridge, 1994); B. Bradshaw & J. Morrill, eds, *The British Problem, c.1534–1707: State Formation in the Atlantic Archipelago* (Basingstoke, 1996); B. Bradshaw & P. Roberts, eds, *British Consciousness and Identity: The Making of Britain, 1533–1707* (Cambridge, 1998); A. Grant & K.J. Stringer, eds, *Uniting the Kingdom? The Making of British History* (London, 1995); A.I. Macinnes & J. Ohlmeyer, eds, *The Stuart Kingdoms in the Seventeenth Century: Awkward Neighbours* (Dublin, 2002).
2. R. Cust & A. Hughes, 'Introduction: After Revisionism', in R. Cust & A. Hughes, eds, *Conflict in Early Stuart England* (London, 1989), pp.1–47; A. Woolrych, *Britain in Revolution, 1625–1660* (Oxford, 2002), pp.1–6.
3. Cf. G. Burgess, ed., *The New British History: Founding a Modern State, 1603–1715* (London, 1999); S.J. Connolly, ed., *Kingdoms United? Great Britain and Ireland since 1500: Integration and Diversity* (Dublin, 1999); S.G. Ellis & S. Barber, eds, *Conquest and Union: Fashioning a British State, 1485–1725* (London, 1995); R.M. Smuts, ed., *The Stuart Court and Europe: Essays in Politics and Political Culture* (Cambridge, 1996); R.G. Asch, ed., *Three Nations – A Common History? England, Scotland, Ireland and British History, c.1600–1920* (Bochum, 1993).
4. G. Parker, 'The World beyond Whitehall: British Historiography and European Archives', in Smuts, ed., *The Stuart Court and Europe*, pp.274–82.
5. Cf. J. Scott, *England's Troubles: Seventeenth-Century English Political Instability in a European Context* (Cambridge, 2000); J. Goodare, *State and Society in Early Modern Scotland* (Oxford, 1999).
6. Cf. K. Brown, 'Seducing the Scottish Clio: Has Scottish History Anything to Fear from the New British History?', in Burgess, ed., *The New British History*, pp.238–65; M. Lee Jr, 'Scotland, the Union and the Idea of a General Crisis', in R.A. Mason, ed., *Scots and Britons: Scottish Political Thought and the Union of 1603* (Cambridge, 1994), pp.41–87.
7. Cf. M. Lynch & J. Goodare, eds, *The Reign of James VI* (East Linton, 1999).
8. Cf. J. Ohlmeyer, 'Introduction: A Failed Revolution?', in J. Ohlmeyer, ed., *Ireland from Independence to Occupation, 1641–1660* (Cambridge, 1995), pp.1–23.
9. C. Russell, 'Is British History International History?', in Macinnes & Ohlmeyer, eds, *The Stuart Kingdoms in the Seventeenth Century*, pp.62–9.
10. A. Calder, *Revolutionary Empire: The Rise of the English-Speaking Empire from the Fifteenth Century to the 1780s* (London, 1988), pp.79–288.

11. J.G.A. Pocock, 'The Limits and Divisions of British History: In Search of an Unknown Subject', *AHR*, 87 (1982), pp.311–36.
12. J. Morrill, *The Nature of the English Revolution* (London, 1993), pp.252–72, and *idem*, 'The Britishness of the English Revolution', in Asch, ed., *Three Nations – A Common History?*, pp.83–115.
13. R. Frost, 'Confessionalization and the Army in the Polish–Lithuanian Commonwealth, 1550–1667', in J. Bahlcke & A. Strohmeyer, eds, *Konfessionalisierung in Ostmitteleuropa: Wirkungen des religiösen Wandels im 16. und 17. Jahrhundert in Staat, Gesellschaft und Kultur* (Stuttgart, 1999), pp.139–60; E. Opalinski, 'Von der Krise der ständischen Monarchien bis zur Revolution (ca. 1600–1789)', in R.G. Asch, ed., *Der europäische Adel im Ancien Regime* (Böhlau, 2001), pp.77–104.
14. M. Peltonen, *Classical Humanism and Republicanism in English Political Thought, 1570–1640* (Cambridge, 1995), pp.229–70.
15. C. Brady, 'The Decline of the Irish Kingdom', in M. Greengrass, ed., *Conquest and Coalescence: The Shaping of the State in Early Modern Europe* (London, 1991), pp.94–115; S.G. Ellis, 'Tudor State Formation and the Shaping of the British Isles', in Ellis & Barber, eds, *Conquest and Union*, pp.40–63.
16. Cf. D.L. Smith, *A History of the Modern British Isles, 1603–1707: The Double Crown* (Oxford, 1998); B.P. Levack, *The Formation of the British State: England, Scotland and the Union, 1603–1707* (Oxford, 1987).
17. Cf. C. Russell, *The Causes of the English Civil Wars* (Oxford, 1990); *idem*, *Unrevolutionary England, 1603–1642* (London, 1990); and *idem*, *The Fall of the British Monarchies, 1637–1642* (Oxford, 1991).
18. Cf. A. Fletcher, *The Outbreak of the English Civil War* (London, 1981); A. Hughes, *The Causes of the English Civil War* (Basingstoke, 1991); D. Hirst, *England in Conflict, 1603–1660: Kingdom, Community, Commonwealth* (London, 1999).
19. S. James, *The Atlantic Celts: Ancient People or Modern Invention?* (Madison, WI, 1999), pp.43–59.
20. J.R. Young, ed., *Celtic Dimensions of the British Civil Wars* (Edinburgh, 1997).
21. J.G.A. Pocock, 'The Atlantic Archipelago and the War of the Three Kingdoms', in B. Bradshaw & J. Morrill, eds, *The British Problem, c.1534–1707* (Basingstoke, 1996), pp.172–91; J. Morrill, 'The War(s) of the Three Kingdoms', in Burgess, ed., *The New British History*, pp.65–91.
22. Cf. S. Murdoch, ed., *Scotland and the Thirty Years' War, 1618–1648* (Leiden, 2001); J. Ohlmeyer, *Civil War and Restoration in the Three Stuart Kingdoms: The Political Career of Randal MacDonnell, First Marquis of Antrim, 1609–83* (Cambridge, 1993).
23. A. Williamson, 'The Jewish Dimension of the Scottish Apocalypse: Climate, Covenant and World Renewal', in Y. Kaplan, H. Mechoulan & R.H. Popkins, eds, *Menasseh Ben Israel and His World* (New York, 1989), pp.7–30; J.R. Young, 'The Scottish Parliament and European Diplomacy, 1641–1647: The Palatinate, the Dutch Republic and Sweden', in Murdoch, ed., *Scotland and the Thirty Years' War, 1618–1648*, pp.77–106.
24. Cf. N. Canny, 'The Attempted Anglicization of Ireland in the Seventeenth Century: An Exemplar of "British History"', in Asch, ed., *Three Nations – A Common History?*, pp.49–82; J. Smyth, 'The Communities of Ireland and the British State, 1660–1707', in Bradshaw & Morrill, eds, *The British Problem, c.1534–1707*, pp.246–61.

25. A. Williamson, 'Patterns of British Identity: "Britain" and its Rivals in the Sixteenth and Seventeenth Centuries', in Burgess, ed., *The New British History*, pp.138–73.

26. N. Canny, 'The Origins of Empire: An Introduction', in N. Canny, ed., *The Origins of Empire: British Overseas Empire to the Close of the Seventeenth Century* (Oxford, 1998), pp.18–19; Patrick Copland, *Virginia's God be Thanked* (London, 1622); *idem, A Declaration of Monies* (London, 1622).

27. A. Milton, ' "The Universal Peacemaker"? John Dury and the Politics of Irenicism in England', in M. Greengrass, M. Leslie & T. Raylor, eds, *Samuel Hartlib and Universal Reformation* (Cambridge, 1994), pp.1–25; J.M. Batten, *John Dury: Advocate of Christian Reunion* (Chicago, 1944), pp.13–83.

28. DR, TKUA, Alm.Del. I Indtil 1670, no. 141, 'Breve med Bilag fra engelsk Praest Johannes Duraeus, 1634–39'; BL, J. Dury, Epistolae Pace Ecclesiastica, Sloane MS 654, ff. 216–17; John Dury, *A Summary Discourse concerning the work of peace ecclesiastical, how it may concurre with the aim of a civill confederation amongst Protestants. Presented to the consideration of my lord ambassador Sir T. Row at Hamburg 1639* (Cambridge, 1641); H. Trevor-Roper, *Archbishop Laud, 1573–1645* (Basingstoke, 1988), pp.213–70.

29. William Lithgow, *The Pilgrimes Farewell, to his Native Countrey of Scotland* (Edinburgh, 1618); T.C. Smout, N.C. Landsman & T.M. Devine, 'Scottish Emigration in the Seventeenth and Eighteenth Centuries', in N. Canny, ed., *Europeans on the Move: Studies on Migration, 1500–1800* (Oxford, 1994), pp.70–112.

30. Cf. M. Kishlansky, *The Rise of the New Model Army* (Cambridge, 1979), pp.26–51.

31. William Lithgow, *The Totall Discourse, Of the Rare Adventures, and powerfull peregrinations of long nineteen Yeares Travayles, from Scotland, to the most Famous Kingdomes in Europe, Asia, and Africa* (London, 1632); *idem, The Present Survey of London and England's State* (London, 1643).

1 British Perceptions

1. A.I. Macinnes, 'The Multiple Kingdoms of Britain and Ireland: "The British Problem" ', in B. Coward, ed., *The Blackwell Companion to Stuart Britain* (London, 2003), pp.3–25.

2. J. Wormald, 'The Union of 1603', in Mason, ed., *Scots and Britons*, pp.17–40; J. Goss, *World Historical Atlas, 1662* (London, 1990), pp.90–91. Wales were the losers in this British accommodation as the Welsh quarterings were dropped from the English imperial crown of the Tudors.

3. R.A. Mason, *Kingship and the Commonweal: Political Thought in Renaissance and Reformation Scotland* (East Linton, 1998), pp.242–69.

4. D.R. Woolf, *The Idea of History in Early Stuart England: Erudition, Ideology, and 'The Light of Truth' from the Accession of James I to the Civil War* (Toronto, 1990), pp.55–64, 115–27.

5. Cf. William Camden, *Britain, or, A Chronological description of the most flourishing kingdomes, England, Scotland and Ireland, and the islands adjoining, out of the depth of antiquity* (London, 1610, 1637); *idem, The abridgement of Camden's Britannia* (London, 1626); *idem, Camden's Britannia newly translated into English with large additions and improvements* (London, 1695). Constantine the Great was

reputed to be the son of the British princess the Venerable Helen, a pious Christian who had suppressed the idols at Jerusalem, salvaged the true cross and erected churches on the spot where Christ was crucified at Calvary and at the site of the manger in Nazareth. She was instrumental in converting her husband, Emperor Constantinus Chlorus.

6. Cf. John Speed, *The Theatre of the Empire of Great Britain: presenting an exact geography of the kingdomes of England, Scotland, Ireland and the isle adjoyning* (London, 1616, 1627); *idem*, *England, Wales, Scotland and Ireland described and abridged* (London, 1632).

7. C. Moreland & D. Bannister, *Antique Maps* (London, 2000), pp.209, 213–16; Goss, *World Historical Atlas*, pp.72–3.

8. [Wye Saltonstall], *Historia Mundi: Or Mercator's Atlas* (London, 1635), pp.38–43, 68–87.

9. Woolf, *The Idea of History in Early Stuart England*, pp.64–72; J. Adamson, 'Chivalry and Political Culture in Caroline England', in K. Sharpe & P. Lake, eds, *Culture and Politics in Early Stuart England* (Basingstoke, 1994), pp.161–97.

10. Q. Skinner, *Foundations of Modern Political Thought*, 2 vols (Cambridge, 1977–8), vol. 2, pp.135–73, 276–84; Peltonen, *Classical Humanism and Republicanism in English Political Thought*, pp.119–58.

11. M. Smuts, 'Court-Centred Politics and the Uses of Roman Histories, c.1590–1630', in Sharpe & Lake, eds, *Culture and Politics in Early Stuart England*, pp.21–43; R. Cust, 'News and Politics in Early-Seventeenth-Century England', in R. Cust & A. Hughes, eds, *The English Civil War* (London, 1997), pp.233–60.

12. K. Sharpe, *Remapping Early Modern England: The Culture of Seventeenth Century Politics* (Cambridge, 2000), pp.294–341; B. Worden, 'Ben Jonson Among the Historians', in Sharpe & Lake, eds, *Culture and Politics in Early Stuart England*, pp.67–89.

13. D. Allan, *Philosophy and Politics in Later Stuart Scotland* (East Linton, 2000), pp.89–109.

14. J.H. Burns, *The True Law of Kingship: Concepts of Monarchy in Early Modern Scotland* (Oxford, 1996), pp.222–54; J. Wormald, 'James VI and I, *Basilikon Doron* and *The Trew Law of Free Monarchies*: The Scottish Context and the English Translation', in L.L. Peck, ed., *The Mental World of the Jacobean Court* (Cambridge, 1991), pp.36–54.

15. D.J. Gordon, *The Renaissance Imagination* (Berkeley, CA, 1975), pp.36–7.

16. R.A. Mason, 'Scotching the Brut: Politics, History and National Myth in Sixteenth-Century Britain', in R.A. Mason, ed., *Scotland and England, 1286–1815* (Edinburgh, 1987), pp.60–84; S.C. Rowell, 'The Grand Duchy of Lithuania and Baltic Identity, c.1500–1600', in A.I. Macinnes, T. Riis & F.G. Pedersen, eds, *Ships, Guns and Bibles in the North Sea and Baltic States, c.1350–c.1700* (East Linton, 2000), pp.65–92.

17. P. McGinnis & A. Williamson, 'Britain, Race, and the Iberian World Empire', in Macinnes & Ohlmeyer, eds, *The Stuart Kingdoms in the Seventeenth Century*, pp.70–93.

18. Burns, *The True Law of Kingship*, pp.283–95; R.A. Mason, 'Imagining Scotland: Scottish Political Thought and the "Problem of Britain", 1560–1650', in Mason, ed., *Scots and Britons*, pp.3–16.

19. W. Malley, 'The British Problem in Three Tracts on Ireland by Spenser, Bacon and Milton', in Bradshaw & Roberts, eds, *British Consciousness and Identity: The Making of Britain, 1533–1707*, pp.159–84; C. Rawson, *God, Gulliver and Genocide: Barbarism and the European Imagination, 1492–1945* (Oxford, 2001), pp.79–91, 108–13.

20. *The British Union: A Critical Edition and Translation of David Hume of Godscroft's De Unione Insulae Britannicae*, ed. P.J. McGinnis & A. Williamson (Aldershot, 2002), pp.1–53; Allan, *Philosophy and Politics in Later Stuart Scotland*, pp.47–58, 116–21.

21. L. Eriksonas, 'National Heroes and National Identity: A Comparative Framework for Smaller Nations' (PhD diss., University of Aberdeen, DCE [Doctorate of the Community of Europe], 2000), pp.7–13, 50–67. James I had brought the printing of the heroic epics under royal control in 1611, and further runs were commissioned to support the Britannic stance of absentee monarchy in 1618 and 1620. However, an independent printing of *The Wallace* occurred in Aberdeen in 1630, when Charles I was becoming detached from the Scottish political nation. In 1639, the Red Bull Company put on *The Valiant Scot* at the Fortune Theatre in London. This play, which had been written two years earlier, had escaped royal censorship as it appeared to portray Wallace as a justified fighter against tyranny but unwilling to co-operate with the endeavours of Edward I of England to resolve conflict with the Scots through peaceful means. Intended as a timely warning to Charles I to attend to potential breakdown with his Scottish subjects, who were nonetheless expected to accede to the moral force of monarchy, the performance actually turned into an appreciation of the Covenanting movement, at least in the eyes of Puritan commentators, and served as a foretaste of rapport between Scottish Covenanters and English Parliamentarians.

22. [Bonaventure & Abraham Elzevirus], *Respublica, sive Status Regni Scotia et Hiberniae* (Leiden, 1627); Johannes Blaeu, *Scotiae Quae Est Europae, Liber XII* (Amsterdam, 1654, 1662); Goss, *World Historical Atlas*, pp.84–5.

23. K. Skovgaard-Petersen, *Historiography at the Court of Christian IV* (Copenhagen, 2002), pp.23–40, 92–3, 152–7, 179–88, 369–74.

24. H.S. Pawlisch, *Sir John Davies and the Conquest of Ireland: A Study in Legal Imperialism* (Cambridge, 1985), pp.55–64, 84–100.

25. B. Ó Buachalla, *Foras Feasa ar Éirinn, History of Ireland: Foreword* (Dublin, 1987), pp.1–8; B. Cunningham, *The World of Geoffrey Keating* (Dublin, 2000), pp.31–40, 83–101.

26. T. Ó h-Annráchain, 'Rebels and Confederates: The Stance of the Irish Clergy in the 1640s', in Young, ed., *Celtic Dimensions of the British Civil Wars*, pp.96–115; A. Clarke, 'Patrick Darcy and the Constitutional Relationship between Ireland and Britain', in J. Ohlmeyer, ed., *Irish Political Thought in the Seventeenth Century* (Cambridge, 2000), pp.35–55.

27. B. Ó Buachalla, *Aisling Ghearr: Na Stiobhartaigh Agus an tAos Leinn, 1603–1788* (Dublin, 1996), pp.148–94; J.P. Somerville, *Politics and Ideology in England, 1603–1640* (London, 1986), pp.117–20.

28. A. Clarke, 'Colonial Identity in Early Seventeenth-Century Ireland', in T.W. Moody, ed., *Nationality and the Pursuit of National Independence* (Belfast, 1978), pp.57–72; Cunningham, *The World of Geoffrey Keating*, pp.105–12.

29. C. McEachern, 'The Englishness of the Scottish Play: Macbeth and the Poetics of Jacobean Union', in Macinnes & Ohlmeyer, eds, *The Stuart Kingdoms in the Seventeenth Century*, pp.94–112.
30. C. Kidd, *British Identities before Nationalism: Ethnicity and Nationhood in the Atlantic World, 1600–1800* (Cambridge, 1999), pp.77–87; G. Burgess, *The Politics of the Ancient Constitution: An Introduction to English Political Thought, 1603–1641* (University Park, PA, 1992), pp.58–78.
31. S. Kliger, *The Goths in England: A Study in Seventeenth and Eighteenth Century Thought* (New York, 1952), pp.111–12; Richard Verstegan, *Restitution of Decayed Intelligence* (Antwerp, 1605). Subsequent editions were published in London in 1628, 1634, 1653 and 1655.
32. E. Van Mingroot & E. Van Ermen, *Scandinavia in Old Maps and Prints* (Knokke, 1987), pp.8–9; Joannus & Olaus Magnus, *De Omnibus Gothorum Sic Numque Regibus, qui unquam ab initio nationis extitere* (Rome, 1554, 1567), especially Books 20 and 23. The version published in Basle in 1568 was also in Latin, while that published in Paris in 1561 was in French and that in Antwerp in 1562 was in Dutch. The first Swedish version was published at Stockholm in 1620. In his view of the State of Ireland, written in 1596, Edmund Spenser quoted extensively from Olaus Magnus to confirm that the original settlers of Ireland were Scots or Scythians out of Spain, in effect unreconstructed, barbaric Goths (*The Works of the Famous English Poets, Mr Edmund Spenser* (London, 1679), pp.201–58).
33. Skovgaard-Petersen, *Historiography at the Court of Christian IV*, pp.93–5; Ingmar Söhrman, 'The Gothic Tradition: Its Presence in the Baroque Period', in E.M. Ruiz & M.D.P.P. Corrales, eds, *Spain & Sweden in the Baroque Era (1600–1660)* (Madrid, 2000), pp.937–47.
34. Kliger, *The Goths in England*, pp.1–21, 65; Burgess, *The Politics of the Ancient Constitution*, pp.101–2.
35. Burns, *The True Law of Kingship*, pp.255–81; A.I. Macinnes, 'Regal Union for Britain, 1603–38', in Burgess, ed., *The New British History*, pp.33–64.
36. B. Levack, 'Law, Sovereignty and the Union', in Mason, ed., *Scots and Britons*, pp.213–40; B. Galloway, *The Union of England and Scotland, 1606–1608* (Edinburgh, 1986), pp.103–30; *De Unione Regnorum Britanniae Tractatus by Sir Thomas Craig*, ed. C.S. Terry (Edinburgh, 1909).
37. L.L. Peck, 'Kingship, Counsel and Law in Early Stuart Britain', in J.G.A. Pocock, ed., *The Varieties of British Political Thought, 1500–1800* (Cambridge, 1996), pp.80–115.
38. B.H.G. Wormald, *Francis Bacon: History, Politics and Science, 1561–1626* (Cambridge, 1993), pp.154–8; [Sir Francis Bacon], *Three speeches of the Right Honourable, Sir Francis Bacon Knight, then his Majesties Sollicitor Generall, after Lord Verulam, Viscount Saint Alban. Concerning the post-nati naturalization of the Scotch in England, Union of the lawes of the kingdomes of England and Scotland* (London, 1641).
39. R. Eisen, *Gersonides on Providence, Covenant, and the Chosen People: A Study in Medieval Jewish Philosophy and Biblical Commentary* (New York, 1994), pp.1–3, 169–83; R. Gillespie, *Devoted People: Belief and Religion in Early Modern Ireland* (Manchester, 1997), pp.40–62.
40. A. Walsham, *Providence in Early Modern England* (Oxford, 1999), pp.281–325; M. McGiffert, 'God's Controversy with Jacobean England', *AHR*, 88 (1983), pp.1151–74.

41. George Wither, *Britain's Remembrancer* (London, 1628).

42. C. Hill, *Antichrist in Seventeenth-Century England* (Oxford, 1971), pp.78–145. Cf. [Thomas Brightman], *The Reverend Mr Brightmans Judgement or Prophesies, what shall befall Germany, Scotland, Holland, and the churches adhering to them likewise what shall befall England, and the hierarchy therein* (London, 1642); [R.W.], *An Information Concerning the Present State of the Jewish Nation in Europe and Judea* (London, 1658).

43. P. Curry, *Prophecy and Power: Astrology in Early Modern England* (Princeton, NJ, 1989), pp.3–15; H. Rusche, 'Prophecies and Propaganda, 1641 to 1651', *EHR*, 84 (1969), pp.752–70. Vincent Wing moved easily between astrological calculations based on the town of Stamford, but deemed serviceable 'for the whole kingdome of Great Britain', in *An Almanack and Prognostication* (London, 1641), to astronomical rudiments fitted for the meridian of London 'and principally intended for our English nation' in *Harmonicum Coeleste, or, The coelestiall harmony of the visible world* (London, 1651).

44. C. Hill, *The World Turned Upside Down: Radical Ideas during the English Revolution* (London, 1972), pp.70–85, 148–207. Cf. Thomas Tillam, a Weak Labourer in the Lord's Harvest, *The Two Witnesses: Their Prophecy, Slaughter, Resurrection and Ascension* (London, 1651), and William Dewsbury, a Quaker, *A True Prophecie of the Mighty Day of the Lord* (London, 1655).

45. K. Thomas, *Religion and the Decline of Magic: Studies in Popular Beliefs in Seventeenth-Century England* (London, 1991), pp.125–78.

46. *Prophetic Writings of Lady Eleanor Davies*, ed. E.S. Cope (New York, 1995), pp.xi–xxiii; *An Early Modern Englishwoman: A Facsimile Library of Essential Works: Volume 3, Eleanor Davies*, ed. T. Feroh (Ashgate, 2000), pp.ix–xii; N. Smith, *Literature and Revolution in England, 1640–1660* (New Haven, CT, 1994), p.125. Lady Eleanor was married first to the antiquarian and King's Solicitor in Ireland, Sir John Davies, whose death in 1626 she predicted three years in advance. He had disapproved of her prophesying and burned her writings. Her second husband, the Scottish courtier Sir Archibald Douglas, expressed similar disapproval before he became intermittently insane following a seizure in 1631. Her prophesying, based on messages from the book of Daniel in the Old Testament, led to her own periodic incarceration and committal for her trenchant criticisms of Britain and its rulers in the 1630s and 1640s.

47. T. Thornton, 'Reshaping the Local Future: The Development and Uses of Provincial Prophecies, 1300–1900', in B. Taithe & T. Thornton, eds, *Prophecy* (Stroud, 1997), pp.51–67; *Early Modern Women Poets: An Anthology*, ed. J. Stevenson & P. Davidson (Oxford, 2001), pp.116–343.

48. Hugo Grotius, *Two Discourses* (London, 1653), pp.15–18, 24–6.

49. Cf. Robert Butler, *An Almanack for the Yeare of our Lord Christ 1632* (Cambridge, 1632); William Barham, *An Almanack for the Yeere of our Lord and Saviour Christ, 1639* (London, 1639); William Browne, *Britannia's Pastorals*, ed. R.W. Thompson (London, 1772).

50. A.I. Macinnes, 'Gaelic Culture in the Seventeenth Century: Polarization and Assimilation', in Ellis & Barber, eds, *Conquest & Union*, pp.162–94; Walsham, *Providence in Early Modern England*, pp.8–64.

51. HL, Bridgewater & Ellesmere MSS, EL 8743, 8809, 8852, 8882; *Making the News: An Anthology of the Newsbooks of Revolutionary England, 1641–1660,*

ed. J. Raymond (Moreton-in-Marsh, 1993); I. Rachum, 'The Term "Revolution" in Seventeenth-Century English Astrology', *History of European Ideas*, 18 (1994), pp.869–83.

52. Cf. Early English Books Online, www.eebo.org.uk; *Fugitive Poetical Tracts, 1600–1700*, ed. W.C. Hazlett (London, 1875).

53. B. Cunningham, 'Representations of King, Parliament and the Irish People in Geoffrey Keating's *Foras Feasa ar Éirinn* and John Lynch's *Cambrensis Eversus* (1662)', in Ohlmeyer, ed., *Irish Political Thought in the Seventeenth Century*, pp.131–54.

54. J. Casway, 'Gaelic Maccabeanism: The Politics of Reconciliation', in Ohlmeyer, ed., *Irish Political Thought in the Seventeenth Century*, pp.176–88.

55. Gillespie, *Devoted People*, pp.132–40.

56. NLS, Wodrow MSS, quartos, xvi, f.220; xxix, ff.1, 3.

57. Gillespie, *Devoted People*, pp.141–2; Walsham, *Providence in Early Modern England*, p.322.

58. A. Ford, *The Protestant Reformation in Ireland, 1590–1641* (Frankfurt am Main, 1987), pp.194–242; K. Fincham & P. Lake, 'The Ecclesiastical Policies of James I and Charles I', in K. Fincham, ed., *The Early Stuart Church, 1603–1642* (Basingstoke, 1993), pp.71–91.

59. P. Jenkins, 'The Anglican Church and the Unity of Britain: The Welsh Experience, 1560–1714', in Ellis & Barber, eds, *Conquest & Union*, pp.115–38; M. Lee Jr, *Great Britain's Solomon: King James VI and I in his Three Kingdoms* (Urbana, IL, 1990), pp.167–71.

60. John Thornborough, Bishop of Bristol, *A Discourse Shewing the Great Happiness that hath and may still accrue to his Majesties Kingdomes of England and Scotland By re-Uniting them into ane Great Britain* (London, 1604, 1641).

61. Anon., *The Miraculous and Happie Union of England & Scotland* (Edinburgh, 1604).

62. *The Whole Prophecies of Scotland, England, France, Ireland and Denmarke* (Edinburgh, 1617).

63. Thomas Heywood, *The Life of Merlin, sirnamed Ambrosius, His Prophecies and Predictions interpreted and their truth made good by English Annulls* (London, 1641).

64. W. Ferguson, *The Identity of the Scottish Nation: An Historic Quest* (Edinburgh, 1998), pp.38–9.

65. A.H. Williamson, *Scottish National Consciousness in the Age of James VI* (Edinburgh, 1979), pp.140–41.

66. J. MacLeod, *Scottish Theology* (Edinburgh, 1974), pp.28–9, 85, 219; G. Marshall, *Presbyteries and Profits* (Oxford, 1980), pp.74–7, 103–12.

67. J. Wormald, 'Bloodfeud, Kindred and Government in Early Modern Scotland', *Past & Present*, 87 (1980), pp.54–97; P. Miller, 'The Marrow of Puritan Divinity', in G.M. Walker, ed., *Puritanism in Early America* (Toronto, 1973), pp.54–7.

68. Williamson, *Scottish National Consciousness in the Age of James VI*, pp.64–85; J.A. Aikman, *An Historical Account of Covenanting in Scotland from 1556 to 1638* (Edinburgh, 1848), p.65.

69. D. Stevenson, 'Conventicles in the Kirk, 1619–1637', *Records of the Scottish Church History Society*, 18 (1972–4), pp.99–114; A.I. Macinnes, *Charles I and the Making of the Covenanting Movement, 1625–1641* (Edinburgh, 1991), pp.155–8.

70. J.B. Torrance, 'The Covenant Concept in Scottish Theology and Politics and its Legacy', *Scottish Journal of Theology*, 34 (1981), pp.225–43; A.I. Macinnes, 'Covenanting Ideology in Seventeenth-Century Scotland', in Ohlmeyer, ed., *Irish Political Thought in the Seventeenth Century*, pp.191–220.

71. HL, Bridgewater & Ellesmere MSS, EL 7859.

72. A.I. Macinnes, 'Politically Reactionary Brits?: The Promotion of Anglo-Scottish Union, 1603–1707', in Connolly, ed., *Kingdoms United? Great Britain and Ireland since 1500*, pp.43–55.

73. Cf. [Matthew Walbancke], *Sundry Strange Prophecies of Merline, Bede, Becket and others* (London, 1652).

74. P. Collinson, *The Birthpangs of Protestant England: Religious and Cultural Change in the Sixteenth and the Seventeenth Centuries* (Oxford, 1988), pp.20–27; D. Como, 'Puritan, Predestination and the Construction of Orthodoxy in Early Seventeenth-Century England', in P. Lake & M. Questier, eds, *Conformity and Orthodoxy in the English Church, c.1560–1660* (Woodbridge, 2000), pp.64–87.

75. D. Cressy, *Bonfires and Bells: National Memory and the Protestant Calendar in Elizabethan and Stuart England* (London, 1989), pp.93–129, 141–70; Walsham, *Providence in Early Modern England*, pp.225–80. Samuel Garey, pastor at the Wynfarthing in Norfolk, proposed an alternative three days of celebration in *Great Brittans Little Calendar* (London, 1618): 24 March, the day of James I's proclamation in England in 1603; 1 August, the day when James VI escaped from kidnapping by the Earl of Gowrie and his associates in 1583; and 5 November, the day of the Gunpowder Plot in 1605. There was no apparent popular enthusiasm for this Britannic celebration.

76. P. Lake, 'Calvinism and the English Church', *Past & Present*, 114 (1987), pp.32–76. Cf. Peter Moulin, *The Anatomy of Arminianism* (London, 1620, 1635); George Maxwell, *An Apologee or Declaration of the Power and Providence of God in the Government of the World* (Oxford, 1635).

77. N. Tyacke, *Anti-Calvinists: The Rise of English Arminianism, c.1590–1640* (Oxford, 1987), pp.87–105, 181–244; A. Milton, 'The Church of England, Rome and the True Church', in Fincham, ed., *The Early Stuart Church, 1603–42*, pp.187–210.

78. R. Hutton, *The Rise and Fall of Merry England: The Ritual Year, 1400–1700* (Oxford, 1994), pp.153–99; D. Underdown, *Revel, Riot and Rebellion: Popular Politics and Culture in England, 1603–1660* (Oxford, 1985), pp.106–45.

79. Cf. [Bonaventura O'Connor], *An Abstract of Certain Depositions, By vertue of His Majesties Commission, taken upon Oath* (London, 1642); John Booker, *A Bloody Irish Almanack* (London, 1646); Sir George Wharton, *Bellum Hybernicale* (London, 1646).

80. *The Poetry of George Wither*, 2 vols, ed. F. Sidgwick (London, 1902), vol. 1, pp.xiii–liii; Smith, *Literature and Revolution in England*, pp.223–33.

81. S. Barber, 'The Formation of Cultural Attitudes: The Example of the Three Kingdoms in the 1650s', in Macinnes & Ohlmeyer, eds, *The Stuart Kingdoms in the Seventeenth Century*, pp.169–85; B. Worden, 'Providence and Politics in Cromwellian England', *Past & Present*, 109 (1985), pp.55–99.

82. Olaus Magnus, *A Compendious History of the Goths, Swedes and Vandals and other Northern Nations* (London, 1658).

83. Curry, *Prophecy and Power*, pp.19–44; H. Rushe, 'Merlini Anglici: Astrology and Propaganda from 1644 to 1651', *EHR*, 80 (1965), pp.322–33. Lilly was a leading light in the Society of Astrologers which, from 1647 to 1658,

exercised a no less vital influence in favour of the vernacular Gothic than that the Society of Antiquaries had manifested for the classical Britannic formulation in the first decade of regal union. Both were inclusive societies. Whereas the latter had included courtiers and Parliamentarians, the former included Royalists like Wharton and Vincent Wing as well as Commonwealthmen such as John Booker and Nicholas Culpeper. Accordingly, both societies were suspect to the political elite, whether monarchical or republican.

84. Cf. William Lilly, *England's Prophetical Merlin* (London, 1644); *idem, The Starry Messenger* (London, 1645); *idem, The World's Catastrophe, or, Europe's Many Mutations until 1666* (London, 1647); *idem, An Astrological Prediction of the Occurrences in England, Part of the Years 1648, 1649, 1650* (London, 1648); [G.J.], *The Spurious Prognosticator Unmasked* (London, 1660).

85. Cf. William Lilly, *A Prophecy of the White King: and a Dreadfull Dead-man Explained* (London, 1644); *idem, Monarchy or No Monarchy in England* (London, 1651).

86. Thomas, *Religion and the Decline of Magic*, pp.126–7; Edward [Hyde], Earl of Clarendon, *The History of the Rebellion and Civil Wars in England* (Oxford, 1893), p.1; John Rotheram, *The Force of the Argument for the Truth of Christianity Drawn from a Collective View of Prophecy* (Oxford, 1653).

87. *Rider's British Merlin* (London, 1656, 1659, 1661); Hamlett Puleston, *Monarchie Brittanicae Singularis Protectio* (London, 1661).

2 The Britannic Empire, *c.*1629

1. Burgess, *The Politics of the Ancient Constitution*, pp.129–30; Burns, *The True Law of Kingship*, pp.267–8.

2. A.H. Williamson, 'Scots, Indians and Empire: The Scottish Politics of Civilization, 1519–1609', *Past & Present*, 150 (1996), pp.46–83; J. Robertson, 'Empire and Union: Two Concepts of the Early Modern European Political Order', in Robertson, ed., *A Union for Empire: Political Thought and the Union of 1707*, pp.3–37.

3. C. Russell, 'The Anglo-Scottish Union of 1603–43: A Success?', in Fletcher & Roberts, eds, *Religion, Culture & Society in Early Modern Britain*, pp.238–56; P. Donald, *An Uncounselled King: Charles I and the Scottish Troubles, 1637–41* (Cambridge, 1990), pp.1–42.

4. HL, Bridgewater & Ellesmere MSS, EL 6931, 6952.

5. Cf. John Gordon, *Elizabethae Reginae Manes De Religione Et Regno Ad Iacobum Magnum Brittaniarum Regem, Per Ionnem Gordonium Britanno-Scotum* (London, 1604); Sir David Murray, *The Tragicall Death of Sophinisba. Written by David Murray, Scoto-Brittaine* (London, 1611); Alexander Craig, *The Political Recreations of Mr Alexander Craig of Rose-Craig, Scoto Britan* (Aberdeen, 1623). The term 'Scoto-Britannus', first coined by the Presbyterian leader Andrew Melville, was propagated most vociferously at the regal union by Hume of Godscroft.

6. J. Wormald, 'James VI and I: Two Kings or One?', *History*, 68 (1983), pp.187–209; Sommerville, *Politics and Ideology in England*, pp.39–46, 195–9, 303–8.

7. L.A. Ferrell, *Government by Polemic: James I, the King's Preachers, and the Rhetorics of Conformity, 1603–1625* (Stanford, CA, 1998), pp.113–39; P. Bushkovitch & M. Jansson, 'Introduction', in M. Jansson, P. Bushkovitch & N. Rogozhin, eds, *England and the North: The Russian Embassy of 1613–1614* (Philadelphia, 1994), pp.47–71; W.B. Patterson, *King James VI and I and the Reunion of Christendom* (Cambridge, 1998), pp.155–95, 260–92.

8. J.V. Polišenský, 'A Note on Scottish Soldiers in the Bohemian War, 1619–1622', in Murdoch, ed., *Scotland and the Thirty Years' War*, pp.109–15; Lee jr, *Great Britain's Solomon*, pp.261–98.

9. J. Goodare, 'The Nobility and the Absolutist State in Scotland, 1584–1638', *History*, 78 (1993), pp.161–82; G. Burgess, *Absolute Monarchy and the Stuart Constitution* (New Haven, CT, 1996), pp.17–62; R. Lockyer, *James VI and I* (London, 1998), pp.199–210.

10. A.R. MacDonald, *The Jacobean Kirk, 1567–1625: Sovereignty, Polity and Liturgy* (Aldershot, 1998), pp.179–87; D.G. Mullan, *Episcopacy in Scotland: The History of an Idea, 1560–1638* (Edinburgh, 1986), pp.74–113.

11. Macinnes, *Charles I and the Making of the Covenanting Movement*, pp.4, 16–18. Sir Henry Spelman found the landed elite in Scotland no more sympathetic than that of England to his pleas that the churches in both north and south Britain should be fully restored to their pre-Reformation properties (*De non temerandis ecclesiis: A tract, of the rights & respect due unto churches* (Edinburgh, 1616) – notwithstanding his innovative use of the term 'South Britaine' in his preface).

12. Tyacke, *Anti-Calvinists: The Rise of English Arminianism*, pp.87–105; K. Fincham, 'Episcopal Government, 1603–1640', in Fincham, ed., *The Early Stuart Church*, pp.71–91; Patterson, *King James VI and I and the Reunion of Christendom*, pp.31–74.

13. M. McCraith, 'The Gaelic Reaction to the Reformation', in Ellis & Barber, eds, *Conquest and Union*, pp.139–61.

14. A. Ford, 'The Church of Ireland, 1558–1634: A Puritan Church?', in A. Ford, J. McGuire & K. Milne, eds, *As By Law Established: The Church of Ireland since the Reformation* (Dublin, 1995), pp.52–68; J. McCafferty, 'When Reformations Collide', in Macinnes & Ohlmeyer, eds, *The Stuart Kingdoms in the Seventeenth Century*, pp.106–203.

15. T. Cogswell, 'England and the Spanish Match', in Cust & Hughes, eds, *Conflict in Early Stuart England*, pp.107–33; Ferrell, *Government by Polemic*, pp.167–76. Cf. Thomas Scott, *Volivae Angliae. The Desires and Wishes of England against Treacherous Usurpation and formidabil Ambition and Power of the Emperor, the King of Spain and the Duke of Bavaria, dedicated to Great Brittaines Great Hope, Charles Prince of Wales* (Utrecht, 1624).

16. Macinnes, *Charles I and the Making of the Covenanting Movement*, pp.37–41; J. Goodare, 'The Scottish Parliament of 1621', *HJ*, 38 (1995), pp.29–51.

17. K.M. Brown, *Kingdom or Province? Scotland and the Regal Union, 1603–1715* (London, 1992), pp.9–10; A.D. Nicholls, *The Jacobean Union: A Reconsideration of British Civil Policies under the Early Stuarts* (Westport, CT, 1999), pp.23–46.

18. *CSP, Venetian*, vol.19, p.294; K.M. Brown, 'Courtiers and Cavaliers: Service, Anglicisation and Loyalty among the Royalist Nobility', in J. Morrill, ed., *The Scottish National Covenant in its British Context* (Edinburgh, 1990), pp.155–92.

19. BL, Latin Letters of Charles I, 1627–35, Add. MS 38669; DR, TKUA, England, A I, no.3, Breve, til Vels med Bilag fra Medlemmer af det Engelske Kongehus til medlemmer af det danske, 1613–89; Riksarkivet, Stockholm, Anglica, 516, 522, 531/2; *Documenta Bohemica Bellum Tricennale Illustrantia, tomus IV. Der Grosse Kampfe um die Vormacht in Europa 1635–43*, ed. J. Janacek, G. Cechova & J. Koci (Prague, 1978), pp.253–4.

20. S. Murdoch, *Britain, Denmark–Norway and the House of Stuart, 1603–1660* (East Linton, 2000), pp.44–89.

21. S. Murdoch, 'Scottish Ambassadors and British Diplomacy, 1618–1648', in Murdoch, ed., *Scotland and the Thirty Years' War*, pp.27–50; cf. Michael O. Wexionius, *Epitome Descriptiones Sueciae, Gothiae, Fenningiae et Subjectorum Provinciarium* (Åbo, 1650). Thus Grotius, on being exiled from the United Provinces for his Arminian sympathies, was employed as the Swedish representative at the French court.

22. DR, TKUA, England, A II, no.12, Breve fra forskellige engelske Stats og Hofembedsumamd til Kong Christian IV, 1588–1644; DR, TKUA, Alm.Del I Indtil 1670, 'Latina', vol.10, ff.173–4, 185–6, 200–1, 207, 213–14, 221, 229–30; *Kong Christian Den Fjerdes Egenhaendige Breve*, 8 vols, ed. C.F. Bricka & J.A. Fredericia (Copenhagen, 1969–70), vol.1 (1589–1625), p.131. Nottingham had commanded the Royal Navy against the Spanish Armada and was chosen by Elizabeth Tudor on her deathbed to reveal that James VI was her favoured successor.

23. BL, James Hay, Earl of Carlisle, Correspondence, vol.1, 1602–19, Egerton MS 2592, ff.28, 37, 107–8, 127, 132, 195; vol.2, 1619–20, Egerton MS 2593, ff.59, 69; D. Worthington, 'Scottish Clients of the Habsburgs, 1618–1648' (PhD diss., University of Aberdeen, 2001), pp.52–78.

24. S. Adams, 'Spain or the Netherlands? The Dilemmas of Early Stuart Foreign Policy', in H. Tomlinson, ed., *Before the Civil War: Essays in Early Stuart Politics and Government* (London, 1983), pp.89–90; C. Hibbert, *Charles I and the Popish Plot* (Chapel Hill, NC, 1983), p.29.

25. Thomas Scott, *Boanerges, or, The Humble Supplication of the Ministers of Scotland, To the High Court of Parliament in England* (Edinburgh, 1624), and *Aphorisms of State: or certaine secret articles for the reedifying of the Romis Church agreed upon, and approved in councell, by the colledge of cardinalls in Rome, shewed and delivered unto Pope Gregory the 15 a little before his death* (Utrecht, 1624). Scott was then serving as chaplain to the British forces defending Utrecht.

26. Peter Hay of Naughton, *An Advertisement to the Subjects of Scotland, Of the fearfull Dangers threatned to Christian States; and namely, to Great Britane, by the Ambitions of Spayne* (Aberdeen, 1627).

27. A.H. Williamson, 'Scotland, Antichrist and the Invention of Great Britain', in J. Dwyer, R.A. Mason & A. Murdoch, eds, *New Perspectives on the Politics and Culture of Early Modern Scotland* (Edinburgh, 1982), pp.34–58.

28. S. Murdoch, 'James VI and the Formation of a Scottish–British Military Identity', in S. Murdoch & A. Mackillop, eds, *Fighting for Identity: Scottish Military Experience, c.1550–1900* (Leiden, 2002), pp.3–31. Two separate forces were raised for Julich and Cleeves, the first under the English commander Sir Edward Cecil and the second under the joint command of Cecil and two Scots, Colonel William Brog and Colonel Robert Henderson. The British forces in the Kalmar War were under the joint command of the English Lord Willoughby and the Scottish Lord Dingwall.

29. John Taylor, *An English-Mans Love to Bohemia* (Dort, 1620).
30. *CSP, Venetian*, vol.20, pp.26, 77, 143; *CSP, Domestic* (1625–49), p.55.
31. A. Grosjean, 'Scotland: Sweden's Closest Ally?', in Murdoch, ed., *Scotland and the Thirty Years' War*, pp.143–71.
32. S. Murdoch, 'Introduction', in ibid., pp.1–23; S. Murdoch & A. Grosjean, 'Scotland, Scandinavia and Northern Europe, 1580–1707' (SSNE Database), www.abdn.ac.uk/history/datasets/ssne.
33. D. Horsbroch, 'Wish You Were Here? Scottish Reactions to "Postcards" home from the "Germane Warres" ', in Murdoch, ed., *Scotland and the Thirty Years' War*, pp.245–69; R.I. Frost, 'Confessionalism and the Army in the Polish–Lithuanian Commonwealth, 1550–1667', in Bahlcke & Strohmeyer, eds, *Konfessionalisierung in Ostmitteleuropa*, pp.139–60.
34. D. Worthington, 'Alternative Diplomacy? Scottish Exiles at the Courts of the Habsburgs and their Allies, 1618–1648', in Murdoch, ed., *Scotland and the Thirty Years' War*, pp.51–75.
35. G. Henry, *The Irish Military Community in Spanish Flanders, 1586–1621* (Dublin, 1992), pp.43–5; R.A. Stradling, *The Spanish Monarchy and Irish Mercenaries: The Wild Geese in Spain, 1618–1668* (Dublin, 1994), pp.21–9.
36. H. MacDonnell, *The Wild Geese of the Antrim Mac Donnells* (Blackrock, 1996), p.29; Ohlmeyer, *Civil War and Restoration in the Three Stuart Kingdoms*, pp.24–41.
37. S.G. Ellis, 'The Collapse of the Gaelic World, 1450–1650', *IHS*, 31 (1999), pp.449–69, and W.S. Brockington, 'Robert Munro: Professional Soldier, Military Historian and Scotsman', in Murdoch, ed., *Scotland and the Thirty Years' War*, pp.215–41. *Monro His Expedition with the worthy Scots regiment (called Mac-Keyes regiment)* (London, 1637) was written prior to his return to serve the Covenanting movement and is the antidote to the claims of Sir James Turner (*Memoirs of his own Life and Times, 1632–1670*, ed. T. Thomson (London, 1829), p.16) that he joined the Covenanters solely as a soldier of fortune. Turner's memoirs were written after the Restoration to excuse his Covenanting commitment.
38. Goodare, *State and Society in Early Modern Scotland*, pp.254–85; J. Goodare & M. Lynch, 'The Scottish State and its Borderlands, 1567–1625', and M. Lynch, 'James VI and the Highland Problem', both in Lynch & Goodare, eds, *The Reign of James VI*, pp.186–227.
39. Lee jr, *Great Britain's Solomon*, pp.167–71; K. Fincham, *Prelate as Pastor: The Episcopate of James I* (Oxford, 1990), pp.36–41, 96–111.
40. A. Cathcart, 'Crisis of Identity? Clan Chattan's Response to Government Policy in the Scottish Highlands, c.1580–1609', in Murdoch & Mackillop, eds, *Fighting for Identity*, pp.163–84; A.I. Macinnes, *Clanship, Commerce and the House of Stuart, 1603–1788* (East Linton, 1996), pp.11, 59.
41. A. MacCoinnich, ' "His spirit was given only to warre": Conflict and Identity in the Scottish *Gàidhealtachd*, c.1580–c.1630', in Murdoch & Mackillop, eds, *Fighting for Identity*, pp.133–61; J. MacInnes, 'The Gaelic Perception of the Lowlands', in W. Gilles, ed., *Gaelic and Scotland, Alba agus A'Ghàidhlig* (Edinburgh, 1989), pp.89–100.
42. K.M. Brown, *Bloodfeud in Scotland, 1573–1625: Violence, Justice and Politics in Early Modern Scotland* (Edinburgh, 1986), pp.228–9, 243–6; R.T. Spence, 'The Pacification of the Cumberland Borders, 1593–1628', *Northern History*, 13 (1977), pp.59–160; J.R.S.M. Jared, 'The Good of This Service Consists

in Absolute Secrecy: The Earl of Dunbar, Scotland and the Border (1603–1611)', *Canadian Journal of History*, 36 (2001), pp.229–57.

43. Macinnes, *Charles I and the Making of the Covenanting Movement*, pp.50–51; HL, Bridgewater & Ellesmere MSS, EL 7397.

44. N. Canny, 'The Marginal Kingdom: Ireland as a Problem in the First British Empire', in B. Bailyn & P.D. Morgan, eds, *Strangers within the Realm: Cultural Margins of the First British Empire* (Chapel Hill, NC, 1991), pp.35–66; B. MacCuarta, 'The Plantation of Leitrim, 1620–41', *IHS*, 32 (2001), pp.297–320; J. Ohlmeyer, ' "Civilizing of those Rude Partes": Colonization within Britain and Ireland, 1580s–1640s', in Canny, ed., *The Origins of Empire*, pp.124–46.

45. HL, Bridgewater & Ellesmere MSS, EL 7048–7049, 7051, 7058; M. Perceval-Maxwell, *The Scottish Migration to Ulster in the Reign of James I* (London, 1973), pp.8–10, 29–67, 154–6; R. Gillespie, 'Explorers, Exploiters and Entrepreneurs: Early Modern Ireland and its Context, 1500–1700', in B.J. Graham & L.J. Proudfoot, eds, *An Historical Geography of Ireland* (London, 1993), pp.123–57; P. Robinson, *The Plantation of Ulster* (Belfast, 2000), pp.108–28.

46. R. Gillespie, 'Plantation and Profit: Richard Spert's Tract on Ireland, 1608', *Irish Economic and Social History*, 20 (1993), pp.62–71; R.T. Spence, 'The Backward North Modernized? The Cliffords, Earls of Cumberland and the Socage Manor of Carlisle, 1611–43', *Northern History*, 20 (1984), pp.64–87; R. Dodgshon, *From Chiefs to Landlords: Social and Economic Change in the Western Highlands and Islands, c.1493–1820* (Edinburgh, 1998), pp.84–111.

47. J. Dawson, 'Calvinism and the Gaidhealtachd in Scotland', in A. Pettegree, A. Duke & G. Lewis, eds, *Calvinism in Europe, 1540–1620* (Cambridge, 1994), pp.231–53; K.W. Nicholls, *Gaelic and Gaelicised Ireland in the Middle Ages* (Dublin, 1972), pp.21–44, 57–65.

48. *RPCS*, 1st ser., vol.8, pp.737–61; M. Lee jr, 'James VI's Government of Scotland after 1603', *SHR*, 55 (1976), pp.49–53.

49. Macinnes, *Clanship, Commerce and the House of Stuart*, pp.338–75.

50. P. Anderson, *Robert Stewart, Earl of Orkney, Lord of Shetland, 1533–1593* (Edinburgh, 1983), pp.138–42; H.D. Smith, *Shetland Life and Trade, 1550–1914* (Edinburgh, 1984), pp.10–45.

51. W.H. Sherman, *John Dee: The Politics of Reading and Writing in the English Renaissance* (Amherst, 1995), pp.148–200; D. Armitage, *The Ideological Origins of the British Empire* (Cambridge, 2000), pp.208–13.

52. DR, TKUA, Alm.Del I Indtil 1670, 'Latina', vol.10a (1616–31).

53. DR, TKUA, Alm.Del I Indtil 1670, 'Latina', vol.10, ff.33–5, 103–4, 240; *Danmark-Norges Traktater (1626–49)*, ed. L. Laursen (Copenhagen, 1917), pp.87–93.

54. Moreland & Bannister, *Antique Maps*, pp.217–33; T.W. Fulton, *The Sovereignty of the Sea: An Historical Account of the Claims for Dominion of the British Seas* (Edinburgh, 1911), pp.338–75.

55. D. Armitage, 'Making the Empire British: Scotland in the Atlantic World, 1542–1717', *Past & Present*, 155 (1997), pp.34–63; R.S. Dunn, *Sugar and Slaves: The Rise of the Planter Class in the English West Indies, 1624–1713* (Chapel Hill, NC, 1992), pp.3–45.

56. A. Pagden, *Lords of all the World: Ideologies of Empire in Spain, Britain and France, c.1500-c.1800* (New Haven, CT, 1995), pp.29–125; J.P. Greene, *Pursuits of Happiness: The Social Development of Early Modern British Colonies and the Formation of American Culture* (Chapel Hill, NC, 1988), pp.28–46.

57. J. Ohlmeyer, 'Seventeenth-Century Ireland and the New British and Atlantic Histories', *AHR*, 104 (1999), pp.446–62; N. Canny, *Making Ireland British, 1580–1650* (Oxford, 2001), pp.214–15, 297, 312; M. Netzloff, 'Forgetting the Ulster Plantation: John Speed's The Theatre of the Empire of Great Britain (1611) and the Colonial Archive', *Journal of Medieval and Early Modern Studies*, 31 (2001), pp.313–48.

58. A. Games, *Migration and the Origins of the English Atlantic World* (Cambridge, MA, 1999), pp.13–41; W.R. Scott, *The Constitution and Finance of English, Scottish and Irish Joint-Stock Companies to 1720*, 3 vols (Cambridge, 1911–12), vol.1, pp.129–49.

59. [Charles I], *By the King a proclamation for the better encouragemet, and aduancement of the trade of the East-Indie Companie, and for the preuention of excesse of priuate trade* (London, 1632); [Sir William Alexander], *The Earl of Stirling's Register of Royal Letters, Relative to the Affairs of Scotland and Nova Scotia from 1615 to 1635*, ed. C. Rogers, 2 vols (Edinburgh, 1873), vol.1, pp.150–51; vol.2, p.608; Nicholls, *The Jacobean Union*, pp.168–71.

60. R. Davis, *The Rise of Atlantic Economies* (London, 1973), pp.96–8; N. Canny, 'Asia, the Atlantic and the Subjects of the British Monarchy', in Coward, ed., *Companion*, pp.45–66.

61. A. Kulikoff, *From British Peasants to Colonial American Farmers* (Chapel Hill, NC, 2000), pp.39–72; cf. Robert Baillie, *A Dissuasive from the Errours of the Times* (London, 1645).

62. R. Brenner, *Merchants and Revolution: Commercial Change, Political Conflict, and London's Overseas Traders, 1550–1653* (Princeton, NJ, 1993), pp.93–102; K.O. Kupperman, *Providence Island, 1630–1641: The Other Puritan Colony* (Cambridge, 1993), pp.267–94.

63. T.K. Rabb, *Enterprise & Empire: Merchants and Gentry Investment in the Expansion of England, 1575–1630* (Cambridge, MA, 1967), pp.1–101; N. Canny, *Kingdom and Colony: Ireland in the Atlantic World* (Baltimore & London, 1988), pp.44–59.

64. J.G. Reid, *Acadia, Maine and New England: Marginal Colonies in the Seventeenth Century* (Toronto, 1981), pp.20–42, 81–2, 88–90. Cf. Sir William Alexander, *An Encouragement to Colonies* (London, 1624).

65. N.E.S. Griffiths & J.G. Reid, 'New Evidence on New Scotland, 1629', *William and Mary Quarterly*, 3rd ser., 39 (1992), pp.492–508; *Stirling's Register of Royal Letters*, ed. Rogers, vol.2, pp.463, 544–8, 599.

66. Reid, *Acadia, Maine and New England*, pp.49–51, 246–9, 186–7.

67. Macinnes, *Charles I and the Making of the Covenanting Movement*, pp.120–22; R. Law, 'The First Scottish Guinea Company of 1634–9', *SHR*, 76 (1997), pp.185–202.

68. Dunn, *Sugar and Slaves*, pp.49–53; NAS, Hay of Haystoun Papers, GD 34/920–33. Likewise, more than English settlement is indicated by the subsequent naming of parishes in the Caribbean after the saints of the British Isles.

69. *Tabeller over Skibsfart og Varetransport gennem Oresund, 1492–1660*, 3 vols, ed. N.E. Bang & K. Korst (Copenhagen, 1906–22), vol.1, pp.266–389; vol.2, pp.352–607.
70. Games, *Migration and the Origins of the English Atlantic World*, pp.143–7, 202–3.
71. DR, TKUA, Alm.Del. I Indtil 1670, no. 141; S. Murdoch, 'Kith and Kin: John Durie and the Scottish Community in Scandinavia and the Baltic, 1624–34', in P. Salmon & T. Barrow, eds, *Britain and the Baltic: Studies in Commercial, Political and Cultural Relations, 1500–2000* (Sunderland, 2003), pp.21–46; Robert Farlie, *Kalendarium Humanae Vitae* (London, 1638).
72. William Lithgow, *A True and Experimentall Discourse, upon the beginning, proceeding and Victorious event of this last siege of Breda* (London, 1637).

3 The Prerogative Rule of Charles I, 1629–1638

1. D.L. Smith, *The Stuart Parliaments, 1603–1689* (London, 1999), pp.118–19; Russell, *Unrevolutionary England, 1603–1642*, pp.31–57.
2. A. Clarke, *The Old English in Ireland* (London, 1966), pp.47–52; V. Treadwell, *Buckingham and Ireland, 1616–1628: A Study in Anglo-Irish Politics* (Dublin, 1998), pp.277–93.
3. Macinnes, *Charles I and the Making of the Covenanting Movement*, pp.77–82; K. Sharpe, *The Personal Rule of Charles I* (New Haven, CT, & London, 1992), pp.3–62.
4. Even England was not without a constitutional assembly, albeit the Convocation of the Stannaries summoned for Cornwall in 1636 was concerned purely with economic regulation, judicial privileges and prescriptive rights pertaining to the working of tin within the county rather than to national affairs of state (HL, Huntington Manuscripts, HM 30664).
5. Burns, *The True Law of Kingship*, pp.278–81.
6. J. Richards, ' "His Nowe Majestie" and the English Monarchy: The Kingship of Charles I before 1640', *Past & Present*, 113 (1986), pp.70–96; T. Cogswell, 'The Politics of Propaganda: Charles I and the People in the 1620s', *Journal of British Studies*, 29 (1990), pp.187–215.
7. R. Cust, *The Forced Loan and English Politics, 1626–1628* (Oxford, 1989), pp.13–90, 324–31; M. Kishlansky, 'Tyranny Denied: Charles I, Attorney General Heath, and the Five Knights' Case', *HJ*, 42 (1999), pp.53–83; J.P. Kenyon, ed., *The Stuart Constitution* (Cambridge, 1966), pp.7–86.
8. P. Christianson, 'Arguments on Billeting and Martial Law in the Parliament of 1628', *HJ*, 37 (1994), pp.539–67; J. Flemion, 'A Savings to Satisfy All: The House of Lords and the Meaning of the Petition of Right', *Parliamentary History*, 10 (1991), pp.27–44; L.S. Popofsky, 'The Crisis over Tonnage and Poundage in Parliament in 1629', *Past & Present*, 126 (1990), pp.44–75.
9. R. Smuts, *Court Culture and the Origins of a Royalist Tradition in Early Stuart England* (Philadelphia, 1987), pp.258–62; F. Pogson, 'Making and Maintaining Political Alliances during the Personal Rule of Charles I: Wentworth's Associations with Laud and Cottington', *History*, 84 (1999), pp.52–73.

10. J.F. Merritt, 'Power and Communication: Thomas Wentworth and Gov-
     ernment at a Distance during the Personal Rule, 1629–1635', in J.F.
     Merritt, ed., *The Political World of Thomas Wentworth, Earl of Strafford,
     1621–1641* (Cambridge, 1996), pp.109–32; *The Earl of Strafforde's Letters and
     Dispatches*, ed. W. Knowler, 2 vols (London, 1739), vol.1, pp.65–7. Went-
     worth was at his most vindictive in securing the criminal prosecution which
     removed Francis Annesley, 1st Viscount Mountnorris, from public life in
     December 1635.
11. Clarendon, *The History of the Rebellion*, vol.1, pp.194–5.
12. Macinnes, *Charles I and the Making of the Covenanting Movement*, pp.36–7.
13. M. Lee jr, *The Road to Revolution: Scotland under Charles I, 1625–37* (Urbana
     & Chicago, IL, 1985), pp.46–8, 69–71, 126. Menteith laid claim to the
     earldom of Strathearn as direct heir male of David, a younger son of
     Robert II, King of Scots in the late fourteenth century. This claim, though
     initially accepted by Charles I in 1629, raised complications about the royal
     succession which Menteith expressed indiscreetly at the end of 1632. For
     Earl David had been the eldest son of the second marriage of Robert II,
     whose first marriage was of questionable validity. When his drunken
     remarks that 'he had the reddest blood in Scotland' were reported at court,
     neither the leading officials in Edinburgh nor his close associates among
     the Scottish courtiers made any effort to check his removal from office. The
     treasonable imputations of his boast were not prosecuted after he surren-
     dered his title of Strathearn in return for that of the Earl of Airth, demit-
     ted his offices.
14. Macinnes, *Charles I and the Making of the Covenanting Movement*, pp.82–6.
15. DR, TKUA, England A II, no.12, Breve fra forskellige engelske Stats og
     Hofembedsumamd til Kong Christian IV, 1588–1644.
16. *Kong Christian Den Fjerdes Egenhaendige Breve*, 2 (1626–31), pp.41–2, 51–2, 131;
     DR, TKUA, Alm.Del I Indtil 1670, 'Latina' vol.10 (1616–31), ff.162, 166,
     185–6, 198, 207, 213–14; TKUA, Skotland A I, no.4a, Akter og Doku-
     menter nedr det politiske Forhold til Scotland, 1572–1640. The Irish per-
     spective appeared more favourable in the light of negotiations for the
     Graces, although a member of the Protestant planter classes, Richard
     Boyle, Earl of Cork, was more concerned with issues of entrepreneurship
     than with military recruitment or religious toleration. In his correspon-
     dence with Christian IV, he suggested that Youghall, whose harbour he
     thought magnificent, should become the routine port of repair for Danish
     ships returning from the Indian Ocean, where they could be met con-
     veniently by the escort ships which usually picked them up between Ulster
     and the Hebrides.
17. DR, TKUA, England A II, no.13, Akter og Dokumenter nedr det politiske
     Forhold til England, 1620–38; *Kong Christian Den Fjerdes Egenhaendige Breve*, 1
     (1589–1625), pp.472–3. By a treaty of 1621, confirmed in November 1625,
     Charles I was committed to pay 300,000 guilders ($£30,000$) monthly to
     supply Christian IV with around 28,000–30,000 foot and 7000–8000 horse
     from his British dominions. By May 1638, this sum with interest had ac-
     cumulated to 429,000 thalers ($£100,941$), albeit English treasury sources
     claimed that 448,582 thalers ($£105,549$) were eventually paid.
18. J. Cramsie, *Kingship and Crown Finance under James VI and I, 1603–1625*
     (Woodbridge, 2002), pp.1–11, 28–39, 50–66; Lockyer, *James VI and I,*

pp.78–99. In Scotland, where the absence of the court had made commutation commonplace, rents and provisions from crown lands were commuted at a king's fiars price notably higher than the fiars prices being established in sheriff courts for the commutation of rentals in each Scottish county from the 1620s.

19. M.J. Braddick, *The Nerves of State: Taxation and the Financing of the English State, 1558–1714* (Manchester, 1996), pp.68–90. Thus, the patent procured in 1613 through generous bribes at court by William Cockayne, London alderman and merchant adventurer in the Baltic, was reputed to raise customs revenues through the finishing of cloth in England and the prohibition on exports of unfinished cloth. Instead, Cockayne's scheme compounded recession in the clothing industry and did little more than impose additional taxes on unfinished cloth exported under licence until the patent was rescinded after three years following parliamentary pressure (Hirst, *England in Conflict, 1603–1660*, pp.23, 89–90, 97). A more prolonged controversy was the leather patent granted for 31 years in 1620 to John, Lord Erskine, the eldest son of John Erskine, 7th Earl of Mar and Scottish treasurer, in order to improve the tanning process. This patent effectively imposed a stamp duty on tanned leather marketed in Scotland, whether produced domestically or imported. Although Erskine was deemed to have established a superior process by 1629, continuing complaints about excessive rates of stamp duty had made his patent a declared grievance at the Conventions of Estates in 1625 and 1630. Charles I agreed not to renew the patent in 1634, but a further seven years were to elapse before the Covenanting movement terminated Erskine's patent and all other contentious monopolies (Macinnes, *Charles I and the Making of the Covenanting Movement*, pp.38–9, 106–8).

20. Hirst, *England in Conflict*, pp.110–20; Macinnes, *Charles I and the Making of the Covenanting Movement*, pp.104–5, 114–15.

21. M.J. Braddick, *State Formation and Social Change in Early Modern England, c.1550–1700* (Cambridge, 2000), pp.202–13; Macinnes, *Charles I and the Making of the Covenanting Movement*, pp.41–3.

22. B. Coward, *Early Stuart England, 1603–1640* (London, 1980), pp.137–8; Hirst, *England in Conflict*, pp.121–9; Macinnes, *Charles I and the Making of the Covenanting Movement*, pp.67, 104–6.

23. M.B. Young, 'Charles I and the Erosion of Trust, 1625–1628', *Albion*, 22 (1990), pp.217–35.

24. Roger Maynwaring, *Religion and Alegiance: In Two Sermons Preached before the Kings Maiestie* (London, 1627).

25. HL, Bridgewater & Ellesmere MSS, EL 7728; Hirst, *England in Conflict*, pp.131–2. The fiscal association of Arminianism with popery at court was sustained by the monopoly awarded in 1632 to the English treasurer, Richard Weston, Earl of Portland, and his Catholic clients for a soap that proved incapable of cleaning clothes despite bringing in £33,000 to the royal coffers.

26. Macinnes, *Charles I and the Making of the Covenanting Movement*, pp.49–76, 103–4.

27. NLS, Sir James Balfour on Nobility, Adv. MS 15.2.14; K.M. Brown, *Noble Society in Scotland: Wealth, Family and Culture from the Reformation to the Revolution* (Edinburgh, 2000), pp.1–21.

28. Rape, murder, arson and robbery came within the competence of the regalities. Only charges of treason were reserved for the crown. Lords of regality could be given judicial rights over lands and baronies beyond their own estates. Such baronies, though losing their judicial autonomy, continued to operate within the hierarchical framework of the regality. These lords also had extensive powers of recall, having the right to repledge from central and local courts of the crown not only cases affecting their tenants and feuars, but also those citing neighbouring barons and other freeholders within their territorial spheres of influence.

29. Claims that the uplifting or leading of teinds was a perennial cause of civil disturbance and occasional blood-letting must be treated with caution, however (Lee jr, *The Road to Revolution*, p.34). The commutation of teinds from kind into money through the mechanism of fiars prices was beginning to offset delays in uplifting teinds.

30. *RPCS*, 2nd ser., vol.1, pp.352, 509–16.

31. HMC, *Manuscripts of the Earls of Mar and Kellie* (London, 1904), pp.135–6,139.

32. [Walter Balcanqual], *A Declaration concerning the Late Tumults in Scotland* (Edinburgh, 1639), p.15.

33. NAS, Cunninghame-Grahame MSS, GD 22/2/518 & /781; Sir James Balfour, *Historical Works*, ed. J. Haig, 4 vols (Edinburgh, 1824–5), vol.2, pp.151–4. When the whole Scheme was eventually brought before the coronation parliament in 1633, Charles authorised only minor amendments that restricted the right of heritors to purchase their own teinds on lands held in feu from bishops, burghs, universities and hospitals. All authorised purchases had to be completed within two years of the teinds being valued.

34. NAS, Sederunt Book of the High Commission of Teinds, 1633–50, TE 1/2, ff.17, 23, 28, 31, 35.

35. Macinnes, *Charles I and the Making of the Covenanting Movement*, pp.115–16. When Charles decreed in February 1634 that his annuity should become a composition rather than a direct tax, no more than 88 landowners took up his offer to be quit of his annuity for the payment of a lump sum equivalent to seven years' exaction. By July 1635, Charles had resorted more in hope than expectation to the farming of his annuity, which yielded no perceptible financial benefit.

36. *RPCS*, 2nd ser., vol.5, pp.409, 424–30; vol.6, pp.21, 36, 56–7, 78, 175–6, 378, 426, 453, 472, 481.

37. There were 58 categories of offence liable to prosecution for breaches since 1621 and another six deemed sufficiently heinous as to have no retrospective limits on prosecution – namely, sporting firearms without licence, exorbitant usury, exporting gold and silver, poaching from river and loch, smuggling to defraud customs, and concealing loans of money that were liable to the tax on annualrents.

38. Hull University Library, Maxwell-Constable of Everingham MSS, DDEV/79/D; Macinnes, *Charles I and the Making of the Covenanting Movement*, pp.92–6. After deducting legal charges, compositions yielded just over £1068: the aggravation of political dissent they caused had more than outweighed anticipated financial benefits.

39. Scott, *England's Troubles*, pp.113–14.

40. Robert Baillie, *Letters and Journals, 1637–62*, ed. D. Laing, 3 vols (Edinburgh, 1841–2), vol.1, pp.476–8; John Row, *The History of the Kirk of Scotland, 1558–1637*, ed. D. Laing (Edinburgh, 1842), pp.350–51. Loudoun's speech emphasised the constitutional impropriety of Charles swearing to preserve 'all canonical privileges' in his coronation oath, especially as no comparable concession was required for the maintenance of the rights and privileges of the lay estates. As canonical privileges remained unspecified, Loudoun held that any concession beyond that of the Reformed coronation oaths approved in 1567 and ratified in 1581 and 1592 opened up the prospects of the bishops reclaiming the spiritual and temporal rights to property enjoyed by the pre-Reformation clergy. By such a selective appeal to constitutional precedents, Loudoun identified the bishops as the common threat to the landed privileges of the laity and, simultaneously, associated their unbounded ambition with the spectre of popery.

41. [University of Oxford], *Solis Britannici Perigaeum sive Itinirantes Caroli Auspicatissima Periodus* (Oxford, 1633); Andrew Boyd, *Ad Augustissimum Monarcham Carolum Majori Britanniae* (Edinburgh, 1633).

42. William Lithgow, *Scotlands welcome to her native sonne, and soveraigne lord, King Charles* (Edinburgh, 1633). Lithgow also argued that rack-renting and credit frauds had turned Berwick into a frontier town garrisoned by spendthrifts rather than soldiers. Teind redistribution was becoming embroiled in recrimination and litigation to the detriment of learning, social welfare and the godly commonwealth. His promotion of plantation found contemporaneous English expression through fen drainage in East Anglia, which was undermined by royal interference, and the Scottish scheme to straighten the River Forth, mooted but not implemented in 1636 (M.E. Kennedy, 'Charles I and Local Government: The Draining of the East and West Fens', *Albion*, 15 (1983), pp.19–31; D. Stevenson, 'A Note on a Scheme to Straighten the River Forth in 1636', *Scottish Economic and Social History*, 17 (1997), pp.65–8).

43. Macinnes, *Charles I and the Making of the Covenanting Movement*, pp.86–9. On the recommendation of the king, the bishops chose eight nobles who, in turn, chose eight bishops. All the bishops owed their position to royal patronage. The eight nobles selected were predominantly, but not exclusively, courtiers. The eight nobles and eight bishops then chose commissioners from eight shires and eight burghs. Although these latter selections did provide the committee with a representative cross-section of Scottish localities, gentry with a track record of support for the court were preferred.

44. Row, *History of the Kirk*, pp.366–7; *Memoirs of the Maxwells of Pollock*, ed. W. Fraser, 2 vols (Edinburgh, 1863), vol.2, pp.232–40.

45. Balfour, *Historical Works*, vol.2, p.200; Clarendon, *History of the Rebellion*, vol.1, pp.138–43, 184; William Scott, *An Apologetical Narration of the State and Government of the Kirk of Scotland since the Reformation*, ed. D. Laing (Edinburgh, 1846), pp.293–5, 336–8.

46. Row, *History of the Kirk*, pp.376–81.

47. John Spalding, *History of the Troubles and Memorable Transactions in Scotland and England*, ed. J. Skene, 2 vols (Edinburgh, 1828–9), vol.1, pp.17–20; Row, *History of the Kirk*, pp.351–2, 362–3, 368–70, 376–8. Ministers were to con-

tinue to wear black gowns when preaching, but surplices were to be worn when administering the sacraments, reading divine service or carrying out burials.

48. HL, Stowe Collection, Temple Papers, STT: Religious Papers (10–11).
49. David Calderwood, *The Pastor and the Prelate, or, Reformation and Conformitie* (Edinburgh, 1636); D.G. Mullan, *Scottish Puritanism* (Oxford, 1999), pp.13–44; M. Todd, *The Culture of Protestantism in Early Modern Scotland* (New Haven, CT, 2002), pp.24–83, 402–13.
50. Baillie, *Letters and Journals*, vol.1, pp.424–36; Sir John Scot of Scotstarvit, *The Staggering State of Scottish Statesmen, from 1550 to 1650*, ed. C. Rogers (Edinburgh, 1872), p.61.
51. NAS, Hamilton Papers, GD 406/1/315; Sir William Brereton, *Travels in Holland, the United Provinces, England, Scotland and Ireland, 1634–35*, ed. E. Hawkins (London, 1844), pp.100–01. These rumours were not without foundation as Charles I was proposing to confer the abbacy of Lindores, the only temporal lordship revoked by legal compulsion, on Andrew Learmouth, minister of Libberton in Mid-Lothian.
52. Sharpe, *The Personal Rule of Charles I*, pp.456–63; H. Langelüddecke, '"Patchy and Spasmodic?" The Response of Justices of the Peace to Charles I's Book of Orders', *EHR*, 113 (1998), pp.1231–48.
53. Hirst, *England in Conflict*, pp.140–44; TWA, Company of Hostmen of Newcastle-upon-Tyne, GU/HO/12; NAS, Hay of Haystoun Papers, GD 34/889, /913.
54. S.P. Salt, 'Sir Simon D'Ewes and the Levying of Ship Money, 1635–1640', *HJ*, 37 (1994), pp.253–87; *Ship Money Papers and Richard Greville's Notebook*, ed. C.G. Bonsey & J.G. Jenkins (Buckingham Record Society, 1965), pp.22, 56, 59.
55. William Prynne, *An Humble Remonstrance Against the Tax of Ship-money Lately Imposed* (London, 1643); HL, Stowe Collection: Temple Papers, STT: Ship Money L8C10. Prynne was subsequently convicted in Star Chamber for attacking the bishops in print, for which he was branded, had the rest of his ears removed, was fined £5000 and sentenced to life imprisonment.
56. *Historical Collections*, ed. J. Rushworth, 4 vols (London, 1680–91), vol.2, pp.359–64; N.P. Bard, 'The Ship Money Case and William Fiennes, Viscount Saye and Seale', *Bulletin of the Institute of Historical Research*, 50 (1977), pp.177–84.
57. A.J. Fielding, 'Opposition to the Personal Rule of Charles I: The Diary of Robert Woodford, 1637–41', *HJ*, 31 (1988), pp.769–88; A. Hughes, 'Thomas Dugard and his Circle in the 1630s', *HJ*, 29 (1986), pp.771–93; Woolrych, *Britain in Revolution*, pp.75–82; HL, Bridgewater & Ellesmere MSS, EL 7275, 7414. In September 1637 the Council for Wales and the Marches reported a noted reluctance in counties, cities and towns to make the expected and necessary contribution for the repair of St Paul's Cathedral in London (ibid., EL 7417).
58. Henry Parker, *The Case of Ship Money Briefly Discoursed* (London, 1640); M. Mendle, *Henry Parker and the English Civil War* (Cambridge, 1995), pp.32–50.
59. L.L. Peck, 'Beyond the Pale: John Cusacke and the Language of Absolutism in Early Stuart Britain', *HJ*, 41 (1998), pp.121–49; N. Canny, 'The Attempted Anglicisation of Ireland in the Seventeenth Century: An Exemplar of "British History"', in Merritt, ed., *The Political World of Thomas*

Wentworth, Earl of Strafford, pp.157–86; J. Morrill, 'A British Patriarchy? Ecclesiastical Imperialism under the Early Stuarts', in Fletcher & Roberts, eds, *Religion, Culture and Society in Early Modern Britain*, pp.209–37. As an indication of Ireland's standing within the Stuart dominions, Wentworth sponsored a North American colony in the vicinity of Virginia that was to be called New Albion, licensed by the Irish crown and serviced from Ireland. This colony, albeit settled primarily by English adventurers, was still a distinctive settlement in 1650 (*The Earl of Strafforde's Letters and Dispatches*, ed. Knowler, vol.1, pp.72–3; Beauchamp Plantagenet, *A Description of the Province of New Albion* (London, 1650)).

60. H. Kearney, *Strafford in Ireland, 1633–41: A Study in Absolutism* (Manchester, 1959, 2nd edn Cambridge, 1989), pp.42–68; A. Clarke, 'Sir Piers Crosby, 1590–1646: Wentworth's "Tawney Ribon"', *IHS*, 26 (1988), pp.142–60; *The Earl of Strafforde's Letters and Dispatches*, ed. Knowler, vol.1, pp.310–28. A military and colonial adventurer who shared the same penchant for malevolent plotting as his Scottish associate Lord Ochiltree, Sir Piers Crosby had led the Irish contingents fighting in the British expeditionary forces at La Rochelle in 1627. He remained well connected at court to the circle around Queen Henrietta Maria led by the Marquess of Hamilton and Henry Rich, 1st Earl of Holland, who were the principal critics of Wentworth's stewardship in Ireland.

61. J. McCafferty, '"God bless your free Church of Ireland": Wentworth, Laud, Bramhall and the Irish Convocation of 1634', in *The Political World of Thomas Wentworth, Earl of Strafford*, pp.187–208; A.L. Capern, 'The Caroline Church: James Ussher and the Irish Dimension', *HJ*, 39 (1996), pp.57–85; HL, Hastings Irish Papers, box 7/HA 15162–3, 15165, 15168.

62. *Autobiography of the Life of Mr Robert Blair*, ed. T. McCrie (Edinburgh, 1848), pp.57–148; *Select Biographies*, ed. W.K. Tweedie, 2 vols (Edinburgh, 1845–7), vol.1, pp.134–57, 344; Patrick Adair, *A True Narrative of the Rise and Progress of the Presbyterian Church in Ireland (1623–1670)*, ed. W.D. Killen (Belfast, 1866), pp.16–51.

63. *The Earl of Strafforde's Letters*, vol.2, pp.33–4; J.H. Ohlmeyer, 'Strafford, the "Londonderry Business" and the "New British History"', in *The Political World of Thomas Wentworth, Earl of Strafford*, pp.209–29.

64. *RPCS*, 2nd ser., vol.4, pp.56–7; Macinnes, *Charles I and the Making of the Covenanting Movement*, pp.108–14. Whereas Charles was to seek finance for 45 warships totalling 20,450 tons, crewed by 9830 men and costing £221,500 annually from 1634, he projected a deep-sea fleet of 200 busses (fishing vessels), ranging from 30 to 50 tons, employing around 1600 men and boys, costing £134,000 but with anticipated yearly profits of around £165,000. The promotion of the common fishing cannot be dissociated from the secret treaty with Spain, negotiated by Cottington at the outset of 1631, in which Charles condoned the partition of the United Netherlands as the price of restoring his sister's family to the Palatinate.

65. *RPCS*, 2nd ser., vol.4, pp.181, 208, 308–9, 541–2, 546–8, 551–2, 554–6.

66. Scott, *Joint-Stock Companies to 1720*, vol.2, pp.365–71; *RPCS*, 2nd ser., vol.6, pp.279–80, 292, 335, 346, 457. The leading English officials who formed the provincial associations were the treasurer, Richard Weston, Earl of Portland; the earl marshal, Thomas Howard, Earl of Arundel & Surrey; the chamberlain, Philip Herbert, Earl of Pembroke & Montgomery; and

the attorney-general, William Noy. All three associations were defunct by 1641.

67. Spalding, *The History of the Troubles*, vol.1, pp.40, 44; Macinnes, *Charles I and the Making of the Covenanting Movement*, pp.119–23. The value of Scottish silver coin, set against the Dutch *riksdaller* as the international standard, was reduced initially from 58 to 56 shillings, then to 54 shillings. This maladroit devaluation was tantamount to an indirect tax of 7 per cent on all commercial transactions.

68. HMC, Ninth Report, part ii, appendix, *Traquhair Muniments* (London, 1887), pp.247, 253; NAS, Hamilton Papers, GD 406/1/357, /1000, /8165; Macinnes, *Charles I and the Making of the Covenanting Movement*, pp.116–19, 141. Negotiations between the associations of both countries were broken off acrimoniously in April because of the English demands to limit Scottish imports.

69. *State Trials*, ed. W. Cobbett, 33 vols (London, 1809–28), vol.3, pp.593–603, 689–712; Gilbert Burnet, *History of My Own Times*, 2 vols (London, 1838), vol.1, pp.12–14; Balfour, *Historical Works*, vol.2, pp.216–19.

70. *Diary of Sir Thomas Hope of Craighall, 1634–45*, ed. T. Thomson (Edinburgh, 1843), pp.45–6, 51, 58; Row, *History of the Kirk*, pp.385–6, 392–406. Forewarned by Laud's securing of the appointment of William Juxon, Bishop of London, as treasurer in England, Traquhair outmanoeuvred Bishop Maxwell of Ross for this office when it became vacant in 1636.

71. *The Works of William Laud D.D.*, ed. J. Bliss, 5 vols (Oxford, 1853), vol.3, pp.278, 310–15, 372–6, 427–8; Baillie, *Letters and Journals*, vol.1, pp.4–8.

4 Covenants and Confederations, 1638–1643

1. Baillie, *Letters and Journals*, ed. Laing, vol.1, pp.30, 113; Sharpe, *The Personal Rule of Charles I*, pp.285–6, 305–8, 837–9; Hibbert, *Charles I and the Popish Plot*, pp.38–71; P. Lake, 'The Laudian Style: Order, Uniformity and the Pursuit of Holiness in the 1630s', in Fincham, ed., *The Early Stuart Church*, pp.161–85.

2. Row, *History of the Kirk*, pp.392–406; John Gordon, *History of Scots Affairs, 1637–41*, ed. J. Robertson & G. Grub, 3 vols (Aberdeen, 1841), vol.1, pp.3–7; Macinnes, *Charles I and the Making of the Covenanting Movement*, pp.147–9, 158–61. The contents of the Service Book became known in advance of publication through a combination of impolitic delays in drafting, deliberate leakage of episcopal intentions from within the Privy Council and wanton incompetence on the part of the principal printer. Robert Young had allowed discarded sheets from his printing house to be recycled as wrapping paper for tobacco and spices purchased from Edinburgh shops.

3. D. Stevenson, *The Scottish Revolution, 1637–44: The Triumph of the Covenanters* (Newton Abbot, 1973), pp.64–79; Donald, *An Uncounselled King*, pp.70–88.

4. M. Butler, 'A Case Study in Caroline Political Theatre: Braithwaite's Mercurius Britannicus (1641)', *HJ*, 27 (1984), pp.947–53; Sharpe, *The Personal Rule of Charles I*, pp.230–31, 794–7. Robert Sidney, 2nd Earl of Leicester, who briefly succeeded Wentworth as lord-lieutenant of Ireland in 1641,

reputedly sponsored its production in Paris while serving as ambassador to France.

5. *Letters of Samuel Rutherford*, ed. A.A. Bonar, 2 vols (Edinburgh, 1863), vol.1, pp.59, 69, 102–5, 107, 111, 117, 134, 148–9, 159, 163, 167, 214, 274, 277; *Diary of Sir Archibald Johnston of Wariston, 1632–39*, ed. J.M. Paul (Edinburgh, 1911), pp.206, 250, 256–9, 262.

6. John Leslie, Earl of Rothes, *A Relation of Proceedings Concerning the Affairs of the Kirk of Scotland from August 1637 to July 1638*, ed. J. Nairne (Edinburgh, 1830), pp.4–23, 47–50; Macinnes, *Charles I and the Making of the Covenanting Movement*, pp.166–73.

7. D. Stevenson, *King or Covenant? Voices from the Civil War* (East Linton, 1996), pp.151–73, has postulated that Wariston was a manic depressive. The jury is still out.

8. *A Source Book of Scottish History*, ed. W.C. Dickinson & G. Donaldson, 3 vols (Edinburgh, 1961), vol.3, pp.95–104; *APS*, vol.5 (1626–40), pp.272–6; Burns, *The True Law of Kingship*, pp.122–52, 185–221.

9. Rothes, *A Relation of Proceedings*, pp.90–92, 96–8, 100–02, 211; Archibald Campbell, Marquess of Argyle, *Instructions to a Son, containing rules of conduct in public and private life* (London, 1661), pp.30–36; D. Stevenson, *The Covenanters: The National Covenant and Scotland* (Edinburgh, 1988), pp.35–44.

10. Alexander Henderson, *Sermons, Prayers and Pulpit Addresses*, ed. R.T. Martin (Edinburgh, 1867), pp.9–30.

11. Rothes, *A Relation of Proceedings*, pp.100–86; *Diary of Sir Archibald Johnston of Wariston*, ed. Paul, pp.349–404; Gordon, *History of Scots Affairs*, vol.1, pp.64–134; HL, Stowe Collection: Temple Papers, STT Personal box 9 (21). The six Aberdeen Doctors were John Forbes of Corse, Robert Baron, William Leslie, James Sibbald, Alexander Scrooge and Alexander Ross. All six were graduates of either King's or Marischall College in Aberdeen. Forbes was Professor of Divinity and Leslie was Principal of King's College, while Baron was the first Professor of Theology in the more recently founded Marischall College.

12. *The Confession of the Kirk of Scotland subscribed by the King's Majesty and his Household in the year of God 1580. With a Designation of such acts of Parliament as are expedient, for justifying the Union, after mentioned. And subscribed by the Nobles, Barrons, Gentlemen, Burgesses, Ministers and Commons, in the year of God, 1638* (Edinburgh, 1638); [Balcanqual], *A Declaration concerning the late tumults in Scotland*, pp.186–205.

13. *The Hamilton Papers*, ed. S.R. Gardiner (London, 1880), pp.26–37, 42–7; Baillie, *Letters and Journals*, vol.1, pp.103–8, 112, 115–16.

14. Rothes, *A Relation of Proceedings*, pp.29, 128, 166, 169; Baillie, *Letters and Journals*, vol.1, pp.99–176, 469–72; *The Memoirs of Henry Guthry, Late Bishop of Dunkeld*, ed. G. Crawford (Glasgow, 1747), pp.46–7. The election of ruling elders was justified by recourse to Andrew Melville's *Second Book of Discipline* (1578) and a selective interpretation of the enactment from the general assembly of 1597, whereby three ministers, one noble or laird and one burgess were to be elected commissioners within every presbytery. Only three presbyteries failed to send any commissioners. Hamilton received solid backing from only six presbyteries and three royal burghs – all from the north-east of Scotland.

15. *Diary of Sir Archibald Johnston of Wariston*, ed. Paul, pp.374–402; Gordon, *History of Scots Affairs*, vol.2, pp.3–187; Mullan, *Episcopacy in Scotland*, pp.190–93.
16. Russell, *The Causes of the English Civil War*, pp.28–9; Sharpe, *The Personal Rule of Charles I*, pp.827–31, 895–9.
17. Cf. *De intentie van het coninghrijcke van Scotlands armade. Waer in vertoont wert de oorsake waerom zy in Enghelandt comen, . . . ende op wat conditie zy daer wederom uyttrecken sullen. Verclaert aen hare broeders van, Enghelandt, by de commissarissen van 't laetste Parlement* . . . (n.p., 1640); DR, TKUA, England A I, no.3, 'Breve fra Karl I til Christian IV, 1639–41'; *Kong Christian Den Fjerdes Egenhaendige Breve*, vol.4 (1639–40), pp.272–6, 359–60, 364–9, 378–9, 395–6, 425–6; Archives Du Royaume De Belgique, Don Ferdinand: Correspondence avec les Trois Ambassadeurs Ci-Dessus Nommes 1640–1641, bundle 377, ff.157–60, 163–4; *Lettres, Instructions Diplomatiques et Papiers D'Etat Du Cardinal de Richelieu (1638–1642)*, ed. M. Avenel (Paris, 1867), pp.688–90.
18. Cf. [Archibald Johnston of Wariston], *Remonstrantie vande edelen, baronnen, state, kercken-dienaers, ende gemeente in het Coningryck van Schotland: Verclarende dat sy onschuldigh syne van de crimen daer mede sy in't laetste Engelsche Placcaet (vanden 27 february) beswaert werden. Gevisiteert na de Ordonnantie vande Generale Vergaderinge van den Raedt van Staten in Schotland* (Edinburgh & Amsterdam, 1639); *Informatie, aen alle oprechte christenen in het coningrijcke van Engelandt. Door de edelen, baronnen, staten, leeraers, ende gemeente in het coninckrijcke van Schotlandt. Waer in zy hare onschuldt te kennen gheven* . . . (Edinburgh, 1639); [Alexander Henderson], *Vertoog van de vvettelyckheyt van onsen tocht in Engelant* (Edinburgh, 1640); DR, TKUA, A II, no.14, Akter og Dokumenter nedr. Det politiske Forhold til England, 'Korfit Ulfelds or Gregers Krabbes Sendelse til England, 1640'; Murdoch, *Britain, Denmark–Norway and the House of Stuart*, pp.90–116.
19. Cf. *Briefwisseling van Hugo Grotius*, ed. B.L. Meulenbroek & P.P. Witkam (The Hague, 1976–81), (1639) pp.422–7; (1640) pp.200–09, 251–3, 273–82, 303–4; Stevenson, *The Scottish Revolution*, pp.184–7.
20. Hibbard, *Charles I and the Popish Plot*, pp.168–238; Scott, *England's Troubles*, pp.94–7.
21. HL, Bridgewater & Ellesmere MSS, EL 7352, 7815, 7824, 7853, 7857–7858; EUL, Instructions of the Committee of Estates of Scotland, 1640–41, Dc.4.16, pp.52–3, 92; John Corbet, *The Epistle congratulatorie of Lysimachus Niccanor of the Societie of Jesu, to the Covenanters of Scotland* (Oxford, 1641); Anon., *The Passionate Remonstrance made by his Holiness in the conclave in Rome, upon the late proceedings and great Covenant of Scotland with a reply of Cardinal de Barbarini in name of the Roman Clergy* (Edinburgh, 1641).
22. *The Earl of Strafforde's Letters and Dispatches*, ed. Knowler, vol.2, pp.187, 287.
23. J. Scally, 'Counsel in Crisis: James, third Marquis of Hamilton and the Bishops' Wars, 1638–1640', in Young, ed., *Celtic Dimensions of the British Civil Wars*, pp.18–34; Patrick Gordon of Ruthven, *A Short Abridgement of Britane's Distemper, 1639–1649*, ed. J. Dunn (Aberdeen, 1844), pp.6–16.
24. A. Grosjean, 'General Alexander Leslie, the Scottish Covenanters and the Riksråd Debates, 1638–40', in Macinnes, Riis & Pedersen, eds, *Ships, Guns and Bibles in the North Sea and Baltic States*, pp.115–38; DR, TKUA, Skotland, A II, no. 4a, Akter og Dokumenter nedr. det politiske Forhold til Skotland, 1572–1640; *Kancelliets Brevbøger: Vedrørende Danmarks Indre Forhold*

(1637–39), ed. E. Marquard (Copenhagen, 1944), pp.171, 213, 348, 672–3, 722. Field-Marshal Leslie's son was married to Rothes's daughter.

25. S. Murdoch, 'Scotland, Scandinavia and the Bishops' Wars, 1638–40', in Macinnes & Ohlmeyer, eds, *The Stuart Kingdoms in the Seventeenth Century*, pp.113–34; *Kong Christian Den Fjerdes Egenhaendige Breve*, vol.4 (1636–40), pp.195–6, 272–6, 304–5, 359–60, 364–9, 378–9; DR, TKUA, England A II, no.14, Akter of Dokumenter til England, 1631–40.

26. NAS, Hamilton Papers, GD 406/1/10491, /10816; *Proceedings of the Short Parliament*, ed. E.S. Cope & W.H. Coates (London, 1977), p.77.

27. NLS, Salt & Coal: Events, 1635–62, MS 2263, ff.73–84; NAS, Breadalbane MSS, GD 112/1/510, /514, /520; Macinnes, *Charles I and the Making of the Covenanting Movement*, pp.190–92.

28. DH, Loudoun Deeds, bundle 2/10; HL, Bridgewater & Ellesmere MSS, EL 7734, 7798; *Minute Book kept by the War Committee of the Covenanters in the Stewartry of Kirkcudbright in the Years 1640 and 1641* (Kirkcudbright, 1855), pp.50–51, 103–8; Henderson, *Sermons, Prayers and Pulpit Addresses*, pp.144–70; *The Earl of Strafforde's Letters and Dispatches*, ed. Knowler, vol.2, pp.396, 399–407. The hopes of Charles to mobilise at least 30,000 men at the outset of the Bishops' Wars failed to materialise. His troops in 1639 were at least a third less than the anticipated number. Although Wentworth had established garrisons on the Irish side of the North Channel, he sent no more than 500 Irish troops to protect Carlisle. The Covenanting army was superior not just in numbers along the Borders in July, but in the additional forces raised to suppress dissent in the north-east as a supplement to the vanguard of 2400 men first raised in February 1639. The 25,000 troops the Covenanters assembled on the Borders in August 1640 considerably outnumbered the forces raised by Charles to resist invasion.

29. E.M. Furgol, 'Scotland turned Sweden: The Scottish Covenanters and the Military Revolution, 1638–1651', in Morrill, ed., *The Scottish National Covenant in its British Context*, pp.134–55; M.C. Fissel, *The Bishops' Wars: Charles I's Campaigns against Scotland, 1638–40* (Cambridge, 1994), pp.26–9, 39–53, 195–214; M. Bennett, *The Civil Wars in Britain & Ireland, 1638–1651* (Oxford, 1997), pp.41–8, 64–8; HL, Bridgewater & Ellesmere MSS, EL 7851, 7857.

30. Macinnes, *Charles I and the Making of the Covenanting Movement*, pp.183–213; Morrill, *The Nature of the English Revolution*, pp.252–7; T. ó hAnnracháin, 'Rebels and Confederates: The Stance of the Irish Clergy in the 1640s', in Young, ed., *Celtic Dimensions of the British Civil War*, pp.96–115.

31. NAS, Hamilton Papers, GD 406/1/326, /1010; NAS, Breadalbane MSS, GD 112/1/516, /525; Macinnes, *Clanship, Commerce and the House of Stuart*, pp.75–6, 94–5; *The Earl of Strafforde's Letters and Dispatches*, ed. Knowler, vol.2, pp.187, 210, 220, 246–8, 278, 281, 289–91, 299–306, 321–5, 353–9.

32. DH, Loudoun Deeds, bundles 1/10; ICA, Letters – Marquess's Period, 1638–1645, bundles 6/90, 12/10; EUL, Instructions of the Committee of Estates of Scotland, 1640–41, Dc.4.16, p.74. Johnston of Wariston, Robert Douglas and his former tutor, Robert Barclay, provost of Irvine, served as his main agents respectively within the Estates of the gentry, the clergy and the burgesses.

33. Samuel Rutherford, *Lex Rex: The Law and the Prince* (Edinburgh, 1848), pp.56, 98–9, 143–8, 199, 222–3; Argyle, *Instructions to a Son*, pp.134–43; J.

Coffey, 'Samuel Rutherford and the Political Thought of the Scottish Covenanters', in Young, ed., *Celtic Dimensions of the British Civil Wars*, pp.75–95.

34. NLS, Wodrow MSS, quarto xxiv, f.165; EUL, Instructions of the Committee of Estates of Scotland, 1640–41, Dc.4.16, p.1.

35. J.R. Young, *The Scottish Parliament, 1639–1661: A Political and Constitutional Analysis* (Edinburgh, 1996), pp.1–18; Macinnes, *Charles I and the Making of the Covenanting Movement*, pp.194–7; BL, Scotland, Rents & Tenths 1639, Add. MS 33262, ff.1–65; NAS, Breadalbane MSS, GD 112/1/523, /536; HL, Loudoun Scottish Collection, box 43, LO 12565, 12870; HL, Bridgewater & Ellesmere MSS, EL 7737, 7809, 7813.

36. J.R. Young, 'The Scottish Parliament in the Seventeenth Century: European Perspectives', in Macinnes, Riis & Pedersen, eds, *Ships, Guns and Bibles in the North Sea and the Baltic States*, pp.139–72. Robert Balfour, Lord Balfour of Burleigh, a longstanding opponent of unfettered prerogative rule, was elected to preside over parliament. Henceforth, business was to be initiated from the floor of the unicameral Scottish parliament. All business devolved to committees was to be reported back for full deliberation prior to voting. Each section of the Committee of Estates governed autonomously, save for the declaration of war and the conclusion of peace, which required the assent of the whole Committee.

37. *APS*, vol.5, pp.264; 280–82, c.23–4; 285–90, c.26–33, 39, 41.

38. HL, Bridgewater & Ellesmere MSS, EL 7859, 7810, 7838, 7842–7849, 7869, 7872; R.T. Spence, 'Henry, Lord Clifford and the First Bishops' War, 1639', *Northern History*, 31 (1995), pp.138–56; D. Scott, '"Hannibal at our Gates": Loyalists and Fifth-Columnists During the Bishops' Wars: The Case of Yorkshire', *Historical Research*, 70 (1997), pp.269–93.

39. Baillie, *Letters and Journals*, ed. Laing, vol.1, pp.255–61; vol.2, pp.470–71; *The Intentions of the Army of the Kingdom of Scotland declared to their Brethren in England* (Edinburgh, 1640); Sir John Borough, *Notes on the Treaty carried on at Ripon between King Charles and the Covenanters of Scotland, A.D. 1640*, ed. J. Bruce (London, 1869), pp.70–77.

40. Russell, *The Fall of the British Monarchies*, pp.27–205, 303–29; Hirst, *England in Conflict*, pp.156–90; Woolrych, *Britain in Revolution*, pp.189–233.

41. J. Peacey, 'The Outbreak of the Civil Wars in the Three Kingdoms', in Coward, ed., *Companion*, pp.290–308; N. Canny, 'What Really Happened in Ireland in 1641?', in Ohlmeyer, ed., *Ireland: From Independence to Occupation*, pp.24–42.

42. J. Raymond, *Pamphlets and Pamphleteers in Early Modern Britain* (Cambridge, 2003), pp.172–92.

43. *The Earl of Strafforde's Letters and Dispatches*, ed. Knowler, vol.2, pp.394–405; HL, Hastings Irish Papers, box 7/HA 15043; HL, Bridgewater & Ellesmere MSS, EL 7840; M. Perceval-Maxwell, *The Outbreak of the Irish Rebellion of 1641* (Montreal, 1944), pp.67–82.

44. HL, Huntington Manuscripts, HM 1554, Anon. Diary of the Long Parliament, pp.109–22; *The Short Parliament (1640) Diary of Sir Thomas Aston*, ed. J.D. Maltby (London, 1988), pp.3, 6–7, 63–4, 124–5, 131–2, 145.

45. NLS, Wodrow MSS, folio lxiv, f.82; HL, Bridgewater & Ellesmere MSS, EL 7811, 7819–7821, 7823–7830, 7836; Gordon, *History of Scots Affairs*, vol.3, pp.7–9, 32–6, 125, 133–46, 148–53.

46. HL, Bridgewater & Ellesmere MSS, EL 7833–7835, 7837, 7841; *The Oxinden Letters, 1607–1642*, ed. D. Gardiner (London, 1933), pp.174–5; Sharpe, *The Personal Rule of Charles I*, pp.877–84.
47. Canny, *Making Ireland British*, pp.237, 295–8; Donald, *An Uncounselled King*, pp.191–6, 218–20, 245–50. Since the promulgation of the National Covenant, the Covenanting leadership had received regular, but not always reliable, intelligence from English sympathisers and Scottish courtiers usually channelled through Eleazar Borthwick, formerly chaplain to the Scottish forces in Sweden. Indeed, Borthwick sought to convince his former patron, the Marquess of Hamilton, that it was not fitting for 'a trew patriot' to offend God and lose the hearts of his countrymen by leading invasion forces on behalf of Charles I (NAS, Hamilton Papers, GD 406/1/920, /1101).
48. Stevenson, *The Scottish Revolution*, pp.205–6, 213; J.S.A. Adamson, 'The *Vindiciae Veritatis* and the Political Creed of Viscount Saye and Sele', *Historical Research*, 60 (1987), pp.45–63; EUL, Instructions of the Committee of Estates of Scotland, 1640–41, Dc.4.16, pp.4–5; DH, Loudoun Papers, bundle 1/8; John Selden, *A Briefe Discourse Concerning the Power of the Peeres and Comons of Parliament, in point of Judicature* (London, 1640). The supplication, which was actually drawn up by the nobles and gentry (including Pym, Hampden, and Fiennes) leading the English opposition to the prerogative rule, was subscribed by six nobles – Essex, Warwick, Saye & Sele, Brooke, Saville and Edward Montagu, Viscount Mandeville (later 2nd Earl of Manchester) – viewed as sympathetic to and supportive of Covenanting intervention.
49. J.S.A. Adamson, 'The Baronial Context of the English Civil War', in Cust & Hughes, eds, *The English Civil War*, pp.83–110; HL, Loudoun Scottish Collection, box 5, LO 8053; HL, Bridgewater & Ellesmere MSS, EL 7740–7741, 7743, 7862–7864, 7871; Balfour, *Historical Works*, ed. Haig, vol.2, pp.383–424.
50. HL, Bridgewater & Ellesmere MSS 7757, 7874; Northumbria Archives, Berwick-upon-Tweed, Guild Book 1627–43, B1/9, ff.194, 197–8; EUL, Instructions of the Committee of Estates of Scotland, 1640–41, Dc.4.16, pp.11, 30–31.
51. Perceval-Maxwell, *The Outbreak of the Irish Rebellion*, pp.82–91; P. Little, 'The Earl of Cork and the Fall of the Earl of Strafford, 1638–41', *HJ*, 39 (1996), pp.619–35. The Irish commissioners ranged from the future Catholic Confederate Sir Donagh McCarthy (later Viscount Muskerry) to the future regicide Sir Hardress Waller, and included the Scottish settler Sir James Montgomery of Rosemount, who had opposed the imposition of the 'black oath' which had proscribed covenanting and required unconditional loyalty to Charles I.
52. BL, Original Documents relating to Scotland, the Borders & Ireland, 16th and 17th centuries, Add. MS 5754, f.40; BL, Nicholas Papers, Egerton MS 2533, ff.89–92; DH, Loudoun Papers, bundle 1/5; EUL, Instructions of the Committee of Estates of Scotland, 1640–41, Dc.4.16, pp.5, 16, 29; HL, Bridgewater & Ellesmere MS 7430; *The Earl of Strafforde's Letters and Dispatches*, ed. Knowler, vol.2, pp.324, 328, 382–5.
53. *Proceedings in the Opening Session of the Long Parliament, 1640–41*, ed. M. Jannson, 3 vols (Rochester, 1999–2000); T. Cogswell, *Home Divisions: Aris-*

tocracy, the State and Provincial Conflict (Manchester, 1998), pp.276–82; I. Roots, *The Great Rebellion* (Stroud, 1995), pp.32–42.

54. EUL, Instructions of the Committee of Estates of Scotland, 1640–41, Dc.4.16, pp.31–2, 81–3, 94, 98; NAS, Hamilton Papers, GD 406/1/1397.

55. Morrill, *The Nature of the English Revolution*, pp.45–90.

56. Russell, *The Fall of the British Monarchies*, pp.83–6, 139–42, 150, 187, 195, 198, 200, 218, 334–5.

57. EUL, Instructions of the Committee of Estates of Scotland, 1640–41, Dc.4.16, pp.101, 105; *The Oxinden Letters*, ed. Gardiner, p.282; M. Mendle, 'A Machiavellian in the Long Parliament before the Civil War', *Parliamentary History*, 8 (1989), pp.116–24; W. Palmer, 'Oliver St. John and the Legal Language of Revolution in England: 1640–1642', *Historian*, 51 (1989), pp.263–82. In addition to most of the 12 peers who signed the supplication of August 1640, this group could draw on the support of not only Hampden, St John and Fiennes, but also of emergent radicals like Sir Arthur Haselrig and committed Puritans like the diarist Sir Simonds D'Ewes in the Commons.

58. D.L. Smith, *Constitutional Royalism and the Search for Settlement, c.1640–1649* (Cambridge, 1994), pp.39–80, 91–106; R. Tuck, *Philosophy and Government, 1572–1651* (Cambridge, 1993), pp.225–35; Woolrych, *Britain in Revolution*, pp.170–73, 183–6; Hirst, *England in Conflict*, pp.165–7, 173–5. Bristol and Thomas Wriothesley, 4th Earl of Southampton, can be counted among this conservative grouping in the Lords, as can William Seymour, 3rd Earl (later Marquess) of Hertford, who was formerly aligned to the group of peers who had petitioned Charles for the recall of parliament in August 1640. His younger brother Sir Francis Seymour (later Lord Seymour of Trowbridge), who had instigated debate in the 'Short Parliament' by extolling the supremacy of parliament as the highest law court for the redress of grievances, was a prominent associate in the Commons, along with Lucius Carey (Viscount Falkland), Sir John Strangeways, George Digby and Sir John Culpepper.

59. *Memoirs of Henry Guthry*, ed. Crawford, pp.65, 87–98; E.J. Cowan, *Montrose: For Covenant and King* (London, 1977), pp.96–101, 108–18; Donald, *An Uncounselled King*, pp.292–7. The Scottish plotters were attempting to open lines of communication with the Anglo-Scottish courtier James Stewart, 4th Duke of Lennox, who, as the recently created Duke of Richmond in the English peerage, was closely linked to the 'constitutional Royalists'.

60. Russell, *Unrevolutionary England*, pp.281–302; BL, Political and State Papers, 16th and 17th Centuries: Ramsay Papers, vol.25, Add. MS 33469, ff.49–50; DH, Loudoun Papers, bundle 1/5.

61. *Kong Christian Den Fjerdes Egenhaendige Breve*, vol.4, pp.395–6; DR, TKUA, England A II, no. 14, Akter og Dokumenter vedrgrende det politiske Forhold til England, 1631–40, 'E. Rosenkrantz, Diurnall occurances of the parliament holden at Westminster 1640 from the beginnings to the present time'.

62. EUL, Instructions of the Committee of Estates of Scotland, 1640–41, Dc.4.16, pp.57, 60–63, 88–91; BL, Speeches in Parliament, 1558–1695, Stowe MS 361, ff.90–91; HL, Bridgewater & Ellesmere MSS, EL 7752–7753, 7760; *The Great Account Delivered to the English Lords by the Scottish Commissioners* (London, 1641). Negotiations ongoing since January 1639

between Christian IV and Sir Thomas Roe as British ambassador, which had been primarily concerned with the activities of the Merchant Adventurers Company based at Hamburg, were broadened in August 1641 to seek relief from Sound tolls for Scottish as well as English merchants (DR, TKUA, Alm.Del I Indtil 1670, 'Latina' vol.11 (1632–51), ff.139, 152–5, 177–81, 189–90).

63. EUL, Instructions of the Committee of Estates of Scotland, 1640–41, Dc.4.16, pp.79–83, 86, 94, 100–01, 105–7; DH, Loudoun Papers, bundle 1/6; HL, Bridgewater & Ellesmere MSS, EL 7755–7756; [Archibald Campbell], *An Honourable speech made in the Parlament of Scotland by the Earle of Argile . . . the thirtieth of September 1641. Touching the prevention of nationall dissention, and perpetuating the happie peace and union betwixt the two kingdomes, by the frequent holding of Parlaments* (London, 1641); Levack, *The Formation of the British State*, pp.110, 130–31.

64. EUL, Instructions of the Committee of Estates of Scotland, 1640–41, Dc.4.16, pp.93, 97; *Rikskanseleren Axel Oxenstiernas Skrifter och Brefvexling*, II, 9 (Kingl. Vitterhets Historie och Antiquitetsakademien, Stockholm, 1898), pp.486–8; *Kong Christian den Fjerdes Egenhaendige Breve*, vol.5, pp.142–4; BL, John Dury, Epistolae Pace Ecclesiastica, Sloane MS 654, ff.216–217.

65. Balfour, *Historical Works*, ed. Haig, vol.3, pp.4–45; NAS, Hamilton Papers, GD 406/1/1378; Sir Simonds D'Ewes, *Speech delivered in the House of Commons 7 July 1641, being resolved into a committee . . . in the Palatine case* (London, 1641).

66. NAS, Hamilton Papers, GD 406/1/1440–1; Anon., *The Truth of the Proceedings in Scotland containing the Discovery of the late Conspiracie* (Edinburgh, 1641); Donald, *An Uncounselled King*, pp.313–16. Hamilton's brother William, Earl of Lanark (later 2nd Duke of Hamilton), was also a target.

67. Young, *The Scottish Parliament*, pp.30–53; Gilbert Burnet, *The Memoirs of the Lives and Actions of James and William, Dukes of Hamilton and Castleherald* (London, 1838), pp.46, 184–7. Charles's formal acceptance of the realities of political power in Scotland was manifest in his liberal bestowal of honours and pensions on the Covenanting leadership who had masterminded his defeat, militarily and constitutionally. Argyll was promoted to marquess and Loudoun to earl, General Leslie became Earl of Leven, Wariston was knighted and Henderson was appointed royal chaplain in Scotland.

68. *The Nicholas Papers: Correspondence of Sir Edward Nicholas, Secretary of State*, ed. G.F. Warner, 2 vols (London, 1886), vol.1, pp.25, 33–4, 58–9; Balfour, *Historical Works*, ed. Haig, vol.3, pp.64, 92, 125, 128–30, 134–5, 143–6; D. Stevenson, *Scottish Covenanters and Irish Confederates* (Belfast, 1981), pp.43–50.

69. BL, Observations of the State of Ireland, April 1640, Stowe MS 29, f.2; R. Gillespie, 'Destabilizing Ulster', in B. MacCuarta, ed., *Ulster, 1641: Aspects of the Rising* (Belfast, 1997), pp.107–22; Canny, *Making Ireland British*, pp.461–534.

70. Russell, *The Fall of the British Monarchies*, pp.373–94; Perceval-Maxwell, *The Outbreak of the Irish Rebellion*, pp.129–239; HL, Bridgewater & Ellesmere MSS, EL 7466, 7539, 7543. Parliament remained unresponsive to extensive lobbying by John Egerton, 1st Earl of Bridgewater, the last president of the Council, and by the circuit judges for Wales and the Marches that the government of the principality over the past century 'doeth much

manifest how much the neighbourhood of a Courte of Justice doeth further a reducinge and civilizinge of a People'. The Council for the North was also abolished, as were the Court of the Duchy of Lancaster and the Court of Exchequer of the County Palatine of Chester.

71. M. Perceval-Maxwell, 'Ireland and the Monarchy in the Early Stuart Multiple Kingdom', *HJ*, 34 (1991), pp.279–95; M. Ó Siochrú, *Confederate Ireland, 1642–9: A Constitutional and Political Analysis* (Dublin, 1999), pp.21–6, 237–40.

72. *The History of the Irish Confederation and the War in Ireland* (1641–9), ed. J.T. Gilbert, 7 vols (Dublin, 1882–91), vol.1, pp.279, 289; Canny, *Making Ireland British*, pp.404–8, 553–6, 561; A. Clarke, 'The 1641 Rebellion and Anti-Popery in England', in MacCuarta, ed., *Ulster, 1641*, pp.139–57.

73. Sir Simon Harcourt, *March 18. A letter sent from Sr. Simon Harcourt, to a worthy member of the House of Commons. With a true relation of the proceedings of the English army, under his command to this present March* (London, 1641); Edward Conway, 2nd Viscount Conway, *A Relation from the Right Honourable the Lord Viscount Conway, of the Proceedings of the English Army in Ulster from June 17 to July 30* (London, 1642); Stevenson, *Scottish Covenanters and Irish Confederates*, pp.51–65. Although Alexander Leslie, Earl of Leven, was the designated supreme commander of the Scottish forces, he only spent three months in Ireland between August and November 1642.

74. *A Contemporary History of Affairs in Ireland from A.D. 1641 to 1652*, ed. J.T. Gilbert, 3 vols (Dublin, 1879–80), vol.1, pp.450–53; Ó Siochrú, *Confederate Ireland, 1642–9*, pp.205–15 ; J.H. Ohlmeyer, 'The Civil Wars in Ireland', in J. Kenyon & J.H. Ohlmeyer, eds, *The Civil Wars: A Military History of England, Scotland and Ireland, 1638–1660* (Oxford, 1998), pp.73–102.

75. Kenyon, ed., *The Stuart Constitution*, pp.226–50; Smith, *Constitutional Royalism and the Search for Settlement*, pp.80–91; Bonaventura O' Connor, *A Wonderful Discovery of a Terrible Plot against Hull by the Designs of Lord Digby, Many Papists and Others of the Malignant Party* (London, 1642).

76. Henry Parker, *The Danger to England observed, upon its Deserting the High Court of Parliament* (London, 1642); *The Oxinden Letters*, ed. Gardiner, pp.311–12; M. Mendle, 'The Great Council of Parliament and the First Ordinances: The Constitutional Theory of the Civil War', *Journal of British Studies*, 31 (1992), pp.133–62.

77. Kenyon, ed., *The Stuart Constitution*, pp.21–3; HL, Bridgewater & Ellesmere MSS, EL 7763–7764, 7803; and Stowe Collection: Temple Papers, STT Ship Money L8C10; W. Kelly, 'James Butler, twelfth Earl of Ormond, the Irish Government and the Bishops' Wars, 1638–1640', in Young, ed., *Celtic Dimensions of the British Civil Wars*, pp.35–54; A.J. Hopper, ' "Fitted for Desperation": Honour and Treachery in Parliament's Yorkshire Command, 1642–43', *History*, 86 (2001), pp.138–54.

78. R. Hutton, *The Royalist War Effort, 1642–1646* (London, 1999), pp.22–48; *Declaration of the Lords and Commons assembled in Parliament concerning His Majesties advancing with his Army toward London: with Direction that all Trained Bands and Volunteers be put into a Readinesse* (London, 1642); Anon., *The King of Denmark's Resolution concerning Charles King of Great Britain, Wherein is Declared the Determination for the setting forth of a fleet towards England* (London, 1642).

79. Kenyon, ed., *The Stuart Constitution*, pp.274–84; Bennett, *The Civil Wars in Britain and Ireland*, pp.150–55. Notorious delinquents contributing money

to or appearing for the Royalist cause were to have their estates sequestered and placed under the management of commissioners who remitted surplus rents to the Parliamentary treasury established at the London Guildhall.

80. John Pym, *A Most Learned and Religious Speech spoken by Mr. Pym, at a Conference of both Houses of Parliament the 23 of . . . September. Declaring unto them the Necessity and Benefit of the Union of his Majesties three kingdomes, England, Scotland, and Ireland in matters of Religion and Church-Government* (London, 1642); Henry Parker, *The Generall Junto, or, The Councell of Union: chosen equally out of England, Scotland and Ireland, for the Better Compacting of Three Nations into One Monarchy* (London, 1642); *The Scots Resolution Declared in a Message Sent from the Privie Councell of the Kingdome of Scotland, to His Majestie at Yorke . . . wherein is expressed their earnest Desires both to his Maiestie and Parliament, That they would be pleased to joyne in a perfect Unione, it being the chiefe meanes to give an overthrow to the Enemies of the three Kingdoms* (Edinburgh, 1642); NAS, Hamilton Papers, GD 406/1/1688, /1742–3, /1782, /1808, /1887.

81. NAS, Hamilton Papers, GD 406/1/1828, /1840, /1846; HL, Loudoun Scottish Papers, box 29, LO 10503; *The Proceedings of the Commissioners, appointed by the Kings Maiesty and Parliament of Scotland, for conserving the articles of the Treaty and Peace betwixt the kingdomes of Scotland and England* (London, 1643). Interlocking control of both these interval committees was reinforced by the radicals' dominance over the Commission for the Public Affairs of the Kirk, constituted formally as the Interval Committee for the general assembly in August 1642, which promoted Covenanting solidarity with the Parliamentarians.

82. Young, *The Scottish Parliament*, pp.54–70; BL, Historical Papers, Egerton MS 2884, f.19; *A Declaration of the Lords of His Majesties Privie-Councell in Scotland and Commissioners for the conserving the Articles of the Treaty: For the Information of His Majesties good Subjects of this Kingdom. Together with a Treacherous and damnable Plot* (Edinburgh, 1643); Robert Munro, *A Letter of Great Consequence sent . . . out of the Kingdom of Ireland, to the Honorable, the Committee for the Irish Affairs in England, concerning the State of Rebellion there. Together with the relation of a Great Victory he obtained, and of his taking the Earl of Antrim, about whom was found Divers Papers which discovered a Dangerous Plot against the Protestants in all his Majesties Dominions* (London, 1643).

83. D. Stevenson, 'The Early Covenanters and the Federal Union of Britain', in Mason, ed., *Scotland and England*, pp.163–81; Brown, *Kingdom or Province?*, pp.81–3; J. Morrill, 'The Britishness of the English Revolution, 1640–1660', in Asch, ed., *Three Nations – A Common History?*, pp.83–115. A federative reconfiguration can be viewed as an association or confederation of executive powers authorised by the Scottish Estates and the English parliament that did not involve the subordination or incorporation of these separate constitutional assemblies. A federalist position would have subordinated them to a British assembly. Full parliamentary union, as achieved in 1707, required the incorporation or merger of the Scottish Estates with the English parliament. Federalism did not feature in contemporary British political vocabulary until the early eighteenth century.

84. *APS*, vol.6 (i) (1641–7), pp.41–3, 47–9.

85. G. Schramm, 'Armed Conflict in East-Central Europe: Protestant Noble Opposition and Catholic Royalist Factions, 1604–20', & I. Auerbach, 'The Bohemian Opposition, Poland–Lithuania, and the Outbreak of the Thirty

Years War', both in R.J.W. Evans & T.V. Thomas, eds, *Crown, Church and Estates: Central European Politics in the Sixteenth and Seventeenth Centuries* (London, 1991), pp.176–225; *The Journal of John Winthrop, 1630–1649*, ed. R.S. Dunn, J. Savage & L. Yeandle (Cambridge, MA, 1996), pp.429–40. In 1635, John Winthrop junior, the son of the principal architect of the New England confederation, had toured among the conventicling communities of Scottish and Irish settlers in Ulster, and Sir Henry Vane junior had served briefly and controversially as governor of the Massachusetts colony between 1635 and 1637.

86.   ICA, Letters – Marquess's Period, 1638–1645, bundle 7/145; Anon., *A great discoverie of a plot in Scotland, by miraculous means* (London, 1641); Anon., *The mysterie of iniquity, yet working in the kingdomes of England, Scotland, and Ireland, for the destruction of religion truly protestant* (London, 1643); Anon., *A full relation of the late expedition of the Right Honourable, the Lord Monroe, Majore-Generall of all the Protestant forces in the povince of Ulster with their several marches and skirmishes with the bloody Irish rebels . . . also, two declarations and an oath of confederacy whereby they bind themselves utterly to ruine and destroy the Protestants in that kingdome* (London, 1644); Anon., *A declaration made by the Rebells in Ireland against the English and Scottish Protestants, Inhabitants within that kingdome. Also a treacherous oath . . . lately contrived by the Confederate Rebells in a Council held at Kilkenny* (Waterford, rprt London, 1644); Anon., *The bloody diurnall from Ireland being papers of propositions, order, and oath, and severall bloody acts, and proceedings of the Confederate Catholics assembled at Kilkenny* (Kilkenny, rprt London, 1647); Clement Walker, *Relations and observations, historicall and politick, upon the Parliament, begun anno Dom. 1640 . . . Together with An appendix to The history of Independency, being a brief description of some few of Argyle's proceedings before and since he ioyned in confederacy with the Independent junto in England. With a parallel betwixt him and Cromwell, and a caveat to all his seduced adherents* (London, 1648).

5   The Wars for the Three Kingdoms, 1644–1651

1.   Pocock, 'The Atlantic Archipelago and the War of the Three Kingdoms', in Bradshaw & Morrill, eds, *The British Problem*, pp.184–9; E.J. Cowan, 'The Solemn League and Covenant', in Mason, ed., *Scotland and England, 1286–1815*, pp.182–202.

2.   Edward Bowles, *The Mysterie of Iniquity, Yet Working in the Kingdomes of England, Scotland, and Ireland, for the Destruction of Religion Truly Protestant* (London, 1643).

3.   NAS, Hamilton Papers, GD 406/1/1916; Young, *The Scottish Parliament*, pp.70–78. The Committee of Estates, which was to be periodically renewed over the next eight years – in 1644, 1647, 1648, 1649 and 1651 – remained the nucleus of oligarchic centralism in Scotland, notwithstanding the devolution of executive power onto specialist commissions for financial, diplomatic and ecclesiastical affairs. The periodic reinvigoration of local government – in 1644, 1646, 1648 and 1649 – underscored the accountability of the shire committees of war to the Committee of Estates (A.I. Macinnes, 'The Scottish Constitution, 1638–1651: The Rise and Fall of Oligarchic Centralism', in Morrill, ed., *The Scottish National Covenant in its British Context*, pp.106–33).

4. Anon., *The Love and Faithfulnes of the Scottish Nation, The Excellency of the Covenant, The Union between England and Scotland cleared, by Collections, from the Declarations of Parliament and Speeches of severall Independent Brethren* (London, 1646); HL, Loudoun Scottish Collection, box 16, LO 9998. The Covenanting army was committed to sending 18,000 foot and 2100 horse; around 300 Scottish officers were also infiltrated into the Parliamentary forces. The Covenanting intervention was to be maintained at £30,000 per month from the revenues of papists and other malignants. However, the Covenanting leadership was also committed to negotiating a loan of £200,000 jointly with the English Parliamentarians in continental money markets.

5. BL, Ordinances of Parliament, 1642–9, Add. MS 5492, ff.11, 54–5, 115–16; *Die Sabbati 30 December 1643. Ordered that the Adventurers of this House for lands in Ireland, and the body of Adventurers in London, doe meete at Grocers-Hall on Thursday in the afternoon at two of the clock, and take into their serious consideration by what wayes and meanes the British Army in Ulster, opposing the cessation may be maintained and encouraged to process in prosecution of that warre of Ireland against the Rebels, and to prepare some propositions to be presented to the House* (London, 1643). A further 10,000 Covenanting troops were despatched to England in the summer of 1644.

6. *The Declaration of the Kingdomes of Scotland and England* (Edinburgh, 1644).

7. HL, Bridgewater & Ellesmere MSS, EL 7732, 7773–7774; BL, Family of Pitt, Official Papers, 17th Century, Add. MS 29975, ff.88–9; Stephen Marshall, *A Sacred Panegyrick* (London, 1644); Thomas Mocket, *A View of the Solemn League and Covenant* (London, 1644); E. Vallance, 'Protestations, Vow, Covenant and Engagement: Swearing Allegiance in the English Civil War', *Historical Research*, 75 (2002), pp.408–24.

8. L. Kaplan, *Politics and Religion during the English Revolution: The Scots and the Long Parliament, 1643–1645* (New York, 1976), *passim*; D. Stevenson, *Revolution and Counter-Revolution in Scotland, 1644–1651* (London, 1977), pp.1–81; Smith, *Constitutional Royalism and the Search for Settlement*, pp.109–218.

9. Kishlansky, *The Rise of the New Model Army*, pp.22–102; I. Gentles, *The New Model Army in England, Ireland and Scotland, 1645–1653* (Oxford, 1992), pp.1–86; Bennett, *The Civil Wars in Britain & Ireland*, pp.169–229; J.S. Wheeler, *The Irish and British Wars, 1637–1654: Triumph, Tragedy and Failure* (London, 2002), pp.94–157.

10. D. Scott, 'The "Northern Gentlemen", the Parliamentary Independents and Anglo-Saxon Relations in the Long Parliament', *Historical Journal*, 42 (1999), pp.347–75; S. Barber, 'The People of Northern England and Attitudes towards the Scots, 1639–1651: "The Lamb and the Dragon cannot be Reconciled"', *Northern History*, 35 (1999), pp.93–118.

11. *The Journal of Sir Simonds D'Ewes from the Beginning of the Long Parliament to the opening of the Trial of the Earl of Strafford*, ed. W. Notestein (London, 1923), p.9; George Wither, *The British Appeals with Gods Mercifull Replies on the behalfe of the Commonwealth of England* (London, 1650), pp.12–13; M. Perceval-Maxwell, 'Ireland and Scotland, 1638–1648', in Morrill, ed., *The Scottish National Covenant in its British Context*, pp.193–211. At the same time, the Scottish Covenanters had a more disciplined military record in terms of massacres and atrocities than either the Royalists or the Parliamentarians in England. Of the 18 attested massacres during the first phase of the civil

war in England, the Scots were only held responsible for two – following the siege of Newcastle in October 1644 and after the skirmish at Canon Frome, Herefordshire, in June 1645. The Royalists, who instigated the atrocities at Barthomley, Cheshire, on Christmas Day 1643, were involved in nine incidents, the most notorious being the massacre at Bolton, Lancashire, in May 1644, when estimates of the number of victims ran from three to four figures. The Scots, despite persistent problems with their funding, were also considerably more professional in their restraint in comparison to the Parliamentary forces before and after the creation of the New Model Army. In only one of the four incidents cited prior to 1645, that at Cheriton, Hampshire, instigated under Sir William Waller in March 1644, did casualties run into three figures. But victims did run into the hundreds in two out of the three incidents following the creation of the New Model Army, notably after Sir Thomas Fairfax's victory at Naseby and Oliver Cromwell's capture of Basing House, Hampshire, in October 1645 (W. Coster, 'Massacre and Codes of Conduct in the English Civil War', in M. Levene & P. Roberts, eds, *The Massacre in History* (Oxford, 1999), pp.89–105; C. Carlton, *Going to the Wars: The Experience of the British Civil Wars, 1638–1651* (London, 1994), pp.34–7, 257–60). In Ireland, after the swapping of atrocities in May 1642 by the British forces under Edward, Lord Conway, at Newry, the Irish under Phelim O'Neill at Armagh and the Covenanting regiment raised by the Marquess of Argyll on the Rathlin Isles, the professionalism of the respective Ulster commanders Robert Munro and Owen Roe O'Neill ensured restraint was exercised on both sides over the next five years. Although confessionalism remained a bitterly and brutally decisive issue, both the Covenanting and the Confederate forces had a backbone of veterans from the Thirty Years War who were wary of reciprocal atrocities, an experienced as well as an orderly influence not evident to the same extent in England (Stevenson, *Scottish Covenanters and Irish Confederates*, pp.103–30; G. Parker, 'Early Modern Europe', in M. Howard, G.J. Andreopoulos & M.R. Shulman, eds, *The Laws of War: Constraints on Warfare in the Western World* (New Haven, CT, 1994), pp.40–58). Moreover, the Covenanting armies in Ireland and England seemingly never indulged in the humiliating stripping of survivors which had characterised the acts of atrocity against Protestant planters during the Irish rebellion of 1641–2 and the Royalist victory over Essex at Lostwithiel in Cornwall on 31 August 1644 (B. Donagan, 'Codes and Conduct in the English Civil War', *Past & Present*, 118 (1988), pp.64–95; Canny, *Making Ireland British*, pp.541–50). The Cornish civilian population who joined in this degradation were not deemed beyond reconciliation by Parliamentarians disgusted by their barbarous behaviour. In contrast, the Irish fighting in England and Wales were subjected to a no quarter ordinance issued by the 'Long Parliament' on 24 October 1644.

12. DH, Loudoun Deeds, bundle 1/1; *Tabeller over Skibsfart og Varetransport gennem Oresund*, vol.1, pp.266–389. Scottish shipping to the Baltic had enjoyed parity with that of England at the outset of Charles I's reign. It had continued to rise throughout the 1630s despite being overtaken by English shipping. A downward spiral from the emergence of the Covenanting movement onwards had been reversed from 1641. But shipping ventures plummeted during the three years of Covenanting intervention in England

from 1644, when Scottish trade through the Sound fell markedly behind the English and was even overtaken by the Portuguese. Portuguese shipping had lagged considerably behind that of Scotland prior to the emergence of the Covenanting movement.

13. BL, Naval Papers, 1643–77, Add. MS 22546, f.5; TWA, Hostmen's Company, Old Book, 1600–*c*.1690, GU/HO/1/1, ff.206–8, 242–4; *The Correspondence of the Scots Commissioners in London, 1644–1646*, ed. H.W. Meikle (Edinburgh, 1907), pp.31, 39–41; C. Dalhede, *Handelsfamiljer på Stormaktstiden Europamarknad*, 2 vols (Partille, 2001), vol.2, pp.294–5, 303, 306–7, 311, 414–15, 319.

14. A. Grosjean, *An Unofficial Alliance: Scotland and Sweden, 1569–1654* (Leiden, 2003), pp.195–206; BL, Nicholas Papers, Egerton MS 2533, f.365; DR, TKUA, Alm.Del I Indtil 1670, 'Latina' vol.11, ff.272–4, 310–15, 335–7, and TKUA, England, A II, no. 15, Akter og Dokumenter vedr. det politiske Forhold til England, 1641–8. The Scottish commissioners led by Loudoun were John, Lord Maitland (later 2nd Earl and 1st Duke of Lauderdale), Johnston of Wariston and Mr Robert Barclay. Another six commissioners, headed by Argyll, were added in July 1644. Although Charles I had been informed officially by the Covenanters of the embassy to France, Lothian was imprisoned at Oxford on his return when calling to pay his respects to the king in November 1643.

15. Cf. *Making the News*, ed. Raymond, pp.110–12; [Robert Devereux], *A Letter from his Excellency, Robert Earl of Essex, to the Honourable House of Commons concerning the sending of a Commission forthwith to Sir William Waller* (London, 1644). This distinctive Scottish perspective was upheld by the newsbook *The Scottish Dove*. Possibly initiated by the peripatetic William Lithgow, its moralistic British concerns were sustained by its London editor, George Smith.

16. Alexander Henderson, *A Sermon Preached to the Honourable House of Commons, At their late solemne Fast, Wednesday, December 27 1643* (London, 1644). The other Scottish clerics attending the Westminster Assembly were Robert Baillie, Robert Douglas, George Gillespie and Samuel Rutherford, all powerful preachers and polemicists.

17. DH, Loudoun Papers, bundles 1/26–7, 7/161, and Loudoun Deeds, bundle 1700/2; *Correspondence of the Scots Commissioners in London*, ed. Meikle, pp.6, 10–13, 22–7, 33–4, 45, 50, 53, 57–8. The trial in England of peers from another kingdom remained a live issue, as is evident from the prosecution of Connor Maguire, Lord Enniskillen, in 1645 for treasonable acts committed in Ireland (D.A. Orr, 'England, Ireland, Magna Carta, and the Common Law: The Case of Connor, Lord Maguire, second Baron of Enniskillen', *Journal of British Studies*, 39 (2000), pp.389–421). At the same time, the estates of Irish peers in England were protected through British family affiliations (P. Little, '"Blood and Friendship": The Earl of Essex's Protection of the Earl of Clanricarde's Interests, 1641–6', *EHR*, 112 (1997), pp.927–41).

18. Sir Benjamin Rudyard, *A Speech concerning a West Indies association, at a committee of the whole House in the Parliament, 21 January* (London, 1641); *An Ordinance of the Lords & Commons assembled in Parliament, whereby Robert, Earl of Warwick is made governor in chiefe, and lord high admiral of all those islands and other plantations, inhabited, planted or belonging to any His Majesties the King of England's subjects, within the bounds, and upon the coasts of America* (London, 1643). Simul-

taneously, an invitation was opportunely extended to the well-affected in straitened circumstances and to the public-spirited to transport themselves, their servants or agents to the Caribbean, 'for propagating the Gospell, and increase of trade'. The only concession to Scottish interests during the Treaty of London was a clerical petition, supported by 70 English divines, that Alexander Henderson 'and some other worthy ministers of Scotland' should be associated with any scheme to promote Reformation as well as plantations in the West Indies. When resubmitted in 1644, the petition's supporters were now cited as 'many English and Scottish divines' ([William Castell], *A Petition of W.C. exhibited to the High Court of Parliament now assembled, for the propagating of the Gospel in America and the West Indies* (London, 1641); *Certaine Inducements to Well Minded People* (London, 1643); William Castell, *A Short Discoverie of the Coasts and Continent of America, from the equinoctiall northward and the adjacent isles* (London, 1644)). By this juncture, however, Scottish colonial aspirations were shifting from the West to the East Indies, with two trading schemes, one inspired by Danish practice, the other by French enterprise, under active consideration by the Scottish Estates (*APS*, vol.6 (i), c.118, p.344; c.164–6, pp.372–5).

19. *Correspondence of the Scots Commissioners in London*, ed. Meikle, pp.9, 29, 59–63; HL, Ellesmere & Bridgewater MSS, EL 7776; D.L. Smith, '"The More Posed and Wised Advice": The Fourth Earl of Dorset and the English Civil Wars', *HJ*, 34 (1991), pp.797–829. The king's principal negotiators were two 'constitutional Royalists', Thomas Wriothesley, 4th Earl of Southampton, and the Anglo-Scot James Stuart, 4th Duke of Lennox and 1st Duke of Richmond, whose endeavours to play on the sympathy of his Scottish countrymen for the Stuart monarchy were unproductive (HL, Bridgewater & Ellesmere MSS, EL 7776; DH, Loudoun Deeds, bundle 2/9).

20. J. Adamson, 'The Triumph of Oligarchy: The Management of War and the Committee of Both Kingdoms, 1644–1645', in C.R. Kyle & J. Peacey, eds, *Parliament at Work: Parliamentary Committees, Political Power & Public Access in Early Modern England* (Woodbridge, 2002), pp.101–27; M. Kishlansky, *A Monarchy Transformed: Britain, 1603–1714* (London, 1996), pp.155–6, 163–4; PRO, Committee of Both Kingdoms, Entry Book: letters received 1644 September – 1645 February, SP 21/7, pp.75–9, 112–13, 153, 194–6, and Committee of the House of Commons for Scottish Affairs: Order Book 1643 October – 1645 December, SP 23/1A, pp.18–21, 48, 50, 58, 63, 71, 77, 102. Developed on the English side from the Committee of Safety, the Committee of Both Kingdoms was obliged to share direction of the war effort, initially with the Committee to Reform the Lord General Essex's Army, which dealt with the composition of regiments, and then with the Army Committee, which was primarily concerned with supply. Meeting the costs of the Covenanting armies in England and Ireland remained the responsibility of the Committee at Goldsmith's Hall for Scottish Affairs.

21. Northumbria Archives, Berwick-upon-Tweed, Guild Book, 1627–43, B1/9, ff.258, 261, and Guild Book, 1643–51, B1/10, ff.2–4; PRO, State Papers Domestic, Supplementary: Orders, Warrants and Receipts for Payment of the Scots Army in England, 1643–8, SP 46/106, ff.150, 255, 257; *The Correspondence of the Scots Commissioners in London*, ed. Meikle, pp.2–4, 39, 46–8, 68–9, 82–3, 88–9, 93, 102, 107, 141, 202; D. Scott, 'The Barwis

Affair: Political Allegiance and the Scots During the British Civil Wars',
EHR, 115 (2000), pp.843–63.

22. Young, 'The Scottish Parliament and European Diplomacy', in Murdoch,
ed., *Scotland and the Thirty Years' War*, pp.87–92; *The Journal of Thomas
Cunningham of Campvere*, ed. E.J. Courthope (Edinburgh, 1928), pp.5–7,
14–16, 82–8, 109–17, 251.

23. Riksarkivet, Stockholm, Anglica 521; Grosjean, *An Unofficial Alliance*,
pp.206–13.

24. DR, TKUA, England, A I, no.3, Breve, til Vels med Bilag fra Medlemmer
af det Engelske Kongehus til medlemmer af det danske, 1613–89, and
TKUA, England, A II, no. 15, Akter og Dokumenter vedr. det politiske
Forhold til England, 1641–8; *Kong Christian Den Fjerdes Egenhaendige Breve*,
vol.4, pp.423–5, 513–15; Murdoch, *Britain, Denmark–Norway and the House of
Stuart*, pp.124–38. English merchant communities overseas also reciprocated this Gothic tendency. Thus, the members of the Merchant Adventurers' Company based in Hamburg were continuing to refuse universal
subscription to the Solemn League and Covenant in the summer of 1645,
although they were prepared to recognise that effective power in England
had passed to the Parliamentarians (HL, Stowe Collection: Temple Papers.
STT: Miscellaneous Papers, L9B5). However, the governor and merchants
of the Levant Company, though their business was an English monopoly,
did apply to the Committee of Both Kingdoms at the outset of 1646
to effect a change of ambassador to Turkey (PRO, State Papers, Turkey
(1641–62), SP 97/17).

25. PRO, Committee of Both Kingdoms, Entry Book: letters received 1644,
June–September, SP 21/16, pp.145–7; HL, Loudoun Scottish Collection,
box 21, LO 11367; *The Quarrel between The Earl of Manchester and Oliver
Cromwell: An Episode of the English Civil Wars*, ed. D. Mason (London, 1875),
pp.62–70, 78–95; *The Correspondence of the Scots Commissioners in London*, ed.
Meikle, pp.50–53; Kaplan, *Politics and Religion during the English Revolution*,
pp.55–96.

26. M. Kishlansky, 'The Case of the Army Truly Stated: The Creation of the
New Model Army', *Past & Present*, 81 (1978), pp.51–74; I. Gentles, 'The
Choosing of the Officers for the New Model Army', *Historical Research*, 67
(1994), pp.264–85. The New Model Army combined and pruned the
armies of Essex, Manchester and Sir William Waller. Two additional contingents were retained: the Western Army commanded by Edward Massey
concentrated on the recovery of Royalist areas, while the Northern Army
under Sydenham Poyntz manifestly served notice on Covenanting intervention (Wheeler, *The Irish and British Wars*, pp.125–9).

27. BL, Historical Autographs, 16th–18th Centuries, Add. MS 28103, f.41;
Bennett, *The Civil Wars in Britain & Ireland*, pp.220–29; J. Morrill, *The Revolt
of the Provinces: Conservatives and Radicals in the English Civil War* (London,
1976), pp.98–114; Hutton, *The Royalist War Effort*, pp.155–65; Hirst, *England
in Conflict*, pp.220–24, 229–30. The centralised support structure for the
New Model Army enabled the Parliamentarians to retain a firm hold of
counties, such as Staffordshire, whose loyalty was by no means assured
prior to 1645 (AUL, microfilm, Stuart Papers from the Denys Eyre Bower
Collection, Chiddingstone Castle, Kent. Reel 1, County Record Office,
Staffordshire, 793/8–78).

28. PRO, State Papers Domestic, Supplementary: Orders, Warrants and Receipts for Payment of the Scots Army in England, 1643–8, SP 46/106, ff.129–32, 134, 228, 268, 314–15; *An Ordinance of the Lords and Commons assembled in Parliament for the further supply of the British army in Ireland* (London, 1645); Wheeler, *The Irish and British Wars*, pp.129–31. Most of the £200,000 loaned to pay for Scottish intervention was recouped from the 14 counties under Parliamentary control at the outset of 1644, which were situated in the south-east around London and its commercial hinterland. Rutland was the only defaulting county and arrears were less than £10,000 (a shortfall of less than 5 per cent). However, the first four months' assessment, from March 1644, encountered significant arrears for an assessment of almost £69,000 that ran to just under £18,000 (a shortfall in excess of 16 per cent). The three additional Midland counties subject to this assessment, like Rutland, wholly defaulted. A second four-monthly assessment, which commenced in August 1645 from the same 17 counties, led to further arrears close to £26,000 (a shortfall of more than 37 per cent). In addition to these defaults, the first four months' assessment failed to meet the agreed rate of £31,000 per month that the Covenanting army was to receive by £55,000. Although the monthly rate for 1645 was reduced to £21,000 following the withdrawal of troops to engage in the Scottish civil war, the sums assessed for the second four months still failed to meet this rate by £15,000.

29. DH, Loudoun Papers, A525/1; *The Correspondence of the Scots Commissioners in London*, ed. Meikle, pp.21, 35–8, 54–7, 72–3, 89–93, 124–30, 144 5, 160–61, 166–7; Bennett, *The Civil Wars in Britain and Ireland*, pp.182–4.

30. John Shawe, *Brittains Remembrancer: Or, The National Covenant, As it was laid out in a sermon preached in the minster at Yorke . . . upon Friday Sept. 20 1644* (London, 1644), and *The Three Kingdomes Case: or, Their sad calamities, together with their causes and cure. Laid down in a sermon preached at a publique fast at Kingston upon Hull* (London, 1646); *The Journal of Thomas Juxon, 1644–47*, ed. K. Lindley & D. Scott (Cambridge, 1999), pp.27–9, 61–2, 75, 78, 81–7, 114–17; Morrill, *The Revolt of the Provinces*, pp.118–22.

31. HL, Bridgewater & Ellesmere MSS, EL 7778; DH, Loudoun Papers, A15/4, bundle 44/1, and Loudoun Deeds, bundle 1/16; [Robert Devereux], *A Paper delivered in the Lord's House by the Earle of Essex, Lord Generall, at the offering up of his Commission* (London, 1645).

32. DH, Loudoun Papers, A15/4, /15; Bulstrode Whitelocke, *Memorials of the English Affairs from the beginning of the Reign of Charles I to the Happy Restoration of King Charles the Second*, 4 vols (Oxford, 1853), vol.1, pp.460–67; *The Journal of Thomas Juxon*, ed. Lindley & Scott, pp.94–5, 102–5; W.M. Lamont, 'The Puritan Revolution: A Historiographical Essay', in Pocock, ed., *The Varieties of British Political Thought*, pp.119–45; E. Vallance, ' "An Holy and Sacramental Paction": Federal Theology and the Solemn League and Covenant in England', *EHR*, 116 (2000), pp.50–75. The adversarial nature of the divisions between Presbyterians and Independents was laid bare in the summer of 1645, when Thomas, Lord Saville, at the prompting of Saye & Sele for the latter party, attempted to implicate Denzil Holles and Bulstrode Whitelocke in secret dealings with the Scots to negotiate terms of peace with Charles I (M. Mahoney, 'The Saville Affair and the Politics of the Long Parliament', *Parliamentary History*, 7 (1988), pp.212–27).

33. *Making the News*, ed. Raymond, pp.339–48; Henry Parker, John Sadler & Thomas May, *The King's Cabinet Opened* (London, 1645).

34. BL, Historical Letters and Papers, 1633–55, Add. MS 33596, ff.7–8; *The Diplomatic Correspondence of Jean de Montereul and the Brothers De Bellièvre, French Ambassadors in England and Scotland, 1645–48*, ed. J.G. Fotheringham, 2 vols (Edinburgh, 1898–9), vol.1, pp.5–195; vol.2, pp.569–83; *The Correspondence of the Scots Commissioners in London*, ed. Meikle, pp.150, 153, 160, 163, 179–80. The principal Covenanting agent in France was Sir Robert Moray, lieutenant-colonel of the Scots Guards. Prior to Uxbridge, the Scottish commissioners in London had been particularly resistant to French overtures that they unilaterally conclude a peace treaty with Charles I. Indeed, prior to the arrival of Montereul, the relationship of the Committee of Estates with the French envoy de Boisivon, sent to Scotland in the wake of the Solemn League and Covenant, had varied from abrasive to outright hostility. The Scots had imprisoned the envoy in York when he attempted to reach Charles I in the summer of 1644 (ibid., vol.2, pp.539–68).

35. DH, Loudoun Papers, A15/5, /7-11, /16 & bundle 1/25; *The Correspondence of the Scots Commissioners in London*, ed. Meikle, pp.82–3, 97–8, 109–11, 118–23, 133–4, 137–9, 147; Whitelocke, *Memorials of the English Affairs*, vol.2, pp.542–3; Wheeler, *The Irish and British Wars*, pp.148–50; Stevenson, *Revolution and Counter-Revolution in Scotland*, pp.61–3. Newark surrendered the day after Charles came into Scottish custody.

36. DH, Loudoun Papers, green suitcase, bundle 1/21, and Loudoun Deeds, bundles 1/7, 1700/1; Baillie, *Letters and Journals*, ed. Laing, vol.2, pp.103, 195, 211, 229–30, 234, 242, 250, 265–6, 270, 286, 299, 317–20, 326, 335–41, 357, 360–62, 485; vol.3, pp.10–11; *The Correspondence of the Scots Commissioners in London*, ed. Meikle, pp.43, 71, 155; Kaplan, *Politics and Religion during the English Revolution*, pp.128–44. The Scottish commissioners were certainly familiar with the Committee for Examination and Parliamentary Justice, which had had the determination of loyalty and censorship of the written and spoken word among its ideological functions since 1642.

37. DH, Loudoun Papers, A213/4, bundle 1/23–4, and green suitcase, bundle 1/20; *The Correspondence of the Scots Commissioners in London*, ed. Meikle, pp.104–5, 148–52, 173–7, 181–2, 186–200; Whitelocke, *Memorials of the English Affairs*, vol.1, pp.548–9, 557, 564, 578; Smith, *Constitutional Royalism and the Search for a Settlement*, pp.128–31, 149–50, 183–7; P. Little, 'The English Parliament and the Irish Constitution', in M. Ó Siochrú, ed., *Kingdoms in Crisis: Ireland in the 1640s* (Dublin, 2000), pp.106–21.

38. [Archibald Campbell], *The Lord Marquess of Argyle's Speech to A Grand Committee of Both Houses of Parliament* (London, 1646); ICA, Letters – Marquess's Period, 1646–9, bundle 8/192; *Making the News*, ed. Raymond, pp.349–50; J.R. Young, 'The Scottish Parliament and the Covenanting Revolution: The Emergence of a Scottish Commons', in Young, ed., *Celtic Dimensions of the British Civil Wars*, pp.164–84; Stevenson, *Revolution and Counter-Revolution in Scotland*, pp.63–72. Scotophobia was evident in various measures. A relatively innocuous publication by a Scottish writer, David Buchanan, explaining the emerging differences between the Uxbridge and Newcastle propositions was deemed insulting by the Commons and burned by the common hangman. The Lords declined to accept the vote of the

Commons on 19 May to dispense with the services of the Covenanting army, having determined 12 days earlier that no move should be made by the New Model Army to interpose itself between the Scottish forces and the Borders. The monthly maintenance for the Scots had been reduced to £15,000 at the outset of 1646.

39. [John Campbell], *The Lord Chancellor of Scotland his first Speech: At a Conference in the Painted Chamber with a Committee of Both Houses, Octob. 1. 1646* (London, 1646); DH, Loudoun Deeds, bundle 1/2; BL, Royal and Noble Autographs, 1646–1768, Add. MS 19399, f.4; D. Scott, ' "Particular Businesses" in The Long Parliament: The Hull Letters, 1644–1648', in C.R. Kyle, ed., *Parliament, Politics and Elections, 1604–1648* (Cambridge, 2001), pp.321–4, 329–31; [William Prynne], *Scotland's ancient obligation to England and publicke acknowledgement thereof, for their brotherly assistance to, and deliverance of them, with the expence of their blood, and hazard of the state and tranquility of their realm, from the bondage of the French, in the time of their greatest extremity, 1560* (London, 1646).

40. *The Journal of Thomas Juxon*, ed. Lindley & Scott, pp.133–7, 145–8; Richard Codrington, *The Life and Death of the Illustrious Robert, Earl of Essex* (London, 1646); Richard Vines, *The Hearse of the Renowned, The Right Honourable Robert Earle of Essex* (London, 1646).

41. DH, Loudoun Papers, A213/3, and Loudoun Deeds, bundle 1/17, /20; ICA, Letters – Marquess's Period, 1646–9, bundle 8/209; NAS, Hamilton Papers, GD 406/1/2104, /2108, /2114, /2145; *The Diplomatic Correspondence of Jean de Montereul*, ed. Fotheringham, vol.1, pp.238–367; vol.2, pp.583–94; *The Correspondence of the Scots Commissioners in London*, ed. Meikle, pp.201–16; Anon., *Papers from the Scottish Quarters, containing the substance of two votes made by the Estates at Edinburgh at their general meeting this present Septemb. 1646* (London, 1646). The first instalment of £200,000 was actually paid between 30 January and 3 February 1647, on the surrender of the northern garrisons but prior to the Covenanting forces crossing the border; the second went by default.

42. Hutton, *The Royalist War Effort*, pp.86–109; A.I. Macinnes, 'Scottish Gaeldom, 1638–1661: The Vernacular Response to the Covenanting Dynamic', in Dwyer, Mason & Murdoch, eds, *New Perspectives in Scottish History in the Politics and Culture of Early Modern Scotland*, pp.59–94.

43. HL, Hastings Irish Papers, box 8/HA 14987 & box 9/HA 15009; S. Wheeler, 'Four Armies in Ireland', in Ohlmeyer, ed., *Ireland from Independence to Occupation*, pp.43–65. As no mention was made of the disposition of forces in Mayo, Cavan and Fermanagh, the Protestant presence there presumably went by default. The Protestant/Catholic divide must also be treated with caution as Ormond relied heavily in negotiations on his principal facilitator, Colonel John Barry, a Catholic Royalist from Munster, and was supported in Connacht by perhaps the foremost Catholic Royalist, the Earl of Clanricarde. In Ulster, while Antrim shuttled between the Royalist and Confederate camps, his fellow Catholic planter the Earl of Castlehaven was a committed Confederate (W. Kelly, 'John Barry: An Irish Catholic Royalist in the 1640s', in Ó Siochrú, ed., *Kingdoms in Crisis*, pp.158–75; D.F. Cregan, 'The Confederate Catholics of Ireland: The Personnel of the Confederation, 1642–9', *IHS*, 29 (1995), pp.492–512).

44. HL, Hastings Irish Papers, box 7/HA 15051& box 8/HA 14929, 1500-1, 15030, 15904; PRO, Committee of Both Kingdoms, Entry Books, letters received 1644, SP21/16, f.144; P. Lenihan, 'Confederate Military Strategy, 1643–7', in Ó Siochrú, ed., *Kingdoms in Crisis*, pp.158–75; Wheeler, *The Irish and British Wars*, pp.99–102, 121–3; Stevenson, *Scottish Covenanters and Irish Confederates*, pp.139–63.

45. DH, Loudoun Papers, bundle 1/2; *The Correspondence of the Scots Commissioners in London*, ed. Meikle, pp.5–7, 16, 37–8; D. Stevenson, *Alasdair MacColla and the Highland Problem in the Seventeenth Century* (Edinburgh, 1980), pp.69–70, 73, 99–101. The Irish Royalists, who steadfastly refused to campaign with the Confederates in Ireland until a firm peace had been concluded between them, supported the link with Montrose which opened up the prospect of ridding the provinces of Ulster and Connacht of local robber bands, sometimes known as Tories, who were exploiting endemic warfare for their own personal gain (*The Letter-Book of the Earl of Clanricarde, 1643–47*, ed. J. Lowe (Dublin, 1983), pp.138–9, 144–5, 168–71).

46. Macinnes, *Clanship, Commerce and the House of Stuart*, pp.98–108; E.M. Furgol, 'The Northern Highland Covenanting Clans, 1639–1651', *Northern Scotland*, 7 (1987), pp.19–31; NAS, Hamilton Papers, GD 406/1/1635; BL, Miscellaneous Letters etc., 1566–1804, Add. MS 36450, ff.16–17. Royalism was also able to tap into traditional respect for social order, reinforced by cultural distinctiveness in Cornwall and, perhaps more patchily, in Wales (M.J. Stoyle, ' "Pagans or Paragons?": Images of the Cornish during the English Civil War', *EHR*, 111 (1996), pp.299–323; H. Thomas, *A History of Wales, 1485–1660* (Cardiff, 1972), pp.197–205).

47. Gordon of Ruthven, *A Short Abridgement of Britane's Distempers*, pp.152–4, 160–61, 168–72. The blood lust of the Covenanters was not confined to the Irish. A contingent of Covenanting irregulars led by James Campbell of Ardkinglass massacred over 100 Lamonts after that Royalist clan surrendered their strongholds of Ascog and Toward in the Cowal district of Argyllshire in June 1646. During his mopping up operations on the western seaboard in June 1647, Lieutenant-Colonel David Leslie condoned the massacre of over 300 clansmen, mainly MacDougalls, on their surrender of Dunaverty Castle in the Kintyre peninsula, which they had garrisoned for MacColla (A.I. Macinnes, 'Clan Massacres and British State Formation', in Levene & Roberts, eds, *The Massacre in History*, pp.127–48).

48. Ohlmeyer, *Civil War and Restoration in the Three Stuart Kingdoms*, pp.6–10, 172–83; NAS, Hamilton Papers, GD 406/1/1972; Cowan, *Montrose*, pp.154, 232–4; Stevenson, *Alasdair MacColla*, pp.258–62.

49. NAS, Hamilton Papers, GD 406/1/1610; TFA, TD 4666; BL, Ordinances of Parliament, 1642–9, Add. MS 5492, ff.115–16.

50. Adair, *A True Narrative of the Rise and Progress of the Presbyterian Church in Ireland*, pp.69–134; J.R. Young, 'Invasions: Scotland and Ireland, 1641–1691', in P. Lenihan, ed., *Conquest and Resistance: War in Seventeenth Century Ireland* (Leiden, 2001), pp.53–86.

51. *The Correspondence of the Scots Commissioners in London*, ed. Meikle, pp.219, 222–3; HL, Loudoun Scottish Collection, box 30, LO 10335–7; box 41, LO 10067; box 43, LO 7601; and Hastings Irish Papers, box 8/HA 14972; PRO, Committee of Both Kingdoms, Entry Book, letters received 1644–5, SP21/17, pp.153, 194–6, 205, and Committee of the House of Commons

for Scottish Affairs: Order Book, 1643–5, SP 23/1A, pp.18, 20–21, 50, 58, 63; DH, Loudoun Papers, A213/2.

52. J.H. Ohlmeyer, 'Ireland Independent: Confederate Foreign Policy and International Relations during the Mid-seventeenth Century', in Ohlmeyer, ed., *Ireland from Independence to Occupation*, pp.89–111; T. Ó hAnnracháin, 'Disrupted and Disruptive: Continental Influences on the Confederate Catholics of Ireland', in Macinnes & Ohlmeyer, eds, *The Stuart Kingdoms in the Seventeenth Century*, pp.135–50. This tendency towards crusading was also notable in clerical reports on the Irish forces which accompanied Alasdair MacColla when he intervened in the Scottish civil war of 1644–5 (*Memoirs of Scottish Catholics in the Seventeenth and Eighteenth Centuries*, ed. W.F. Leith, 2 vols (London, 1909), vol.1, pp.221–5, 263–358).

53. G. Parker, *Empire, War and Faith in Early Modern Europe* (London, 2003), pp.169–91; P. Lenihan, *Confederate Catholics at War, 1641–49* (Cork, 2001), pp.22–72, 117–45; P. Edwards, 'Logistical Supply', in Kenyon & Ohlmeyer, eds, *The Civil Wars*, pp.234–71; HL, Hastings Irish Papers, box 8/HA 14776.

54. R. Armstrong, 'Ormond, the Confederate Peace Talks and Protestant Royalism', in Ó Siochrú, ed., *Kingdoms in Crisis*, pp.122–40; I. Roy, 'George Digby, Royalist Intrigue and the Collapse of the Cause', in I. Gentles, J. Morrill & B. Worden, eds, *Soldiers, Writers and Statesmen of the English Revolution* (Cambridge, 1998), pp.69–90; *The Letter-Book of the Earl of Clanricarde*, ed. Lowe, pp.155–68, 190–215.

55. BL, View of the Condition of Ireland from 1640, Sloane MS 3838, ff.23, 31, 79; *The King's Letter to the Marquesse of Ormond and the Marquesse of Ormonds Letter to Monroe Relating the King's whole Design, concerning all the three Kingdoms* (London, 1646); Ó Siochrú, *Confederate Ireland*, pp.18–19, 229–36; M. O'Riordan, ' "Political" Poems in the Mid-seventeenth Century Crisis", in Ohlmeyer, ed., *Ireland from Independence to Occupation*, pp.112–27. Rinuccini carried majority support but never unanimous backing from the 13 Irish Catholic bishops (T. Ó hAnnracháin, 'Lost in Rinuccini's Shadow: The Irish Clergy, 1645–9', in Ó Siochrú, ed., *Kingdoms in Crisis*, pp.176–91).

56. Wheeler, *The Irish and British Wars*, pp.175–8, 195–8; T. Ó hAnnracháin, 'The Strategic Involvement of Confederate Powers in Ireland, 1596–1691', in Lenihan, ed., *Conquest and Resistance*, pp.25–52; *The Diplomatic Correspondence of Jean De Montereul*, ed. Fotheringham, vol.2, pp.21, 31, 35, 41, 95, 171, 228, 256, 435–6, 439; HL, Hastings Irish Papers, box 8/HA14116, 14667, 15355; box 9/HA 14345, 14998. Colonel Michael Jones was the brother of Dean Henry Jones, one of the prime movers who compiled the 1641 depositions which grossly exaggerated the extent of Protestant massacres during the Irish rebellion.

57. J. Adamson, 'Strafford's Ghost: The British Context of Viscount Lisle's Lieutenancy of Ireland', in Ohlmeyer, ed., *Ireland from Independence to Occupation*, pp.128–60; R. Armstrong, 'Ireland at Westminster: The Long Parliament's Irish Committee, 1641–1647', in Kyle & Peacey, eds, *Parliament at Work*, pp.79–99; Sir John Temple, *The Irish Rebellion* (London, 1646); *A Warning to the Parliament of England. A discovery of the ends and designes of the Popish partie both abroad, and at home, in the raising and formenting our late war, and still-continuing troubles: in an oration made to the generall Assembly of the French clergy in Paris, by Monsieur Jaques du Perron, Bishop of Angolesme, and Grand Almosner to*

the Queen of England (London, 1647); PRO, Derby House Committee for Irish Affairs, Letters Sent 1647, Mar. 22–1648, Aug. 1, SP21/27, ff.8, 11, 49, 57, 79–80, 89.

58. PRO, Derby House Committee for Irish Affairs, Letters Sent 1647–8, SP21/27, ff.14, 24, 123–9, 132–3; BL, Miscellaneous Letters and Papers, Add. MS 33506, f.26; Sir Thomas Adams, *Plain dealing or a fair warning to the gentlemen of the Committee for Union* (London, 1647). The defaulting counties in chronological order were Devon, Worcester, Derby, Cambridge, Warwick, Wiltshire, Berkshire, Dorset, Surrey, Kent, Northampton, Cornwall, Worcester and Norfolk: that is, more than a third of all English counties and representative of every region except the north and Wales.

59. Whitelocke, *Memorials of the English Affairs*, vol.2, pp.182–93; [Clement Walker], *The History of Independency, with the Rise, Growth and Practices of that powerful and restlesse Faction* (London, 1648), pp.31, 75, 78–9; J.S.A. Adamson, 'The English Nobility and the Projected Settlement of 1647', *HJ*, 30 (1987), pp.567–602. The Presbyterians also became too closely identified with Ormond in their management of Irish affairs (P. Little, 'The Marquess of Ormond and the English Parliament, 1645–1647', in T.C. Barnard & J. Fenlon, eds, *The Dukes of Ormonde, 1610–1745* (Woodbridge, 2000), pp.83–99).

60. Smith, *Constitutional Royalism and the Search for Settlement*, pp.132–6, 195–6; M. Kishlansky, 'The Army and the Levellers: The Roads to Putney', *HJ*, 22 (1979), pp.795–824; A. Woolrych, *Soldiers and Statesmen: The General Council of the Army and its Debates, 1647–48* (Oxford, 1987), pp.214–99.

61. Kliger, *The Goths in England*, pp.260–86; Kenyon, ed., *The Stuart Constitution*, pp.288–324; *The Clarke Papers*, ed. C.H. Firth, 4 vols (London, 1891–1901), vol.1, pp.226–418. Ireton's political philosophy was also expounded further in the debates with the Independent ministers in the Army's General Council at Whitehall, 14–15 December 1648 (ibid., vol.2, pp.71–132). The term 'Leveller' was an abusive epithet applied to democratic agitators and polemicists like John Lilburne who repudiated the communism advocated by Gerard Winstanley as leader of the Diggers who deemed his group the 'True Levellers'. The pro-Leveller newsbook claimed the title of *The Moderate*.

62. Scott, *England's Troubles*, pp.269–89; Tuck, *Philosophy and Government*, pp.173, 244–51.

63. S. Barber, *Regicide and Republicanism: Politics and Ethics in the English Revolution, 1646–1659* (Edinburgh, 1998), pp.40–65, 157–8, 177–8; A. Sharp, 'The Levellers and the End of Charles I', in J. Peacey, ed., *The Regicides and the Execution of Charles I* (Basingstoke, 2001), pp.181–201; N. Carlin, 'The Levellers and the Conquest of Ireland in 1649', *HJ*, 39 (1987), pp.269–88. The *Agreement of the People* was redrafted on two occasions between the Putney Debates and the regicide.

64. Anon., *The Scots-Mans Remonstrance* (London, 1647); Riksarkivet, Stockholm, Anglica 521; Burnet, *Memoirs of the Dukes of Hamilton*, pp.365–78; J. Scally, 'Constitutional Revolution, Party and Faction in the Scottish Parliaments of Charles I', in C. Jones, ed., *The Scots and Parliament* (Edinburgh, 1996), pp.54–73.

65. *A Source Book of Scottish History*, ed. Dickinson & Donaldson, vol.3, pp.134–9; Baillie, *Letters and Journals*, ed. Laing, vol.3, pp.444–50; NAS, Hamilton

Papers, GD 406/1/1193, /2156, /2212, /2254, /2368, /10806. In his address to 'the Lords & Gentlemen Commons of the Scots Parliament, together with the Officers of the Army' on 31 July 1648, Charles I made no mention of covenanting, far less hinting at a future commitment to his taking the Covenants (BL, Miscellaneous Autograph Letters, Add. MS 24422, f.1).

66. Anon., *The British Bell-man* (London, 1648); PRO, Derby House Committee for Irish Affairs, Letters Sent 1647–8, SP21/27, ff.129–30; M. Bennett, 'Dampnified Villagers: Taxation and Wales during the First Civil War', *Welsh History Review*, 19 (1998), pp.29–43.

67. [Marchmont Nedham], *Anti-Machiavelli, or, Honesty Against Policy* (London, 1647); [Walker], *The History of Independency*, pp.80–81, 100–01, 118–20, 123–6; *A Letter from the House of Commons assembled in the Parliament of England at Westminster, To the Right Honourable and Right Reverend, the Lords, Ministers and others of the present General Assemble of the Church of Scotland sitting at Edinburgh* (London, 1648); *The Clarke Papers*, ed. Firth, vol.2, pp.251–2; NAS, Hamilton Papers, GD 406/1/2284, /2389, /2403, /2408, /2442, /2454.

68. James Turner, *Memoirs of His Own Life and Times, 1632–1670*, ed. T. Thomson (London, 1829), pp.49–75; S. Barber, ' "A bastard kind of militia", Localism, and Tactics in the Second Civil War', in Gentles, Morrill & Worden, eds, *Soldiers, Writers and Statesmen of the English Revolution*, pp.133–50; Wheeler, *The Irish and British Wars*, pp.182–92, 200–02; Bennett, *The Civil Wars in Britain and Ireland*, pp.284–305. The Prince of Wales did join the naval mutineers, who were able to make their presence felt in the Channel Islands.

69. NLS, Scottish Parliament 1648, MS 8482, ff.1–82; *The Clarke Papers*, ed. Firth, vol.2, pp.52–3; Gordon, *Britane's Distemper*, pp.212–13; *A Letter Sent from Lieutenant Generall Cromwell to The Marquis of Argyle, and General Lesley* (London, 1648); A.I. Macinnes, 'The First Scottish Tories?', *SHR*, 67 (1988), pp.56–66; Young, *The Scottish Parliament*, pp.189–227. While the Kirk gained a right of veto over office holding, the general assembly remained a supplicant, not a director, in the shaping of public policy. The ideological principle underlying the Act of Classes was that acquiescence in the directives of the Covenanting movement was insufficient. Those seeking public office had to demonstrate a positive commitment to radicalism. Loudoun was among the first to make public repentance for his part in the Engagement.

70. [Walker], *The History of Independency*, pp.140, 156–8, 166–74; Smith, *Constitutional Royalism and the Search for a Settlement*, pp.138–40, 196–7. The Presbyterian shift away from the Heads of Proposals had already been signposted by the Four Bills in December 1647 but truncated by the passage through the 'Long Parliament' of no addresses to the king in the following month. Bulstrode Whitelocke was among those members formerly associated with the Presbyterian party who were not purged from the 'Rump Parliament', which was not a cipher for the Army.

71. Whitelocke, *Memorials of the English Affairs*, vol.2, pp.468–516; J. Adamson, 'The Frightened Junto: Perception of Ireland, and the Last Attempts at Settlement with Charles I', & S. Kelsey, 'Staging the Trial of Charles I', both in Peacey, ed., *The Regicides and the Execution of Charles I*, pp.36–93.

72. *A Letter from Scotland: and the Votes of the Parliament for Proclaiming Charles the Second, King of Great Britain, France & Ireland* (London, 1649); *The Vindication and Declaration of the Scots Nation* (Edinburgh, 1649); [Charles II], *The King of Scots his Message and Remonstrance to the Parliament of that Kingdome, conveened at Edenburge, for a perfect Union, and Agreement, between Prince and People and his desires to all his loving Subjects of that Nation, requiring their due obedience towards him, as their law-full King and Governor* (London, 1649). Overtures from the Scottish commissioners in London that the Covenanting leadership should be consulted were ignored and the messengers imprisoned.

73. [Marchmont Nedham], *Digitus Dei: or, God's Justice upon Treachery and Treason, Exemplified in the Life and Death of the late James, Duke of Hamilton* (London, 1649); Anon., *The Bounds & bonds of Publique Obedience* (London, 1649); Whitelocke, *Memorials of the English Affairs*, vol.2, pp.532–48; DR, TKUA, England, A I, no.3, Breve, til Vels med Bilag fra Medlemmer af det Engelske Kongehus til medlemmer af det danske, 1613–89. Of the new Council of State, 22 members (including Whitelocke) had not voted for the trial and execution of Charles I, 19 had.

74. HL, Hastings Irish Papers, box 9/HA 14167, 14954, 14992, 14999, 15308–9, 15311, 15313, 15354, 15357, 15426; *The Clarke Papers*, ed. Firth, vol.2, pp.202–6; [Walker], *The History of Independency*, pp.86–7, 121–2; Gentles, *The New Model Army in England, Ireland and Scotland*, pp.350–84; Wheeler, *The Irish and British Wars*, pp.209–20. Charles I had recognised the independence of Portugal from Spain in 1642.

75. Murdoch, *Britain, Denmark–Norway and the House of Stuart*, pp.150–59; Grosjean, *An Unofficial Alliance*, pp.221–7; Stevenson, *Revolution and Counter-Revolution in Scotland*, pp.145–8, 161–3; *The Scots Remonstrance or Declaration* (London, 1650); BL, Holme Hall Papers, vol.1, 1518–1773, Add. MS 40132, ff.1–5, and Nicholas Papers, Egerton MS 2542, ff.17–19.

76. Balfour, *Historical Works*, ed. Haig, vol.4, pp.92–109, 141–60, 174–8; *A Source Book of Scottish History*, ed. Dickinson & Donaldson, vol.3, pp.144–6; BL, Correspondence of R. Lang, Secretary of State, 1649–61, Add. MS 37047, ff.22, 149, and T. Astle, Historical Collections, 1642–1769, Add. MS 34713, ff.3–8.

77. *The Covenants and the Covenanters*, ed. J. Kerr (Edinburgh, 1896), pp.348–98; *The Government of Scotland under the Covenanters, 1637–1651*, ed. D. Stevenson (Edinburgh, 1982), pp.105–73; BL, Collection of Historical and Parliamentary Papers, 1620–60, Egerton MS 1048, ff.134–41.

6   Commonwealth and Protectorate, 1651–1660

1. J. Peacey, 'Reporting a Revolution: A Failed Propaganda Campaign', in Peacey, ed., *The Regicides and the Execution of Charles I*, pp.161–80; [John Gauden], *Eikon Basilike: The portraicture of His sacred Maiestie in his solitudes and sufferings* (London, 1649); Peter Heylyn, *A Short View of the life and reign of King Charles (the second monarch of Great Britain) from his birth to his burial* (London, 1658); Arthur Wilson, *The History of Great Britain being the life and reign of King James the First, relating to what passed from his first access to the Crown, till his death* (London, 1653).

2. *A Declaration of his Imperiall Majestie, the most High and Mighty Potentate Alexea, Emperor of Russia, and great Duke of Muscovia &c. wherein is conteined his detestation of the murther of Charles the first, King of Great Britain and Ireland* (London, 1650); TFA, Papers TD 3756; *The Perfect Diurnall of some passages and proceedings of, and in relation to, the armies of England, Ireland and Scotland* (London, 1650), no. 31 (8–15 July), p.358, and no. 34 (29 July – 5 August), p.395.

3. Murdoch, *Britain, Denmark–Norway and the House of Stuart*, pp.146–9; *A Declaration of the Proceedings of Thirteen Christian Kings, Princes, and Dukes, and the present state and condition of the King of Scots* (London, 1651); DR, TKUA, England, A I, no.3, Breve, til Vels med Bilag fra Medlemmer af det Engelske Kongehus til medlemmer af det danske, 1613–89.

4. DR, TKUA, Alm.Del I Indtil 1670, 'Latina' vol.13 (1652–61), ff.74–5, 89, 103, 107–8, 278, 338–9; Whitelocke, *Memorials of the English Affairs*, vol.3, pp.207–11.

5. John Shawe, *Britannia Rediviva: of the Proper and Sovereign Remedy for the Healing and Recovering of these three distracted Nations* (London, 1649); Anon., *A brief narration of the mysteries of state carried on by the Spanish faction in England, since the reign of Queen Elizabeth to this day for supplanting of the magistracy and ministry, the laws of the land, and the religion of the Church of England* (London, 1651); E. Vernon, 'The Quarrel of the Covenant: The London Presbyterians and the Regicide', in Peacey, ed., *The Regicides and the Execution of Charles I*, pp.202–24.

6. Marchmont Nedham, *The Case of the Common-Wealth of England Stated* (London, 1650); Henry Parker, *Scotlands holy war. A discourse truly, and plainly remonstrating, how the Scots out of a corrupt pretended zeal to the Covenant have made the same scandalous and odious to all good men: and how by religious pretexts of saving the peace of Great Britain they have irreligiously involved us all in a most pernicious warre* (London, 1651); S. Kelsey, 'The Foundation of the Council of State', in Kyle & Peacey, eds, *Parliament at Work*, pp.129–48.

7. DR, TKUA, England, AII no.16, Akter og Dokumenter vedr. det politiske Forhold til England, 1649–59; John Milton, *A Manifesto of the Lord Protector of the Commonwealth of England, Scotland, Ireland &c.* (London, 1738, trans. from the original Latin version of 1655).

8. *Records of the Commissions of the General Assemblies for the years 1650–52*, ed. J. Christie (Edinburgh, 1909), pp.557–62; *Register of the Consultations of the Ministers of Edinburgh, and some other Brethren of the Ministry, 1652–60*, ed. J. Christie, 2 vols (Edinburgh, 1921, 1930), vol.1, pp.292–340; vol.2, pp.143–75; Canny, *Making Ireland British*, pp.556–9, 572–8.

9. J.S. Wheeler, *Cromwell in Ireland* (Dublin, 1999), pp.191–7; S. Barber, 'Scotland and Ireland under the Commonwealth: A Question of Loyalty', in Ellis & Barber, eds, *Conquest and Union*, pp.195–221; É. Ó Ciardha, 'Tories and Moss-troopers in Scotland and Ireland in the Interregnum: A Political Dimension', in Young, ed., *Celtic Dimensions of the British Civil Wars*, pp.141–63; Cuthbert Sydenham, *The false brother, or, A new map of Scotland, drawn by an English pencil* (London, 1651).

10. D. Hirst, 'The English Republic and the Meaning of Britain', in Bradshaw & Morrill, eds, *The British Problem*, pp.192–219; J.S. Wheeler, 'Sense of Identity in the Army of the English Republic', in Macinnes & Ohlmeyer, eds, *The Stuart Kingdoms in the Seventeenth Century*, pp.151–68; Barber, *Regicide and Republicanism*, pp.191–5. The term 'British republike' did enjoy a

brief currency at the beginning of the Protectorate (cf. George Wither, *The Protector* (London, 1655)). Officers and soldiers regularly articulated their opinions in petitions, pamphlets and newsletters.

11. *The Perfect Diurnall* (London, 1650), no. 31 (8–15 July), pp.359–60, and no. 34 (29 July – 5 August), pp.402–3; (London, 1652), no. 108 (29 December 1651 – 5 January 1652), pp.1560–62, 1567–8, 1570; Whitelocke, *Memorials of the English Affairs*, vol.3, pp.247–8, 381–2, 392, 404–5. Having taken over the command of that portion of the navy which had defected to the Royalists in 1648, Prince Rupert had effectively resorted to privateering from the Irish Seas to the Caribbean.

12. S. Kelsey, 'Unkingship', in Coward, ed., *Companion*, pp.331–49; B. Coward, *The Cromwellian Protectorate, 1653–59* (Manchester, 2002), pp.155–6.

13. Whitelocke, *Memorials of the English Affairs*, vol.3, pp.100, 132, 152, 159, 260–73; S. Kelsey, *Inventing a Republic: The Political Culture of the English Commonwealth, 1649–1653* (Stanford, CA, 1997), pp.85–113.

14. George Wither, *To the Soveraigne Maiesty of the Parliament of the English Republike, (by the grace of God) Keepers of the Liberties of England* (London, 1651). When Ireton died, he was accorded a state funeral as an Army grandee on 6 March 1652 that echoed the defiant splendour of the ceremonial in that for Essex as a Parliamentary grandee in October 1646 (*Diary and Correspondence of John Evelyn, F.R.S.*, ed. W. Bray (London, n.d.), p.188).

15. Barber, *Regicide and Republicanism*, pp.160–61, 174–91; B. Worden, *The Rump Parliament, 1648–1653* (Cambridge, 1974), pp.82, 219–20, 225–32; E. Vallance, 'Oaths, Casuistry, and Equivocation: Anglican Responses to the Engagement Controversy', *HJ*, 44 (2001), pp.59–79.

16. Hirst, *England in Conflict*, pp.264–5, 271; A. Woolrych, *Commonwealth to Protectorate* (Oxford, 1986), pp.8, 294; HL, Bridgewater & Ellesmere MSS, EL 8539, 8542; John Dury, *Considerations concerning the present Engagement whether it may be lawfully entered into: Yea or No?* (London, 1649), and *A Second Parcel of Objections against the taking of the Engagement answered* (London, 1650).

17. T.C. Barnard, *Cromwellian Ireland: English Government and Reform in Ireland, 1649–1660* (Oxford, 1975), pp.67–8, 95–8, 148; BL, Petitions, 1648–54, Add. MS 34326, f.3; HL, Hastings Irish Papers, box 9/HA 14349–52, 14354–6, 14358, 15356; Adair, *A True Narrative*, pp.135–237; *The Declaration of the British in the North of Ireland, With some queries of Colonel Moncke, and the answers of the British to the queries* (London, 1649). However, as the Commonwealth gave way to the Protectorate, the presbytery of Ulster took advantage of renewed offers of toleration, not by formally engaging with the Republican regime but by adopting self-denying ordinances that promoted passive resistance. The acts passed in Bangor in 1654 were designed to neutralise, if not avoid, the spread of the Protestor–Resolutioner controversy as returning exiles and new recruits were attracted from Scotland. So successful were these measures that Presbyterianism on the Scottish model expanded throughout and beyond the confines of Ulster. Whereas there were no more than 24 ministers during the Commonwealth, there were at least 80 during the Protectorate. By 1659, the presbytery had become the synod.

18. *The Clarke Papers*, ed. Firth, vol.3, pp.22, 81–2, 96; vol.4, pp.49–55; Whitelocke, *Memorials of the English Affairs*, vol.3, pp.392–3, 410, 414–15, 419. Some Independents antipathetic to Scottish interests, and particularly

wary that free trade would favour Scottish salt to the prejudice of the salt works on the Tyne, did suggest that precedence after England be accorded to Ireland, which was reputedly the better country and had been planted chiefly by the English.

19. BL, Collection of Historical and Parliamentary Papers, 1620–60, Egerton MS 1048, ff.142–8; Woolrych, *The British Revolution*, pp.500–01.

20. F.D. Dow, *Cromwellian Scotland, 1651–1660* (Edinburgh, 1979), pp.30–36; Brown, *Kingdom or Province?*, pp.136–7.

21. DH, Loudoun Papers, bundle A15/2; ICA, Letters – Marquess's Period, 1650–58, bundles 13/18; NAS, Breadalbane MSS, GD 112/1/568; Anon., *The Antiquity of Englands Superiority over Scotland and The Equity of Incorporating Scotland or other Conquered Nations, into the Commonwealth of England* (London, 1652).

22. HL, Loudoun Scottish Collection, box 32, LO 9054; BL, Hardwicke Papers, vol. 516, Add. MS 35864, ff.1–12; *Scotland and the Commonwealth, 1651–53*, ed. C.H. Firth (Edinburgh, 1895), pp.15–185. The absence of some deputies was explicable by illness, and special allowance was sought for the absence of deputies from small coastal burghs engaged in herring fishing. Special pleading was also undertaken for smaller shires remote from Edinburgh who usually sent only one commissioner to the Scottish parliament, and likewise for smaller and distant burghs.

23. PRO, Anglo-Scottish Committee of Parliament appointed to confer with the deputies from Scotland: minute book, 1652 October 14–1653, April 8, SP 25/138, pp.3–64; BL, Letters and State Papers: Birch Collection, Add. MS 4158, ff.101–3. Although with 400 MPs English dominance was not endangered, the quorum of 60 proposed for the reconstituted 'Rump Parliament' technically allowed parliament to function without English MPs.

24. Young, *The Scottish Parliament*, pp.297–303; TFA, Papers, TD 3758–60; BL, Maitland and Lauderdale Papers, 1532–1688, Add. MS 35125, f.54.

25. PRO, Anglo-Scottish Committee of Parliament, SP 25/138, pp.62–3; DH, Loudoun Deeds, bundle 2/6; A.H. Williamson, 'Union with England Traditional, Union with England Radical: Sir James Hope and the Mid-Seventeenth Century British State', *EHR*, 110 (1995), pp.303–12; Woolrych, *Commonwealth to Protectorate*, pp.177–81.

26. Macinnes, *Clanship, Commerce and the House of Stuart*, pp.110–14; Mitchell Library, Glasgow, John Graham of Duchrie. Account of the Earl of Glencairn's expedition to the Highlands of Scotland, 1653–4, Special Collection SR 163, pp.1–21; BL, Letters & State Papers, Birch Collection, Add. MS 4156, f.73.

27. Whitelocke, *Memorials of the English Affairs*, vol.4, pp.98–10; Dow, *Cromwellian Scotland*, pp.17–22, 44, 53, 67–8, 107, 244; Woolrych, *Britain in Revolution*, pp.567–73, 589–92. Arguably, the main benefit of political incorporation and English oversight of Scottish government in kirk and state was the phasing out of witchcraft trials, which had reached a peak during the patriotic accommodation of 1649–50. The reputed resurgence in witchcraft had less to do with demonology than as a form of parochially sponsored euthanasia in which the less favoured members of communities, such as the old, the infirm and the unbalanced, were sacrificed at a time of scarce resources, rampant plague, and perhaps even clerical impotence

over the running of civil affairs (Glasgow University Archives, Beith Parish MSS, P/CN, II/139/3–14).

28. BL, Papers of General Desborough, 1651–60, Egerton MS 2519, ff.19, 21, 23, 25, 29–30, and Miscellaneous Letters and Papers, Add. MS 41295, ff.129–30; HL, Loudoun Scottish Collection, box 37/LO 9201; *Scotland and the Protectorate*, ed. C.H. Firth (Edinburgh, 1899), pp.147–8, 226, 270, 272–6, 286, 303, 321; Woolrych, *Commonwealth to Protectorate*, p.298. The full extent of Argyll's military showdown with Cromwellian forces in 1652 was only admitted during the endeavours of the military command in Scotland to have him excluded from the 1659 parliament.

29. Woolrych, *Commonwealth to Protectorate*, pp.274–311; B.M. Downing, *The Military Revolution and Political Change: Origins of Democracy and Autocracy in Early Modern Europe* (Princeton, NJ, 1992), pp.168–79; Coward, *The Cromwellian Protectorate*, pp.119–38.

30. B.S. Capp, *Cromwell's Navy: The Fleet and the English Revolution, 1648–1660* (Oxford, 1989), pp.42, 66–72; Brenner, *Merchants and Revolution*, pp.577–8, 622–3; S. Pincus, *Protestantism and Patriotism: Ideologies and the Making of English Foreign Policy, 1650–1668* (Cambridge, 1996), pp.40–50; *Akstykker og Oplysinger til Rigsrådets of Staendermødernerns Historie i Frederick III's tid*, ed. C.R. Hansen, 2 vols (Copenhagen, 1959, 1975), vol.2, pp.562–3; [Richard Wylde], *The humble petition and remonstrance of Richrd Wylde, merchant and adventurer in the East-India trade laying open the many wilfull neglects, ill-managed actions and improvident courses, the governors and committees of the East-India Company, have heretofore, and still do practice in all their way of trade to the East-Indies, to the exceeding great prejudice of the adventurer and nation in generall* (London, 1654).

31. J.B. Collins, *The State in Early Modern France* (Cambridge, 1995), pp.65–78; J.-F. Schaub, *La France Espagnole* (Paris, 2003), pp.309–19; Pincus, *Protestantism and Patriotism*, pp.15–39.

32. DR, TKUA, A II, no. 16, Akter og Dokumenter nedr. det politiske Forhold til England (1649–59), bundle 'Erik Rosenkrantz og Peder Sendelse til England, 1652'; *Danmark–Norges Traktater*, vol.4, pp.626–43; Thomas Jenner, *Londons blame, if not its shame: manifested by the great neglect of the fishery, which affordeth to our neighbor nation yeerly, the revenue of many millions, which they take up at our doors, whilst with the sluggard, we fold our hands in our bosoms and will not stretch them forth to our mouths* (London, 1651).

33. Pincus, *Protestantism and Patriotism*, pp.51–79; B. Worden, 'Marchmont Nedham and the Beginnings of English Republicanism, 1649–1656', in D. Wootton, ed., *Republicanism, Liberty and Commercial Society, 1649–1776* (Stanford, CA, 1994), pp.45–81; Anon., *The Seas Magazine Opened: or, the Hollander dispossest of his usurped trade of fishing upon the English seas* (London, 1653).

34. Wheeler, *The Irish and British Wars*, pp.251–6; *Danmark–Norges Traktater*, vol.5, pp.15–42: HL, Bridgewater & Ellesmere MSS, EL 8185–6, and Stowe Collection: Temple Papers, STT Personal box 11 (15), and Hastings Irish Papers, box 9/HA 14355.

35. Anon., *The Fifth Monarchy, or Kingdom of Christ in Opposition to the Beasts, Asserted* (London, 1659); Woolrych, *Commonwealth to Protectorate*, pp.56–75, 278–333; Hirst, *England in Conflict*, pp.278–82; J. Sproxton, 'From Calvin to Cromwell through Beard', *Journal of European Studies*, 25 (1995), pp.17–33; B. Coward, *Oliver Cromwell* (Harlow, 1991), pp.91–8.

36.   Kenyon, ed., *The Stuart Constitution*, pp.333–5, 342–8; Woolrych, *Commonwealth to Protectorate*, pp.23–4, 357–60, 366–78; P. Gaunt, *Oliver Cromwell* (Oxford, 1996), pp.153–69; Anon., *Britania triumphalis: a brief history of the warres and other state-affairs of Great Britain. From the death of the late King, to the dissolution of the last Parliament* (London, 1654). Under the Instrument, parliament was now to meet for at least five months on a triennial basis rather than biennially for at least four months.

37.   G. Burgess, 'Repacifying the Polity: The Responses of Hobbes and Harrington to the "Crisis of the Common Law"', in Gentles, Morrill & Worden, eds, *Soldiers, Writers and Statesmen of the English Revolution*, pp.202–28; Q. Skinner, '"*Scientia civilis*" in Classical Rhetoric and in the Early Hobbes', in N. Phillipson & Q. Skinner, eds, *Political Discourse in Early Modern Britain* (Cambridge, 1993), pp.67–93.

38.   A. Fukuda, *Sovereignty and the Sword: Harrington, Hobbes and Mixed Government in the English Civil Wars* (Oxford, 1997), pp.52–68; Tuck, *Philosophy and Government*, pp.320–25; Kliger, *The Goths in England*, pp.139–46.

39.   Pincus, *Protestantism and Patriotism*, pp.114–91; *Articles of Peace, Union and Confederation, concluded and agreed between his Highness Oliver Lord Protector of the common-wealth of England, Scotland & Ireland, and the dominions thereto belonging. And the Lords of the States General of the United Provinces of the Netherlands* (London, 1654); *Danmark–Norges Traktater*, vol.5, pp.134–61; *Akstykker og Oplysinger til Rigsrådets of Staendermødernerns Historie i Frederick III's tid*, vol.2, pp.1011–29.

40.   DR, TKUA, A II, no. 16, Akter og Dokumenter nedr. det politiske Forhold til England (1649–59), bundle 'Forhandlinger med de engleske Afsendinge, Philip Meadow, Edward Montague, Algernon Sidney, Robert Honywood og Thomas Boone, 1659', and TKUA, Alm.Del I Indtil 1670, 'Latina' vol.13, ff.309–12, 320, 325–6, 355–9; *Swedish Diplomats at Cromwell's Court, 1655–56: The Missions of Peter Julius Coyet and Christer Bonde*, ed. M. Roberts (London, 1988), pp.7–8, 31–2, 38–43, 124–44, 192–9; Whitelocke, *Memorials of the English Affairs*, vol.4, pp.224–73. By a separate convention to the treaty, supplies of naval stores from Sweden such as tar, pitch, hemp and sails, which were usually carried in Dutch ships, were declared contraband for the duration of England's hostilities with Spain.

41.   *The Clarke Papers*, ed. Firth, vol.3, pp.21–38, 105–6, 197–208; Woolrych, *Britain in Revolution*, pp.616–23, 692–4. Charles II sold Dunkirk back to France at the Restoration.

42.   Milton, *A Manifesto of the Lord Protector of the Commonwealth*, pp.5–25; K.O. Kupperman, 'Errand to the Indies: Puritan Colonization from Providence Island through the Western Design', *William and Mary Quarterly*, 45 (1988), pp.70–99; Capp, *Cromwell's Navy*, pp.86–106. Further compensation was gained in the Canaries in April 1657, when a naval force under the command of Robert Blake scuppered the Spanish treasure fleet in the strongly defended harbour of Santa Cruz in Tenerife.

43.   [John Dury], *A Summary Account of Mr John Dury's former and latter negotiations for procuring of the true gospell peace* (London, 1657), and *The Effect of Master Dury's negotiation for the unity of Protestantism in a Gospel Interest in brief is this* (London, 1657), and *The Interest of England in the Protestant Cause* (London, 1659); K. Brauer, *Die Unionstätigkeit John Duries unter dem Protektorat Cromwells* (Marburg, 1907), pp.191–244. Cromwell was powerless to do anything

other than sponsor fundraising throughout the Protectorate after the massacre of the Protestantly inclined Waldenses of Piedmont by the Duke of Savoy in 1655.

44. A. Hughes, 'Religion, 1640–1660', in Coward, ed., *Companion*, pp.350–73; G. DesBrisay, 'Catholics, Quakers and Religious Persecution in Restoration Aberdeen', *Innes Review*, 7 (1996), pp.136–68. The Quakers, whom Cromwell identified as a threat to civil government and military discipline, were the one British religious legacy of the 1650s. Their evangelising message having been spread through the New Model Army, they survived in pockets into the Restoration era, not only among the planters in Ireland but within the indigenous population in Scotland as well.

45. J.R. Collins, 'The Church Settlement of Oliver Cromwell', *History*, 87 (2002), pp.18–40; D.L. Smith, 'Oliver Cromwell, The First Protectorate Parliament and Religious Reform', *Parliamentary History*, 19 (2001), pp.38–48; L. Brace, *The Idea of Property in Seventeenth-century England* (Manchester, 1998), pp.86–111. No more than £200,000 had been awarded annually to Cromwell for the maintenance of the civil and military establishment. It was only during the Interregnum that the crown lands in England were sold close to their true value. At the Restoration, they reverted to being as much a source of patronage as of revenue.

46. C. Durston, *Cromwell's Major-Generals: Godly Government during the English Revolution* (Manchester, 2001), pp.15–37, 97–126; A. Woolrych, 'The Cromwellian Protectorate: A Military Dictatorship?', *History*, 75 (1990), pp.207 31. Horse-racing, cock-fighting, bear-baiting and stage plays were banned as occasions for unlawful assemblies that encouraged subversion and wickedness. Highways and roads were to be freed of robbers and vagabonds were to be compelled to work or be expelled overseas. All premises dispensing beer or wine outside the towns were to be suppressed, and only alehouses in towns that lodged travellers and were of good repute should be licensed.

47. C.S. Egloff, 'The Search for a Cromwellian Settlement: Exclusions from the Second Protectorate Parliament', *Parliamentary History*, 17 (1998), pp.178–97; Durston, *Cromwell's Major-Generals*, pp.206–27. The rule of the major-generals in no way discouraged private individuals from searching for redress in the law courts against officials neglecting their duties or abusing their power (J.A. Shedd, 'Thwarted Victors: Civil and Criminal Prosecution against Parliament's Officials during the English Civil War and Commonwealth', *Journal of British Studies*, 41 (2002), pp.139–69).

48. Woolrych, *Britain in Revolution*, pp.638–45; R.E. Mayers, 'Real and Practicable, not Imaginary and Notional: Sir Henry Vane, *A Healing Question*, and the Problems of the Protectorate', *Albion*, 28 (1996), pp.37–72; D. Armitage, 'The Cromwellian Protectorate and the Languages of Empire', *HJ*, 35 (1992), pp.531–55.

49. J.G.A. Pocock & G.J. Schochet, 'Interregnum and Restoration', in Pocock, ed., *The Varieties of British Political Thought*, pp.146–79; B. Worden, 'James Harrington and *The Commonwealth of Oceana*', in Wootton, ed., *Republicanism, Liberty and Commercial Society*, pp.82–110; Fukuda, *Sovereignty and the Sword*, pp.91–110; Kliger, *The Goths in England*, pp.155–63.

50. J. Scott, 'The Rapture of Motion: James Harrington's Republicanism', in Phillipson & Skinner, eds, *Political Discourse in Early Modern Britain*,

pp.139–63; J.C. Davis, 'Equality in an Unequal Commonwealth: James Harrington's Republicanism and the Meaning of Equality', in Gentles, Morrill & Worden, eds, *Soldiers, Writers and Statesmen of the English Revolution*, pp.229–42; B. Worden, 'Harrington's *Oceana*: Origins and Aftermath, 1651–1660', in Wootton, ed., *Republicanism, Liberty and Commercial Society*, pp.111–38. The principle of rotation applied also to the central judiciary and to local magistrates whose judicial functions were to be entirely separate from those of the executive and the legislature. Idiosyncratically, the senate could initiate and debate but not vote on issue, while the representative assembly had only the power to vote.

51. Kenyon, ed., *The Stuart Constitution*, pp.350–57; Whitelocke, *Memorials of the English Affairs*, vol.4, pp.315–36; *The Clarke Papers*, ed. Firth, vol.3, pp.89–99; Woolrych, *Britain in Revolution*, pp.638–63; Gaunt, *Oliver Cromwell*, pp.180–204. Divisions between Cromwell and the parliament as constituted by the Instrument of Government, already strained by the latter's prosecution and imprisonment of the Socinian James Biddle for denying the divinity of Christ in September 1654, were brought to breaking point by the subsequent prosecution of the Quaker James Naylor for blasphemy. In October 1656, during an evangelical revival in the West Country, Naylor had entered Bristol riding on an ass, for which he was duly condemned to be branded, mutilated, flogged and imprisoned for life. While Cromwell was not personally sympathetic to either Biddle or Naylor, he was extremely concerned, as he forcibly made clear to a meeting of the Army command in February 1657, that parliament's indiscriminate assault on religious sectaries would draw no distinction between moderates and extremists. Baptists and Congregationalists might become as open to prosecution as Socinians and Quakers (Coward, *Oliver Cromwell*, pp.122–3, 146–9).

52. Hirst, *England in Conflict*, pp.311–27; J.S. Morrill, 'Postlude: Between War and Peace, 1651–1662', in Kenyon & Ohlmeyer, eds, *The Civil Wars*, pp.306–28.

53. B. Worden, 'The Politics of Marvell's Horation Ode', *HJ*, 27 (1984), pp.525–47; J. Raymond, 'Framing Liberty: Marvell's *First Anniversary* and the Instrument of Government', *Huntington Library Quarterly*, 62 (1999), pp.313–50; Barber, *Regicide and Republicanism*, pp.193–4.

54. Edmund Waller, *A Panegyrick to my Lord Protector by a gentleman that loves peace, union and the prosperity of the English nation* (London, 1655); Sir Richard Hawkins, *A Discourse of the National Excellencies of England* (London, 1658); Thomas Le White, *A Brief Character of Englands Distraction being the copy of a letter sent into the country by a gentleman of the Middle Temple* (London, 1660); J.C. Davis, *Oliver Cromwell* (London, 2001), pp.116–70.

55. L.L. Knoppers, 'The Politics of Portraiture: Oliver Cromwell and the Plain Style', *Renaissance Quarterly*, 51 (1998), pp.1282–319; *The Diary and Correspondence of John Evelyn*, ed. Bray, p.208; 'The Life of Master John Shaw', in *Yorkshire Diaries and Autobiographies in the Seventeenth and Eighteenth Centuries* (Durham, 1877), p.152.

56. Mr James Fraser, *Chronicles of the Frasers: The Wardlaw Manuscript, 916–1674*, ed. W. Mackay (Edinburgh, 1905), pp.403, 409–10, 412–13, 417–19; Macinnes, 'Gaelic Culture in the Seventeenth Century', in Ellis & Barber, eds, *Conquest & Union*, pp.180–81; Canny, *Kingdom and Colony*, pp.107–8.

57. S. Pincus, 'Neither Machiavellian Moment nor Possessive Individualism: Commercial Society and the Defenders of the English Commonwealth', *AHR*, 103 (1998), pp.705–36, and 'From Holy Cause to Economic Interest: The Study of Population and the Invention of the State', in A. Houston & S. Pincus, eds, *A Nation Transformed: England after the Restoration* (Cambridge, 2001), pp.277–98.

58. Gervaise Markham, *A Way to Get Wealth: containing the Sixe Principall Vocations or Callings, in which everie good Husband or House-wife may lawfully employ themselves* (London, 1631, 1648); Robert Lewes, *The Merchants Mappe of Commerce wherein, the universall maner and matter of trade, is compendiously handled* (London, 1638).

59. Sir Ralph Maddison, *Englands looking in and out presented to the High Court of Parliament now assembled* (London, 1640); Robert Lewes, *The Treasure of Trafficke. Or a discourse of forraigne trade* (London, 1641); Sir Thomas Roe, *Speech in Parliament wherein he sheweth the cause of the decay of coyne and trade in this land, especially of merchant trade* (London, 1641).

60. John Battie, *The Merchants Remonstrance. Wherein is set forth the inevitable miseries which may suddenly befall this kingdomee by want of trade, and decay of manufacture* (London, 1644, 1648); Thomas Johnson, *A Discourse Consisting of Motives for the Enlargement and Freedome of Trade, Especially that of cloth, and other woollen manufactures, engrossed at present contrary to the law of nature, the law of nations, and the lawes of this kingdom* (London, 1645); *APS*, vol.5, pp.240, 654, c.128; Braddick, *The Nerves of State*, pp.119–28.

61. Henry Parker, *Of a Free Trade. A discourse seriously recommending to our nation the wonderful benefits of trade, especially of a rightly governed and ordered trade* (London, 1648); Henry Robinson, *Brief Considerations, concerning the advancement of trade and navigation humbly tendred unto all ingenious patriots* (London, 1649), and *Certain proposalls in order to the peoples freedome and accommodation in some particulars with the advancement of trade and navigation in this commonwealth in general* (London, 1652); William Potter, *The Key of Wealth: or, A new way, for improving of trade* (London, 1650), and *The trades-man's jewel: or a safe, easie, speedy and effectual means, for the incredible advancement of trade, and multiplication of riches* (London, 1650), and *Humble proposalls to the hnourable Councell for Trade and all merchants and others who desire to improve their estates* (London, 1651). Potter's proposals for a land bank were endorsed by Sir Cheney Culpepper, an intellectual associate of Samuel Hartlib and John Durie and a member of the Commission for the Advancement and Regulation of Trade, which met under the auspices of the 'Rump Parliament' in 1650–51. Culpepper had also anticipated Parker in contending in 1646 that monopolising corporations of merchants encroached upon the liberty of the subject (*The Letters of Sir Cheney Culpepper, 1641–1657*, ed. M.J. Braddick & M. Greengrass, in *Seventeenth-Century Political and Financial Papers: Camden Miscellany XXXIII* (Cambridge, 1996), pp.132–3, 139, 269–70).

62. Thomas Violet, *The Advancement of Merchandize: or, Certain propositions for the improvement of trade of this Common-wealth, humbly presented to the right honourable the Council of State* (London, 1651); Thomas Scott, *The Spaniards Cruelty and Treachery to the English in the time of peace and war* (London, 1654); Richard Baker, *The Marchants Humble Petition and Remonstrance to his late Highnesse, with an accompt of the losses of their shipping, and estates, since the war with Spain* (London, 1659).

63. John Marius, *Advice Concerning Bills of Exchange* (London, 1655); Zachary Crofton, *Excise Anatomiz'd, and Trade Epitomiz'd: declaring, that the unequall imposition of excise, to be the only cause of the ruine of trade, and universall impoverishment of this whole nation* (London, 1659); John Bland, *Trade Revived, or, A way proposed to restore, increase, inrich, strengthen and preserve the decayed and even dying trade of this our English nation* (London, 1659, 1660); Thomas Willsford, *The Scales of Commerce and Trade* (London, 1660).

64. James Howell, *Londinopolis, an historicall discourse or perlustration of the city of London, the imperial chamber, and chief emporium of Great Britain* (London, 1657); W. Blith, *The English improver improved or the survey of husbandry surveyed discovering the improueableness of all lands* (London, 1652); D. Hirst, 'Locating the 1650s in England's Seventeenth Century', *History*, 81 (1996), pp.359–83.

65. *APS*, vol.6 (ii), p.745; Williamson, 'Union with England Traditional', pp.311–12, 320.

66. BL, Petitions 1648–54, Add. MS 34326, f.3, and Surveys of Properties 1655–*c.*1661, Add. MS 4765, ff.16–17, 20–21; John Woodhouse, *The Map of Ireland with the exact dimensions of the provinces therein contained* (London, 1653); Woolrych, *Britain in Revolution*, pp.573–9; A. Clarke, *Prelude to Restoration in Ireland: The End of the Commonwealth, 1659–1660* (Cambridge, 1999), pp.4–17. Land forfeited in ten counties – Antrim, Armagh, Down, Meath, Westmeath, King's, Queen's, Tipperary, Limerick and Waterford – was designated to meet public debts, with one half of the forfeited lands in each county being assigned to meet the claims of the adventurers and the other to cover army arrears of pay. Lots were drawn initially to benefit 1043 adventurers, but the remainder assigned to officers and soldiers was insufficient and further promises to reimburse were made from forfeited lands in Cavan, Fermanagh, Monaghan, Louth, Longford, Kilkenny, Cork and Sligo and later still from Londonderry, Tyrone, Wexford, Kerry and Kilkenny.

67. HL, Hastings Irish Papers, box 8/HA14973, 14931, 15044, 15226, 15293–4, 15297–9, 15304, 15644; Samuel Hartlib, *A Discoverie for Division or Setting out of land, as to the best form* (London, 1653); Richard Lawrence, *The Interest of England in the Irish Transplantation, stated* (London & Dublin, 1655); Vincent Gookin, *The Great Case of Transplantation in Ireland Discussed* (London, 1655), and *The author and case of transplanting the Irish into Connaught vindicated, from the unjust aspersions of Col. Richard Laurence* (London, 1655); Canny, *Making Ireland British*, pp.556–9.

68. HL, Hastings Irish Papers, box 9/HA 15052 & box 10/HA 14363, 14989; Barnard, *Cromwellian Ireland*, pp.10–15, 20–23, 297–305; K. McKenny, 'The Seventeenth-century Land Settlement in Ireland: Towards a Statistical Interpretation', in Ohlmeyer, ed., *Ireland from Independence to Occupation*, pp.181–200. A major disincentive to new English planters wanting to develop cloth manufactures was the relatively high rates of taxation through the monthly assessment in Ireland in proportion to the amounts levied as cess in England, which were purportedly as much as 75 per cent more by 1656, when the monthly assessment was increased from £10,000 per month to £12,000, with another £1000 increase to be added in each of the following two years.

69. T.C. Barnard, 'The Protestant Interest, 1641–1660', and A. Clarke, '1659 and the Road to Restoration', both in Ohlmeyer, ed., *Ireland from Independence to Occupation*, pp.218–64.

70. BL, Collection of Historical and Parliamentary Papers, 1620–60, 'Instructions for Scotland, October 5, 1659', Egerton MS 1048, ff.176–80; *A Declaration to the People, concerning the great and present expedition: with the gallant resolutions of the Parliament; as it was graciously voted in their Honourable House, and communicated to his Highness, the Lord Protector* (London, 1659); Peter Chamberlen, *The Declaration and Proclamation of the Army of God, owned by the Lord of Host in many victories* (London, 1659).

71. BL, Letters and State Papers: the Birch Collection, Add. MS 4156, f.112, and Papers Relating to the Revenue etc, Add. MS 11597, ff.1–10; Hirst, *England in Conflict*, pp.311, 314; T. Venning, *Cromwellian Foreign Policy* (New York, 1995), pp.238–50. Cromwell's decisive intervention on the side of the French at the battle of the Dunes in June 1658 did secure Dunkirk as an English bridgehead and hastened the subsequent Peace of the Pyrenees between France and Spain.

72. George Monck, *General Monck's last letter to His Excellency the Lord Fleetwood* (London, 1659); *A Message Sent from the King of Scots, and the Duke of York's Court in Flanders* (Aberdeen, 1659); William Prynne, *A brief narrative of the manner how divers Members of the House of Commons, that were illegally and unjustly imprisoned or secluded by the Armies force in December 1648 and May 7, 1659, coming upon Tuesday the 27ᵗʰ of December . . . were again forcibly shut out* (London, 1659); *Making the News*, ed. Raymond, pp.435, 443; R. Hutton, *The Restoration: A Political & Religious History of England and Wales, 1658–1667* (Oxford, 1985), pp.42–67.

73. BL, Historical Letters and Papers 1556–1753, Egerton MS 2618, f.57; *Memoirs of Sir Ewen Cameron of Lochiel*, ed. J. Macknight (Edinburgh, 1842), pp.148–53; Dow, *Cromwellian Scotland*, pp.254–7; Clarke, *Prelude to Restoration in Ireland*, pp.92–168.

74. Kenyon, ed., *The Stuart Constitution*, pp.357–8; *A Phanatique League & Covenant, Solemnly entered into by the Assertors of the Good Old Cause* (London, 1659); William Sprigg, *A Modest Plea for an equal common-wealth against monarchy* (London, 1659).

75. *The Diary and Correspondence of John Evelyn*, ed. Bray, p.233; [M.H.], *The History of the Union of the four famous Kingdoms of England, Wales, Scotland and Ireland wherein is demonstrated that by the prowess and prudence of the English, those four distinct and discordant nations have upon several conquests been entirely united and devolved into one commonwealth* (London, 1659, 1660).

Conclusion: A Britannic Restoration?

1. [University of Oxford], *Britannia Rediviva* (Oxford, 1660); Anon., *The Funeral of the Good Old Cause, or, A Covenant of Both Houses of Parliament against the Solemn League and Covenant* (London, 1661).

2. HL, Hastings Irish Papers, box 22/HA 15352; Hutton, *The Restoration*, pp.125–84; G. Holmes, *The Making of a Great Power: Late Stuart and Early Georgian Britain, 1660–1722* (Harlow, 1993), pp.27–43. In like manner, James, Duke of York, as Lord High Admiral, was advised by a commis-

sion for the Royal Navy staffed by experts as during the 1650s, albeit these experts included both former Royalists and Parliamentarians.

3. HL, Stowe Collection: Temple Papers, STT Ship Money L8C10; J.L. Malcolm, 'Charles II and the Reconstruction of Royal Power', *HJ*, 35 (1992), pp.307–30; D. Hirst, 'The Conciliatoriness of the Cavalier Commons Reconsidered', *Parliamentary History*, 6 (1987), pp.221–35.

4. William Prynne, *The first tome of an exact chronological vindication and historical demonstration of our British, Roman, Saxon, Danish, Norman, English kings supreme ecclesiastical jurisdiction, in, over all spiritual, or religious affairs, causes, persons, as well as temporal within their realms of England, Scotland, Ireland, and other dominions* (London, 1665); N.H. Keeble, *The Restoration: England in the 1660s* (Oxford, 2002), pp.109–31.

5. HL, Hastings Irish Papers, box 11/HA 14779, 14958, 15993; J.M. Buckroyd, 'Bridging the Gap: Scotland, 1659–1660', *SHR*, 66 (1987), pp.1–25; A.I. Macinnes, 'Repression and Conciliation: The Highland Dimension, 1660–1688', *SHR*, 65 (1986), pp.167–95.

6. DH, Loudoun Papers, bundle 1/19; R. Lee, 'Retreat from Revolution: The Scottish Parliament and the Restored Monarchy, 1661–1663', in Young, ed., *Celtic Dimensions of the British Civil Wars*, pp.164–85; Young, *The Scottish Parliament*, pp.304–23.

7. S.S. Webb, *The Governors-General: The English Army and the Definition of Empire, 1569–1681* (Chapel Hill, NC, 1979), pp.329–466; J. Smyth, *The Making of the United Kingdom, 1660–1800* (Harlow, 2001), pp.77–87.

8. HL, Hastings Irish Papers, box 11/HA 14126, 14368, 14372–5, 15026–8, 15037, 15177; Adair, *The Presbyterian Church in Ireland*, pp.238–304.

9. K. McKenny, 'Charles II's Irish Cavaliers: The 1649 Officers and the Restoration Land Settlement', *IHS*, 28 (1993), pp.409–25; L.J. Arnold, 'The Irish Court of Claims of 1663', *IHS*, 24 (1985), pp.417–30. Scottish planters were prominent players in the land issue, most notably Hugh Montgomery, 1st Earl of Mount-Alexander, who was part of the delegation from the Irish parliament who negotiated the terms of settlement with the court and Privy Council in London. When he died in September 1663, his widow wrote to Ormond, now restored as lord-lieutenant, requesting that her husband's funeral might be solemnised in Dublin. She was instructed instead that she should follow the steps of his fathers in arranging for the burial of her husband among the Ulster Scots, a clear indication of the Gothic nature of the Protestant ascendancy in Ireland (HL, Hastings Irish Papers, box 14/HA15363, box 16/HA 15366 and box 17/HA 14389).

10. DR, TKUA, England, A I, no.3, Breve, til Vels med Bilag fra Medlemmer af det Engelske Kongehus til medlemmer af det danske, 1613–89. Official accounts of events in the three kingdoms and of approved intelligence from abroad, published weekly from January 1662 to July 1663, adopted the seemingly neutral standpoint of *The Kingdoms intelligencer of the affairs now in agitation in England, Scotland and Ireland* (London, 1662–3).

11. Rutgerius Hermannides, *Britannia Magna* (Amsterdam, 1661); Samuel [von] Puffendorf, *An Introduction to the History of the Principal Kingdoms and States of Europe* (London, 1699).

12. John Ogilby, *The King's Coronation: Being an Exact Account of the Cavalcades with a Description of the Triumphal Arches, and Speeches prepared by the City of London,*

for his late Majesty Charles the Second (Edinburgh, 1685); J.P. Montaño, 'The Quest for Consensus: The Lord Mayor's Day Show in the 1670s', in G. Maclean, ed., *Culture and Society in the Stuart Restoration: Literature, Drama and History* (Cambridge, 1995), pp.31–51; Keeble, *The Restoration*, pp.51–3. John Ogilby subsequently published a detailed survey of the main roads of England and Wales under the rubric of *Britannia* (London, 1675).

13. HL, Hastings Irish Papers, box 19/Ha 14432 & box 20/HA 14175, 14445–8, 14450, 14452, 14455–60.

14. BL, Maitland & Lauderdale Papers, 1532–1688, Add. MS 35125, f.74; N.C. Landsman, 'The Middle Colonies: New Opportunities for Settlement, 1660–1700', in Canny, ed., *The Origins of Empire*, pp.351–74; Moreland & Bannister, *Antique Maps*, pp.158–60.

15. Scott, *The Constitutions and Finance of English, Scottish and Irish Joint-Stock Companies*, vol.2, pp.361–82; Anon., *His Majesties Propriety and Dominion on the British Seas Asserted* (London, 1665).

16. J. Kelly, 'The Origins of the Act of Union: An Examination of Unionist Opinion in Britain and Ireland, 1650–1800', *IHS*, 25 (1987), pp.236–63; A.I. Macinnes, 'Politically Reactionary Brits? The Promotion of Anglo-Scottish Union, 1603–1707', in Connolly, ed., *Kingdoms United?*, pp.50–55.

Bibliography

1. Primary Sources

1.1 Archival Material

Aberdeen University Library

Microfilm. Stuart Papers from the Denys Eyre Bower Collection, Chiddingstone Castle, Kent. Reel 1, County Record Office, Staffordshire, 793/8–78

Archives du Royaume de Belgique

Don Ferdinand: Correspondence avec les Trois Ambassadeurs Ci-Dessus Nommés, 1640–1641

British Library, London

Letters and State Papers: Birch Collection, Add. MSS 4156, 4158
Surveys of Properties, 1655–c.1661, Add. MS 4765
Ordinances of Parliament, 1642–9, Add. MS 5492
Original Documents relating to Scotland, the Borders & Ireland, 16th and 17th centuries, Add. MS 5754
Papers Relating to the Revenue etc., Add. MS 11597
Royal and Noble Autographs, 1646–1768, Add. MS 19399
Naval Papers, 1643–77, Add. MS 22546
Miscellaneous Autograph Letters, Add. MS 24422
Historical Autographs, 16th–18th centuries, Add. MS 28103
Family of Pitt, Official Papers, 17th century, Add. MS 29975
Scotland, Rents & Tenths, 1639, Add. MS 33262
Political and State Papers, 16th and 17th centuries: Ramsay Papers, vol. 25, Add. MS 33469
Miscellaneous Letters and Papers, Add. MS 33506
Historical Letters and Papers, 1633–55, Add. MS 33596
Petitions, 1648–54, Add. MS 34326
T. Astle, Historical Collections, 1642–1769, Add. MS 34713
Maitland and Lauderdale Papers, 1532–1688, Add. MS 35125
Hardwicke Papers, vol. 516, Add. MS 35864
Miscellaneous Letters, etc., 1566–1804, Add. MS 36450
Correspondence of R. Lang, Secretary of State, 1649–61, Add. MS 37047
Latin Letters of Charles I, 1627–35, Add. MS 38669
Holme Hall Papers, vol. 1, 1518–1773, Add. MS 40132
Miscellaneous Letters and Papers, Add. MS 41295

Collection of Historical and Parliamentary Papers, 1620–60, Egerton MS 1048
Papers of General Desborough, 1651–60, Egerton MS 2519
Nicholas Papers, Egerton MSS 2533, 2542
James Hay, Earl of Carlisle, Correspondence, 2 vols, 1602–20, Egerton MSS 2592–2593
Historical Letters and Papers, 1556–1753, Egerton MS 2618
Historical Papers, Egerton MS 2884
Observations of the State of Ireland, April 1640, Stowe MS 29
Speeches in Parliament, 1558–1695, Stowe MS 361
J. Dury, Epistolae Pace Ecclesiastica, Sloane MS 654
View of the Condition of Ireland from 1640, Sloane MS 3838

Dansk Rigsarkivet, Copenhagen
Tyske Kancellis Udenrigske Afdeling
  England, A I, no.3; & A II, nos. 12–16
  Skotland A I, no. 4a
  Alm.Del. I Indtil 1670, 'Latina' vols 10–13, & no. 141, 'Breve med Bilag fra engelsk Praest Johannes Duraeus, 1634–39'

Dumfries House, Cumnock, Ayrshire
Loudoun Deeds & Papers

Edinburgh University Library
Instructions of the Committee of Estates of Scotland, 1640–41, Dc.4.16.

Glasgow University Archives
Beith Parish MSS

Hull University Library
Maxwell-Constable of Everingham MSS

Huntington Library, San Marino, California
Bridgewater & Ellesmere MSS
Hastings Irish Papers
Huntington Manuscripts, HM 1554
Huntington Manuscripts, HM 30664
Loudoun Scottish Collection
Stowe Collection: Temple Papers. STT: Religious Papers; Personal; Ship Money, L8C10; Miscellaneous Papers, L9B5

Inveraray Castle Archives, Inveraray, Argyllshire
Letters – Marquess's Period, 1638–58

Mitchell Library, Glasgow
John Graham of Duchrie, Account of the Earl of Glencairn's Expedition to the Highlands of Scotland, 1653–4, Special Collection, SR 163

National Archives of Scotland, Edinburgh

Breadalbane MSS, GD 112
Cunninghame-Grahame MSS, GD 22
Hamilton Papers, GD 406
Hay of Haystoun Papers, GD 34
Sederunt Book of the High Commission of Teinds, 1633–50, TE 1/2

National Library of Scotland, Edinburgh

Sir James Balfour on Nobility, Adv. MS 15.2.14
Salt & Coal: Events, 1635–62, MS 2263
NLS, Scottish Parliament, 1648, MS 8482
Wodrow MSS, folio lxiv, quartos xvi, xxiv, xxix

Northumbria Archives, Berwick-upon-Tweed

Guild Books, 1627–51, B1/9–10

Public Record Office, London

Committee of Both Kingdoms, Entry Books, 1644–5, SP 21/16–17
Derby House Committee for Irish Affairs, Letters Sent, 1647–8, SP 21/27
Committee of the House of Commons for Scottish Affairs: Order Book, 1643–5, SP 23/1A
Anglo-Scottish Committee of Parliament: minute book, 1652–3, SP 25/138
State Papers Domestic, Supplementary: Orders, Warrants and Receipts for Payment of the Scots Army in Ireland & England, 1642–8, SP 46/106
State Papers, Turkey, 1641–62, SP 97/17

Riksarkivet, Stockholm

Anglica, 516, 521–2, 531/2

Tollemache Family Archives, Buckminster, Grantham, Lincolnshire

Papers TD 3756, 3758–3760

Tyne & Wear Archives, Newcastle

Hostmen's Company, Old Book, 1600–*c*.1690, GU/HO/1/1
Company of Hostmen of Newcastle-upon-Tyne, GU/HO/12

1.2   Pamphlets

Adams, Sir Thomas. *Plain dealing, or, A fair warning to the gentlemen of the Committee for Union* (London, 1647)
A Declaration of his Imperiall Majestie, the most High and Mighty Potentate Alexea, Emperor of Russia, and great Duke of Muscovia &c. wherein is conteined his detestation of the murther of Charles the first, King of Great Britain and Ireland (London, 1650)
A Declaration of the Lords of His Majesties Privie-Councell in Scotland and Commissioners for the conserving of the Articles of the Treaty: For the Information of His Majesties good Subjects of this Kingdom. Together with a Treacherous and damnable Plot (Edinburgh, 1643)

A Declaration of the Proceedings of Thirteen Christian Kings, Princes, and Dukes, and the present state and condition of the King of Scots (London, 1651)

A Declaration to the People, concerning the great and present expedition: with the gallant resolutions of the Parliament; as it was graciously voted in their Honourable House, and communicated to his Highness, the Lord Protector (London, 1659)

A Letter from Scotland: and the Votes of the Parliament for Proclaiming Charles the Second, King of Great Britain, France & Ireland (London, 1649)

A Letter from the House of Commons assembled in the Parliament of England at Westminster, To the Right Honourable and Right Reverend, the Lords, Ministers and others of the present General Assemble of the Church of Scotland sitting at Edinburgh (London, 1648)

A Letter Sent from Lieutenant Generall Cromwell to The Marquis of Argyle, and General Lesley (London, 1648)

A Message Sent from the King of Scots, and the Duke of York's Court in Flanders (Aberdeen, 1659)

Alexander, Sir William. *An Encouragement to Colonies* (London, 1624)

Anon. *A brief narration of the mysteries of state carried on by the Spanish faction in England, since the reign of Queen Elizabeth to this day for supplanting of the magistracy and ministry, the laws of the land, and the religion of the Church of England* (London, 1651)

Anon. *A declaration made by the Rebells in Ireland against the English and Scottish Protestants, Inhabitants within that kingdome. Also a treacherous oath . . . lately contrived by the Confederate Rebells in a Council held at Kilkenny* (Waterford, reprinted London, 1644)

Anon. *A full relation of the late expedition of the Right Honourable, the Lord Monroe, Majore-Generall of all the Protestant forces in the povince of Ulster with their several marches and skirmishes with the bloody Irish rebels . . . also, two declarations and an oath of confederacy whereby they bind themselves utterly to ruine and destroy the Protestants in that kingdome* (London, 1644)

Anon. *A great discoverie of a plot in Scotland, by miraculous means* (London, 1641)

Anon. *A Phanatique League & Covenant, Solemnly entered into by the Assertors of the Good Old Cause* (London, 1659)

Anon. *A Warning to the Parliament of England. A discovery of the ends and designes of the Popish partie both abroad, and at home, in the raising and formenting our late war, and still-continuing troubles: in an oration made to the generall Assembly of the French clergy in Paris, by Monsieur Jaques du Perron, Bishop of Angolesme, and Grand Almosner to the Queen of England* (London, 1647)

Anon. *Britania triumphalis: a brief history of the warres and other state-affairs of Great Britain. From the death of the late King, to the dissolution of the last Parliament* (London, 1654)

Anon. *His Majesties Propriety and Dominion on the British Seas Asserted* (London, 1665)

Anon. *Papers from the Scottish Quarters, containing the substance of two votes made by the Estates at Edinburgh at their general meeting this present Septemb. 1646* (London, 1646)

Anon. *The Antiquity of Englands Superiority over Scotland and The Equity of Incorporating Scotland or other Conquered Nations, into the Commonwealth of England* (London, 1652)

Anon. *The bloody diurnall from Ireland being papers of propositions, order, and oath, and severall bloody acts, and proceedings of the Confederate Catholics assembled at Kilkenny* (Kilkenny, reprinted London, 1647)

Anon. *The Bounds & bonds of Publique Obedience* (London, 1649)

Anon. *The British Bell-man* (London, 1648)

Anon. *The Fifth Monarchy, or, Kingdom of Christ in Opposition to the Beasts, Asserted* (London, 1659)

Anon. *The Funeral of the Good Old Cause, or, A Covenant of Both Houses of Parliament against the Solemn League and Covenant* (London, 1661)

Anon. *The King of Denmark's Resolution concerning Charles King of Great Britain, Wherein is Declared the Determination for the setting forth of a fleet towards England* (London, 1642)

Anon. *The Love and Faithfulnes of the Scottish Nation, The Excellency of the Covenant, The Union between England and Scotland cleared, by Collections, from the Declarations of Parliament and Speeches of severall Independent Brethren* (London, 1646)

Anon. *The Miraculous and Happie Union of England & Scotland* (Edinburgh, 1604)

Anon. *The mysterie of iniquity, yet working in the kingdomes of England, Scotland, and Ireland, for the destruction of religion truly protestant* (London, 1643)

Anon. *The Passionate Remonstrance made by his Holiness in the conclave in Rome, upon the late proceedings and great Covenant of Scotland with a reply of Cardinal de Barbarini in name of the Roman Clergy* (Edinburgh, 1641)

Anon. *The Scots-Mans Remonstrance* (London, 1647)

Anon. *The Seas Magazine Opened, or, The Hollander dispossest of his usurped trade of fishing upon the English seas* (London, 1653)

Anon. *The Truth of the Proceedings in Scotland containing the Discovery of the late Conspiracie* (Edinburgh, 1641)

An Ordinance of the Lords & Commons assembled in Parliament, whereby Robert, Earl of Warwick is made governor in chiefe, and lord high admiral of all those islands and other plantations, inhabited, planted or belonging to any His Majesties the King of England's subjects, within the bounds, and upon the coasts of America (London, 1643)

An Ordinance of the Lords and Commons assembled in Parliament for the further supply of the British army in Ireland (London, 1645)

Articles of Peace, Union and Confederation, concluded and agreed between his Highness Oliver Lord Protector of the common-wealth of England, Scotland & Ireland, and the dominions thereto belonging. And the Lords of the States General of the United Provinces of the Netherlands (London, 1654)

[Bacon, Sir Francis]. *Three speeches of the Right Honourable, Sir Francis Bacon Knight, then his Majesties Sollicitor Generall, after Lord Verulam, Viscount Saint Alban. Concerning the post-nati naturalization of the Scotch in England, Union of the lawes of the kingdomes of England and Scotland* (London, 1641)

Baillie, Robert. *A Dissuasive from the Errours of the Times* (London, 1645)

Baker, Richard. *The Marchants Humble Petition and Remonstrance to his late Highnesse, with an accompt of the losses of their shipping, and estates, since the war with Spain* (London, 1659)

[Balcanqual, Walter]. *A Declaration concerning the Late Tumults in Scotland* (Edinburgh, 1639)

Barham, William. *An Almanack for the yeere of our Lord and Saviour Christ, 1639* (London, 1639)

Battie, John. *The Merchants Remonstrance. Wherein is set forth the inevitable miseries which may suddenly befall this kingdome by want of trade, and decay of manufacture* (London, 1644, 1648)

Bland, John. *Trade Revived, or, A way proposed to restore, increase, inrich, strengthen and preserve the decayed and even dying trade of this our English nation* (London, 1659, 1660)

Blith, W. *The English improver improved, or, The survey of husbandry surveyed discovering the improueableness of all lands* (London, 1652)

[Brightman, Thomas]. *The Reverend Mr Brightmans Judgement or Prophesies, what shall befall Germany, Scotland, Holland, and the churches adhering to them likewise what shall befall England, and the hierarchy therein* (London, 1642)

Booker, John. *A Bloody Irish Almanack* (London, 1646)

Bowles, Edward. *The Mysterie of Iniquity, Yet Working in the Kingdomes of England, Scotland, and Ireland, for the Destruction of Religion Truly Protestant* (London, 1643)

Boyd, Andrew. *Ad Augustissimum Monarcham Carolum Majori Britanniae* (Edinburgh, 1633)

Butler, Robert. *An Almanack for the yeare of our Lord Christ, 1632* (Cambridge, 1632)

Calderwood, David. *The Pastor and the Prelate, or, Reformation and Conformitie* (Edinburgh, 1636)

[Campbell, Archibald]. *An Honourable speech made in the Parlament of Scotland by the Earle of Argile . . . the thirtieth of September 1641. Touching the prevention of nationall dissention, and perpetuating the happie peace and union betwixt the two kingdomes, by the frequent holding of Parlaments* (London, 1641)

[Campbell, Archibald]. *The Lord Marquess of Argyle's Speech to A Grand Committee of Both Houses of Parliament* (London, 1646)

Campbell, Archibald, Marquis of Argyle. *Instructions to a Son, containing rules of conduct in public and private life* (London, 1661)

[Campbell, John]. *The Lord Chancellor of Scotland his first Speech: At a Conference in the Painted Chamber with a Committee of Both Houses, Octob. 1. 1646* (London, 1646)

[Castell, William]. *A Petition of W.C. exhibited to the High Court of Parliament now assembled, for the propagating of the Gospel in America and the West Indies* (London, 1641)

Castell, William. *A Short Discoverie of the Coasts and Continent of America, from the equinoctiall northward and the adjacent isles* (London, 1644)

Certaine Inducements to Well Minded People (London, 1643)

Chamberlen, Peter. *The Declaration and Proclamation of the Army of God, owned by the Lord of Host in many victories* (London, 1659)

[Charles II]. *The King of Scots his Message and Remonstrance to the Parliament of that Kingdome, conveened at Edenburge, for a perfect Union, and Agreement, between Prince and People and his desires to all his loving Subjects of that Nation, requiring their due obedience towards him, as their law-full King and Governor* (London, 1649)

Codrington, Richard. *The Life and Death of the Illustrious Robert, Earl of Essex* (London, 1646)

Conway, Edward, 2nd Viscount Conway. *A Relation from the Right Honourable the Lord Viscount Conway, of the Proceedings of the English Army in Ulster from June 17 to July 30* (London, 1642)

Copland, Patrick. *Virginia's God be Thanked* (London, 1622)

Copland, Patrick. *A Declaration of Monies* (London, 1622)

Corbet, John. *The Epistle congratulatorie of Lysimachus Niccanor of the Societie of Jesu, to the Covenanters of Scotland* (Oxford, 1641)

Craig, Alexander. *The Political Recreations of Mr Alexander Craig of Rose-Craig, Scoto Britan* (Aberdeen, 1623)

Crofton, Zachary. *Excise Anatomiz'd, and Trade Epitomiz'd: declaring, that the unequall imposition of excise, to be the only cause of the ruine of trade, and universall impoverishment of this whole nation* (London, 1659)

De intentie van het coninghrijcke van Scotlands armade. Waer in vertoont wert de oorsake waerom zy in Enghelandt comen, . . . ende op wat conditie zy daer wederom uyt-trecken sullen. Verclaert aen hare broeders van, Enghelandt, by de commissarissen van 't laetste Parlement, . . . (n.p., 1640)

Declaration of the Lords and Commons assembled in Parliament concerning His Majesties advancing with his Army toward London: with Direction that all Trained Bands and Volunteers be put into a Readinesse (London, 1642)

[Devereux, Robert]. *A Letter from his Excellency, Robert Earl of Essex, to the Honourable House of Commons concerning the sending of a Commission forthwith to Sir William Waller* (London, 1644)

[Devereux, Robert]. *A Paper delivered in the Lord's House by the Earle of Essex, Lord Generall, at the offering up of his Commission* (London, 1645)

D'Ewes, Sir Simonds. *Speech delivered in the House of Commons 7 July 1641, being resolved into a committee . . . in the Palatine case* (London, 1641)

Dewsbury, William. *A True Prophecie of the Mighty Day of the Lord* (London, 1655)

Die Sabbati 30 December 1643. Ordered that the Adventurers of this House for lands in Ireland, and the body of Adventurers in London, doe meete at Grocers-Hall on Thursday in the afternoon at two of the clock, and take into their serious consideration by what wayes and meanes the British Army in Ulster, opposing the cessation may be maintained and encouraged to process in prosecution of that warre of Ireland against the Rebels, and to prepare some propositions to be presented to the House (London, 1643)

Dury, John. *A Summary Discourse concerning the work of peace ecclesiastical, how it may concurre with the aim of a civill confederation amongst Protestants. Presented to the consideration of my lord ambassador Sir T. Row at Hamburg, 1639* (Cambridge, 1641)

Dury, John. *Considerations concerning the present Engagement whether it may be lawfully entered into: Yea or No?* (London, 1649)

Dury, John. *A Second Parcel of Objections against the taking of the Engagement answered* (London, 1650)

[Dury, John]. *A Summary Account of Mr John Dury's former and latter negotiations for procuring of the true gospell peace* (London, 1657)

[Dury, John]. *The Effect of Master Dury's negotiation for the unity of Protestantism in a Gospel Interest in brief is this* (London, 1657)

[Dury, John]. *The Interest of England in the Protestant Cause* (London, 1659)

Farlie, Robert. *Kalendarium Humanae Vitae* (London, 1638)

Garey, Samuel. *Great Brittans Little Calendar* (London, 1618)

[Gauden, John]. *Eikon Basilike: The portraicture of His sacred Maiestie in his solitudes and sufferings* (London, 1649)

Gookin, Vincent. *The Great Case of Transplantation in Ireland Discussed* (London, 1655)

Gookin, Vincent. *The author and case of transplanting the Irish into Connaught vindicated, from the unjust aspersions of Col. Richard Laurence* (London, 1655)

Gordon, John. *Elizabethae Reginae Manes De Religione Et Regno Ad Iacobum Magnum Briattniarum Regem, Per Ionnem Gordonium Britanno-Scotum* (London, 1604)

Grotius, Hugo. *Two Discourses* (London, 1653)

[H., M.] *The History of the Union of the four famous Kingdoms of England, Wales, Scotland and Ireland wherein is demonstrated that by the prowess and prudence of the English, those four distinct and discordant nations have upon several conquests been entirely united and devolved into one commonwealth* (London, 1659, 1660)

Harcourt, Sir Simon. *March 18. A letter sent from Sr. Simon Harcourt, to a worthy member of the House of Commons. With a true relation of the proceedings of the English army, under his command to this present March* (London, 1641)

Hartlib, Samuel. *A Discoverie for Division or Setting out of land, as to the best form* (London, 1653)

Hawkins, Sir Richard. *A Discourse of the National Excellencies of England* (London, 1658)

Hay of Naughton, Peter. *An Advertisement to the Subjects of Scotland, Of the fearfull Dangers threatned to Christian States; and namely, to Great Britane, by the Ambitions of Spayne* (Aberdeen, 1627)

[Henderson, Alexander]. *Vertoog van de vvettelyckheyt van onsen tocht in Engelant* (Edinburgh, 1640)

Henderson, Alexander. *A Sermon Preached to the Honourable House of Commons, At their late solemne Fast, Wednesday, December 27 1643* (London, 1644)

Heylyn, Peter. *A Short View of the life and reign of King Charles (the second monarch of Great Britain) from his birth to his burial* (London, 1658)

Heywood, Thomas. *The Life of Merlin, sirnamed Ambrosius, His Prophecies and Predictions interpreted and their truth made good by English Annulls* (London, 1641)

Informatie, aen alle oprechte christenen in het coningrijcke van Engelandt. Door de edelen, baronnen, staten, leeraers, ende gemeente in het coninckrijcke van Schotlandt. Waer in zy hare onschuldt te kennen gheven . . . (Edinburgh, 1639)

Howell, James. *Londinopolis, an historivall discourse or perlustration of the city of London, the imperial chamber, and chief emporium of Great Britain* (London, 1657)

[J., G.] *The Spurious Prognosticator Unmasked* (London, 1660)

Jenner, Thomas. *Londons blame, if not its shame: manifested by the great neglect of the fishery, which affordeth to our neighbor nation yeerly, the revenue of many millions, which they take up at our doors, whilst with the sluggard, we fold our hands in our bosoms and will not stretch them forth to our mouths* (London, 1651)

Johnson, Thomas. *A Discourse Consisting of Motives for the Enlargement and Freedome of Trade, Especially that of cloth, and other woollen manufactures, engrossed at present contrary to the law of nature, the law of nations, and the lawes of this kingdom* (London, 1645)

[Johnston of Wariston, Archibald]. *Remonstrantie vande edelen, baronnen, state, kerckendienaers, ende gemeente in het Coningryck van Schotland: Verclarende dat sy onschuldigh syne van de crimen daer mede sy in't laetste Engelsche Placcaet (vanden 27 february) beswaert werden. Gevisiteert na de Ordonnantie vande Generale Vergaderinge van den Raedt van Staten in Schotland* (Edinburgh & Amsterdam, 1639)

Lawrence, Richard. *The Interest of England in the Irish Transplantation, stated* (London & Dublin, 1655)

Lewes, Robert. *The Merchants Mappe of Commerce wherein, the universall maner and matter of trade, is compendiously handled* (London, 1638)

Lewes, Robert. *The Treasure of Trafficke, or, A discourse of forraigne trade* (London, 1641)

Le White, Thomas. *A Brief Character of Englands Distraction being the copy of a letter sent into the country by a gentleman of the Middle Temple* (London, 1660)

Lilly, William. *A Prophecy of the White King: and a Dreadfull Dead-man Explained* (London, 1644)

Lilly, William. *England's Prophetical Merlin* (London, 1644)

Lilly, William. *The Starry Messenger* (London, 1645)

Lilly, William. *The World's Catastrophe, or, Europe's Many Mutations until 1666* (London, 1647)

Lilly, William. *An Astrological Prediction of the Occurrences in England, Part of the Years 1648, 1649, 1650* (London, 1648)

Lilly, William. *Monarchy or No Monarchy in England* (London, 1651)

Lithgow, William. *The Pilgrimes Farewell, to his Native Countrey of Scotland* (Edinburgh, 1618)

Lithgow, William. *The Totall Discourse, Of the Rare Adventures, and powerfull peregrinations of long nineteen Yeares Travayles, from Scotland, to the most Famous Kingdomes in Europe, Asia, and Africa* (London, 1632)

Lithgow, William. *Scotlands welcome to her native sonne, and soveraigne lord, King Charles* (Edinburgh, 1633)

Lithgow, William. *A True and Experimentall Discourse, upon the beginning, proceeding and Victorious event of this last siege of Breda* (London, 1637)

Lithgow, William. *The Present Survey of London and England's State* (London, 1643)

Maddison, Sir Ralph. *Englands looking in and out presented to the High Court of Parliament now assembled* (London, 1640)

Marius, John. *Advice Concerning Bills of Exchange* (London, 1655)

Markham, Gervaise. *A Way to Get Wealth: containing the Sixe Principall Vocations or Callings, in which everie good Husband or House-wife may lawfully employ themselves* (London, 1631, 1648)

Marshall, Stephen. *A Sacred Panegyrick* (London, 1644)

Maxwell, George. *An Apologee or Declaration of the Power and Providence of God in the Government of the World* (Oxford, 1635)

Maynwaring, Roger. *Religion and Alegiance: In Two Sermons Preached before the Kings Maiestie* (London, 1627)

Milton, John. *A Manifesto of the Lord Protector of the Commonwealth of England, Scotland, Ireland &c.* (London, 1738, translated from the original Latin version of 1655)

Mocket, Thomas. *A View of the Solemn League and Covenant* (London, 1644)

Monck, George. *General Monck's last letter to His Excellency the Lord Fleetwood* (London, 1659)

Moulin, Peter. *The Anatomy of Arminianism* (London, 1620, 1635)

Munro, Robert. *A Letter of Great Consequence sent . . . out of the Kingdom of Ireland, to the Honorable, the Committee for the Irish Affairs in England, concerning the State of Rebellion there. Together with the relation of a Great Victory he obtained, and of his taking the Earl of Antrim, about whom was found Divers Papers which discovered a Dangerous Plot against the Protestants in all his Majesties Dominions* (London, 1643)

Murray, Sir David. *The Tragicall Death of Sophinisba. Written by David Murray, Scoto-Brittaine* (London, 1611)

[Nedham, Marchmont]. *Anti-Machiavelli, or, Honesty Against Policy* (London, 1647)

[Nedham, Marchmont]. *Digitus Dei, or, God's Justice upon Treachery and Treason, Exemplified in the Life and Death of the late James, Duke of Hamilton* (London, 1649)

Nedham, Marchmont. *The Case of the Common-Wealth of England Stated* (London, 1650)

Ogilby, John. *The King's Coronation: Being an Exact Account of the Cavalcades with a Description of the Triumphal Arches, and Speeches prepared by the City of London, for his late Majesty Charles the Second* (Edinburgh, 1685)

Parker, Henry. *The Case of Ship Money Briefly Discoursed* (London, 1640)

Parker, Henry. *The Danger to England observed, upon its Deserting the High Court of Parliament* (London, 1642)

Parker, Henry. *The Generall Junto, or, The Councell of Union: chosen equally out of England, Scotland and Ireland, for the Better Compacting of Three Nations into One Monarchy* (London, 1642)

Parker, Henry, Sadler, John & May, Thomas. *The King's Cabinet Opened* (London, 1645)

Parker, Henry. *Scotlands holy war. A discourse truly, and plainly remonstrating, how the Scots out of a corrupt pretended zeal to the Covenant have made the same scandalous and odious to all good men: and how by religious pretexts of saving the peace of Great Britain they have irreligiously involved us all in a most pernicious warre* (London, 1651)

Parker, Henry. *Of a Free Trade. A discourse seriously recommending to our nation the wonderful benefits of trade, especially of a rightly governed and ordered trade* (London, 1648)

Plantagenet, Beauchamp. *A Description of the Province of New Albion* (London, 1650)

Potter, William. *The Key of Wealth, or, A new way, for improving of trade* (London, 1650)

Potter, William. *The trades-man's jewel, or, A safe, easie, speedy and effectual means, for the incredible advancement of trade, and multiplication of riches* (London, 1650)

Potter, William. *Humble proposalls to the honourable Councell for Trade and all merchants and others who desire to improve their estates* (London, 1651)

Puleston, Hamlett. *Monarchie Brittanicae Singularis Protectio* (London, 1661)

Prynne, William. *An Humble Remonstrance Against the Tax of Ship-money Lately Imposed* (London, 1643)

[Prynne, William]. *Scotland's ancient obligation to England and publicke acknowledgement thereof, for their brotherly assistance to, and deliverance of them, with the expence of their blood, and hazard of the state and tranquility of their realm, from the bondage of the French, in the time of their greatest extremity, 1560* (London, 1646)

Prynne, William. *A brief narrative of the manner how divers Members of the House of Commons, that were illegally and unjustly imprisoned or secluded by the Armies force in December 1648 and May 7, 1659, coming upon Tuesday the 27th of December . . . were again forcibly shut out* (London, 1659)

Prynne, William. *The first tome of an exact chronological vindication and historical demonstration of our British, Roman, Saxon, Danish, Norman, English kings supreme ecclesiastical jurisdiction, in, over all spiritual, or religious affairs, causes, persons, as well as temporal within their realms of England, Scotland, Ireland, and other dominions* (London, 1665)

Pym, John. *A Most Learned and Religious Speech spoken by Mr. Pym, at a Conference of both Houses of Parliament the 23 of . . . September. Declaring unto them the Necessity and Benefit of the Union of his Majesties three kingdomes, England, Scotland, and Ireland in matters of Religion and Church-Government* (London, 1642)

O'Connor, Bonaventura. *A Wonderful Discovery of a Terrible Plot against Hull by the Designs of Lord Digby, Many Papists and Others of the Malignant Party* (London, 1642)

[O'Connor, Bonaventura]. *An Abstract of Certain Depositions, By vertue of His Majesties Commission, taken upon Oath* (London, 1642)

Rider's British Merlin (London, 1656, 1659, 1661)

Robinson, Henry. *Brief Considerations, concerning the advancement of trade and navigation humbly tendred unto all ingenious patriots* (London, 1649)

Robinson, Henry. *Certain proposalls in order to the peoples freedome and accommodation in some particulars with the advancement of trade and navigation in this commonwealth in general* (London, 1652)

Roe, Sir Thomas. *Speech in Parliament wherein he sheweth the cause of the decay of coyne and trade in this land, especially of merchant trade* (London, 1641)

Rotheram, John. *The Force of the Argument for the Truth of Christianity Drawn from a Collective View of Prophecy* (Oxford, 1653)

Rudyard, Sir Benjamin. *A Speech concerning a West Indies association, at a committee of the whole House in the Parliament, 21 January* (London, 1641)

Scott, Thomas. *Aphorisms of State, or, Certaine secret articles for the reedifying of the Romis Church agreed upon, and approved in councell, by the colledge of cardinalls in Rome, shewed and delivered unto Pope Gregory the 15 a little before his death* (Utrecht, 1624)

Scott, Thomas. *Boanerges, or, The Humble Supplication of the Ministers of Scotland, To the High Court of Parliament in England* (Edinburgh, 1624)

Scott, Thomas. *Volivae Angliae. The Desires and Wishes of England against Treacherous Usurpation and formidabil Ambition and Power of the Emperor, the King of Spain and the Duke of Bavaria, dedicated to Great Brittaines Great Hope, Charles Prince of Wales* (Utrecht, 1624)

Scott, Thomas. *The Spaniards Cruelty and Treachery to the English in the time of peace and war* (London, 1654)

Selden, John. *A Briefe Discourse Concerning the Power of the Peeres and Comons of Parliament, in point of Judicature* (London, 1640)

Shawe, John. *Brittains Remembrancer, or, The National Covenant, As it was laid out in a sermon preached in the minster at Yorke . . . upon Friday Sept. 20 1644* (London, 1644)

Shawe, John. *The Three Kingdomes Case, or, Their sad calamities, together with their causes and cure. Laid down in a sermon preached at a publique fast at Kingston upon Hull* (London, 1646)

Shawe, John. *Britannia Rediviva: of the Proper and Sovereign Remedy for the Healing and Recovering of these three distracted Nations* (London, 1649)

Spelman, Sir Henry. *De non temerandis ecclesiis: A tract, of the rights & respect due unto churches* (Edinburgh, 1616)

Sprigg, William. *A Modest Plea for an equal common-wealth against monarchy* (London, 1659)

Sydenham, Cuthbert. *The false brother, or, A new map of Scotland, drawn by an English pencil* (London, 1651)

Taylor, John. *An English-Mans Love to Bohemia* (Dort, 1620)

Temple, Sir John. *The Irish Rebellion* (London, 1646)

The Confession of the Kirk of Scotland subscribed by the King's Majesty and his Household in the year of God 1580. With a Designation of such acts of Parliament as are expedient, for justifying the Union, after mentioned. And subscribed by the Nobles, Barrons, Gentlemen, Burgesses, Ministers and Commons, in the year of God, 1638 (Edinburgh, 1638)

The Declaration of the British in the North of Ireland, With some queries of Colonel Moncke, and the answers of the British to the queries (London, 1649)

The Declaration of the Kingdomes of Scotland and England (Edinburgh, 1644)

The Great Account Delivered to the English Lords by the Scottish Commissioners (London, 1641)

The Intentions of the Army of the Kingdom of Scotland declared to their Brethren in England (Edinburgh, 1640)

The Kingdoms intelligencer of the affairs now in agitation in England, Scotland and Ireland (London, 1662–3)

The King's Letter to the Marquesse of Ormond and the Marquesse of Ormonds Letter to Monroe Relating the King's whole Design, concerning all the three Kingdoms (London, 1646)

The Perfect Diurnall of some passages and proceedings of, and in relation to, the armies of England, Ireland and Scotland (London, 1650)

The Scots Resolution Declared in a Message Sent from the Privie Councell of the Kingdome of Scotland, to His Majestie at Yorke . . . wherein is expressed their earnest Desires both to his Maiestie and Parliament, That they would be pleased to joyne in a perfect Unione, it being the chiefe meanes to give an overthrow to the Enemies of the three Kingdoms (Edinburgh, 1642)

The Proceedings of the Commissioners, appointed by the Kings Maiesty and Parliament of Scotland, for conserving the articles of the Treaty and Peace betwixt the kingdomes of Scotland and England (London, 1643)

The Scots Remonstrance or Declaration (London, 1650)

The Vindication and Declaration of the Scots Nation (Edinburgh, 1649)

Thornborough, John, Bishop of Bristol. *A Discourse Shewing the Great Happiness that hath and may still accrue to his Majesties Kingdomes of England and Scotland By re-Uniting them into ane Great Britain* (London, 1604, 1641)

Tillam, Thomas. *The Two Witnesses: Their Prophecy, slaughter, Resurrection and Ascension* (London, 1651)

[University of Oxford]. *Solis Britannici Perigaeum sive Itinirantes Caroli Auspicatissima Periodus* (Oxford, 1633)

[University of Oxford]. *Britannia Rediviva* (Oxford, 1660)

Vines, Richard. *The Hearse of the Renowned, The Right Honourable Robert Earle of Essex* (London, 1646)

Violet, Thomas. *The Advancement of Merchandize, or, Certain propositions for the improvement of trade of this Common-wealth, humbly presented to the right honourable the Council of State* (London, 1651)

[W., R.] *An Information Concerning the Present State of the Jewish Nation in Europe and Judea* (London, 1658)

[Walbancke, Matthew]. *Sundry Strange Prophecies of Merline, Bede, Becket and others* (London, 1652)

[Walker, Clement]. *The History of Independency, with the Rise, Growth and Practices of that powerful and restlesse Faction* (London, 1648)

Walker, Clement. *Relations and observations, historicall and politick, upon the Parliament, begun anno Dom. 1640 . . . Together with An appendix to The history of Independency, being a brief description of some few of Argyle's proceedings before and since he ioyned in confederacy with the Independent junto in England. With a parallel betwixt him and Cromwell, and a caveat to all his seduced adherents* (London, 1648)

Waller, Edmund. *A Panegyrick to my Lord Protector by a gentleman that loves peace, union and the prosperity of the English nation* (London, 1655)

Wharton, Sir George. *Bellum Hybernicale* (London, 1646)

Willsford, Thomas. *The Scales of Commerce and Trade* (London, 1660)

Wilson, Arthur. *The History of Great Britain being the life and reign of King James the First, relating to what passed from his first access to the Crown, till his death* (London, 1653)

Wing, Vincent. *An Almanack and Prognostication* (London, 1641)

Wing, Vincent. *Harmonicum Coeleste, or, The coelestiall harmony of the visible world* (London, 1651)

Wither, George. *Britain's Remembrancer* (London, 1628)

Wither, George. *The British Appeals with Gods Mercifull Replies on the behalfe of the Commonwealth of England* (London, 1650)

Wither, George. *To the Soveraigne Maiesty of the Parliament of the English Republike (by the grace of God) Keepers of the Liberties of England* (London, 1651)

Wither, George. *The Protector* (London, 1655)

[Wylde, Richard]. *The humble petition and remonstrance of Richard Wylde, merchant and adventurer in the East-India trade, laying open the many wilfull neglects, ill-managed actions and improvident courses, the governors and committees of the East-India Company, have heretofore, and still do practice in all their way of trade to the East-Indies, to the exceeding great prejudice of the adventurer and nation in generall* (London, 1654)

1.3   Published Records

A Contemporary History of Affairs in Ireland from A.D. 1641 to 1652, ed. J.T. Gilbert, 3 vols (Dublin, 1879–80)

A Source Book of Scottish History, ed. W.C. Dickinson & G. Donaldson, 3 vols (Edinburgh, 1961)

Acts of the Parliament of Scotland, ed. T. Thomson & C. Innes, 12 vols (Edinburgh, 1814–72)

Adair, Patrick. *A True Narrative of the Rise and Progress of the Presbyterian Church in Ireland (1623–1670)*, ed. W.D. Killen (Belfast, 1866)

Akstykker og Oplysinger til Rigsrådets of Staendermødernerns Historie i Frederick III's tid, ed. C.R. Hansen, 2 vols (Copenhagen, 1959, 1975)

[Alexander, Sir William]. *The Earl of Stirling's Register of Royal Letters, Relative to the Affairs of Scotland and Nova Scotia from 1615 to 1635*, ed. C. Rogers, 2 vols (Edinburgh, 1873)

An Early Modern Englishwoman: A Facsimile Library of Essential Works: volume 3, Eleanor Davies, ed. T. Feroh (Ashgate, 2000)

Autobiography of the Life of Mr Robert Blair, ed. T. McCrie (Edinburgh, 1848)

Baillie, Robert. *Letters and Journals, 1637–62*, ed. D. Laing, 3 vols (Edinburgh, 1841–2)

Balfour, Sir James. *Historical Works*, ed. J. Haig, 4 vols (Edinburgh, 1824–5)

Blaeu, Johannes. *Scotiae Quae Est Europae, Liber XII* (Amsterdam, 1654, 1662)

Borough, Sir John. *Notes on the Treaty carried on at Ripon between King Charles and the Covenanters of Scotland, A.D. 1640*, ed. J. Bruce (London, 1869)

Brereton, Sir William. *Travels in Holland, the United Provinces, England, Scotland and Ireland, 1634–35*, ed. E. Hawkins (London, 1844)

Briefwisseling van Hugo Grotius (1639–40), ed. B.L. Meulenbroek & P.P. Witkam (The Hague, 1976–81)

Browne, William. *Britannia's Pastorals*, ed. R.W. Thompson (London, 1772)

Burnet, Gilbert. *History of My Own Times*, 2 vols (London, 1838)

Burnet, Gilbert. *The Memoirs of the Lives and Actions of James and William, Dukes of Hamilton and Castleherald* (London, 1838)

Calendar of State Papers Domestic Series, of the reign of Charles I, ed. J. Bruce & W.D. Hamilton, 17 vols (London, 1858–82)

Calendar of State Papers and Manuscripts relating to English Affairs existing in the Archives and Collections of Venice, and in other Libraries of Northern Italy, ed. A.B. Hinds (London, 1913–23)

Camden, William. *Britain, or, A Chronological description of the most flourishing kingdomes, England, Scotland and Ireland, and the islands adjoining, out of the depth of antiquity* (London, 1610, 1637)

Camden, William. *The abridgement of Camden's Britannia* (London, 1626)

Camden, William. *Camden's Britannia newly translated into English with large additions and improvements* (London, 1695)

[Charles I]. *By the King a proclamation for the better encouragemet, and aduancement of the trade of the East-Indie Companie, and for the preuention of excesse of priuate trade* (London, 1632)

Correspondence of the Scots Commissioners in London, 1644–1646, ed. H.W. Meikle (Edinburgh, 1907)

Danmark-Norges Traktater (1626–49), ed. L. Laursen (Copenhagen, 1917)

De Unione Regnorum Britanniae Tractatus by Sir Thomas Craig, ed. C.S. Terry (Edinburgh, 1909)

Diary and Correspondence of John Evelyn, F.R.S., ed. W. Bray (London, n.d.)

Diary of Sir Archibald Johnston of Wariston, 1632–39, ed. J.M. Paul (Edinburgh, 1911)

Diary of Sir Thomas Hope of Craighall, 1634–45, ed. T. Thomson (Edinburgh, 1843)

Documenta Bohemica Bellum Tricennale Illustrantia, tomus IV. Der Grosse Kampfe um die Vormacht in Europa 1635–43, ed. J. Janacek, G. Cechova & J. Koci (Prague, 1978)

Early Modern Women Poets: An Anthology, ed. J. Stevenson & P. Davidson (Oxford, 2001)

[Elzevirus, Bonaventure & Abraham]. *Respublica, sive Status Regni Scotia et Hiberniae* (Leiden, 1627)

Fraser, Mr James. *Chronicles of the Frasers: The Wardlaw Manuscript, 916–1674*, ed. W. Mackay (Edinburgh, 1905)

Fugitive Poetical Tracts, 1600–1700, ed. W.C. Hazlett (London, 1875)

Gordon, John. *History of Scots Affairs, 1637–41*, ed. J. Robertson & G. Grub, 3 vols (Aberdeen, 1841)

Gordon of Ruthven, Patrick. *A Short Abridgement of Britane's Distemper, 1639–1649*, ed. J. Dunn (Aberdeen, 1844)

Henderson, Alexander. *Sermons, Prayers and Pulpit Addresses*, ed. R.T. Martin (Edinburgh, 1867)

Hermannides, Rutgerius. *Britannia Magna* (Amsterdam, 1661)

Historical Manuscripts Commission, *Manuscripts of the earls of Mar and Kellie* (London, 1904)

Historical Manuscripts Commission, Ninth Report, part ii, appendix, *Traquhair Muniments* (London, 1887)

Historical Collections, ed. J. Rushworth, 4 vols (London, 1680–91)

[Hyde], Edward, Earl of Clarendon. *The History of the Rebellion and Civil Wars in England* (Oxford, 1893)

Kancelliets Brevbøger: Vedrørende Danmarks Indre Forhold (1637–39), ed. E. Marquard (Copenhagen, 1944)

Kong Christian Den Fjerdes Egenhaendige Breve, ed. C.F. Bricka & J.A. Fredericia, 8 vols (Copenhagen, 1969–70)

Leslie, John, Earl of Rothes. *A Relation of Proceedings Concerning the Affairs of the Kirk of Scotland from August 1637 to July 1638*, ed. J. Nairne (Edinburgh, 1830)

Lettres, Instructions Diplomatiques et Papiers D'Etat Du Cardinal de Richelieu (1638–1642), ed. M. Avenel (Paris, 1867)

Letters of Samuel Rutherford, ed. A.A. Bonar, 2 vols (Edinburgh, 1863)

Magnus, Joannus & Olaus. *De Omnibus Gothorum Sic Numque Regibus, qui unquam ab initio nationis extitere* (Rome, 1554, 1567)

Magnus, Olaus. *A Compendious History of the Goths, Swedes and Vandals and other Northern Nations* (London, 1658)

Making the News: An Anthology of the Newsbooks of Revolutionary England, 1641–1660, ed. J. Raymond (Moreton-in-Marsh, 1993)

Memoirs of the Maxwells of Pollock, ed. W. Fraser, 2 vols (Edinburgh, 1863)

Memoirs of Scottish Catholics in the Seventeenth and Eighteenth Centuries, ed. W.F. Leith, 2 vols (London, 1909)

Memoirs of Sir Ewen Cameron of Lochiel, ed. J. Macknight (Edinburgh, 1842)

Minute Book kept by the War Committee of the Covenanters in the Stewartry of Kirkcudbright in the Years 1640 and 1641 (Kirkcudbright, 1855)

[Munro, Robert]. *Monro His Expedition with the worthy Scots regiment (called Mac-Keyes regiment)* (London, 1637)

Murdoch, S. & Grosjean, A. 'Scotland, Scandinavia and Northern Europe, 1580–1707' (SSNE Database), www.abdn.ac.uk/history/datasets/ssne

Ogilby, John. *Britannia* (London, 1675)

Parliament, Politics and Elections, 1604–1648, ed. C.R. Kyle (Cambridge, 2001)

Proceedings in the Opening Session of the Long Parliament, 1640–41, ed. M. Jannson, 3 vols (Rochester, 1999–2000)

Proceedings of the Short Parliament, ed. E.S. Cope & W.H. Coates (London, 1977)

Prophetic Writings of Lady Eleanor Davies, ed. E.S. Cope (New York, 1995)

Puffendorf, Samuel [von]. *An Introduction to the History of the Principal Kingdoms and States of Europe* (London, 1699)

Records of the Commissions of the General Assemblies for the years 1650–52, ed. J. Christie (Edinburgh, 1909)

Register of the Consultations of the Ministers of Edinburgh, and some other Brethren of the Ministry, 1652–60, ed. J. Christie, 2 vols (Edinburgh, 1921, 1930)

Registers of the Privy Council of Scotland, 1st ser., ed. D. Masson, 14 vols (Edinburgh, 1877–98); 2nd ser., ed. D. Masson & P.H. Brown, 8 vols (Edinburgh, 1899–1908)

Rikskanseleren Axel Oxenstiernas Skrifter och Brefvexling, II, 9 (Kingl. Vitterhets Historie och Antiquitetsakademien, Stockholm, 1898)

Row, John. *The History of the Kirk of Scotland, 1558–1637*, ed. D. Laing (Edinburgh, 1842)

Rutherford, Samuel. *Lex Rex: The Law and the Prince* (Edinburgh, 1848)

[Saltonstall, Wye]. *Historia Mundi, or, Mercator's Atlas* (London, 1635)

Scot of Scotstarvit, Sir John. *The Staggering State of Scottish Statesmen, from 1550 to 1650*, ed. C. Rogers (Edinburgh, 1872)

Scotland and the Commonwealth, 1651–53, ed. C.H. Firth (Edinburgh, 1895)

Scotland and the Protectorate, ed. C.H. Firth (Edinburgh, 1899)

Scott, William. *An Apologetical Narration of the State and Government of the Kirk of Scotland since the Reformation*, ed. D. Laing (Edinburgh, 1846)

Select Biographies, ed. W.K. Tweedie, 2 vols (Edinburgh, 1845–7)

Seventeenth-Century Political and Financial Papers: Camden Miscellany XXXIII (Cambridge, 1996)

Ship Money Papers and Richard Greville's Notebook, ed. C.G. Bonsey & J.G. Jenkins (Buckingham Record Society, 1965)

Spalding, John. *History of the Troubles and Memorable Transactions in Scotland and England*, ed. J. Skene, 2 vols (Edinburgh, 1828–9)

Speed, John. *The Theatre of the Empire of Great Britain: presenting an exact geography of the kingdomes of England, Scotland, Ireland and the isle adjoyning* (London, 1616, 1627)

Speed, John. *England, Wales, Scotland and Ireland described and abridged* (London, 1632)

State Trials, ed. W. Cobbett, 33 vols (London, 1809–28)

Swedish Diplomats at Cromwell's Court, 1655–56: The Missions of Peter Julius Coyet and Christer Bonde, ed. M. Roberts (London, 1988)

Tabeller over Skibsfart og Varetransport gennem Oresund, 1492–1660, ed. N.E. Bang & K. Korst, 3 vols (Copenhagen, 1906–22)

The British Union: A Critical Edition and Translation of David Hume of Godscroft's De Unione Insulae Britannicae, ed. P.J. McGinnis & A. Williamson (Aldershot, 2002)

The Clarke Papers, ed. C.H. Firth, 4 vols (London, 1891–1901)

The Covenants and the Covenanters, ed. J. Kerr (Edinburgh, 1896)

The Diplomatic Correspondence of Jean de Montereul and the Brothers De Bellièvre, French Ambassadors in England and Scotland, 1645–48, ed. J.G. Fotheringham, 2 vols (Edinburgh, 1898–9)

The Earl of Strafforde's Letters and Dispatches, ed. W. Knowler, 2 vols (London, 1739)

The Government of Scotland under the Covenanters, 1637–1651, ed. D. Stevenson (Edinburgh, 1982)

The Hamilton Papers, ed. S.R. Gardiner (London, 1880)

The History of the Irish Confederation and the War in Ireland (1641–49), ed. J.T. Gilbert, 7 vols (Dublin, 1882–91)

The Journal of John Winthrop, 1630–1649, ed. R.S. Dunn, J. Savage & L. Yeandle (Cambridge, MA, 1996)

The Journal of Sir Simonds D'Ewes from the Beginning of the Long Parliament to the Opening of the Trial of the Earl of Strafford, ed. W. Notestein (London, 1923)

The Journal of Thomas Cunningham of Campvere, ed. E.J. Courthope (Edinburgh, 1928)

The Journal of Thomas Juxon, 1644–47, ed. K. Lindley & D. Scott (Cambridge, 1999)

The Letter-Book of the Earl of Clanricarde, 1643–47, ed. J. Lowe (Dublin, 1983)

The Memoirs of Henry Guthry, Late Bishop of Dunkeld, ed. G. Crawford (Glasgow, 1747)

The Nicholas Papers, Correspondence of Sir Edward Nicholas, Secretary of State, ed. G.F. Warner, 2 vols (London, 1886)

The Oxinden Letters, 1607–1642, ed. D. Gardiner (London, 1933)

The Poetry of George Wither, ed. F. Sidgwick, 2 vols (London, 1902)

The Quarrel between the Earl of Manchester and Oliver Cromwell: An Episode of the English Civil Wars, ed. D. Mason (London, 1875)

The Short Parliament (1640) Diary of Sir Thomas Aston, ed. J.D. Maltby (London, 1988)

The Stuart Constitution, ed. J.P. Kenyon (Cambridge, 1966), pp.7–86.

The Whole Prophecies of Scotland, England, France, Ireland and Denmarke (Edinburgh, 1617)

The Works of William Laud D.D., ed. J. Bliss, 5 vols (Oxford, 1853)

The Works of the Famous English Poets, Mr Edmund Spenser (London, 1679)

Turner, Sir James. *Memoirs of his Own Life and Times, 1632–1670*, ed. T. Thomson (London, 1829)

Verstegan, Richard. *Restitution of Decayed Intelligence* (Antwerp, 1605 & London, 1628, 1634, 1653, 1655)

Wexionius, Michael O. *Epitome Descriptiones Sueciae, Gothiae, Fenningiae et Subjectorum Provinciarium* (Åbo, 1650)

Whitelocke, Bulstrode. *Memorials of the English Affairs from the Beginning of the Reign of Charles I to the Happy Restoration of King Charles the Second*, 4 vols (Oxford, 1853)

Woodhouse, John. *The Map of Ireland with the exact dimensions of the provinces therein contained* (London, 1653)
Yorkshire Diaries and Autobiographies in the Seventeenth and Eighteenth Centuries (Durham, 1877)

2. Secondary Sources

2.1   Theses

Eriksonas, L. 'The National Heroes and National Identity: A Comparative Framework for Smaller Nations' (PhD diss., University of Aberdeen, DCE, 2000)

Worthington, D. 'Scottish Clients of the Habsburgs, 1618–1648' (PhD diss., University of Aberdeen, 2001)

2.2   Monographs

Aikman, J.A. *An Historical Account of Covenanting in Scotland from 1556 to 1638* (Edinburgh, 1848)

Allan, D. *Philosophy and Politics in Later Stuart Scotland* (East Linton, 2000)

Anderson, P. *Robert Stewart, Earl of Orkney, Lord of Shetland, 1533–1593* (Edinburgh, 1983)

Armitage, D. *The Ideological Origins of the British Empire* (Cambridge, 2000)

Barber, S. *Regicide and Republicanism: Politics and Ethics in the English Revolution, 1646–1659* (Edinburgh, 1998)

Barnard, T.C. *Cromwellian Ireland: English Government and Reform in Ireland, 1649–1660* (Oxford, 1975)

Batten, J.M. *John Dury: Advocate of Christian Reunion* (Chicago, 1944)

Bennett, M. *The Civil Wars in Britain & Ireland, 1638–1651* (Oxford, 1997)

Brace, L. *The Idea of Property in Seventeenth-Century England* (Manchester, 1998)

Braddick, M.J. *The Nerves of State: Taxation and the Financing of the English State, 1558–1714* (Manchester, 1996)

Braddick, M.J. *State Formation and Social Change in Early Modern England, c.1550–1700* (Cambridge, 2000)

Brauer, K. *Die Unionstätigkeit John Duries unter dem Protektorat Cromwells* (Marburg, 1907)

Brenner, R. *Merchants and Revolution: Commercial Change, Political Conflict, and London's Overseas Traders, 1550–1653* (Princeton, NJ, 1993)

Brown, K.M. *Bloodfeud in Scotland, 1573–1625: Violence, Justice and Politics in Early Modern Scotland* (Edinburgh, 1986)

Brown, K.M. *Kingdom or Province? Scotland and the Regal Union, 1603–1715* (London, 1992)

Brown, K.M. *Noble Society in Scotland: Wealth, Family and Culture from the Reformation to the Revolution* (Edinburgh, 2000)

Burgess, G. *The Politics of the Ancient Constitution: An Introduction to English Political Thought, 1603–1641* (University Park, PA, 1992)

Burgess, G. *Absolute Monarchy and the Stuart Constitution* (New Haven, CT, 1996)

Burns, J.H. *The True Law of Kingship: Concepts of Monarchy in Early Modern Scotland* (Oxford, 1996)

Calder, A. *Revolutionary Empire: The Rise of the English-Speaking Empire from the Fifteenth Century to the 1780s* (London, 1988)

Canny, N. *Kingdom and Colony: Ireland in the Atlantic World* (Baltimore & London, 1988)

Canny, N. *Making Ireland British, 1580–1650* (Oxford, 2001)

Capp, B.S. *Cromwell's Navy: The Fleet and the English Revolution, 1648–1660* (Oxford, 1989)

Carlton, C. *Going to the Wars: The Experience of the British Civil Wars, 1638–1651* (London, 1994)

Clarke, A. *The Old English in Ireland* (London, 1966)

Clarke, A. *Prelude to Restoration in Ireland: The End of the Commonwealth, 1659–1660* (Cambridge, 1999)

Cogswell, T. *Home Divisions: Aristocracy, the State and Provincial Conflict* (Manchester, 1998)

Collins, J.B. *The State in Early Modern France* (Cambridge, 1995)

Collinson, P. *The Birthpangs of Protestant England: Religious and Cultural Change in the Sixteenth and the Seventeenth Centuries* (Oxford, 1988)

Cowan, E.J. *Montrose: For Covenant and King* (London, 1977)

Coward, B. *Early Stuart England, 1603–1640* (London, 1980)

Coward, B. *Oliver Cromwell* (Harlow, 1991)

Coward, B. *The Cromwellian Protectorate, 1653–59* (Manchester, 2002)

Cramsie, J. *Kingship and Crown Finance under James VI and I, 1603–1625* (Woodbridge, 2002)

Cressy, D. *Bonfires and Bells: National Memory and the Protestant Calendar in Elizabethan and Stuart England* (London, 1989)

Cunningham, B. *The World of Geoffrey Keating* (Dublin, 2000)

Curry, P. *Prophecy and Power: Astrology in Early Modern England* (Princeton, NJ, 1989)

Cust, R. *The Forced Loan and English Politics, 1626–1628* (Oxford, NJ, 1989)

Davis, J.C. *Oliver Cromwell* (London, 2001)

Davis, R. *The Rise of Atlantic Economies* (London, 1973)

Dalhede, C. *Handelsfamiljer på Stormaktstiden Europamarknad*, 2 vols (Partille, 2001)

Dodgshon, R. *From Chiefs to Landlords: Social and Economic Change in the Western Highlands and Islands, c.1493–1820* (Edinburgh, 1998)

Donald, P. *An Uncounselled King: Charles I and the Scottish Troubles, 1637–41* (Cambridge, 1990)

Dow, F.D. *Cromwellian Scotland, 1651–1660* (Edinburgh, 1979)

Downing, B.M. *The Military Revolution and Political Change: Origins of Democracy and Autocracy in Early Modern Europe* (Princeton, NJ, 1992)

Dunn, R.S. *Sugar and Slaves: The Rise of the Planter Class in the English West Indies, 1624–1713* (Chapel Hill, NC, 1992)

Durston, C. *Cromwell's Major-Generals: Godly Government during the English Revolution* (Manchester, 2001)

Eisen, R. *Gersonides on Providence, Covenant, and the Chosen People: A Study in Medieval Jewish Philosophy and Biblical Commentary* (New York, 1994)

Ferguson, W. *The Identity of the Scottish Nation: An Historic Quest* (Edinburgh, 1998)

Ferrell, L.A. *Government by Polemic: James I, the King's Preachers, and the Rhetorics of Conformity, 1603–1625* (Stanford, CA, 1998)

Fincham, K. *Prelate as Pastor: The Episcopate of James I* (Oxford, 1990)

Fissel, M.C. *The Bishops' Wars: Charles I's Campaigns against Scotland, 1638–40* (Cambridge, 1994)

Fletcher, A. *The Outbreak of the English Civil War* (London, 1981)

Ford, A. *The Protestant Reformation in Ireland, 1590–1641* (Frankfurt am Main, 1987)

Fukuda, A. *Sovereignty and the Sword: Harrington, Hobbes and Mixed Government in the English Civil Wars* (Oxford, 1997)

Fulton, T.W. *The Sovereignty of the Sea: An Historical Account of the Claims for Dominion of the British Seas* (Edinburgh, 1911)

Galloway, B. *The Union of England and Scotland, 1606–1608* (Edinburgh, 1986)

Games, A. *Migration and the Origins of the English Atlantic World* (Cambridge, MA, 1999)

Gaunt, P. *Oliver Cromwell* (Oxford, 1996)

Gentles, I. *The New Model Army in England, Ireland and Scotland, 1645–1653* (Oxford, 1992)

Gillespie, R. *Devoted People: Belief and Religion in Early Modern Ireland* (Manchester, 1997)

Goodare, J. *State and Society in Early Modern Scotland* (Oxford, 1999)

Gordon, D.J. *The Renaissance Imagination* (Berkeley, CA, 1975)

Goss, J. *World Historical Atlas, 1662* (London, 1990)

Greene, J.P. *Pursuits of Happiness: The Social Development of Early Modern British Colonies and the Formation of American Culture* (Chapel Hill, NC, 1988)

Grosjean, A. *An Unofficial Alliance: Scotland and Sweden, 1569–1654* (Leiden, 2003)

Henry, G. *The Irish Military Community in Spanish Flanders, 1586–1621* (Dublin, 1992)

Hibbert, C. *Charles I and the Popish Plot* (Chapel Hill, NC, 1983)

Hill, C. *Antichrist in Seventeenth-Century England* (Oxford, 1971)

Hill, C. *The World Turned Upside Down: Radical Ideas during the English Revolution* (London, 1972)

Hirst, D. *England in Conflict, 1603–1660: Kingdom, Community, Commonwealth* (London, 1999)

Holmes, G. *The Making of a Great Power: Late Stuart and Early Georgian Britain, 1660–1722* (Harlow, 1993)

Hughes, A. *The Causes of the English Civil War* (Basingstoke, 1991)

Hutton, R. *The Restoration: A Political & Religious History of England and Wales, 1658–1667* (Oxford, 1985)

Hutton, R. *The Rise and Fall of Merry England: The Ritual Year, 1400–1700* (Oxford, 1994)

Hutton, R. *The Royalist War Effort, 1642–1646* (London, 1999)

James, S. *The Atlantic Celts: Ancient People or Modern Invention?* (Madison, WI, 1999)

Kaplan, L. *Politics and Religion during the English Revolution: The Scots and the Long Parliament, 1643–1645* (New York, 1976)

Kearney, H. *Strafford in Ireland, 1633–41: A Study in Absolutism* (Manchester, 1959; 2nd edn Cambridge, 1989)

Keeble, N.H. *The Restoration: England in the 1660s* (Oxford, 2002)

Kelsey, S. *Inventing a Republic: The Political Culture of the English Commonwealth, 1649–1653* (Stanford, CA, 1997)

Kidd, C. *British Identities before Nationalism: Ethnicity and Nationhood in the Atlantic World, 1600–1800* (Cambridge, 1999)

Kishlansky, M. *The Rise of the New Model Army* (Cambridge, 1979)

Kishlansky, M. *A Monarchy Transformed: Britain, 1603–1714* (London, 1996)

Kliger, S. *The Goths in England: A Study in Seventeenth and Eighteenth Century Thought* (New York, 1952)

Kulikoff, A. *From British Peasants to Colonial American Farmers* (Chapel Hill, NC, 2000)

Kupperman, K.O. *Providence Island, 1630–1641: The Other Puritan Colony* (Cambridge, 1993)

Lee jr, M. *The Road to Revolution: Scotland under Charles I, 1625–37* (Urbana & Chicago, IL, 1985)

Lee jr, M. *Great Britain's Solomon: King James VI and I in his Three Kingdoms* (Urbana, IL, 1990)

Lenihan, P. *Confederate Catholics at War, 1641–49* (Cork, 2001)

Levack, B.P. *The Formation of the British State: England, Scotland and the Union, 1603–1707* (Oxford, 1987)

Lockyer, R. *James VI and I* (London, 1998)

MacDonald, A.R. *The Jacobean Kirk, 1567–1625: Sovereignty, Polity and Liturgy* (Aldershot, 1998)

MacDonnell, H. *The Wild Geese of the Antrim Mac Donnells* (Blackrock, 1996)

Macinnes, A.I. *Charles I and the Making of the Covenanting Movement, 1625–1641* (Edinburgh, 1991)

Macinnes, A.I. *Clanship, Commerce and the House of Stuart, 1603–1788* (East Linton, 1996)

MacLeod, J. *Scottish Theology* (Edinburgh, 1974)

Marshall, G. *Presbyteries and Profits* (Oxford, 1980)

Mason, R.A. *Kingship and the Commonweal: Political Thought in Renaissance and Reformation Scotland* (East Linton, 1998)

Mendle, M. *Henry Parker and the English Civil War* (Cambridge, 1995)

Moreland, C. & Bannister, D. *Antique Maps* (London, 2000)

Morrill, J. *The Revolt of the Provinces: Conservatives and Radicals in the English Civil War* (London, 1976)

Morrill, J. *The Nature of the English Revolution* (London, 1993)

Mullan, D.G. *Episcopacy in Scotland: The History of an Idea, 1560–1638* (Edinburgh, 1986)

Mullan, D.G. *Scottish Puritanism* (Oxford, 1999)

Murdoch, S. *Britain, Denmark–Norway and the House of Stuart, 1603–1660* (East Linton, 2000)

Nicholls, A.D. *The Jacobean Union: A Reconsideration of British Civil Policies under the Early Stuarts* (Westport, CT, 1999)

Nicholls, K.W. *Gaelic and Gaelicised Ireland in the Middle Ages* (Dublin, 1972)

Ó Buachalla, B. *Foras Feasa ar Éirinn, History of Ireland: Foreword* (Dublin, 1987)

Ó Buachalla, B. *Aisling Ghearr: Na Stiobhartaigh Agus an tAos Leinn, 1603–1788* (Dublin, 1996)

Ó Siochrú, M. *Confederate Ireland, 1642–9: A Constitutional and Political Analysis* (Dublin, 1999)

Ohlmeyer, J. *Civil War and Restoration in the Three Stuart Kingdoms: The Political Career of Randal MacDonnell First Marquis of Antrim, 1609–83* (Cambridge, 1993)

Pagden, A. *Lords of all the World: Ideologies of Empire in Spain, Britain and France, c.1500–c.1800* (New Haven, CT, 1995)

Parker, G. *Empire, War and Faith in Early Modern Europe* (London, 2003)

Patterson, W.B. *King James VI and I and the Reunion of Christendom* (Cambridge, 1998)

Pawlisch, H.S. *Sir John Davies and the Conquest of Ireland: A Study in Legal Imperialism* (Cambridge, 1985)

Peltonen, M. *Classical Humanism and Republicanism in English Political Thought, 1570–1640* (Cambridge, 1995)

Perceval-Maxwell, M. *The Scottish Migration to Ulster in the Reign of James I* (London, 1973)

Perceval-Maxwell, M. *The Outbreak of the Irish Rebellion of 1641* (Montreal, 1944)

Pincus, S. *Protestantism and Patriotism: Ideologies and the Making of English Foreign Policy, 1650–1668* (Cambridge, 1996)

Rabb, T.K. *Enterprise & Empire: Merchants and Gentry Investment in the Expansion of England, 1575–1630* (Cambridge, MA, 1967)

Rawson, C. *God, Gulliver and Genocide: Barbarism and the European Imagination, 1492–1945* (Oxford, 2001)

Raymond, J. *Pamphlets and Pamphleteers in Early Modern Britain* (Cambridge, 2003)

Reid, J.G. *Acadia, Maine and New England: Marginal Colonies in the Seventeenth Century* (Toronto, 1981)

Robinson, P. *The Plantation of Ulster* (Belfast, 2000)

Roots, I. *The Great Rebellion* (Stroud, 1995)

Russell, C. *The Causes of the English Civil Wars* (Oxford, 1990)

Russell, C. *Unrevolutionary England, 1603–1642* (London, 1990)

Russell, C. *The Fall of the British Monarchies, 1637–1642* (Oxford, 1991)

Schaub, J-F. *La France Espagnole* (Paris, 2003)

Scott, J. *England's Troubles: Seventeenth-century English Political Instability in a European Context* (Cambridge, 2000)

Scott, W.R. *The Constitution and Finance of English, Scottish and Irish Joint-Stock Companies to 1720*, 3 vols (Cambridge, 1911–12)

Sharpe, K. *The Personal Rule of Charles I* (New Haven, CT, & London, 1992)

Sharpe, K. *Remapping Early Modern England: The Culture of Seventeenth Century Politics* (Cambridge, 2000)

Sherman, W.H. *John Dee: The Politics of Reading and Writing in the English Renaissance* (Amherst, 1995)

Skinner, Q. *Foundations of Modern Political Thought*, 2 vols (Cambridge, 1977–8)

Skovgaard-Petersen, K. *Historiography at the Court of Christian IV* (Copenhagen, 2002)

Smith, D.L. *Constitutional Royalism and the Search for Settlement, c.1640–1649* (Cambridge, 1994)

Smith, D.L. *A History of the Modern British Isles, 1603–1707: The Double Crown* (Oxford, 1998)

Smith, D.L. *The Stuart Parliaments, 1603–1689* (London, 1999)

Smith, H.D. *Shetland Life and Trade, 1550–1914* (Edinburgh, 1984)

Smith, N. *Literature and Revolution in England, 1640–1660* (New Haven, CT, 1994)

Smuts, R. *Court Culture and the Origins of a Royalist Tradition in Early Stuart England* (Philadelphia, 1987)

Smyth, J. *The Making of the United Kingdom, 1660–1800* (Harlow, 2001)

Somerville, J.P. *Politics and Ideology in England, 1603–1640* (London, 1986)

Stradling, R.A. *The Spanish Monarchy and Irish Mercenaries: The Wild Geese in Spain, 1618–1668* (Dublin, 1994)

Stevenson, D. *The Scottish Revolution, 1637–44: The Triumph of the Covenanters* (Newton Abbot, 1973)

Stevenson, D. *Revolution and Counter-Revolution in Scotland, 1644–1651* (London, 1977)

Stevenson, D. *Alasdair MacColla and the Highland Problem in the Seventeenth Century* (Edinburgh, 1980)

Stevenson, D. *Scottish Covenanters and Irish Confederates* (Belfast, 1981)

Stevenson, D. *The Covenanters: The National Covenant and Scotland* (Edinburgh, 1988)

Stevenson, D. *King or Covenant? Voices from the Civil War* (East Linton, 1996)

Thomas, H. *A History of Wales, 1485–1660* (Cardiff, 1972)

Thomas, K. *Religion and the Decline of Magic: Studies in Popular Beliefs in Seventeenth-Century England* (London, 1991)

Todd, M. *The Culture of Protestantism in Early Modern Scotland* (New Haven, CT, 2002)

Treadwell, V. *Buckingham and Ireland, 1616–1628: A Study in Anglo-Irish Politics* (Dublin, 1998)

Trevor-Roper, H. *Archbishop Laud, 1573–1645* (Basingstoke, 1988)

Tuck, R. *Philosophy and Government, 1572–1651* (Cambridge, 1993)

Tyacke, N. *Anti-Calvinists: The Rise of English Arminianism, c.1590–1640* (Oxford, 1987)

Underdown, D. *Revel, Riot and Rebellion: Popular Politics and Culture in England, 1603–1660* (Oxford, 1985)

Van Mingroot, E. & Van Ermen, E. *Scandinavia in Old Maps and Prints* (Knokke, 1987)

Venning, T. *Cromwellian Foreign Policy* (New York, 1995)

Walsham, A. *Providence in Early Modern England* (Oxford, 1999)

Webb, S.S. *The Governors-General: The English Army and the Definition of Empire, 1569–1681* (Chapel Hill, NC, 1979)

Wheeler, J.S. *Cromwell in Ireland* (Dublin, 1999)

Wheeler, J.S. *The Irish and British Wars, 1637–1654: Triumph, Tragedy and Failure* (London, 2002)

Williamson, A.H. *Scottish National Consciousness in the Age of James VI* (Edinburgh, 1979)

Worden, B. *The Rump Parliament, 1648–1653* (Cambridge, 1974)

Wormald, B.H.G. *Francis Bacon: History, Politics and Science, 1561–1626* (Cambridge, 1993)

Woolf, D.R. *The Idea of History in Early Stuart England: Erudition, Ideology, and 'The Light of Truth' from the Accession of James I to the Civil War* (Toronto, 1990)

Woolrych, A. *Commonwealth to Protectorate* (Oxford, 1986)

Woolrych, A. *Soldiers and Statesmen: The General Council of the Army and its Debates, 1647–48* (Oxford, 1987)

Woolrych, A. *Britain in Revolution, 1625–1660* (Oxford, 2002)

Young, J.R. *The Scottish Parliament, 1639–1661: A Political and Constitutional Analysis* (Edinburgh, 1996)

2.3   Edited Books

Asch, R.G., ed. *Three Nations – A Common History? England, Scotland, Ireland and British History, c.1600–1920* (Bochum, 1993)

Asch, R.G., ed. *Der europäische Adel im Ancien Régime* (Böhlau, 2001)

Bahlcke, J. & Strohmeyer, A., eds. *Konfessionalisierung in Ostmitteleuropa: Wirkungen des religiosen Wandels im 16. und 17. Jahrhundert in Staat, Gesellschaft und Kultur* (Stuttgart, 1999)

Bailyn, B. & Morgan, P.D., eds. *Strangers within the Realm: Cultural Margins of the First British Empire* (Chapel Hill, NC, 1991)

Barnard, T.C. & Fenlon, J., eds. *The Dukes of Ormonde, 1610–1745* (Woodbridge, 2000)

Bradshaw, B. & Morrill, J., eds. *The British Problem, c.1534–1707: State Formation in the Atlantic Archipelago* (Basingstoke, 1996)

Bradshaw, B. & Roberts, P., eds. *British Consciousness and Identity: The Making of Britain, 1533–1707* (Cambridge, 1998)

Burgess, G., ed. *New British History: Founding a Modern State, 1603–1715* (London, 1999)

Connolly, S.J., ed. *Kingdoms United? Great Britain and Ireland since 1500: Integration and Diversity* (Dublin, 1999)

Canny, N., ed. *Europeans on the Move: Studies on Migration, 1500–1800* (Oxford, 1994)

Canny, N., ed. *The Origins of Empire: British Overseas Empire to the Close of the Seventeenth Century* (Oxford, 1998)

Coward, B., ed. *The Blackwell Companion to Stuart Britain* (London, 2003)

Cust, R. & Hughes, A., eds. *Conflict in Early Stuart England* (London, 1989)

Cust, R. & Hughes, A., eds. *The English Civil War* (London, 1997)

Dwyer, J., Mason, R.A. & Murdoch, A., eds. *New Perspectives on the Politics and Culture of Early Modern Scotland* (Edinburgh, 1982)

Ellis, S.G. & Barber, S., eds. *Conquest and Union: Fashioning a British State, 1485–1725* (London, 1995)

Evans, R.J.W. & Thomas, T.V., eds. *Crown, Church and Estates: Central European Politics in the Sixteenth and Seventeenth Centuries* (London, 1991)

Fincham, K., ed. *The Early Stuart Church, 1603–1642* (Basingstoke, 1993)

Fletcher, A. & Roberts, P., eds. *Religion, Culture and Society in Early Modern Britain* (Cambridge, 1994)

Ford, A., McGuire, J. & Milne, K., eds. *As By Law Established: The Church of Ireland since the Reformation* (Dublin, 1995)

Gentles, I., Morrill, J. & Worden, B., eds. *Soldiers, Writers and Statesmen of the English Revolution* (Cambridge, 1998)

Gilles, W., ed. *Gaelic and Scotland, Alba agus A'Ghàidhlig* (Edinburgh, 1989)

Graham, B.J. & Proudfoot, L.J., eds. *An Historical Geography of Ireland* (London, 1993)

Grant, A. & Stringer, K.J., eds. *Uniting the Kingdom? The Making of British History* (London, 1995)

Greengrass, M., ed. *Conquest and Coalescence: The Shaping of the State in Early Modern Europe* (London, 1991)

Greengrass, M., Leslie, M. & Raylor, T., eds. *Samuel Hartlib and Universal Reformation* (Cambridge, 1994)

Houston, A. & Pincus, S., eds. *A Nation Transformed: England after the Restoration* (Cambridge, 2001)

Howard, M., Andreopoulos, G.J. & Shulman, M.R., eds. *The Laws of War: Constraints on Warfare in the Western World* (New Haven, CT, 1994)

Jansson, M., Bushkovitch, P. & Rogozhin, N., eds. *England and the North: The Russian Embassy of 1613–1614* (Philadelphia, 1994)

Jones, C., ed. *The Scots and Parliament* (Edinburgh, 1996)

Kaplan, Y., Mechoulan, H. & Popkins, R.H., eds. *Menasseh Ben Israel and His World* (New York, 1989)

Kenyon, J. & Ohlmeyer, J., eds. *The Civil Wars: A Military History of England, Scotland and Ireland, 1638–1660* (Oxford, 1998)

Kyle, C.R. & Peaccy, J., eds. *Parliament at Work: Parliamentary Committees, Political Power & Public Access in Early Modern England* (Woodbridge, 2002)

Lake, P. & Questier, M., eds. *Conformity and Orthodoxy in the English Church, c.1560–1660* (Woodbridge, 2000)

Lenihan, P., ed. *Conquest and Resistance: War in Seventeenth Century Ireland* (Leiden, 2001)

Levene, M. & Roberts, P., eds. *The Massacre in History* (Oxford, 1999)

Lynch, M. & Goodare, J., eds. *The Reign of James VI* (East Linton, 1999)

MacCuarta, B., ed. *Ulster, 1641: Aspects of the Rising* (Belfast, 1997)

Macinnes, A.I., Riis, T. & Pedersen, F.G., eds. *Ships, Guns and Bibles in the North Sea and Baltic States, c.1350–c.1700* (East Linton, 2000)

Macinnes, A.I. & Ohlmeyer, J., eds. *The Stuart Kingdoms in the Seventeenth Century: Awkward Neighbours* (Dublin, 2002)

Maclean, G., ed. *Culture and Society in the Stuart Restoration: Literature, Drama and History* (Cambridge, 1995)

Mason, R.A., ed. *Scotland and England, 1286–1815* (Edinburgh, 1987)

Mason, R.A., ed. *Scots and Britons: Scottish Political Thought and the Union of 1603* (Cambridge, 1994)

Merritt, J.F., ed. *The Political World of Thomas Wentworth, Earl of Strafford, 1621–1641* (Cambridge, 1996)

Moody, T.W., ed. *Nationality and the Pursuit of National Independence* (Belfast, 1978)

Morrill, J., ed. *The Scottish National Covenant in its British Context* (Edinburgh, 1990)

Murdoch, S., ed. *Scotland and the Thirty Years' War, 1618–1648* (Leiden, 2001)

Murdoch, S. & Mackillop, A., eds. *Fighting for Identity: Scottish Military Experience, c.1550–1900* (Leiden, 2002)

Ó Siochrú, M., ed. *Kingdoms in Crisis: Ireland in the 1640s* (Dublin, 2000)

Ohlmeyer, J., ed. *Ireland from Independence to Occupation, 1641–1660* (Cambridge, 1995)

Ohlmeyer, J., ed. *Irish Political Thought in the Seventeenth Century* (Cambridge, 2000)

Peacey, J., ed. *The Regicides and the Execution of Charles I* (Basingstoke, 2001)

Peck, L.L., ed. *The Mental World of the Jacobean Court* (Cambridge, 1991)

Pettegree, A., Duke, A. & Lewis, G., eds. *Calvinism in Europe, 1540–1620* (Cambridge, 1994)

Phillipson, N. & Skinner, Q., eds. *Political Discourse in Early Modern Britain* (Cambridge, 1993)

Pocock, J.G.A., ed. *The Varieties of British Political Thought, 1500–1800* (Cambridge, 1996)

Ruiz, E.M. & Corrales, M.D.P.P., eds. *Spain & Sweden in the Baroque Era (1600–1660)* (Madrid, 2000)

Salmon, P. & Barrow, T., eds. *Britain and the Baltic: Studies in Commercial, Political and Cultural Relations, 1500–2000* (Sunderland, 2003)

Sharpe, K. & Lake, P., eds. *Culture and Politics in Early Stuart England* (Basingstoke, 1994)

Smuts, R.M., ed. *The Stuart Court and Europe: Essays in Politics and Political Culture* (Cambridge, 1996)

Taithe, B. & Thornton, T., eds. *Prophecy* (Stroud, 1997)
Tomlinson, H., ed., *Before the Civil War: Essays in Early Stuart Politics and Government* (London, 1983)
Walker, G.M., ed. *Puritanism in Early America* (Toronto, 1973)
Wootton, D., ed. *Republicanism, Liberty and Commercial Society, 1649–1776* (Stanford, CA, 1994)
Young, J.R., ed. *Celtic Dimensions of the British Civil Wars* (Edinburgh, 1997)

2.4 Journal Articles

Adamson, J.S.A. 'The English Nobility and the Projected Settlement of 1647', *HJ*, 30 (1987), pp.567–602
Adamson, J.S.A. 'The *Vindiciae Veritatis* and the Political Creed of Viscount Saye and Sele', *Historical Research*, 60 (1987), pp.45–63
Armitage, D. 'The Cromwellian Protectorate and the Languages of Empire', *HJ*, 35 (1992), pp.531–55
Armitage, D. 'Making the Empire British: Scotland in the Atlantic World, 1542–1717', *Past & Present*, 155 (1997), pp.34–63
Arnold, L.J. 'The Irish Court of Claims of 1663', *IHS*, 24 (1985), pp.417–30
Barber, S. 'The People of Northern England and Attitudes towards the Scots, 1639–1651: "The Lamb and the Dragon cannot be Reconciled"', *Northern History*, 35 (1999), pp.93–118
Bard, N.P. 'The Ship Money Case and William Fiennes, Viscount Saye and Sele', *Bulletin of the Institute of Historical Research*, 50 (1977), pp.177–84
Bennett, M. 'Dampnified Villagers: Taxation and Wales during the First Civil War', *Welsh History Review*, 19 (1998), pp.29–43
Buckroyd, J.M. 'Bridging the Gap: Scotland, 1659–1660', *SHR*, 66 (1987), pp.1–25
Butler, M. 'A Case Study in Caroline Political Theatre: Braithwaite's Mercurius Britannicus (1641)', *HJ*, 27 (1984), pp.947–53
Capern, A.L. 'The Caroline Church: James Ussher and the Irish Dimension', *HJ*, 39 (1996), pp.57–85
Carlin, N. 'The Levellers and the Conquest of Ireland in 1649', *HJ*, 39 (1987), pp.269–88
Christianson, P. 'Arguments on Billeting and Martial Law in the Parliament of 1628', *HJ*, 37 (1994), pp.539–67
Clarke, A. 'Sir Piers Crosby, 1590–1646: Wentworth's "Tawney Ribon"', *IHS*, 26 (1988), pp.142–60
Cogswell, T. 'The Politics of Propaganda: Charles I and the People in the 1620s', *Journal of British Studies*, 29 (1990), pp.187–215
Collins, J.R. 'The Church Settlement of Oliver Cromwell', *History*, 87 (2002), pp.18–40
Cregan, D.F. 'The Confederate Catholics of Ireland: The Personnel of the Confederation, 1642–9', *IHS*, 29 (1995), pp.492–512
DesBrisay, G. 'Catholics, Quakers and Religious Persecution in Restoration Aberdeen', *Innes Review*, 7 (1996), pp.136–68
Donagan, B. 'Codes and Conduct in the English Civil War', *Past & Present*, 118 (1988), pp.64–95
Egloff, C.S. 'The Search for a Cromwellian Settlement: Exclusions from the Second Protectorate Parliament', *Parliamentary History*, 17 (1998), pp.178–97

Ellis, S.G. 'The Collapse of the Gaelic World, 1450–1650', *IHS*, 31 (1999), pp.449–69

Fielding, A.J. 'Opposition to the Personal Rule of Charles I: The Diary of Robert Woodford, 1637–41', *HJ*, 31 (1988), pp.769–88

Flemion, J. 'A Savings to Satisfy All: The House of Lords and the Meaning of the Petition of Right', *Parliamentary History*, 10 (1991), pp.27–44

Furgol, E.M. 'The Northern Highland Covenanting Clans, 1639–1651', *Northern Scotland*, 7 (1987), pp.19–31

Gentles, I. 'The Choosing of the Officers for the New Model Army', *Historical Research*, 67 (1994), pp.264–85

Gillespie, R. 'Plantation and Profit: Richard Spert's Tract on Ireland, 1608', *Irish Economic and Social History*, 20 (1993), pp.62–71

Goodare, J. 'The Nobility and the Absolutist State in Scotland, 1584–1638', *History*, 78 (1993), pp.161–82

Goodare, J. 'The Scottish Parliament of 1621', *HJ*, 38 (1995), pp.29–51

Griffiths, N.E.S. & Reid, J.G. 'New Evidence on New Scotland, 1629', *William and Mary Quarterly*, 3rd ser., 39 (1992), pp.492–508

Hirst, D. 'The Conciliatoriness of the Cavalier Commons Reconsidered', *Parliamentary History*, 6 (1987), pp.221–35

Hirst, D. 'Locating the 1650s in England's Seventeenth Century', *History*, 81 (1996), pp.359–83

Hopper, A.J. '"Fitted for Desperation": Honour and Treachery in Parliament's Yorkshire Command, 1642–43', *History*, 86 (2001), pp.138–54

Hughes, A. 'Thomas Dugard and his Circle in the 1630s', *HJ*, 29 (1986), pp.771–93

Jared, J.R.S.M. 'The Good of This Service Consists in Absolute Secrecy: The Earl of Dunbar, Scotland and the Border (1603–1611)', *Canadian Journal of History*, 36 (2001), pp.229–57

Kelly, J. 'The Origins of the Act of Union: An Examination of Unionist Opinion in Britain and Ireland, 1650–1800', *IHS*, 25 (1987), pp.236–63

Kennedy, M.E. 'Charles I and Local Government: The Draining of the East and West Fens', *Albion*, 15 (1983), pp.19–31

Kishlansky, M. 'The Case of the Army Truly Stated: The Creation of the New Model Army', *Past & Present*, 81 (1978), pp.51–74

Kishlansky, M. 'The Army and the Levellers: The Roads to Putney', *HJ*, 22 (1979), pp.795–824

Kishlansky, M. 'Tyranny Denied: Charles I, Attorney General Heath, and the Five Knights' Case', *HJ*, 42 (1999), pp.53–83

Knoppers, L.L. 'The Politics of Portraiture: Oliver Cromwell and the Plain Style', *Renaissance Quarterly*, 51 (1998), pp.1282–1319

Kupperman, K.O. 'Errand to the Indies: Puritan Colonization from Providence Island through the Western Design', *William and Mary Quarterly*, 45 (1988), pp.70–99

Lake, P. 'Calvinism and the English Church', *Past & Present*, 114 (1987), pp.32–76

Langelüddecke, H. '"Patchy and Spasmodic?" The Response of Justices of the Peace to Charles I's Book of Orders', *EHR*, 113 (1998), pp.1231–48

Law, R. 'The First Scottish Guinea Company of 1634–9', *SHR*, 76 (1997), pp.185–202

Lee jr, M. 'James VI's Government of Scotland after 1603', *SHR*, 55 (1976), pp.49–53

Little, P. 'The Earl of Cork and the Fall of the Earl of Strafford, 1638–41', *HJ*, 39 (1996), pp.619–35

Little, P. '"Blood and Friendship": The Earl of Essex's Protection of the Earl of Clanricarde's Interests, 1641–6', *EHR*, 112 (1997), pp.927–41

MacCuarta, B. 'The Plantation of Leitrim, 1620–41', *IHS*, 32 (2001), pp.297–320

Macinnes, A.I. 'Repression and Conciliation: The Highland Dimension, 1660–1688', *SHR*, 65 (1986), pp.167–95

Macinnes, A.I. 'The First Scottish Tories?', *SHR*, 67 (1988), pp.56–66

Mahoney, M. 'The Saville Affair and the Politics of the Long Parliament', *Parliamentary History*, 7 (1988), pp.212–27

Malcolm, J.L. 'Charles II and the Reconstruction of Royal Power', *HJ*, 35 (1992), pp.307–30

Mayers, R.E. 'Real and Practicable, not Imaginary and Notional: Sir Henry Vane, *A Healing Question*, and the Problems of the Protectorate', *Albion*, 28 (1996), pp.37–72

McGiffert, M. 'God's Controversy with Jacobean England', *AHR*, 88 (1983), pp.1151–74

McKenny, K. 'Charles II's Irish Cavaliers: The 1649 Officers and the Restoration Land Settlement', *IHS*, 28 (1993), pp.409–25

Mendle, M. 'A Machiavellian in the Long Parliament before the Civil War', *Parliamentary History*, 8 (1989), pp.116–24

Mendle, M. 'The Great Council of Parliament and the First Ordinances: The Constitutional Theory of the Civil War', *Journal of British Studies*, 31 (1992), pp.133–62

Netzloff, M. 'Forgetting the Ulster Plantation: John Speed's The Theatre of the Empire of Great Britain (1611) and the Colonial Archive', *Journal of Medieval and Early Modern Studies*, 31 (2001), pp.313–48

Ohlmeyer, J. 'Seventeenth-Century Ireland and the New British and Atlantic Histories', *AHR*, 104 (1999), pp.446–62

Orr, D.A. 'England, Ireland, Magna Carta, and the Common Law: The Case of Connor Lord Maguire, second Baron of Enniskillen', *Journal of British Studies*, 39 (2000), pp.389–421

Palmer, W. 'Oliver St. John and the Legal Language of Revolution in England: 1640–1642', *Historian*, 51 (1989), pp.263–82

Peck, L.L. 'Beyond the Pale: John Cusacke and the Language of Absolutism in Early Stuart Britain', *HJ*, 41 (1998), pp.121–49

Perceval-Maxwell, M. 'Ireland and the Monarchy in the Early Stuart Multiple Kingdom', *HJ*, 34 (1991), pp.279–95

Pincus, S. 'Neither Machiavellian Moment nor Possessive Individualism: Commercial Society and the Defenders of the English Commonwealth', *AHR*, 103 (1998), pp.705–36

Pocock, J.G.A. 'The Limits and Divisions of British History: In Search of an Unknown Subject', *AHR*, 87 (1982), pp.311–36

Pogson, F. 'Making and Maintaining Political Alliances during the Personal Rule of Charles I: Wentworth's Associations with Laud and Cottington', *History*, 84 (1999), pp.52–73

Popofsky, L.S. 'The Crisis over Tonnage and Poundage in Parliament in 1629', *Past & Present*, 126 (1990), pp.44–75

Rachum, I. 'The Term "Revolution" in Seventeenth-Century English Astrology', *History of European Ideas*, 18 (1994), pp.869–83

Raymond, J. 'Framing Liberty: Marvell's *First Anniversary* and the Instrument of Government', *Huntington Library Quarterly*, 62 (1999), pp.313–50

Richards, J. '"His Nowe Majestie" and the English Monarchy: The Kingship of Charles I before 1640', *Past & Present*, 113 (1986), pp.70–96

Rushe, H. 'Merlini Anglici: Astrology and Propaganda from 1644 to 1651', *EHR*, 80 (1965), pp.322–33

Rusche, H. 'Prophecies and Propaganda, 1641 to 1651', *EHR*, 84 (1969), pp.752–70

Salt, S.P. 'Sir Simon D'Ewes and the Levying of Ship Money, 1635–1640', *HJ*, 37 (1994), pp.253–87

Scott, D. '"Hannibal at our Gates": Loyalists and Fifth-Columnists During the Bishops' Wars: The Case of Yorkshire', *Historical Research*, 70 (1997), pp.269–93

Scott, D. 'The "Northern Gentlemen", the Parliamentary Independents and Anglo-Saxon Relations in the Long Parliament', *HJ*, 42 (1999), pp.347–75

Scott, D. 'The Barwis Affair: Political Allegiance and the Scots During the British Civil Wars', *EHR*, 115 (2000), pp.843–63

Shedd, J.A. 'Thwarted Victors: Civil and Criminal Prosecution against Parliament's Officials during the English Civil War and Commonwealth', *Journal of British Studies*, 41 (2002), pp.139–69

Smith, D.L. '"The More Posed and Wised Advice": The Fourth Earl of Dorset and the English Civil Wars', *HJ*, 34 (1991), pp.797–829

Smith, D.L. 'Oliver Cromwell, the First Protectorate Parliament and Religious Reform', *Parliamentary History*, 19 (2001), pp.38–48

Spence, R.T. 'The Pacification of the Cumberland Borders, 1593–1628', *Northern History*, 13 (1977), pp.59–160

Spence, R.T. 'The Backward North Modernized? The Cliffords, Earls of Cumberland and the Socage Manor of Carlisle, 1611–43', *Northern History*, 20 (1984), pp.64–87

Spence, R.T. 'Henry, Lord Clifford and the First Bishops' War, 1639', *Northern History*, 31 (1995), pp.138–56

Sproxton, J. 'From Calvin to Cromwell through Beard', *Journal of European Studies*, 25 (1995), pp.17–33

Stevenson, D. 'Conventicles in the Kirk, 1619–1637', *Records of the Scottish Church History Society*, 18 (1972–4), pp.99–114

Stevenson, D. 'A Note on a Scheme to Straighten the River Forth in 1636', *Scottish Economic and Social History*, 17 (1997), pp.65–8

Stoyle, M.J. '"Pagans or Paragons?": Images of the Cornish during the English Civil War', *EHR*, 111 (1996), pp.299–323

Torrance, J.B. 'The Covenant Concept in Scottish Theology and Politics and its Legacy', *Scottish Journal of Theology*, 34 (1981), pp.225–43

Vallance, E. '"An Holy and Sacramental Paction": Federal Theology and the Solemn League and Covenant in England', *EHR*, 116 (2000), pp.50–75

Vallance, E. 'Oaths, Casuistry, and Equivocation: Anglican Responses to the Engagement Controversy', *HJ*, 44 (2001), pp.59–79

Vallance, E. 'Protestations, Vow, Covenant and Engagement: Swearing Allegiance in the English Civil War', *Historical Research*, 75 (2002), pp.408–24

Williamson, A.H. 'Scots, Indians and Empire: The Scottish Politics of Civilization, 1519–1609', *Past & Present*, 150 (1996), pp.46–83

Williamson, A.H. 'Union with England Traditional, Union with England Radical: Sir James Hope and the Mid-Seventeenth Century British State', *EHR*, 110 (1995), pp.303–12

Woolrych, A. 'The Cromwellian Protectorate: A Military Dictatorship?', *History*, 75 (1990), pp.207–31

Worden, B. 'The Politics of Marvell's Horation Ode', *HJ*, 27 (1984), pp.525–47

Worden, B. 'Providence and Politics in Cromwellian England', *Past & Present*, 109 (1985), pp.55–99

Wormald, J. 'Bloodfeud, Kindred and Government in Early Modern Scotland', *Past & Present*, 87 (1980), pp.54–97

Wormald, J. 'James VI and I: Two Kings or One?', *History*, 68 (1983), pp.187–209

Young, M.B. 'Charles I and the Erosion of Trust, 1625–1628', *Albion*, 22 (1990), pp.217–35

Index